Francis A. Drexel
LIBRARY

Books For College Libraries
Third Edition

Core Collection

JAMES LARKIN
IRISH LABOUR LEADER
1876–1947

JAMES LARKIN
Irish Labour Leader
1876–1947

by
EMMET LARKIN

THE M.I.T. PRESS
*Massachusetts Institute of Technology
Cambridge, Massachusetts*

Library of Congress Catalog Card Number 64–22134
Printed in Great Britain

To Jack Carney

CONTENTS

PLATES

PREFACE

THE first thing I should point out, perhaps, is that I am not related to the hero of this book. I began this biography of my namesake some dozen years ago when a doctoral candidate at Columbia University. The Irish years of his career were researched in Dublin during the academic year 1952–53, and the British were completed while I was a Fulbright Scholar at the London School of Economics in 1955–56. I presented my dissertation, 'James Larkin and the Irish Labour Movement, 1876–1914,' to Columbia University in 1957 and was awarded my degree in the spring of that year. Since then, in completing the biography, I have considerably revised and rewritten what was originally presented as my dissertation.

I must begin my acknowledgments by paying my respect to the memory of the late John Bartlett Brebner, Gouverneur Morris Professor of History at Columbia University. Professor Brebner was more to me than the sponsor of my dissertation, to which he gave, indeed, his superb critical attention. He was the epitome of what a scholar and a professional man should be. I owe also a profound debt to Professor Jesse D. Clarkson of Brooklyn College, who as Visiting Professor of History at Columbia University in 1956–57, gave my dissertation a meticulous reading and the benefit of his understanding of Irish Labour history. I must also thank Professor Herman Ausubel of Columbia University, for not only giving my dissertation his most careful attention, but for introducing me to the idea of writing this book. Several of my former colleagues at Brooklyn College have read this manuscript, and it has benefited from their suggestions and critical comments. I must especially thank Professor Samuel J. Hurwitz and Professor Howard Zinn, now of Boston University.

To my good friend and mentor, Professor David H. Greene of New York University, who read this manuscript from beginning to

ix

end, and whose editorial comments on almost every page has saved me from much grief and the reader from much pain, I am afraid words will not make amends. I am also deeply indebted editorially to two of my oldest and dearest friends, Mrs. Eloise Segal and Professor Nishan Parlakian of Pace College, whose patience with me and my 'style' was kindness itself.

I received so much help and encouragement in Dublin in the writing of this book that it is hard to know where to begin in my acknowledgments. Let me begin by pointing out, however, that this biography owes materially more to Mr. William O'Brien, former General Secretary of the Irish Transport and General Workers' Union, than to anyone else. Mr. O'Brien not only gave me unstintingly of his time and his wide personal knowledge of the Irish Labour movement, but made available to me the vast resources of his most valuable collection of manuscript and printed materials in Irish Labour history. I must also acknowledge the significant material contributions to this volume by Mr. Desmond Ryan, Mr. James Larkin, Jr., Dr. John Boyle, and the late lamented Thomas Johnson. The many kindnesses of the staff of the National Library of Ireland, and the generous facilities provided for research made it almost a home away from home. I must particularly thank Dr. Richard J. Hayes, the Director, Mr. Ailfrid MacLoichlainn, Assistant Keeper of Manuscripts, and Mr. Thomas O'Neill, Assistant Keeper of Printed Books. On the other side of the Irish Sea, I must thank Mr. H. L. Beales, formerly of the London School of Economics, whose encyclopedic knowledge of subjects, economic and social, has saved me from many a serious fall in British and Irish Labour history.

I must also thank both the American and Irish Governments for allowing me to consult material not ordinarily available to scholars. I must particularly thank Eamon de Valera, President of the Republic of Ireland, who as Prime Minister in 1953 gave me the necessary permission to examine the restricted material concerning James Larkin in the Irish State Paper Office. I must also thank Dr. E. Taylor Parks, Chief, Advisory and Review Branch, Historical Division, for his great personal kindness to me in Washington as well as for granting me permission to examine the records of the Department of State concerning James Larkin which are ordinarily restricted after 1929.

Finally, I must acknowledge the contribution made to this biography by the late Jack Carney and his wife Mina. Jack Carney, more than anyone else, gave me an understanding of what James Larkin was all about. No one, perhaps, knew Larkin better than he did, and though a warm and passionate admirer, he was never blind to the faults and defects in that great man. Jack Carney, then, saw Larkin whole and best, and he did as much as a man could do to help me see him that way, and that is why I have dedicated this book to him. Needless to say, I am alone responsible for all the shortcomings of this biography.

EMMET LARKIN

Bexley House, M.I.T.,
Cambridge, Massachusetts.

PROLOGUE

IN those exciting years before the First World War, Socialism was the most revolutionary element in the European complex. Socialism had posed a threat to the traditional concepts of property and the State since the *Communist Manifesto* and the Revolutions of 1848. But it was not until the turn of the century that the threat actually became a menace. The increasing economic strength of the working classes, and their growing political awareness were, of course, the obvious reasons for the ferment. More important, in the particular sense, at least, was the addition at this time of a still more revolutionary dimension to Socialist thought—Syndicalism. The blow that would destroy Capitalism, the Syndicalists argued, was not to be struck either at the ballot box, or even at the barricades, but rather where the worker was invincible—at the point of production. When the proletariat, therefore, was properly organized along industrial lines, and led by men who could not be corrupted by bourgeois concepts of compromise, it would withdraw its labour, and with folded arms, serenely contemplate the capitalist collapse. This wonderfully simple technique for the achievement of a very complex end—the Social Revolution—gained a very wide following among left-wing Socialists, and particularly among trade union leaders with a revolutionary bent.

Syndicalist theory developed out of the pressing need to make Socialist thought harmonize with proletarian practice. The roots of Syndicalist theory were actually first struck in the pioneer efforts to organize the unskilled worker into industrial unions. This attempt not only produced a dynamic new *rationale* in Socialist thought, but it resulted in the emergence of a remarkably vital new leadership. The old Socialist leadership had been made up almost entirely of converts from the intellectual middle classes. The new men, however, were almost all strictly proletarian in their origins, and could hardly be called intellectuals. They were self-educated, pragmatic, class-conscious, articulate, and individualistic to the point of being anarchic. Since they had come up through the ranks, they were as confident, as dogmatic, and often as arrogant as only self-made men can be. They were full of the truth of their mission and determined to awaken the working classes by preaching their 'divine gospel of discontent.' Their faith was Socialism, their work was industrial unionism, and their vocation was Syndicalism.

The English-speaking world proved very receptive to these prophets of the new order. In America Eugene Debs and 'Big Bill' Haywood, in Britain Tom Mann and Ben Tillett, and in Ireland James Connolly were the outstanding personalities in this broad movement to organize the workers of the world. The most remarkable man, however, among this remarkable generation of proletarian leaders was the Liverpool Irishman—James Larkin. His accomplishment was unique and representative—unique partly because it was representative. His rich and complex personality allowed him to harmonize the three most dissonant themes of his day. For he claimed to be at one and the same time a Socialist, a Nationalist, and a Roman Catholic. It was representative because his career mirrored to a larger extent than did that of his equally colourful comrades those attributes that were the hallmark of this generation of working-class labour leaders. 'It is hard to believe this great man is dead,' wrote Sean O'Casey on the day Larkin died, 'for all thoughts and all activities surged in the soul of this Labour leader. He was far and away above the orthodox Labour leader, for he combined within himself the imagination of the artist, with the fire and determination of a leader of a down-trodden class.'

Born in the slums of a great English city in 1876, like so many Irishmen of his generation, Larkin saw and suffered all that was the lot of his ghettoed class. He received hardly any education, watched his father die of tuberculosis, began to earn his living at the age of eleven, was duly exploited in a precarious labour market, struggled to keep his family from sinking into abject poverty, stowed away to escape unemployment and find adventure, and finally returned to Liverpool to take his place among that vast army of casuals who prowled the docks in search of a day's work. Still, Larkin emerged from this grim reality more fortunate than most, for in these bitter years he found the faith that was to sustain him for a lifetime. His Socialism was rooted deep in his comprehending humanity and in his passionate longing for social justice. As he tried to explain many years later when he was on trial for allegedly attempting to overthrow the United States Government—'And at an early age, I took my mind to this question of the age—why are the many poor? It was true to me. I don't know whether the light of God or the light of humanity or the light of my own intelligence brought it to me, but it came to me like a flash. The thing was wrong because the basis of society was wrong.'

Before he was seventeen Larkin had translated his inspiration into action by joining the Liverpool Branch of the Independent Labour Party. For the next fifteen years he was always to be found in the front rank of militant British Socialists, preaching and prophesying the coming of the Social Revolution. Though Larkin thus early discovered his Socialist faith, he was not to find his work until much later. In earning his bread he graduated from docker to foreman, the youngest on the Liverpool docks. He had not joined the local labour union, the National Union of Dock Labourers, until 1901, although he had been a convinced and militant Socialist for almost ten years. When, however, a strike broke out in his firm in the summer of 1905, he walked out with the men and soon emerged as their leader. The strike was bitterly fought, and when the men lost Larkin was appointed organizer for the National Union. His first assignment, which he successfully completed within a year, was the reorganization of the Scottish ports. Then, early in 1907, he undertook the more difficult task of effecting a reorganization of the Irish ports. He had now found his work, and like all converts to the new cause, Larkin became a veritable St. Paul, in that he would now go and compel them to come in.

In beginning his Irish career at the age of thirty-one, Larkin terminated his long apprenticeship, for he discovered in Ireland the vocation in which his faith and work could find expression—he became an agitator. In the next seven years, until the outbreak of the First World War in 1914, he laboured to build and perfect the most revolutionary labour union of its day—the Irish Transport and General Workers' Union. Larkin thought it was a union's responsibility to do more than merely wring better wages, hours, and conditions from reluctant employers. He viewed his Union as a revolutionary instrument with which he hoped to effect both economic change and social advancement. In his mind equality could never be real unless it was complemented by a genuine fraternity. This fraternity was not to be achieved merely by uniting the workers in a common and militant effort to shake their employers and the State, but also by introducing them to those cultural and educational advantages that give the grandeur and the beauty to life as well as the power and the glory. In those years Sean O'Casey could say, 'here was a man who would put a flower in a vase on a table as well as a loaf on a plate. Here, Sean thought, is the beginning of a broad and busy day, the leisurely evening, the calmer night.'

The building of the Transport Union, and with it the foundations of the Irish Labour movement, was undoubtedly the most creative achievement of Larkin's long life. These seven years, however, both in and out of Ireland, were not only heroic and creative but tragic and violent as well. The terrible paradox was that there could not have been the one without the other. In Ireland those tragic features in the narrative—the human weaknesses, the humiliating defeats, the heart-breaking defections, and cruel reversals of fortune were all redeemed by Larkin's sublime confidence and dogged perseverance. Even at the end of seven painstaking years, when his Union was wrecked by an overwhelming combination of Dublin employers, he could only be brought to grief, not to heel. But the insidious crescendo of violence in these years, that was both to be consumed and born again in the First World War, and which seemed to permeate every class, would neither be stemmed nor redeemed by any act of heroism or sacrifice. For those who were most capable of making such an act were themselves becoming increasingly committed to the use of force in order to effect those changes they felt to be necessary for society. James Larkin, alas, was an outstanding case study in a period which itself was merely the prologue to an era where the continued depreciation of reason has resulted in the apotheosis of force.

The epic struggle of the Dublin workers against their employers in 1913 made Larkin an international figure in the world of labour. For nearly six months 20,000 men and women, on whom some 80,000 others depended for their support, were locked out because they refused to sign a pledge that they would never join Larkin's Union or resign from it if they were already members. In defence of the basic right of the worker to combine, the British Labour Movement contributed over £150,000 and shipped large quantities of food and clothing to their beleaguered brethren in Dublin. By his revolutionary public appeals and his militant demands for extreme measures against the Dublin employers, Larkin and 'Larkinism,' at the end of 1913, were household words in Britain. In America too the left-wing took him up in their journals and periodicals as a prime example of what a Socialist of the meat-eating variety was like. Even Lenin was impressed by Larkin's revolutionary posture in 1913. When the war finally came in August, 1914, Larkin cemented his international reputation as a revolutionary Socialist by immediately and unequivocally denouncing it as a Capitalist plot. With his effectiveness being seriously limited by the wreck of his Union, as well as the obviously inhibiting effects of the war on civil liberties, Larkin decided to tour America to raise some badly needed funds. When he left Ireland in late 1914 he planned to stay in the United States for only a short time, but he remained nearly eight and a half years.

In the United States Larkin was by turns a lecturer, a union organizer, a German secret agent, an Irish propagandist, a Socialist agitator, a founder of the American Communist Party, and a 'martyred' political prisoner. Two themes, however, dominated his American career and gave a kind of coherence to what might otherwise appear to be a mere rootless activity—the war and the Russian Revolution. During the four years in which the war was waged, Larkin agitated and worked against it. By lecturing, propagandizing, and even becoming a German agent, he did all he could to frustrate the war effort. With regard to the Russian Revolution, Larkin enthusiastically agreed with Eugene V. Debs, who had described himself as a Bolshevik from the top of his head to the tips of his toes. During the 'Red Scare' of 1919–20, Larkin was arrested, tried, and convicted of advocating the overthrow of the Government, and sentenced to a term of from five to ten years in Sing Sing, of which he served nearly three years before he was pardoned by Governor Alfred E. Smith in the interests of free speech.

To follow Larkin's American career is indeed to chronicle the decline of Socialism as a political force in the United States. The First World War had seriously shaken the façade of Socialist Unity in the United States, as it had destroyed it almost everywhere else in the world. What temporarily saved it in America was that this country did not immediately become involved, and the Socialist Party did not insist on a 'hard' line in opposition to the war. The Russian Revolution, paradoxically enough, was the beginning of the end for American Socialism. The great event at first seemed to provide a common ground for agreement among all shades of

Socialist opinion, but the Bolshevik seizure of power in November, 1917 soon resulted in a civil war in the Socialist Party of America. While the 'Reds' were numerically superior, the 'Yellows' controlled the Party organization and funds. By the summer of 1919 the Socialist Party was in ruins, and the emergence of two mutually hostile Communist Parties made a shambles of the movement. Larkin, needless to say, always took up his position on the extreme left, and was counted a 'Red' of the deepest hue. He was, indeed, a man who insisted on his version of the truth; and the price he paid was imprisonment, poverty, isolation, and loneliness, but he paid it without a whimper. When he was being deported at Ellis Island in New York in 1923, for example, and an attendant asked about his baggage, Larkin could still reply with a chuckle—'Everything I own is on my back. I'm like the man in Whitman's poem, "Free and light-hearted I take to the open road." '

When he arrived in Ireland, however, he soon discovered it was no longer a land for light-hearted men. A successful revolution against the British had degenerated into a tragic civil war among the Irish. The Irish Labour Movement, pressed by an intolerant Nationalism and an aggressive Catholicism, gave up the ghost of Socialism. The employers, badly frightened by the economic convulsion that had followed on the heels of the First World War, were in a truculent and wage-cutting mood. Larkin had few doubts about what was to be done. The still smouldering civil war must be brought to an end, the Labour Movement must be purged by a strong dose of left-wing laxative, and as for the employers, they must simply be fought—as always. Larkin did as much as one man could do to persuade Eamon de Valera and his Republicans to take up an active political opposition in the Irish Parliament. His efforts, however, to turn Irish Labour in a revolutionary direction only produced in its turn a raging civil war in the Labour Movement. The employers, furthermore, pleading a deteriorating world economic situation beyond their control, and backed by a sympathetic Government, forced their demands for wage cuts on a divided Labour Movement. By 1929 Larkin's power in Dublin was the merest shadow of what it had been, and his influence in the world of Labour was negligible. The Great Depression all but buried him in an unmerciful oblivion.

When Larkin died nearly twenty years later in 1947 most people outside Ireland were surprised, for they had assumed he had been dead for a long time. His last years are a sad testimonial to a man whose way of life was action. Why the fire should have gone out in so vital a man is a question that is as historically important as it is artistically awkward. The answer to that question is also complex. In the early thirties the world in which Larkin believed was disintegrating. The collapse of the old order in the Great Depression did not surprise him because he had been predicting it all his life. The result, however, was not his prophesied Social Revolution, but the rise of a new order, more menacing and more inhumane than the old—Fascism. The European convulsion and its attendant evils were magnified in Ireland by problems implicit in the attempt to consolidate the Revolution recently made against the British. The consequence was that there was little room in Ireland for men or movements intent on perpetuating the Revolution rather than consolidating it. By 1936 Larkin also realized that at sixty he was too old to begin again. Circumstance had deprived him of his role, and time would not allow for the creation of another. To a man whose way of life was action, such a sentence was death.

PART ONE

Apprentice, 1876–1906

In the great things he did for the Irish workers is everlasting life. Not life that will remain as it is now; but life growing into a fuller consciousness of its own work, of its own power, its own right to the ownership of all things.

Sean O'Casey, IRISH TIMES, February 1, 1947

I

LOWER DEPTHS

HOW James Larkin came to be born in Liverpool on January 21, 1876, is simply the story of countless Irish families in the nineteenth century—the pull of the Industrial Revolution and the push of the Great Famine. Barney Larkin, his grandfather, had rented a fair-sized farm in the parish of lower Killeavy, some distance outside Armagh town in Ulster. He had worked his farm, given his sons more than the usual measure of education, been a familiar and welcome sight to his neighbours on Fair days, and attended Mass on Sundays in his top hat and buckled shoes, carrying his silver-mounted walking-stick. In 1847 he watched the Ireland he had known for nearly sixty years change with catastrophic suddenness during the Great Famine. He soon realized that the new Ireland which rose quickly out of the dead ashes of the old had not been resurrected for him or his. Farming and stock-raising became more profitable, indeed, but only if undertaken on a large scale. The primitive and widespread system of barter gave way to a money economy, and the new systems of credit were far more strict and much less personal. The mass exodus after the Famine was hurried by the increasing number of evictions for the non-payment of rent, while those who did manage to hold on were eventually ground out between the machinery of the Encumbered Estates Act, and the rapacious, rent-raising rancher, with his thousands of acres feeding cattle and sheep instead of people.[1]

The system of land tenure traditional in Ulster, and the more sophisticated level of the economy there generally, for a time stayed the worst effects of the vast clearances going on throughout the rest

[1] See Appendices A and B.

3

of Ireland. The 'Ulster Custom,' however, became at best only a short-term advantage in this, the final great enclosure movement in the British Isles. Barney Larkin held out longer than most, but he paid the price that was current in Ireland, the disintegration and partial destruction of his family. His oldest son set out for Liverpool and was never heard from again. Then Hugh and Patrick, and finally James, his youngest son, set out for that same 'capital of Ireland' across the Irish Sea. At last, some thirty years after the Great Famine, Barney Larkin was forced to join his son James in Liverpool, to end his days in respectable poverty. Everything in Ireland was gone, and only the Sunday finery remained—the top hat, the buckled shoes, and the silver-mounted walking-stick, the memory of which was preserved by the wide and wondering eyes of his young grandchildren.

James, who had arrived in Liverpool some ten years before his father Barney was forced to join him, worked as a fitter in an engineering firm. He had married an Irish girl, whom he had met at a christening, and she bore him six children, five of whom survived the terrifying Liverpool infant mortality rate. For twenty years he struggled to support his family on the wage of a pound a week until he died of tuberculosis on his thirty-eighth birthday—Ash Wednesday of 1887. His widow was compensated when the two oldest boys were taken on as apprentices to their father's firm without the customary £50 entrance fee. Hugh was thirteen and James eleven when they began to earn their half-crown a week. James, however, could not adapt himself to the routine, and he soon discovered he could earn more money by doing odd jobs. By turns he was a butcher's assistant, a paper-hanger, a French polisher, and a docker. One day, while working on the dockside, he was struck by a piece of machinery operated by an apprentice engineer. The accident was serious enough to have the apprentice's father pay young Larkin a pound a week for the nineteen weeks he was recuperating. During the days he would read at the Picton Library, and in the evenings listen to the Socialists describe the world he lived in at their open-air meetings. This happy interlude, which Larkin always remembered as his 'crowded hour of glorious life,' soon came to an end. Scarcely sixteen, he returned to the docks to find a day's work.

Young Larkin had already come to understand that there was a vast discrepancy between what should be and what actually was in this world. Before his father's death he had spent three and a half

4

years, which was to be the whole of his formal education, in a 'poverty-stricken,' English Catholic school. 'I was taught,' he explained years later, 'the truth of eternal justice, and I was taught the brotherhood of man was a true and living thing, and the fear of God was a thing that ought to cover all my days and also control my actions.'[1] 'And then,' he said, came the awful revelation, 'I had occasion to go out in the world and found out there was no fatherhood of God and there was no brotherhood of man, but every man in Society was compelled to be like a wolf or hyena.' He also saw that 'the women of our class, daughters of the working class, were out on the street selling their bodies to lustful brutes, earning the price that they might eat bread.' 'Some of the most respectable citizens,' he noted, 'were controlling that industry, and took the product in the brothels around the district.'[2] What, indeed, was there to be said of a system which produced such degradation in the human spirit? The Socialists said it could not be defended, that it would inevitably perish in its own corruption, and Larkin listened. They promised they could close the gap between what should be and what was, and he was heartened. They told him that he could have a part in the making of the brave new world, and he was converted.

Though he had now acquired the faith, Larkin still had to earn his bread. This was becoming an increasingly difficult problem, as unemployment in Britain rose from 2 per cent in 1890 to over 7 per cent in 1893. He finally solved it for himself in the summer of 1893, by stowing away on a steamer whose first port of call was to be Montevideo. When he was discovered, Larkin was put to work passing coals from the bunkers to the engine room. Though the outward passage was peaceful enough, on the way up to Mobile he was required to assist the greaser after a full day passing coals. One night after he had turned in exhausted he was ordered below to relieve one of the firemen. He refused point-blank, and was immediately sent for by the Chief Engineer. As he entered the alley way to the engine room he was seized and ironed to a stanchion in the hold. 'What a night I passed!' he wrote years later. 'The rats

---

[1] Library of the Supreme Court of the State of New York, MS. 3436, New York Supreme Court, Extraordinary Term, *The People of the State of New York* vs. *James J. Larkin, indicted as 'James Larkin,'* New York, April 16, 1920, pp. 718–21. Hereinafter referred to as *People* vs. *Larkin*.

[2] *Ibid.*

came around me in hundreds . . . it makes me shiver even now!'
Larkin jumped ship when it put in at St. Lucia, and lived as a beach-
comber until he signed on a steamer bound for Rio de Janeiro. He
then worked his way up to Galveston, down to Valparaiso, and
picked up a schooner bound for Buenos Aires, where he was hired
by an Irish-American as a five-dollar-a-day mercenary, for one day,
in an abortive insurrection. Eventually he made his way back to
Galveston, and after a tour of the American South shipped out of
Newport News for home after being away for over a year.[1]

The vital question among Liverpool Socialists, when Larkin returned in the late summer of 1894, was what was to be done about
the still very serious unemployment problem.[2] He joined the dis-
cussions in the little café off Lord Street, which later became better
known as the *Clarion* café. Here they planned a series of demonstrations designed to turn the public conscience to the awful plight of the
unemployed. Public protest meetings became the order of the day,
and when a short time later a great deal of publicity was given a
meeting organized to raise funds for the unfortunate victims of an
Italian earthquake, the local Socialists decided to storm the meeting
and demand that the 'starving unemployed' of Liverpool be given
first consideration.[3] Larkin carried a bannerette in the *coup*, which
resulted in a fund being subscribed for the local unemployed. This,
however, only temporarily relieved a chronic situation, and the
unemployed were soon as badly off as they had ever been. Worse
was yet to come, for the winter of 1894–95 was especially severe.
Soup kitchens had to be put into operation in most English cities,
and particularly in the seaports. The Liverpool Socialists inspired
by their local leaders, Bob Manson and John Edwards, fitted out a
covered wagon as a soup kitchen and distributed thousands of bowls
of 'good soup' every day in the most public place in Liverpool,
opposite St. George's Hall in Lime Street. By this they hoped to
strike the sullen social conscience of the 'better off.' This wagon was
the forerunner of the first *Clarion* Van, many of which were soon to
be found in every part of England, manned by dedicated Socialist

[1] George Dallas, 'Larkin's Life History,' Glasgow *Forward*, October 16–23,
1909. See also, for this and the preceding paragraph, *People* vs. *Larkin*, p. 470.

[2] *Forward*, October 9 and 30, 1909. See also DEMOCRAT, 'Notes From the
Front, Liverpool,' *Clarion*, September 15, 1894.

[3] *Forward*, October 9, 1909. See also CITIZEN (James Sexton). 'Notes From the
Front, Liverpool,' *Clarion*, December 8, 1894.

speakers distributing with a missionary zeal vast quantities of their literature.[1]

Before Larkin had gone to sea in 1893, he had joined the Liverpool branch of the Independent Labour Party, which had been founded in June, 1892. When he returned in 1894 he helped his boyhood friend, John Wolfe Tone Morrissey, form the Toxteth branch in Liverpool.[2] Though the Party gained ground nationally between 1892 and 1895, it then began to lose a good deal of its original momentum. The reasons were many, and they had a depressingly cumulative effect. The only other Socialist organization, the doctrinaire Social Democratic Federation, was hostile. The powerful and influential voice of Robert Blatchford, editor of the *Clarion*, the Socialist weekly with the largest circulation in the country, was critical. The President and guiding spirit of the Party, James Keir Hardie, lost his seat in Parliament for West Ham in the general election of 1895. This loss was a severe blow to the prestige of the I.L.P., since Hardie was their only voice in Parliament. After 1895 there was a renewed interest in the trade unions, and many of the more Labour-conscious members of the Party began to neglect politics for the unions. The most notable example of this was Tom Mann, who continued only in a part-time capacity as Secretary of the Party when he founded the Workers' Union of Great Britain and Ireland in 1898. Though he did not join the Workers' Union himself, Larkin did assist in the formation of its Liverpool Branch. Moreover, the Party did not enhance its popularity when it denounced the Boer War as a jingo-imperialist venture, and was in turn denounced by an outraged national conscience. Larkin was arrested and fined several times for his street-corner denunciations of the war. These were, indeed, the difficult years for the I.L.P., but a dedicated core of earnest

[1] Statement by Thomas Johnson, personal interview. See also *Clarion*, January 26, 1895. See also *Liverpool Labour Chronicle*, March 1, 1895, 'The True History of the Socialist Soup Van.' '. . . The public did not believe in the Un-employed. The Guardians of the Poor stated that there was no unusual distress. We wished to convince the Guardians, the City Fathers and the Public at large that there were thousands on the brink of starvation. We succeeded so well that the heart of this great city was touched as it never has been touched before . . .' J.E. (John Edwards).

[2] The first Liverpool branch of the I.L.P. was founded in June, 1892, some six months before the first national conference of the I.L.P. in Bradford, in January, 1893. H. K. Pelling, *The Origins of the Labour Party, 1880–1900* (1954), p. 115. James Larkin is recognized by the I.L.P. as a charter member.

young men of whom Larkin was one, stubbornly held to their faith.

After 1900 the tide began to turn for the Labour Movement in general, and for Larkin in particular. When Keir Hardie regained a seat in Parliament in the general election of that year, and an alliance was made between the Socialists and the trade unionists in the formation of the Labour Representation Committee, the foundations for a Parliamentary Labour Party were finally laid. In 1900 Larkin also helped elect his old friend J. W. T. Morrissey Public Auditor. Morrissey thereby became the first Socialist ever to be elected to public office in Liverpool.[1] Larkin, too, began to make his way in the world. By 1903 he was earning a magnificent £3 10s. a week as a foreman dock-porter in the sheds of T. & J. Harrison Ltd. In the lean years he had of necessity to live an austere life. He neither smoked nor drank, and had few diversions beyond his reading, studying, and talking Socialism. As his earnings had increased he had begun to indulge himself in what had been before unseemly luxuries. He took up smoking a pipe, bought a good black suit and a broad-brimmed hat in the American style, which was to serve him as his life-long trade-mark.

At twenty-seven he was the youngest and toughest boss on the Liverpool docks. His scrupulous honesty and his uncompromising devotion to the cause of temperance won him the respect of his men and his employers. He never paid his men, as was the custom, in a public house, nor did they ever dare to show up for work with the sign or smell of drink on them. There were never any unexplained deductions in their wages, nor were there any kick-backs to ensure the next day's work. His employers were impressed by his ability to get work done, and his reputation for working his men extremely hard soon earned him his nickname, 'The Rusher.' The employers also appreciated the fact that on any boat handled by Larkin thievery was minimal, and needless to say all cargoes involving liquor were assigned to him. Since he was doing so well himself, and his brothers Hugh and Peter, and his sister Delia, were all working, Larkin decided he could afford to get married. He had been keeping

---

[1] *Forward*, October 30, 1909. See also *Report of the Ninth Annual Conference of the Independent Labour Party* (1901), in which the 'Directory of I.L.P. Members on Public Bodies' (p. 62), lists J. W. T. Morrissey for the first time as an elected public official. See also Fred Bower, *Rolling Stonemason* (1936), pp. 191–92, for Larkin's and Bower's experiences in the campaign.

company with Elizabeth Brown, a tall, handsome, red-haired girl, who was three years younger than he, for some time. He had met her in the working-man's restaurant managed by her father, a Baptist lay-preacher. Though she expressed no interest in Socialism he courted her in his own unique way by taking her to all his meetings and speaking engagements. She listened patiently, and they were married on September 8, 1903, in a civil ceremony in Liverpool.[1]

The little time he had outside his work on the docks, his attention to his family, and his Socialist activities, Larkin gave to the Civic Guild of Liverpool. Though his social work kept the poverty and misery of the poor before his eyes, he never became inured to human suffering, nor did his moral indignation ever cool at social injustice. Twenty years later the terrible things he experienced in the Liverpool slums were still vivid in his mind's eye. The following is at once an example of his rhetoric and his deep compassion.

> I and two of these people one night went down into Christian Street. We went down into one of those subterranean dwellings they have in Liverpool, down below the earth, where the people who were born in the image of God and His likeness were drawn down by this economic vortex and driven into this damnable hell down below, driven out of the light of day into these dens that have no background at all, but only have an entrance to get in.
>
> It was dark, bitterly dark. We passed into the first orifice and then the next, and then we heard a moan, and we looked through and saw nothing, it was so dark, and I went out and got a candle and came back, and lit the candle, and then we found it. In the corner laid the body of a woman, and on its dead breast, on its dead breast is the figure of a child, about two months old, sucking, trying to get the life blood out of the breast of the dead woman. And then there were two little girls, one seven years old, and one of nine, and that was in the year 1902, and the City of Liverpool, in a Christian City, in a street called Christian—Christian Street, and Christian people; and they foully murdered that mother and they left these three children to march with the world, and none in that City of a million people cared about that mother or about her children; and even God sent no one down to the gloom, except inasmuch as He had sent us.[2]

Each new horror only served to confirm him again in his Socialist faith.

Even when Larkin amused himself, it was within a serious context.

[1] James Larkin, Jr., personal interview.
[2] *People* vs. *Larkin*, pp. 720–21.

One day, Fred Bower, a stonemason and a Socialist comrade of Larkin's, was working on the site of the new Anglican Cathedral in Liverpool. He had watched Sir Frederick Radcliffe, a Cathedral committee man, deposit a remembrance where the foundation stone would be laid the next day. If the upper classes were allowed such privileges, thought Bower, why not the working classes? That night he visited Larkin and suggested that they, too, should make an offering in the name of the proletariat. Larkin agreed, and contributed copies of the *Clarion* and the *Labour Leader* for June 24, 1904. These were compressed in a piece of tin and the following note was enclosed with them.

To the Finders, Hail!

We, the wage slaves employed on the erection of this cathedral, to be dedicated to the worship of the unemployed Jewish carpenter, hail ye! Within a stone's throw from here, human beings are housed in slums not fit for swine. This message, written on trust-produced paper with trust-produced ink, is to tell ye how we of to-day are at the mercy of trusts. Building fabrics, clothing, food, fuel, transport, are all in the hands of money-mad, soul-destroying trusts. We can only sell our labour power, as wage slaves, on their terms. The money trusts to-day own us. In your own day, you will thanks to the efforts of past and present agitators for economic freedom, own the trusts. Yours will indeed, compared to ours of to-day, be a happier existence. See to it, therefore, that ye, too, work for the betterment of *all*, and so justify your existence by leaving the world the better for your having lived in it. Thus and thus only shall come about the Kingdom of 'God' or 'Good' on Earth. Hail, Comrades, and—Farewell.[1]

Every Sunday Larkin spoke in the neighbourhood of Liverpool. Whether it was Birkenhead, Blackpool, or Widnes, the message was always the same—Socialism. The world was what it was because the basis of society was wrong. A society based on self-interest and the profit motive was an immoral and unclean thing. The vicious system would only perish when the eyes of the working classes were opened. The masses were exploited by an unscrupulous capitalist class and gulled by their kept hand-maidens, the politicians and the Press. Vice, poverty, slums, unemployment, disease, and crime were all the fault of a system in the last stages of moral and economic bankruptcy. That which would save the working classes, the nation, and the world was the nationalization of the means of production,

---

[1] Bower, *op. cit.*, pp. 121–22.

distribution, and exchange. When the workers finally put their own representatives in the seats of the mighty, the Social Revolution would be at hand. The resulting emancipation of the working classes would inevitably bring in its wake the millennium. Then the goodness of man and the largeness of his spirit would at last have uninhibited horizons, and the glorious time spoken of by the poets and the prophets would surely come to pass. Larkin's vision of the millennium was as hazy as that of most British Socialists of his generation. He kept his attention focused sharply on the abominable realities of a decaying industrial system, singing a song of undiluted discontent, and Shelley, Whitman, Francis Adams, and William Morris were his poets. In these years on the hustings he learned all the techniques and tricks of demagogy, the theatrics, the repartee, the rhetoric, and the poetry that were to make him one of the most successful mob-orators of his day.

In 1895 Larkin had expressed the opinion that Trade unionism was a 'played-out economic fallacy.'[1] Like a good many British Socialists he felt the proper way to save the working classes was through organizing a political party devoted to their interests. Many members of the Independent Labour Party, however, with Keir Hardie in the vanguard, argued that the trade unions were not on the wane, and worked hard to convert the unions, and especially their Parliament, the Trades Union Congress, to the idea of a 'Labour Alliance' between Socialists and Trade unionists. Hardie's point of view eventually triumphed when the delegates of the T.U.C. and the various Socialist groups met in February, 1900, and formed the Labour Representation Committee, the nucleus of the future British Labour Party. Larkin had modified his own stand to some extent, at least, when he helped organize a branch of the Workers' Union in Liverpool in 1898, and to a greater extent in 1901, when he joined the National Union of Dock Labourers, though he remained little more than a dues-paying member until 1905.

In the spring of that year trouble was brewing among the dockers employed by the Harrison Line. The National Union had for some time been working for a 'closed shop' in the Harrison sheds, and most of the foremen, who, like Larkin, had begun as dockers, were still members of the Union, though they were now employed in a supervisory capacity. In fact, of the thirty-five foremen employed

[1] Sir James Sexton, *Sir James Sexton, Agitator* (1936), p. 202.

11

by the firm, twenty-eight were paid-up members of the Union. The remaining seven foremen had allowed their membership to lapse. In order to force them to rejoin the Union, upwards of 600 men walked off their jobs on June 28, 1905. The company took the attitude that it was a matter for the foremen themselves to decide, and refused to coerce any foreman into rejoining the Union with a threat of dismissal.[1]

The very next day four to five hundred 'imported labourers' from Hull were provided by the Shipping Federation to break the strike.[2] Larkin had come out with the men, and was elected their delegate to the strike committee. James Sexton, the General Secretary of the National Union, who always proved to be a moderating influence in any fight, appeared cool towards the strike from the beginning.[3] Soon, however, things were humming, and Larkin, who emerged as strike leader, was to learn a great deal about conducting a strike. The strikers tried, as best they could, to make life miserable for the 'blacklegs.' It was the custom at this time to house and feed the 'non-union men' on the ships they were working or in the cargo sheds on the docks. The police kept the strikers from interfering with the 'blacklegs,' but very often the single bottle of beer provided after the evening meal in the cargo sheds only whetted the thirst of these professional strike-breakers, and they would venture, sometimes much to their regret, from the protected confines of the 'dock estate.' One such case was reported the morning after the 'blacklegs' arrived:

> John Winters, one of the men who travelled to Liverpool from Hull, was last evening attacked and severely mauled. At about 7:30 or something like a couple of hours after his arrival, he proceeded to

[1] *Liverpool Courier*, June 29, 1905. See Sexton's resumé of the difficulties.

[2] See Appendix C.

[3] *Courier*, June 29, 1905. Sexton 'was extremely reluctant to make any statement, on the ground that he was anxious to avoid creating irritation.' Sexton also wrote a column for the *Liverpool Weekly Courier*, 'Labour and its Problems,' in which during the course of the strike he restrained himself with great reluctance from any discussion of the strike also. In his autobiography, Sexton said Larkin 'first revealed his extraordinary mentality by organizing a strike of employees of the firm for whom he was acting as foreman, whilst I was away presiding over the 1906 Trade Union Congress at Hanley.' The *Liverpool Daily Post and Mercury*, on August 17, 1905, some seven weeks after the strike began, mentioned that despite his heavy duties because of the strike, Sexton had finished preparing his coming address to the T.U.C.

Wellington Road for the purpose of obtaining something to drink. A large number of people were about and, someone noticing that he was one of the non-union men, the crowd turned on him. Most of the attacking party, it is understood were women. Winters was very badly beaten, receiving a cut 1½ inches in length on the face.[1]

Some two weeks after the strike began, Sir Edward Lee, Lord Mayor of Liverpool, tried to persuade a conference of the strikers' delegates to accept the employers' terms and return to work as 'free labourers.' Larkin was one of the delegates to the conference, which refused to accept such terms. A week later, the strikers were reported as being well supported by their own union and the General Federation of Trade Unions, and there was 'no doubt they will hold out a long time.'[2] The following evening, Larkin, Sexton, and the President of the Liverpool Trades Council addressed a large meeting of strikers and sympathizers in front of St. George's Hall. In his speech Larkin maintained that 'this struggle was an attempt to break the Union, but he believed the men who had ceased work at Harrison's sheds would die in the streets before they would give in.'[3] He went on to criticize the action of the Docks Board and Health and Watch Committees because the conditions prevailing in the Harrison sheds 'would not be tolerated in the compounds of South Africa.' Five days later Larkin maintained the strikers would 'chew the grass in Sefton Park' before they would give in, while announcing that 'a fund was being organized for the purpose of assisting the wives and children of the strikers.'[4] The fund, supported by Liberal, Conservative, and Irish Nationalist alike, collected £600, which was distributed in the form of relief tickets through the local Co-operative Society. The brave words and braver deeds, however, were to no avail as the strike dragged on through August and into September.

Larkin's temper was short and his invective increasingly bitter towards the end. He castigated a striker who wrote an anonymous letter to the Press denouncing the strike and the Union. By way of reply Larkin wrote the editor: 'Sir,—Judging by the remarks of our friend "Sick of the Union" . . . I suggest the union our friend belongs to was the union workhouse, where, bye the bye, when Harrison's has used him up, he will again have to retire.' In replying to a remark by the anonymous striker that he would polish his union button and place it over the mantelpiece for his son to see as an emblematic

---

[1] *Courier*, June 30, 1905.   [2] *Labour Leader*, July 21, 1905.
[3] *Courier*, July 24, 1905.   [4] *Ibid.*, July 27, 1905.

reminder of his father's foolishness, Larkin closed by remarking, 'That eldest boy should be proud of you "Sick of the Union," but the soldier who betrays his comrades is shot like a dog; and that badge you now despise may remind that boy of a creature that was once a man.—I remain, late foreman of T. and J. Harrison, but no blackleg, and not ashamed to sign my name. JAMES LARKIN.'[1] A week later it was all over, and the price the men and their Union had to pay was high, for they had struck for a 'closed shop' and now had to go back as 'free Labourers.'[2]

The strike lasted just over ten weeks and ended in defeat, but during the dispute, Larkin had organized a new branch of the union some 1,200 strong. On the strength of this he was appointed temporary organizer by the Union executive, over the objections of James Sexton, the General Secretary.[3] Soon after the dispute, however, Larkin was Sexton's election agent in a contest for the City Council in St. Anne's Ward, a contest which Sexton won. Just after this a dispute broke out on the municipal docks in Preston and Larkin was sent to take charge. After a few minor clashes, Larkin reorganized the port for the National Union of Dock Labourers and received a permanent appointment as union organizer at £2 10s. a week.[4]

In December, 1905, Larkin returned to Liverpool to act, once again, as Sexton's election agent in the coming general election. Sexton was to stand as the Parliamentary Labour candidate for the West Toxteth Division. Liverpool was solidly Tory at this time except for the Scotland Division, which returned an Irish Nationalist, T. P. O'Connor. R. P. Houston, the sitting member for West Toxteth, had been returned unopposed in 1900 and had piled up a majority of 2,000 in 1895, the last occasion on which he had had to fight for his seat.[5] Sexton, who was never an admirer of Larkin, wrote many years later in his memoirs of the tremendous efforts, honest and otherwise, Larkin made to win the contest:

> Larkin displayed an energy that was almost superhuman. The division was one of the storm centres of religious strife, and the stronghold of the Orange Order, through whom Mr. Houston held the seat. My

[1] *Liverpool Daily Post and Mercury*, September 6, 1905.
[2] *Ibid.*, September 11, 1905.
[3] Sexton, *op. cit.*, p. 203.
[4] Dallas, *loc. cit.*
[5] *The Constitutional Yearbook for 1912*, p. 215.

being a Roman Catholic naturally made the situation still more lively. But nothing could frighten Jim. He plunged recklessly into the fray where the fighting was most furious, organized gigantic processions against Chinese labour on the Rand, faced hostile mobs saturated with religious bigotry who were howling for our blood, and last but by no means least competed with our opponents in the risky game of impersonation then played at almost every election in Liverpool. I am convinced that it was largely owing to Larkin's overwhelming labours that we reduced a Tory majority from four thousand to five hundred, but I would rather not give my opinion on some of the methods he adopted to achieve that highly commendable result.[1]

In 1906 the burning emotional issue in Liverpool was 'Chinese Slavery.' The mine-owners on the Rand had imported Chinese labourers into South Africa because of their willingness and ability to work for practically nothing. The white workers in South Africa saw in this effort to establish a cheap labour market a definite threat to their own precarious standard of living. The Conservatives, and Houston among them, had voted to allow the Chinese to be imported into South Africa. The battle cry against Houston in Liverpool, therefore, became 'Chinese Slavery.' Larkin found a glass-sided hearse, which he fitted out with a makeshift coffin draped with a Union Jack. He employed some fifty unemployed members of the Dockers' Union to make up the funeral cortège at trade union rates. He had their wives make up loose-fitting trousers and jackets on the Chinese style from some cheap yellow cloth, and supplied oakum pigtails which he had made himself. Fred Bower found a dozen picks and shovels, and Larkin some yellow dye for the dockers' hands and faces to make it all the more realistic. On the eve of the election the funeral cortège, headed by a brass band playing the Dead March from *Saul*, wound its way through the Toxteth Division. The theme for the evening was the 'burial of freedom.' The yellow dye, however, did not wash off, and none of the men dared 'shape up' for a Houston-owned boat for a week.[2]

Larkin's strenuous effort, coupled with the fact that the tide was running hard against the Conservatives in 1906, put a formidable dent in the Conservative majority, reducing it to something less than 800.[3] The most unusual thing about Houston, however, was his

[1] Sexton, *op. cit.*, pp. 203–4.
[2] Bower, *op. cit.*, pp. 203–4.
[3] Yearbook, *loc. cit.*, R. P. Houston (C.), 3, 373; J. Sexton (Lab.), 2,592.

rhetoric. This rare piece of eloquence does not deserve to be lost forever.

> Were they to be dismayed by the defeats of Manchester? No, that was not the spirit with which Liverpool would enter on the fight. Their leader in the first engagement had been unhorsed and unseated, and the Manchester Unionist regiment had been annihilated. ('No'.) But on the banks of the Mersey the Unionist Candidates would emulate the example of those noble Romans who stood on the further banks of the Tiber and defended the bridge against the arrays of Tuscany, or those noble Greeks who held the pass at Thermopylae. (Applause.) Had they forgotten the thin red line at Waterloo which broke the charge? When they appeared before the Caesar of public opinion they as Liverpool men were not going to say 'the dying salute thee Caesar,' but 'the winning salute thee Caesar.' (Applause.) They were told the rolling wave of Radicalism approaching from Manchester was going to engulf them in Liverpool, but don't believe it. That wave would break itself on the walls of Liverpool—(applause)—for every man there was a brick. They would dam this rolling tide of Radicalism. The stormy clouds of socialism might roll around them but the Eddystone of Liverpool would shine forth and show the beacon light to guide the rest of England into safety. (Applause.) . . . Since the days of Joshua when the walls of Jericho fell before the blast of trumpets, elections were not won by talking but by hard work. He came down to Liverpool a physical wreck, but the scent of battle had, like a war horse, stirred up the blood which coursed through his veins, blood commingled with that of the Covenanter and the buccaneer—(loud applause)—and that spurred him on. They were there to avenge their comrades who had fallen in the fray in Manchester. (Loud and prolonged applause.)[1]

Houston was wise enough not to depend on his rhetoric alone, however, for his perorations were amply supplemented by the 'hard work' mentioned, and the day following the election, the Tory Press cryptically noted that of election workers, 'the great numerical preponderance rested with the Unionist cause, and the same remark applies to vehicles.' Houston was reported as having 'not fewer than 14 motor cars, 29 traps and carriages, whilst his opponent had two motors and 13 traps at his disposal.'[2] The defeat suffered by Sexton, Larkin, and their followers was softened by the Labour victories elsewhere, and they could find some solace in the thought that though

---

[1] *Liverpool Courier*, January 16, 1906.
[2] *Ibid.*, January 17, 1906.

Houston had been returned he would have very little company in the new House.[1]

After the campaign Larkin was elected General Organizer of the National Union of Dock Labourers. The National Union was organized on a federal basis with the main or head office in Liverpool, and the various branches in the seaports on the Irish Sea. The general policy of the Union was controlled from Liverpool, but the branches were practically autonomous in local affairs and disputes that did not involve serious financial consideration. The chief officers of the Union were the General Secretary, the General President, General Treasurer, and the General Organizer. These officers generally presided over an Executive Committee of about a dozen members which governed the Union between the annual delegate conferences, which elected them to office. Each branch also had a hierarchy of officials and a branch committee, but the number and magnitude usually depended on the size and needs of the particular branch. The key figure in each branch was the branch Secretary, just as on the national level the man who virtually controlled the Union was the General Secretary. The duties of the General Secretary presumably involved periodic visits to the branches to check the accounts, review the administration, and inquire into local labour conditions so as to be better able to formulate the general policy of the National Union. Each branch returned a required percentage of its income to the head office in Liverpool to defray the general expenses of the Union and to build a general strike fund.

James Sexton had been General Secretary of the N.U.D.L. almost since its founding and wielded a great deal of influence with the Executive Committee, if, indeed, he did not control it. Sexton had opposed Larkin's initial appointment as a temporary organizer because, as he wrote years later, he 'strongly suspected' that Larkin 'was playing for his own hand only.'[2] But, continued Sexton, 'to give the devil his due, Larkin was so successful at roping in nonunionists that his appointment was soon made permanent, and for a time he justified his election, though even then the cloven hoof showed itself occasionally in the shape of a self-assertion which went beyond legitimate bounds.' Actually, Sexton recognized in Larkin a threat to his own position in the N.U.D.L. No man with a feeling for power likes to see a strong, independent, and energetic

---

[1] Yearbook, *op. cit.*, p. 255.   [2] Sexton, *op. cit.*, p. 203.

personality come too close to the throne. Sexton sensed Larkin's ambition and feared his obvious desire to lead and dominate. The early antipathy, which Larkin and Sexton felt for each other, was subordinated for a time in a common cause—the building of the National Union of Dock Labourers.

After his election as General Organizer, Larkin proceeded to the reorganization of the moribund Scottish ports. In Aberdeen and Ardrossan he encountered little trouble and things proceeded smoothly, but in Glasgow the task was more difficult. Nearly every shipowner in the port was a member of the Shipping Federation, with its ready supply of 'blacklegs.' The shipowners never hesitated, therefore, to lock out their men when threatened with a strike. The sporadic stoppages of work, generally over the payment of wages, resulted in a great deal of friction between the dockers and the ship-owners. When Larkin had the men properly organized, he was able to reduce the chaos to reasonable proportions, and relations improved to such an extent between the men and their employers that a conference of shipowners and union delegates was arranged for the purpose of recognizing the union as the official bargaining agent for the men. 'Owing to some little difficulties' over arranging the meeting, the conference was postponed, and when it was finally held, Sexton represented the men, since Larkin was in 'another sphere of opera-tions.'[1] At first Larkin had concentrated on the coal-heavers and the crane-men in Glasgow Harbour, and later turned his attention to what was one of the few failures in his organizing career—the iron-ore workers. In reminiscing years later on the death of a friend, he wrote:

> I turned my attention to a body of men who were the most degraded, harrassed body of workers I had ever any experience of in my chequered career—the iron ore workers who discharged the boats from Spain on the Govan side of the River. They were mostly North of Ireland men who lived in the model (?) lodging houses. They were exploited in every cruel way. They were engaged by the hour, and at all hours of the day and night they were put on, according to the number of railway wagons available for loading. No regulations, no considerations given them. They might work one hour loading the wagons available, then stand by for two or three hours, or maybe half a day—get one or more hour's work, draw the few coppers. They were

[1] Report of the Industrial Council on Inquiry into Industrial Agreements, Minutes of Evidence, *Parliamentary Papers*, 1913, XXVIII (Cd. 6953), p. 232.

supposed to get 8*d*. per hour—when working—and what work these men had to carry out cannot be expressed in words. Only men who have shovelled Calcined iron ore or Manganese ore can appreciate their labour. They were in a continual state of semi-starvation and drunkenness. These were the first human beings that I had ever seen drinking methylated spirits or, as it is called in Dublin, 'Spunk'. Many of them never sought even the shelter of a lodging-house, for the doss house charged not less than 4*d*. per night. A few among them—not lost to all sense of manhood—had tried, time and again, to organise their fellows, but failure attended their efforts.[1]

After a short time Larkin found the work even beyond his enormous physical capacity, and had finally to admit the task of organizing these unfortunate men was too much for him.

By the end of 1906 Larkin had completed the reorganization of the Scottish ports, and when the Labour Party decided to hold its eighth annual conference in Belfast in the last week of January, 1907, the union executive thought it was a good opportunity to begin the reorganization of the Irish ports.[2] The National Union of Dock Labourers had organized the Irish ports in the early nineties, but by the turn of the century the Irish branches were moribund.[3] Larkin found the task of organizing the dockers in Belfast and Dublin not much different from that which he had encountered in British ports, for the conditions of employment and the various abuses connected with dock labour were much the same on both sides of the Irish Sea.

The chief complaint of the dockers, and the greatest cause of friction between the men and their employers in almost every port, were the illegal deductions the men had to take in their wages.[4] This came about in several ways, but the most common was the result of fraud on the part of the employer or the stevedore, who functioned as a middleman in the wages paid for piece-work or tonnage. The great majority of the dockers worked at a tonnage rate and were paid on the weight they handled. These men worked

[1] *Irish Worker*, November 22, 1924.

[2] *Ulster Guardian*, February 9, 1907. See also *Forward*, August 17, 1907.

[3] *Ibid.*, February 9, 1907. See also *Forward*, February 16, 1907. 'A union was in existence ten years ago, but went under from various causes.' The minutes of the Dublin Trades Council do not list the N.U.D.L. as a participating society after July 2, 1900.

[4] Report of the Departmental Committee on the Checking of Piece-Work Wages in Dock Labour, *Parliamentary Papers*, 1903, XXXIV (Cd. 4380), p. 2.

in 'gangs' which varied in number from four to twelve, or sometimes more, depending on the class of cargo handled. When they were paid, one of their number, usually the foreman, or 'ganger,' went to the office of the shipowner or stevedore and collected the wages due to his men. The foreman was paid on the tonnage handled and had to accept the word alone of the employer as to the tonnage, since he had no legal right to see a bill of lading or, for that matter, any other relevant document.[1] The abuses in the payment of wages which followed such a system were readily taken advantage of by unscrupulous employers and the only recourse the men had was to threaten the fraudulent employer with a court action. But if the case went to court it would often cost the men more than it was worth.

An even greater deterrent than the cost involved in pursuing justice, however, was the 'victimization' a man was sure to suffer if he openly complained of fraud, or even asked to see the relevant documents.[2] When the 'ganger' was paid by the employer, he customarily proceeded to a public house, where he paid off his men.[3] If the foreman did not actually receive kick-backs, he was at the very least liberally treated to a round of drinks by his 'gang.' This in turn only contributed to the very serious problem of drunkenness among the dockers, besides all the unhappy circumstances that attend the families of men who drink when they cannot afford to do so. It was also customary at this time for 'the men behind the bar' to extend credit to the dockers whom they knew to be working a ship and collect their 'slate' when the foreman came in to pay his men.

Both Larkin and Sexton were appointed in 1907 to be members of the Parliamentary Committee commissioned to investigate these abuses. Larkin also appeared as a witness and was duly questioned by Sexton about the conditions in Belfast when he arrived to reorganize the port for the National Union:

> 529. When you went to Belfast what system did you find with regard to piece-work?—Simple chaos. A stevedore was employed, and he paid the men just what he pleased. There was one man paying $3\frac{1}{2}d.$ a ton

[1] Report of the Departmental Committee on the Checking of Piece-Work Wages in Dock Labour, *Parliamentary Papers*, 1903, XXXIV (Cd. 4380), p. 2.

[2] *Ibid.*

[3] Report of the Departmental Committee on the Checking of Piece-Work Wages in Dock Labour, Minutes of Evidence, *Parliamentary Papers*, 1908, XXXIV (Cd. 4381), p. 4.

to fillers for discharging coal. Another man was paying 4*d*. a ton per man . . .

530. The same ship?—The same ship.

531. There is more than one stevedore in one firm sometimes?— Yes there may be three.

532. These stevedores sometimes have no capital?—Sometimes they have not enough for a week. Sometimes they have to borrow money when a ship comes up.

533. They were employed to evade legal responsibility?—Yes, and they are still kept on.

534. These men are paid by the employer direct the full amount of tonnage discharged?—Yes, a firm at Belfast was paying a man 6*d*. a ton for discharging rails or plate iron. The men were to get 5*d*. a ton. Their agent, who is still employed, was paying 3*d*. a ton for years, and told the men that the firm would not pay more. He was illegally deducting 2*d*. a ton. He was threatened with a summons and he then paid it.

535. The system which you have described generally prevailed before you went to Belfast?—Yes.[1]

The stevedore, or middleman, also came in for his share of criticism by members of the Committee, though in the report the criticism centred mainly on the stevedores of 'little substance' or, as one witness put it, 'the man of straw.' Larkin did not at any time during the Committee hearings, either as a member or a witness, try to conceal the strong contempt he felt for the stevedoring profession, though two representatives of stevedoring unions sat on the same Committee. In rounding off an answer to one question, Larkin bluntly stated, 'We do not want any stevedores,' and in reply to another, 'A stevedore is only an exploiter of the men.'[2] In questioning one witness Larkin asked, 'Do you find as a rule that the stevedore is at fault and not the company?'[3] Later he asked a fellow trade union official, 'Do you think that it would be wiser that the workmen should do the work directly without the intervention of the steve- dores?'[4] When the witness replied to the leading question by saying he thought so, Larkin pressed by asking, 'There is no necessity for a stevedore?' The fellow trade unionist finally closed the obvious circle

[1] Minutes of Evidence, Piece-Work Wages, *op. cit.*, p. 17.
[2] *Ibid.*   [3] *Ibid.*, p. 5.   [4] *Ibid.*, p. 50.

by answering, 'Not in the least. Our people were very foolish when the employers offered them the work in the nineties, and they did not accept it.' Some years later, when he was a power in his own right, Larkin was to return to the vexatious problem of the middleman on the dockside, but solving it was to prove as difficult for him as it has for anyone who has ever tried to eliminate the 'useless' middleman.

By the end of 1906, and at the age of thirty, Larkin had finally brought the apprenticeship phase of his career as an agitator to a conclusion. He was now to begin his journeyman stage not only a convinced Socialist but a trade union official as well. As a Socialist, every day was denunciation day with the promise of a better tomorrow. As a trade union official, every day resulted in another compromise with a system that was dedicated to the frustration of a better tomorrow. Would the Socialist, diluted by the spirit of trade union compromise, eventually come to terms with the despised system? Or would the system purge itself because of the pressure applied by the Socialist and become less despised? Who would reform whom, or, worse yet, perhaps, who would go bankrupt first? The problem of remaining orthodox is like that of remaining young, time is against it. Just as all orthodoxy finds its central truths reduced eventually to abstractions, James Larkin's Socialism became his faith, and his trade unionism became his work. Essentially a Catholic, Larkin believed that both the faith and the work were necessary to the social salvation of the working classes.

PART TWO

Journeyman, 1907–1911

II

BELFAST

IRELAND, in the years following the fall of Parnell, presents an almost unbelievable tableau to the eyes of the historian. With the fall and death of Ireland's 'uncrowned king' in 1891, and the shattering of his magnificent Irish Parliamentary Party into petty factions, the immense energy of the Irish people, which had been for so long channelled to the national cause alone, sought and found new outlets. This release of pent-up energy resulted in the founding and the revitalizing of a score of new movements which permeated nearly every branch of Irish life. The Gaelic League, the Land and Labour Association, the Irish Trade Union Congress, the Co-operative Movement, the Industrial Development Association, the Theosophical Society, the Abbey Theatre, the United Irish League, the Ancient Order of Hibernians, the Independent Orange Order, the All-for-Ireland League, and *Sinn Fein*, were all remarkable movements led by men of energy and ability. All were now able to refresh themselves at the wellspring of national life which had been for too long reserved to the National Being alone. This was truly an exhilarating period and Ireland was never more intellectually alive.

Even Belfast, which had long been in but not of Ireland, shared in and contributed to this general resurgence in Irish vitality. Many strange currents crossed in Belfast in the early years of the present century. In the sweeping Irish revival after the death of Parnell, three important movements pushed to positions of power and influence in the Belfast political arena. The Independent Orange Order, the Ancient Order of Hibernians, and the Labour Party, each in its own interest, challenged the long unquestioned political ascendancy of the old Orange Order, backbone and political machine of the

25

Unionist Party in northern Ireland. By 1906 Orange domination in Belfast was apparently broken, for in the general election of that year three of the four Belfast seats were contested by these varied opponents of the Orange–Unionist political machine. In South Belfast T. H. Sloan, an Independent Orangeman, held his seat, which he had won in a by-election in 1902, by a comfortable majority. In West Belfast, Joseph Devlin, National President of the Ancient Order of Hibernians, was the winner by the narrow margin of 16 votes, and in North Belfast, William Walker, the Belfast Labour Party's choice, came within 300 votes of capturing the Orange stronghold. Only East Belfast could be henceforth counted a safe Unionist seat.[1]

Belfast was not only a seething political volcano in these years, but more than that, a volcano spewing religious bigotry. Even today, nowhere in the world is the abyss which divides Protestant from Catholic deeper or wider than in Belfast. Time has proven a bitter ally to those tolerant souls who hoped that the sectarian strife would succumb finally to its own sterility. Instead, the barren fields of religious bigotry seem to be sown with dragon's teeth, and the yields of bias and hatred continue, growing only more inexplicable with each succeeding generation. During the last fifty years two very powerful historic themes, Socialism and Nationalism, have been hammered and broken on that anvil of militant Protestantism in northern Ireland—the Orange Order. On July 12, during the celebrations of the anniversary of the Battle of the Boyne, one may yet see the Protestant Ulsterman in his Orange sash and bowler hat beating his drums and shouting and singing in the hoarse chorus. It is difficult, indeed, to believe that all this was ever any different and that just after the turn of the century the hard core of Orangeism seemed to soften, and a new era appeared to be in the offing for northern Ireland.[2]

During the course of 1907 the three opponents of the Orange Order in Belfast found in the labour troubles that were to paralyse that city a common vehicle for effecting a temporary anti-Orange alliance. The Labour crisis built up slowly, with three main groups of workers becoming involved, the dockers, the carters, and the coal men. After effectively organizing the port of Belfast and receiving no satisfaction with regard to wage demands, Larkin called some 500 cross-channel dockers out in late June, 1907. The carters then struck

[1] See Appendix D.   [2] See Appendix E.

in sympathy, and the coal men were soon afterwards locked out by an irate Coal Merchants Association. The carters and coal men numbered about 1,000 each. The coal dispute was settled in late July, with the men maintaining their right to combine. The carters won a wage increase, though they failed to enforce a 'closed shop' in the carting trade when they settled their strike in the middle of August. The dockers were the chief victims as they surrendered in September and October, and drifted back to work, if they could find it. In rallying to the support of a widening labour dispute, the Belfast Labour Party, the Independent Orange Order, and the Ancient Order of Hibernians seemed to find a common denominator in the 'cause of the workers.' This newly formed anti-Orange alliance, however, did not survive the ending of the labour troubles. This break-up of an alliance so pregnant with possibilities was the real tragedy and lesson of Belfast in 1907.

When Larkin arrived in Belfast in late January, 1907, he little realized that he would soon be the focus in a revolutionary situation. He began, in his usual way, organizing among the dockers, and attracted some approving attention in Labour circles. 'The visit of Comrade Larkin,' wrote the Belfast correspondent of the *Forward*, '. . . to organize the dockers is bearing good fruit, over 400 of them combining themselves together within the last three weeks. A Union was in existence ten years ago, but went under from various causes.'[1] The labour troubles, which were soon to involve the whole of the port of Belfast, developed out of an almost trivial incident. On Monday afternoon, May 6, 1907, a number of dockers struck work at the York dock of the Belfast Steamship Company because they objected to working with two non-union men.[2] Admitting the men made 'a mistake,' Larkin persuaded them at a meeting the next day to go back to work. When they reported for work the next day, Wednesday morning, however, they discovered their places had been filled by some fifty men sent over by the Shipping Federation from Liverpool. In accusing the Belfast Steamship Company of using the incident as a pretext for 'smashing the Labour Union,' Larkin produced a letter, which he did not explain how he obtained, from the Secretary of the Shipping Federation to his local Secretary for the 'Ulster District.'[3] The letter was dated May 1, 1907, some five days

[1] *Forward* (Glasgow), February 16, 1907. Belfast correspondent.
[2] *Northern Whig* (Belfast), May 7, 1907.
[3] *Irish News* (Belfast), May 9, 1907.

before the men walked out, and it said in part—'As you appear to anticipate a local dispute, we are sending through on Monday Mr. Levine, our general labour superintendent, who will thoroughly investigate the position, and we shall then be prepared to act immediately should the necessity arise.'[1] On Thursday, May 9, 100 more 'blacklegs' were sent over from Hull and Glasgow by the Shipping Federation.

A week after the strike began an attempt was made by the Lord Mayor to settle the dispute by arbitration. Though Larkin was willing, the chairman of the Belfast Steamship Company, Thomas Gallaher, who also had an interest in Belfast's largest tobacco and rope factories, absolutely refused to have anything to do with Larkin, 'and proposed as an alternative that three workingmen from amongst the members of the Dockers' Union should be appointed as a deputation to wait upon him.'[2] The dockers refused to consent to a demand that would in effect give the employer veto power over the trade unionist's basic right to choose his own bargaining agent. The next evening Larkin referred to 'Gallaher' as an 'obscene scoundrel,' and said that 'although St. Patrick was credited with banishing the snakes, there was one he forgot, and that was Gallaher —a man who valued neither country, God, nor creed.'[3] A few days later Larkin was somewhat more humorous when he remarked, 'Now men were going about traducing him, saying his father had been hanged. (Laughter.) Well, he had not been hanged, but if he had it might have been for something good. In any case the man they were fighting would not be hanged, for no honest rope would do it, and no respectable hangman would put his hands to the job. (Laughter and Applause.)'[4]

Towards the end of May, when the strike had been in progress for some three weeks, public interest was reported on the wane, 'but meetings of the men are still held nightly, and extra police are detailed for the protection of the imported labourers.'[5] Public interest was revived when, on May 31, Larkin was arrested for an assault on one of these 'blacklegs' and released on bail.[6] A number of the 'imported men' becoming bored at being confined aboard the S.S. *Caloric*, had decided to venture ashore to get something to drink. The 'blacklegs' entered a 'pub' in Waring Street, and soon

[1] *Irish News* (Belfast), May 9, 1907. [2] *Ibid.*, May 15, 1907.
[3] *Northern Whig*, May 18, 1907. [4] *Ibid.*, May 20, 1907.
[5] *Ibid.*, May 25, 1907. [6] *Irish News*, June 1, 1907.

word was winging that they were in the neighbourhood. A large and threatening crowd surrounded the premises, and the imported men, finding themselves trapped, decided to make a break for it. One, Richard Bamber, failed to escape, and when he was cornered, he drew a knife. Larkin, who was lounging against a convenient lamppost watching the proceedings, saw the crowd fall back, and, on seeing the knife, shouted a warning. When Bamber then made for him, Larkin staggered him with a convenient paving stone. Bamber succeeded in stabbing three men, however, before he was finally felled with a blow from a shovel. A policeman managed to rescue the unfortunate man, and Larkin was duly arrested, and returned for trial, for assaulting Bamber. The Magistrate's hearing was a farce, as were, indeed, most courtroom scenes in Ireland. A witness for Larkin, for example, testified on cross-examination that he was an 'absolutely independent' witness.

> And being an absolutely independent witness, you have no interest in this matter one way or the other?—None.
> And having no interest in it one way or the other, do you happen to be the bailsman of James Larkin?—Yes.[1]

After several delays, which included a change of *venue* to Dublin, Larkin was finally tried and found not guilty in early 1908.[2]

Following Larkin's arrest, and throughout June, tension began to build up on the dockside. 'At the quay during the past few weeks,' commented the *Northern Whig*, 'various grades of workers have been busy sending in ultimatums to their employers, mainly on the question of wages, and in some instances they have been successful in obtaining their demands.'[3] In an attempt to standardize dockers' wages, Larkin sent a circular letter, on June 20, to all the owners engaged in cross-channel traffic 'demanding an advance of wages all round.'[4] The demands were not met and by June 26, the usual supply of 'blacklegs' was provided by the Shipping Federation with the regular detail of police to protect them from the 1,000-odd men now affected by the extension of the dispute. As a further precaution 500 military were called out and detailed to cordon off the quays from the strikers' pickets.

To further complicate matters a good many carters, who carried

---

[1] *Northern Whig*, June 14, 1907. *Irish News* did not carry the report.
[2] *Irish News*, January 15, 1908.   [3] *Northern Whig*, June 20, 1907.
[4] *Ibid.*, June 21, 1907.

goods to and from the docks to the railways and places of business in Belfast, struck work in sympathy with the dockers. For the next few days there was a struggle between Larkin's Dockers' Union and the rather tame 'carters' association . . . that had been in existence for many years' for control of the carters of Belfast.[1] Larkin won, and most of the carters, or at least the most militant of them, joined the Dockers' Union and refused to allow any goods to be carted to or from the firms affected by the strike. At this juncture in the strike Larkin made excellent use of the recently passed Trades Dispute Act (1906), which guaranteed, among other things, the right of 'peaceful picketing,' not as yet well defined under law. Larkin had copies of the Act printed and distributed and then dramatically presented himself and his pickets before the cordon of troops and police, read the Act aloud, and demanded the right to pass.[2] The officers of the military and police were in a real dilemma as to how to proceed, since they were neither familiar with the provisions of the Act nor with their interpretation. After a brief and hurried consultation they allowed Larkin and a small party of his pickets to pass through the lines, to the immense enjoyment of the huge crowd which gathered to witness the proceedings. The carters by this time had made the assignment of protecting the vans too difficult for the infantry and police, and on July 1, the cavalry was called on to escort the vans.[3]

At this point a crisis developed involving Larkin's leadership of the strike. If one judges from Larkin's reactions, the criticism centred mainly on the point that he was backed only by a militant minority of the men involved. The fact that Larkin was a Catholic, always an effective red herring in Belfast, was also dragged in to confuse the issue. Larkin reacted to the criticism and the vague innuendo by resigning his position as strike leader at a mass meeting of the men.[4] The next night Alexander Boyd, a Belfast Socialist, a trade unionist, and a Protestant, who was especially influential among the dockers and carters, announced that Larkin was not going to be allowed to

[1] Report of the Industrial Council of Inquiry into Industrial Agreements, Minutes of Evidence, *Parliamentary Papers*, 1913, XXVIII (Cd. 6953), p. 406. A. M'Dowell, November 26, 1912. M'Dowell, who was the shipping companies' solicitor in Belfast, said the old carters' association 'had been conducted in a most respectable and satisfactory way . . . the carters in the old association were perfectly willing to do carting from those steamers that had been boycotted. . . .'

[2] *Irish News*, June 28, 1907.   [3] *Northern Whig*, July 3, 1907.

[4] *Irish News*, July 3, 1907.

resign. He said that the attempt to divide the men on the question of religion 'would not be successful, because men of all creeds were determined to stand together in fighting the common enemy, the employer who denied the right of the workers to a fair wage.'[1]

In effective control of the strike once again, Larkin resumed the offensive by threatening to close down the port of Belfast with a general strike in the transport trade if the cross-channel companies did not come to terms. In the course of a manifesto to the merchants of Belfast, Larkin said that 'the members of the combined Unions, general cargo, coal quay, and cross-channel traffic, together with the Carters' Union, have decided that, in the event of this dispute being prolonged over the week, to cease work over the entire place.'[2] The employers in the carting trade, through their organization, the Master Carriers' Association, immediately picked up the challenge, as they gave notice that they would enforce a general lockout if the striking carters did not return to work.[3] The next day the carters of some sixty firms struck work, and their effective 'peaceful picketing' resulted in practically no carting being done in the city of Belfast. At the end of the week of grace the coal merchants answered the threat of a general strike by locking their men out over the 12th of July weekend. They also issued an ultimatum, signed by eighteen firms, which struck at the trade unionist's basic right of combination. Since it is such a remarkable piece of arrogance and, further, since it is a definite indication of the type of employer mentality which Larkin had to face in Belfast, and later throughout Ireland, it deserves to be quoted in full:

We have unanimously decided:

1. That no person representing any union or combination will, after this date, be recognized by any of us.

2. That we will exercise our right to employ and dismiss whom we choose, and on whatever terms we choose, and that all persons while employed by us shall work together harmoniously.

3. That, in the event of a strike, whether general or confined to one or more firms, taking place, due to dissatisfaction with the terms or conditions of employment prevailing in the trade without at least three days' written notice having been given by the men to the employers, specifying the grievance complained of, we will immediately lock out all our men.

---

[1] *Irish News*, July 4, 1907. [2] *Northern Whig*, July 4, 1907. [3] *Ibid.*

To enable the men to carefully consider these conditions, work will not be resumed until Monday, the 15th inst., at 10 o'clock a.m. and then only if there shall have been previously shown a general unanimity amongst the men to accept our terms.[1]

In way of reply the men did not even apply for work on the Monday morning designated, and some 1,000 coal men were now added to the 1,000-odd carters also locked out and the 500 dockers striking on the cross-channel quays.

Larkin himself was not in Belfast for the 12th of July celebrations because he had to return to Liverpool to visit his mother who was very ill. The meeting of the old Orange Order on the 12th, however, was remarkable in that there was not even a mention of the strike that was paralysing Belfast.[2] On the other hand the meeting of the Independent Orange Order, with R. Lindsay Crawford and T. H. Sloan presiding, warmly supported the strikers in their speeches and resolutions.[3] Lindsay Crawford, President of the Grand Lodge of Independents, was by this time a strong supporter of Larkin and the strikers. Crawford had taken over the editorship of the Liberal weekly, the *Ulster Guardian*, early in January, 1907, just before Larkin began his work in Belfast.[4] He had strong Labour sympathies and ran a special column called 'Labour World.' On July 20 Crawford, finally exasperated by the employers' attitude, supported the men in his editorial columns and pointed out, 'The best reply to make to the opponents of Mr. Larkin is to point to the fact—admitted by the employers themselves—that they have been compelled to raise wages and reduce hours all round since Mr. Larkin organised the men.' 'If the men were deserving of these better conditions of labour before Mr. Larkin's arrival,' continued Crawford, 'why did they not obtain them? Because they were not organised, and the employers pocketed not only their trade profits but the hard earnings of the men as well.'[5]

To add to the general pandemonium, with some 2,500 men out, including roughly 500 dockers, 1,000 carters, and 1,000 coal labourers, the Belfast police mutinied.[6] The police, or, to be more

[1] *Irish News*, July 12, 1907.   [2] *Northern Whig*, July 13, 1907.
[3] *Irish News*, July 13, 1907.
[4] *Ulster Guardian* (Belfast), December 28, 1907. Crawford mentioned in the course of a libel action against the *Ulster Guardian* that he took over as editor on January 16, 1907.
[5] *Ibid.*, July 20, 1907. 'Case for the Men.'   [6] *Irish News*, July 25, 1907.

precise, the Royal Irish Constabulary, had for some time been dissatisfied with their wages and working conditions. Six months before
the strike, a Royal Commission took evidence on the alleged
grievances of the R.I.C. To the immense annoyance of the police,
the Report had been shelved.[1] It was evident, in the early stages of
the strike, that the Constabulary were dissatisfied with the prevailing
conditions, since there appeared in the *Irish News* a letter to the
editor, obviously by a policeman, complaining bitterly about the
long hours of extra duty entailed by the strike without any form of
compensation and denouncing especially the preferential treatment
accorded the military and the harbour police.[2] Larkin added fuel to
the fire when, on July 16, he noted in a speech to the strikers that the
police were working 18 hours a day while not receiving a penny
extra, and were ready to strike if only they dared.[3] Some days later
the police presented a series of demands to their superiors which
almost took the form of an ultimatum and was viewed by the
authorities as a serious breach of discipline. On July 24 the police
mutinied when an 'attempt to arrest the men's leader,' Constable
Barrett, was prevented by the police themselves, and an 'Acting
Commissioner was knocked down,' in an 'extraordinary barracks
scene.'[4] The authorities withdrew the suspensions they had ordered
among the police and a modicum of order was restored, while they
began to pour thousands of troops into the city. When the authorities
felt they had the situation in hand Constable Barrett was dismissed
and six others were suspended. By August 6, the mutiny had been
suppressed, as 'almost the entire force' in Belfast was transferred to
the outlying country districts in Ireland.[5]

The day after the police mutiny began, significantly enough, the
coal dispute was settled, the men going back on almost the same
terms and conditions that had prevailed before they were locked
out.[6] The masters in this instance were frustrated in their attempt to
force what amounted to a 'yellow-dog' contract, or, as it is known
in Britain, 'the document,' on the men employed in the coal trade.
The two representatives of the General Federation of Trade Unions
who successfully arbitrated the coal dispute now attempted to settle
the carters' strike, which was felt to be the key to the whole situation.

---

[1] Richard Elliot, 'The History of the Belfast Strike,' *Forward*, August 17, 1907.
[2] *Irish News*, June 28, 1907. The letter was signed 'Justitia.'
[3] *Ibid.*, July 17, 1907.   [4] *Ibid.*, July 25, 1907.
[5] *Ibid.*, August 6, 1907.   [6] *Ibid,* July 26, 1907.

A conference was arranged between the Master Carriers' Association and the representatives of the carters. In the beginning the negotiations began to look better as the police mutiny began to look worse. But on Monday, August 5, the conference broke up when the masters presented a new set of rather stiffer terms than those that had been provisionally agreed upon the previous Saturday evening.[1] The men claimed the bad faith and the 'absurd terms' were the result of the success the masters had in persuading 'the authorities to call out the military' between Saturday night and Monday morning. By Monday Belfast had been stripped of the disaffected police, and the men claimed the military 'were allowed to appear on the streets to intimidate the strikers.'[2]

Bitterly, both sides settled down for a fight to the finish. In order to raise the morale and fighting spirit of the men, the Strike Committee called for a monster meeting on Sunday, August 11. The whole of the Labour leadership, with their Independent Orange allies, were in full attendance. Larkin, Boyd, and Lindsay Crawford were the principal speakers, but the surprise of the day was the appearance of Joseph Devlin, the Catholic-Nationalist Member of Parliament for West Belfast. Up to this time Devlin and his Ancient Order of Hibernians had been careful not to commit themselves as to the strike. The *Irish News*, their official organ, had indeed been sympathetic to Larkin and the strike from the beginning, but it was not out of any love for the cause of Labour. These opportunistic Catholic-Nationalists saw only that Labour was effectively fighting the common enemy—the Orange oligarchy in Belfast. This was made perfectly clear when the *Irish News*, in covering Devlin's speech at the strike rally, mentioned only that he 'held the audience in the spell of his eloquence.'[3] Significantly enough, to find a full report of Devlin's speech it is necessary to go to one of the chief Orange newspapers in Belfast, the *Northern Whig*. In what was one of the finest of his many extemporary efforts, Devlin explained that the reason he did not come sooner was that he did not want to give the

[1] *Irish News*, August 6, 1907.

[2] Elliot, *loc. cit.* W. A. Appleton, who was one of the representatives of the General Federation of Trade Unions, wrote some years later that 'the failure to effect a settlement . . . was due . . . to a distinct breach of faith on the part of the employers, who sought to vary the terms of the agreement after most of the conditions had been accepted by a mass meeting of workers and just prior to the final vote being taken.' *Daily Herald* (London).

[3] *Irish News*, August 12, 1907.

'capitalistic' Press the opportunity for raising sectarian differences among the workers.[1] This subordination of Nationalism and Catholicism to the 'cause of the workers,' however, proved an indigestible piece of heresy for the editors of the *Irish News*.

The day after the vast strike meeting, rioting broke out in the Falls Road district, the Catholic working-class section of the city, and clashes were reported between the rioters and the military.[2] The following day, Tuesday, August 12, in the course of five hours' fighting, the military fired on the rioters, killing two and injuring many.[3] Larkin, who had left for Dublin immediately after the Sunday meeting, hurried back, and with the help of Boyd, Walker, and the Catholic clergy, posted pickets in the affected areas to maintain order after the police and military were withdrawn.[4] To prevent the rioting from taking a religious turn, handbills reading, 'Not as Catholics or Protestants, as Nationalists or Unionists, but as Belfast men and workers stand together and don't be misled by the employers' game of dividing Catholic and Protestant,' were posted and distributed in the Falls Road district.[5]

The Board of Trade finally intervened and sent George Askwith, later Sir George and then Lord Askwith, the most able of their arbitrators, to try to settle the dispute. Askwith soon learned that 'under no circumstances would the employers meet Larkin,' and that Larkin 'was tired of both employers and Government officers.' He also found that though nothing 'would or could be done as regards the dockers till they returned to work . . . the carting employers might be willing to settle if a fair tariff could be arranged.'[6] Along with another official of the Board of Trade, Askwith went in search of Larkin and found that

> He was surprised to see us, but after intimating that the British Government and all connected with it might go to hell, launched into long exhortations of the woes of the carters and dockers and denunciations of the bloodthirsty employers, collectively and individually. I said that all this might be true, though, not having been an official for more than ten days, I could scarcely be responsible for the acts of the British Government and in fact wanted some help myself. . . . I

[1] *Northern Whig*, August 12, 1907.   [2] *Irish News*, August 13, 1907.
[3] *Ibid.*, August 14, 1907.   [4] Elliot, *loc. cit.*
[5] *Northern Whig*, August 14, 1907. Quoted also in J. D. Clarkson, *Labour and Nationalism in Ireland* (1925), p. 219.
[6] Lord Askwith, *Industrial Problems and Disputes* (1920), p. 109.

knew that carters are always difficult in a dispute, because of the variety of grades, the strict relative position of grades, and the importance of conditions, such as overtime, distance, care of horses, etc. Mr. Larkin could not tell exactly what the carters wanted, so it was suggested some of them should be got, and we would jointly try to find out. This idea interested him, and it was done. We got chairs from somewhere, and sat down to work it out, sending for some lunch to consume as we worked. So great was Mr. Larkin's zest on this new tack, and so angry did he get at the carters' differences of opinion and changing of proposals, that he did most of the talking, with an occasional phrase from me and gave them lectures which no employer would have dared to utter.[1]

Armed with the resulting document, Askwith arranged a conference between the representatives of the masters and the men, who met in separate rooms, the necessary papers being shuttled back and forth. The details of the agreement were worked out, subject, of course, to final ratification by a full meeting of the parties concerned. Antony MacDonnell, later Lord MacDonnell, was to explain the terms to a *plenum* session of the employers, while Askwith was to deal with the men. Both carters and dockers were summoned to St. Mary's Hall by a crier and bell on the evening of August 15, to hear the proposed terms of the agreement.

The body of the huge hall was filled with carters, while the galleries were crammed with dockers, who got nothing, but who might not accept the view that, if the carters were settled, their course was to return to work, when they would certainly get a corresponding rise from the employers who would do nothing while they were out on strike. They had a long wait, and might be hostile. Afterwards we chaffed Mr. Sexton, a small man, for having taken the precaution of putting two revolvers in his breast pocket. As we entered the hall, Mr. Larkin asked me if I would sit next to him. I said, 'Yes. Why?' 'Because,' he replied, 'I wish you would pull my coat-tails if I say anything wrong.' There was no need for that precaution. In two minutes Mr. Larkin has the men throwing up their caps and roaring applause. He ridiculed the employers and their own representatives, who, he said, would never have known their own minds if I had not told them what to say, the fact being that he himself had settled these uncertain persons. The men wanted to hear every detail, and hence the noise and passage of time before the agreement was ratified.[2]

[1] Lord Askwith, *Industrial Problems and Disputes* (1920), p. 111.
[2] *Ibid.*, p. 112.

Under the terms of the agreement some 1,000 carters returned to work, leaving about 500 dockers still out. The carters 'gained their point in the matter of wages,' but the masters reserved 'the right to employ whom they please, whether union or non-union,' and the men's efforts to effect a 'closed shop' in the carting trade went by the boards.[1] By August 28 an agreement was negotiated for a new wage scale in the coal and iron-ore trades by which the men gained, once again, on the point of wages, while the employers reserved 'the right to employ whom they choose.'[2] The dockers fared badly, however, for, on September 4, a deputation of the men 'waited upon' the Belfast Steamship Company 'and expressed their sorrow for what had happened, their intention if reinstated in their employment of working harmoniously with any fellow employees.'[3] By November 1 most of the dockers followed the course of the men in the Belfast Steamship Company, and appeared before their former employers with their hats in their hands.

After the capitulation of the dockers, it might be expected that the port of Belfast would be in for a long reign of peace and quiet. Such was not the case, for, though after six months' constant strife, the curtain had been rung down on the Belfast strike, the epilogue was yet to be recited. That the men were not yet exhausted was proven when 500 coal men suddenly struck work on November 15, claiming that the masters had broken the July agreement.[4] Two days later, with Larkin in command, 30 carters also came out, while the next day 50 crane men followed suit; the coal men in Newry struck in sympathy and refused to unload a coal vessel from Belfast.[5] Blacklegs were immediately recruited from the surrounding countryside, the Shipping Federation variety being too expensive, besides being reluctant, and another port-wide strike seemed imminent. Larkin was supporting the men, but Sexton arrived on the 26th and took the dispute completely out of his hands. Sexton interviewed Alexander M'Dowell, law adviser to the local employers, and then addressed a large meeting of the strikers. He 'told them that they were to return to work the next day, and that no advantage would be taken of any man. All was to be plain sailing and the past was not

[1] *Irish News*, August 16, 1907.
[2] Report of the Industrial Council, Minutes of Evidence, *op. cit.*, p. 617.
[3] *Northern Whig*, September 5, 1907. Quoted also in Clarkson, *loc. cit.*
[4] *Irish News, November* 16, 1907.
[5] *Ibid.*, November 20, 1907.

to be reaped up.'[1] From the treatment the men received when they reported for work, it was evident that all was not to be 'plain sailing,' and Sexton had misrepresented the facts, since he had not come to any understanding with the representatives of the employers.[2] In this last phase of the Belfast strike, the coal men who refused to swallow their pride were left standing on the dockside to face not only the coming winter but one of the severest trade depressions yet experienced in the British Isles.

Sad as the finale was for the dockers in September, and the curtain call for the coal men in November, sadder still, from the long-run point of view, was the deterioration of the anti-Orange alliance, which during the course of the strike seemed to have found a common denominator in the 'cause of the workers.' On October 28, in Ulster Hall, Joseph Devlin, in the course of a speech that defied definition, blandly repudiated any connection with the strike or Larkin:

> Let me say that I knew nothing whatever about the strike in its inception. I know nothing whatever about the strike in its progress, and I do not think I even know to the present moment what the absolute results of the strike were. I have never spoken to Mr. Larkin in my life but once, and that was about two minutes. I have never received a communication from either Mr. Larkin or anyone connected with the strike during its progress, before it commenced or after it had ended.[3]

The *Irish News* did not miss this speech, but reported the near two-hour effort in nine full columns.

Some six weeks later, in the same Ulster Hall, T. H. Sloan, the Independent Orange member for South Belfast, sounded the beginning of the end for the solid Independent Orange–Labour alliance.[4] Sloan had become extremely 'jealous of Crawford's popularity,' and finally succeeded in getting the Grand Lodge of Independents to

[1] *Irish News*, November 28, 1907.

[2] Report of the Industrial Council, Minutes of Evidence, *op. cit.*, p. 407. A. M'Dowell testified that 'Mr. Sexton came to me in the month of November from Liverpool, and stated that he deplored what had happened in connection with the Belfast section; it was not due to anything in connection with headquarters, but it was a troublesome sectional dispute, and he asked me if I could make arrangements for the restoration of the men. I explained the position to him, and told him that a large number of additional men had been employed, and I could not make any arrangement at all.'

[3] *Irish News*, October 29, 1907.

[4] *Ibid.*, December 17, 1907.

expel him.[1] Many 'labour sympathisers' resigned in protest, and the Independent Orange Order rapidly declined as a force in Ulster Politics. Crawford was fired by the Liberal *Ulster Guardian* in June, 1908, for advocating, as he explained, 'the right of the workers to a living wage and fair conditions of labour.'[2] After several more disappointments in Ireland, Crawford finally emigrated to Canada in May, 1910.[3] Sloan continued on his downhill road and lost his seat to a staunch Unionist in the general election of January, 1910.[4] In the same general election the Labour Party's perennial candidate, William Walker, was unavailable, and Robert Gageby, another popular trade unionist was selected to contest North Belfast. Though Gageby lost, he did well, since Home Rule was once again in the air, and the election was fought bitterly all over Ulster.[5] Only Joseph Devlin, in West Belfast, who fought bigotry with intolerance and matched political machine against political machine, survived the inundation, a Nationalist island in an Orange sea.[6]

The myth that has grown up around James Larkin claims Belfast as one of his great achievements. What happened in Belfast can, of

---

[1] MSS. Thomas Carnduff, *North of the Eire Border*, p. 50. These are Mr. Carnduff's unpublished memoirs, which he was kind enough to let me use. They are extremely valuable in that they throw much light on the inner history and workings of the Independent Orange Order, of which he was a member.

[2] *Freeman's Journal* (Dublin), June 2, 1907. See also Crawford's letter to the London *Times*, April 21, 1907. Also *Forward*, June 13, 1908, quotes from Crawford's pamphlet, 'Liberal and Tory Hypocrisy.' Crawford wrote, 'I have frequently alluded in leading articles to the necessity of grounding the Liberal revival in Ulster on something more patriotic and statesmanlike than the transference of social power and influence from the Tory to the Liberal side by the wholesale creation of magistrates and the shuffling of offices. . . . To denounce landlord rights as tenant wrongs is a cheap passport to political fame for some Liberal employers of Labour, who own no land, but these men if linen merchants and manufacturers, have a different code of ethics in their relations with flax growers and workers.'

[3] William O'Brien and Desmond Ryan, eds., *Devoy's Post Bag 1871–1928* (1953), V, II, pp. 394–95. See Crawford's letter to Devoy offering to write the history of 'The Rise and Fall of the Independent Orange Movement in Ireland.' Crawford mentioned in the course of the letter that he was in straitened circumstances.

[4] Yearbook, *loc. cit.*, South Belfast: J. Chambers, K.C. (C), 5,772; T. H. Sloan (I.C.), 3,553.

[5] *Ibid.*, North Belfast: R. Thompson (C.), 6,275; R. Gageby (Lab.), 3,951.

[6] *Ibid.*, West Belfast: J. Devlin (N.), 4,651; Capt. J. B. Boyd-Carpenter (C.), 4,064; P. J. Magee (I.N.), 75.

course, be conceived in the most grandiose terms. It could include the destruction of political and religious bigotry, organizing the workers for the revolutionary act, and contributing to the dignity and integrity of the working classes. The rub is that Larkin did achieve all these things, but only to a limited extent. He did blend, for example, Orange and Green on a Labour canvas, but the pigment proved soluble in the religious wash. He did explain that he was a Socialist, but his winning better wages and conditions cannot be offered as a laying of the foundations for a change in the social order. He did appeal to what was best in the Belfast workers, but how much their store of dignity and integrity were increased by him is certainly impossible to say. Still, is the attempt to count for nothing? No!—only beware of confusing it with the achievement. In the long run Larkin achieved little of a tangible nature in Belfast, not because he was something less than what he should have been, but because his enemies were too powerful and circumstances too adverse. In the short run he shook Belfast to its roots. There had not been such an upheaval in a hundred years, and there has not been one since.

III

DUBLIN

THOUGH born and raised in the Liverpool slums, Larkin was shocked by the social conditions of Dublin.

> If Dublin men were so proud of their city [he remarked on an early visit], 'why did they not look after the little children who were running about their streets hungry and dirty, and badly clothed; and why did they not put a stop to the disgraceful scenes in O'Connell street, when fellows from the slums of London, in red uniform, were coming along with Irish girls on their arms, whom they would ruin in body and soul?[1]

'It was something terrifying,' he said some weeks later, 'to see how the people lived in the streets and slums.'[2] In these years a walk along Gardiner Street from the quays to Mountjoy Square, only one of the many slums in Dublin, was indeed a sobering experience. Behind the graceful façades of the old Georgian mansions, the former town houses of the gentry and nobility of Ireland, lived the poor and destitute of Dublin. The stately simplicity and restrained elegance of these faded monuments to a former magnificence only emphasized the enormous breach between past and present. The great scarred wooden doors, framed in delicate post and lintel and flanked by the inevitable classical columns, gave entrance to 'an inferno of social degradation.' Architectual delights of another day had become dirty, decayed, wretched tenements—'old, rotten, permeated with . . . physical and moral corruption.'[3]

[1] *Freeman's Journal* (Dublin), August 12, 1907.
[2] *Ulster Guardian* (Belfast), September 21, 1907.
[3] Arnold Wright, *Disturbed Dublin* (1914), p. 29.

The poor crowded into these foul dwellings in incredible numbers. Nearly 26,000 families lived in 5,000 tenements, while over 20,000 families lived in one room, and another 5,000 had only two rooms.[1] Of the 5,000 tenements, over 1,500 were actually condemned as not only unfit for human habitation, but condemned, in fact, as incapable of ever being rendered fit for human habitation. The total of Dublin's 'slum jungle' population came to about 87,000 people, or 30 per cent of that city's population of nearly 300,000. The living conditions of these slum-dwellers approached the sub-human. Water was to be found generally only in the yards of the tenements, while baths were unknown. Toilets were also located in the yards, and their scarcity was attested to by the fact that in nearly every tenement 'human excreta is to be found scattered about the yards . . . and in some cases even in the passages of the house itself.'[2] Heat and light were seldom seen beyond the minimum of cooking requirements and the coldest weather. 'In nearly all of these dwellings the hallways are unlighted and filled nightly with waifs and strays of the city, men, women, and children, seeking a place to lay their heads. The reeking stench of these dens pollutes the air of the streets.'[3]

From these festering tenements oozed all the fearful concomitants of Dublin slum life. Death, disease, immorality, insanity, crime, drunkenness, unemployment, low wages, and high rents rolled on in a seemingly interminable vicious cycle. The Dublin death-rate was fantastic. The average death-rate for the whole of Ireland in the decade 1901–10 was 17·3 persons per thousand of the population. In Dublin it was 24·8 for the same period, while in Belfast, the only city of comparable size in Ireland, it was 20·2.[4] There were two main reasons for the high death-rate in Dublin—infant mortality and tuberculosis. The infant mortality figures for Dublin were appalling. For the whole of Ireland in the ten years 1901–10 infant mortality declined from 101 to 95 per thousand births. In Dublin the figure in 1901 was 168, and in 1910 it fell to only 142. In London, by contrast,

[1] Report of the Departmental Committee of Inquiry into the Housing of the Dublin Working Classes, *Parliamentary Papers*, 1914, XIX (Cd. 7273), p. 3.

[2] *Ibid.*, p. 5.

[3] Robert Monteith, *Casement's Last Adventure* (1932), p. 3.

[4] Supplement to the Forty-Seventh Report of the Registrar-General of Marriages, Births, and Deaths in Ireland, containing Decennial Summaries of the Returns of Marriages, Births, Deaths, and Causes of Death in Ireland, for the years 1901–1910, *Parliamentary Papers*, 1913, XV (Cd. 7121), p. xviii. See also James Connolly, *Labour in Ireland* (1920), pp. 254–58.

the rate declined in the same ten years from 148 to 103. Even Liverpool, which had the worst record for public health in Great Britain, had a lower infant mortality rate than Dublin in 1910, with 140.[1] The second great killer in Dublin in these years was the dreaded 'white plague,' tuberculosis. 'It was a regrettable fact,' noted one observer, 'that in Ireland the death-rate from tuberculosis was roughly 50 per cent higher than it was in Scotland and England.'[2] In Great Britain the number of deaths due to tuberculosis had been steadily falling since 1870, while in Ireland the rate remained practically constant.[3] In Dublin itself, because of tuberculosis, 'the vast majority of deaths occurred among the poorer classes, especially in the families occupying single-room dwellings.'[4]

Death, for the working classes of Dublin, was at least the end of a frightful existence. The most difficult problem for those who had to go on living, however, was unemployment. Ireland presented the curious paradox in these years of having a shortage of labour in the rural areas and an enormous surplus in urban areas. This was the result of the general move from country to city the world over, and in Ireland specifically, the great increase in grazing at the expense of tillage depopulated the countryside in the interests of cattle and sheep. The result was a move to the city and a long tradition of emigration to the United States, Canada, and Great Britain. Dublin, unlike Belfast, had no large staple industries to absorb this neverending stream of cheap labour from the country.[5] The absence of large industries resulted in the labour force in Dublin being mainly non-productive. Since Dublin was a trading rather than an industrial city, the bulk of the labour force was employed in the carrying, or

---

[1] *Parliamentary Papers*, 1913, XV (Cd. 7121), p. xlvii. See also Sir William Thompson, Registrar-General, in *Freeman's Journal*, January 20, 1911.

[2] *Freeman's Journal*, March 16, 1912. Lecture by Dudley Edwards at the Statistical Society.

[3] Supplement, *op. cit.*, p. xxxi. Table shows in Ireland the decade 1871–1880, 26 deaths per 10,000 due to tuberculosis. In 1881–1890, 26·7 per 10,000; 1891–1900, 27·7 per 10,000; and 1901–1910, 26·3 per 10,000. See also Countess of Aberdeen, ed., *Ireland's Crusade Against Tuberculosis* (n.d.), pp. 169–70. See also Interim Report of the Departmental Committee on Tuberculosis, *Parliamentary Papers*, 1912–13, XLVIII (Cd. 6164), pp. 24–26.

[4] *Freeman's Journal*, June 5, 1913. Reports of the Public Health Committee of the Corporation.

[5] *Statistical Abstract of Ireland*, 1952, p. 21. See for Dublin population—1891, 331,314; 1901, 361,219; 1911, 386,386. This is for Dublin Registration Area and not the Metropolitan Area, which is smaller.

transport trade. The total male labour force in Dublin in 1901 was 40,277. Of this total only 9,397 men were employed in industry—printing, engineering, clothing, furnishing, and leather tanning. Some 7,602 men were listed as being permanently engaged in the carrying trade, while the remaining labour force of 23,278 men were classified as labourers, building and general. Of the latter the great majority were in the general category and were mainly employed as casuals in the transport trade.[1]

The periodic trade depressions that rocked the British industrial machine did not have the same disastrous effect on the Irish economy, which was based on agriculture. When trade was good in Britain and the industrial machine was functioning well, there was a mild increase in trade in Ireland. When times were bad in Britain, they had little effect on an economy that had actually been in a state of chronic depression for over thirty years.[2] Unemployment in Dublin was always prevalent, and the reason why it attracted more attention in these years than in others was that the Liberal government, through much of its social legislation, not only turned the minds of serious people towards social problems but also provided the machinery for an examination of these problems.

Exact figures are impossible to find for unemployment either in Great Britain or Ireland during these years. The figures offered must always be taken as only an inference or indication and never as absolute. One acute observer took the breakdown for the labour force in Dublin mentioned above and, using the percentages compiled by the Board of Trade in assessing unemployment in the various trades in Britain, arrived at an unemployment figure for the men engaged in industry as well as the 10 per cent figure for the men in the carrying trade, as compiled by the Board of Trade, to stand for Dublin. Of the 9,397 men in industry in Dublin, therefore, the number of unemployed, at 11 per cent, came to 1,099. For the 7,602 men in the

---

[1] L.P.B., 'Unemployment in Dublin,' *Leader*, February 20, 1909. See also Phillip Hanson, 'Unemployment,' *New Ireland Review*, XXXII, January, February, March, and June, 1910.

[2] Royal Commission of the Poor Laws and Relief of Distress, Appendix, Vol. XIX, B. Report by Mr. Cyril Jackson on the Effects of Employment or Assistance Given to the 'Unemployed' Since 1886 as a Means of Relieving Distress Outside the Poor Law in Ireland, *Parliamentary Papers*, 1909, XLIV (Cd. 4390), 'Unemployment due to large trade fluctuations seems very little in evidence. Belfast, where we might expect to find signs of it, has been expanding its trade for many years.'

carrying trade, 10 per cent came to 760. Among the labourers, building and general, the Board of Trade calculated 15 per cent as the employment figure for Britain. In Dublin, however, it was not an 'overstatement of the situation if we decide on 20 per cent.' Twenty per cent of 23,278 came to 4,656. Thus the grand total of unemployed came to 6,515.[1] This figure was corroborated by an independent set of figures presented by Miss S. C. Harrison, Secretary of the City Labour Yard. Miss Harrison, in compiling figures from the lists of the City Distress Committee and the Trades Hall unemployment register, estimated the unemployment figure at 'practically' 7,000.[2]

By the spring of 1910, when the worst had passed in Britain, Dublin's list of unemployed registered at the Labour Exchange (2,338) was still fourth highest in Great Britain and Ireland.[3] The figures on the rate per 10,000 receiving Poor Law relief for May, 1910, in Dublin were an appalling indication of the destitute condition of the poor. The Dublin rate (306) was only exceeded in Great Britain by East and Central London. What was even worse was that Cork, Waterford, and Limerick exceeded Dublin with a figure of 390 per 10,000.[4] Further, the head of the Dublin Distress Committee reported that the Committee would have 10,000 unemployed to register if they had work for them.[5] Finally, it must be remembered that the problem of unemployment and under employment among the female work force has not even been mentioned.

Because of this 'Stagnant Pool' of casual and under-employed labour, low wages prevailed in Dublin and throughout Ireland. Wage figures, like the unemployment figures, are difficult to find and even more difficult to assess. All the indications are that wages in Ireland were much lower than those paid in Great Britain. In the building trades, for example, the wages in Ireland for unskilled men were anywhere from one-quarter to one-third lower than for the same work in Britain. For the skilled men in the building trades it was anything from one-tenth to one-fifth lower.[6] These figures for the

<hr />

[1] L.P.B., *loc. cit.*

[2] *Freeman's Journal*, April 6, 1909. See also *Freeman's Journal*, December 19, 1911. M. J. O'Lehane in D.T.C.

[3] *Ibid.*, July 28, 1910. This figure was for April, 1910.

[4] *Ibid.*

[5] *Ibid.*, March 4, 1910.

[6] Twelfth Abstract of Labour Statistics of the United Kingdom, 1906–1907, *Parliamentary Papers*, 1908, XCVIII (Cd. 4413), p. 40.

building trades give a general indication of the general rates paid on the docks and in the carrying trade.[1] More specific as to wages in Dublin was a special report prepared for the Poor Law Commissioners who were taking evidence in Ireland.[2] A survey involving 1,254 Dublin families, averaging 4·12 persons, found that the average earnings per family was 22s. 2d. per week, of which 15s. 11½d. was contributed by the head of the family, 5s. 11½d. by the other members, and 3d. by lodgers. The report found that there was 'a very wide range in the family earnings, from under 5s. a week to over 60s. a week, but the larger proportion is under 20s. a week.'[3] How the money was spent was another problem. Twenty-one families were asked to keep an expenditure account. As might be expected, food represented the principal item in the family budget, with no less than 63·38 per cent being devoted to that purpose. The next heaviest item was rent, which absorbed 14·5 per cent of the family income. Together, rent and food accounted for 78 per cent of the whole income, leaving little margin for clothing, fuel, and the other necessities of life. Further, the report found that 98·35 per cent of the total income was spent, leaving only the merest fraction for savings. In the case of the majority of the families whose expenditure exceeded income, the entries under 'Pawn Office and Loans' were suggestive of the remedy resorted to.[4] In an estimate based on a Belfast dietary scale, the cost of bare subsistence for a man and wife and three children was estimated at 22s. 5d. per week. No allowance was made for holidays, doctors' bills, furniture, provision for old age, school fees, or any of the comforts of life. If any of these were enjoyed, it was at the cost of proper food or clothing.[5]

Under such living conditions, and with such an unemployment rate and low wages, the crime rate in Dublin naturally soared. In Ireland as a whole, the crime rate was generally lower than in England or Wales. The indictable offences, or, in other words, the more serious crimes, including murder, rape, larceny, and forgery averaged 21·02 per 10,000 of population for the ten years 1898–

---

[1] *Ulster Guardian*, July 20, 1907. See for Belfast scale of wages for dockers and carters.

[2] Royal Commission on the Poor Laws and Relief of Distress, Appendix, Volume X, Minutes of Evidence with Appendix. This Volume Contains the Oral and Written Evidence of Witnesses Relating to Ireland, *Parliamentary Papers*, 1910, L (Cd. 5070). See Appendix No. II. Papers Handed in by Mr. T. J. Stafford, C.B.

[3] *Ibid.*, p. 147.   [4] *Ibid.*, p. 148.   [5] *Irish Nation*, February 20, 1909.

1907.[1] The figure for more highly urbanized England and Wales in 1908 was 27·2,[2] while the rate for Dublin was about 100 per 10,000.[3] The indictable offences did not include drunkenness. Drunkenness was happily on the decline in Ireland in 1908, though Dublin was still worse off than the general average for the whole of Ireland.[4] More disturbing, however, were the figures involving the number of women and children who frequented public houses in Dublin. Twenty-two public houses in Dublin were observed for two weeks, and 46,574 women and 27,999 children, of whom 5,807 were babies in arms, went into them.[5]

The Belfast figures were much lower and the explanation seemed to be in the fact that there were no public houses in Belfast where groceries were sold. In Dublin nearly every public house in the poorer districts was also a grocery. Only London exceeded Dublin in the average number of children frequenting a public house every hour. The London figure was 9·02 children per house per hour and Dublin was 8·15.[6] Belfast, and even Liverpool, were much lower, with 1·89 and 1·25 respectively. Drink was one of the contributing factors in accounting for the large proportion of lunatics, idiots, and insane people in Dublin. The rate of 63·5 per 10,000 was due, in part, according to Dr. W. R. Dawson, to drinking methylated spirits and sometimes turpentine.[7]

The usual Irish reticence on the subject of sex has made any gathering of figures impossible. It was common knowledge that O'Connell Street and Grafton Street in these years were crowded with prostitutes. In fact one side of O'Connell Street was reserved for

[1] Judicial Statistics, Ireland, 1908. Part I. Criminal Statistics, *Parliamentary Papers*, 1909, CIV (Cd. 4793), p. 9.

[2] Judicial Statistics, England and Wales, 1907. Part I. Criminal Statistics, *Parliamentary Papers*, 1909, CIV (Cd. 4544), p. 11.

[3] Judicial Statistics, Ireland, *op. cit.*, p. 13.

[4] *Ibid.*, pp. 15–16.

[5] Information Obtained from the Police as to the Frequenting of Public-Houses by Women and Children in the Six County Boroughs in Ireland, *Parliamentary Papers*, 1909, LXXIII (Cd. 4787), p. 3.

[6] Information Obtained from Certain Police Forces as to the Frequenting of Public-Houses by Women and Children in England, *Parliamentary Papers*, 1907, LXXXIX (Cd. 3813), p. 3. The calculations on Dublin and Belfast are my own, as the Irish report does not give such a breakdown.

[7] Royal Commission on the Care and Control of the Feeble-Minded. Report of the Medical Investigators with Memorandum Thereon, *Parliamentary Papers*, 1908, VI, Part IV (Cd. 4220), pp. 407–54. Dr. W. R. Dawson.

'respectable people' and the other was given over to the unfortunate women who flocked nightly from the working-class districts in order to supplement their paltry earnings.[1] It was the custom in Dublin during these years for women to board the ships in port and sleep with the crew. Larkin refused to allow any of his dockers to work a ship where such a state of affairs existed and finally managed to check this on the dockside.[2] The streets were also crowded night and day with bands of children, the waifs and strays who had no permanent home or parents and begged and hawked a living from the passers-by.[3] One observer was driven to write:

> [O'Connell Street] is crowded with English soldiers, to whom Irish girls have flocked from the Coombe and other parts of the city, where they have no fit home in which to stay. People have been lately complaining in the Press that they are followed in the street by children, or their elders, trying to gain the tenth part of a penny. It is easy to understand that people should be annoyed not to be left at peace, when they themselves are put 'to the pin of their collar' to keep a good roof over their heads. Nevertheless ought we not all to ask ourselves whether children go about bare-legged and ill-fed through mere perversity, and whether it is a natural, legitimate, and inevitable state of things that some people should be unable to feed themselves and their families?[4]

When Larkin began his work in Dublin amid these social conditions, he was not so fortunate to find, as he had in Belfast, a strong and vigorous Socialist and Labour Movement. James Keir Hardie had, indeed, founded a branch of the Independent Labour Party in Dublin in November, 1894. By August, 1895, however, the branch reported, 'We are now entering a new era as far as Socialism is concerned in Dublin. Our comrades have seen the wisdom of (for the present) dropping all attacks on other political parties, and setting themselves to work to educate the people in the principles of Socialism.'[5] Surprisingly enough this political party was still in existence in December, 1895, but early in 1896 it was eclipsed by the more doctrinaire and less temperate Irish Socialist Republican Party. The

[1] Dublin *Leader*, October 8, 1910.

[2] Barney Conway, personal interview.

[3] Rev. John Gwynn, S.J., 'Our Waifs and Strays,' *Freeman's Journal*, October 14, 1910. The paper was read before the Catholic Truth Society. See also ORMAND, 'Street Begging in Dublin,' *Leader*, June 27, 1917.

[4] D.H.G., 'Too Much Education; Too Little Food,' *Leader*, October 8, 1910.

[5] Buggins, 'Notes from the Front, Dublin,' *Clarion*, August 3, 1895.

founder of the Party, James Connolly, an Edinburgh Irishman, was preparing to emigrate to Chile when he was persuaded to try his hand instead at propagating Socialism among the Irish. He laboured earnestly for seven years, until finally in 1903, with dissension rife among his small band of followers, he decided, in disgust, to emigrate to the United States.[1]

During his seven lean years in Ireland, Connolly not only failed to interest the Dublin workers in Socialism but made even less of an impression on the Dublin trade unionists. When the Local Government Act of 1898 gave the Irish working-man a voice in the election of his municipal representatives, a goodly number of Labour candidates 'were elected in Dublin, Cork, Waterford, and other cities and towns. But there was not the distinctly Labour outlook or the necessary discipline for a national Labour movement.'[2] Before Larkin's arrival, therefore, Irish labour in general, and the Dublin trade unionists in particular, except of course for Belfast, looked to the Irish Party at Westminster for the safeguarding of their interests. The Irish Party, for its part, took care to run several prominent trade unionists and other men with strong Labour sympathies in the working-class constituencies.[3] What Labour Movement there was in Dublin in 1908, however, expressed itself through the Dublin Trades Council, but unlike the Belfast Council there were very few members who were Socialists.

Larkin had made his first trip to Dublin to raise funds for the Belfast strike, while at the same time to organize a branch of the National Union of Dock Labourers.[4] He formally launched the National Union in Dublin on a Sunday evening, August 11, 1907, in the Trades Hall. In sketching the situation faced by the working classes in general, and the dockers and carters in particular, Larkin presented his case in terms of the class struggle. 'The capitalists,' he

[1] William O'Brien, personal interview. Mr. O'Brien showed me the pertinent correspondence, but refused to allow me to quote from it because he is preparing his memoirs.

[2] *Independent Labour Party News*, February, 1899. See *Freeman's Journal*, May 31, 1913, for names of original members of the Dublin Labour Party. Most of them ended up in the Irish Party.

[3] *Labour Leader*, January 19, 1906. D. D. Sheehan and Eugene Crean are listed as 'Other Labour Candidates' elected to Parliament. Both were members of the Irish Party. Crean was a trade unionist. J. P. Nannetti, M.P. of Dublin, was also a prominent trades unionist and member of the Irish Party.

[4] *Freeman's Journal*, July 19, 1907; July 21, 1907; August 5, 1907.

maintained, fresh from his Belfast experience, 'tried to divide them on religious or political grounds, and while they were talking robbed both of them.'[1] 'The total wealth production for 1904,' he pointed out by way of example, 'of the three countries, was estimated by economists at something like eighteen millions of money.' 'There were,' he continued, 'forty million of people in the two islands; of these thirty-seven million were actual workers; the remainder were shirkers, who never worked, and never intended to work.' 'Of the eighteen millions,' said Larkin, referring to the wealth produced 'the workmen got about six millions, and the landlord and the capitalist class got the balance.' What was the result asked Larkin? 'No man in that room,' he replied, 'had a guarantee that tomorrow night he would be in his job.' 'Four out of every 11 men in that room,' he continued, 'were going to die in the workhouse, asylum, or jail unless they altered the laws; and they could only do that if they combined.' He then concluded amidst loud applause by asking them characteristically to 'join the Union—either put up or shut up.'[2]

By the end of September, 1907, on flying trips from Belfast, he enrolled some 2,000 men in the Dublin branch. His appeal to the dockers and carters was simple and direct. He pointed out 'the present condition of society was rotten, and they were determined to alter it.'[3] Though it would cost them 1s. 3d. to join the Union, he guaranteed them the employers would be paying that and more by the end of the year. There was enough work for all, he maintained, and what was necessary was that the work as well as the wages had to be equalized. The Union, Larkin argued, wanted to establish itself as the men's bargaining agent to prevent the employers from victimizing those men who had legitimate grievances. Further, a strike was only a last resort, and if the men were properly organized it would not even be necessary. He concluded by asking them to join the Union, 'not because it was the best but because it was the only possible one for them.'[4]

The first six months of 1908 were hectic for Larkin. Besides trouble-shooting for the National Union in its various ports whenever there were difficulties, attempting to perfect and extend the Union's organization in Ireland, attending various Labour conferences and congresses, he was constantly shuttling back and forth between Dublin, Liverpool, and London. Every Thursday from

[1] *Freeman's Journal*, August 12, 1907.   [2] *Ibid.*
[3] *Ulster Guardian*, September 21, 1907.   [4] *Ibid.*

January to the middle of March, for example, he was in London sitting as a member of the Government's Departmental Committee appointed to investigate dock wages. His family, however, was still living in Liverpool where he was now the father of two sons—James and Denis. In April he attended the annual conference of the Independent Labour Party in Huddersfield as a delegate from the Dublin branch.[1] In early June Larkin attended his second Irish Trades Union Congress as a delegate from the Belfast branch of the National Union. He was refreshing, indeed, as he dissolved the pious humbug of the perpetual proposers of resolutions by insisting on a little common sense. When one delegate, for example, demanded that the Government amend the Small Dwellings Acquisition Act so that tenants could buy the house they occupied, Larkin asked him to face the facts. When the workers did not get sufficient wages to allow them to live, he did not see how anyone could advocate their buying their own houses.[2] What was really needed, he maintained, were good municipal dwellings. 'No man,' he argued, 'had any legal, moral, or divine right to own anything in the way of property or land.'[3] When, however, a resolution on primary education was debated, Larkin revealed how little he understood the complexities of the Irish situation and how little help common sense can be sometimes. In skirting the thorny subject of secular education for Ireland, several supporters of the resolution finally came to the conclusion that it was all really the fault of the Government. It was not the fault of the Government, Larkin bluntly pointed out, 'but the people at home, who allowed the present management of the schools to be run on sectarian basis.' 'Until they would get rid of the clerical power,' he maintained, 'and get more labour representation in connection with education there would be no improvement.' In the course of debating the other resolutions, Larkin spoke his mind and antagonized several delegates by the abruptness of his manner. He made a distinct impression, however, on most of the delegates, for he was elected to the nine-member Parliamentary Committee, which functioned as the Executive of the Irish Trades Union Congress between the annual conferences.

By early July, 1908, Larkin had organized nearly 2,700 men in the Dublin branch. It was common knowledge at this time that the

---

[1] Independent Labour Party, *Report of the Sixteenth Annual Conference*, 1908.
[2] *Report of the Fifteenth Irish Trades Union Congress*, 1908, p. 32.
[3] *Ibid.*, p. 36.

51

employers had 'consistently refused to countenance the trade bodies to which the labourers in their service belonged, and when any of them had occasion to put forward a complaint respecting his treatment or conditions of work, instead of the employer agreeing to hear it as presented by his union, he steadfastly refused, and consented to hear it only as advanced by the individual himself.'[1] As a result of this, the men claimed that there were numerous cases of unjust dismissal, and influence was directly or indirectly brought to bear on the men to deter them from joining the National Union of Dock Labourers.[2] Early in July, 1908, the Dublin Coal Masters' Association decided to break the Dockers' Union in the coal trade by locking their men out.[3] The evening of the day the men were locked out, Larkin maintained that 'it could not be charged against them or their organisation that they had tried to force the hands of the coal merchants.'[4] He went on to point out that 'the coal merchants, like other men of business, combine. We don't dispute their right to do so, but we certainly dispute their right to deny to their employees the right to do the same. That is the sum and total of this dispute.'[5] In answering the coal merchants' charge that the Dockers' Union was trying to establish a 'closed shop' in the coal trade, Larkin said, 'Our men don't object to working with non-unionists.'[6] It will be remembered that in Liverpool Larkin had come out with the men in what was essentially a strike for the 'closed shop.' Since he had become a trade union official, however, he had changed his tactics, for in Belfast he had also emphasized the fact that the Union did not demand a 'closed shop.'

The lockout began the next day when the coal merchants dismissed some 400 men. Larkin seemed anxious to avoid trouble on this occasion, for he was extremely temperate throughout. On Sunday, July 12, at a public meeting held in Beresford Place, Larkin was the spirit of moderation. He appeared on the platform with two prominent Dublin M.P.s, William Field and T. C. Harrington, who represented working-class constituencies and were very pro-Labour. All were perfect examples of self-control except Field, who assumed the role of fire-eater on this occasion, and concluded amidst applause by asking: 'What was ever won in the world without agitation—agitation was the life of freedom and the right arm of progress.'[7]

[1] *Freeman's Journal*, July 8, 1908.   [2] *Ibid.*   [3] *Ibid.*, July 10, 1908.
[4] *Ibid.*   [5] *Ibid.*   [6] *Ibid.*
[7] *Ibid.*, July 13, 1908.

That same evening, Antony MacDonnell, now Lord MacDonnell, managed to secure a truce with a return to the *status quo ante* until the whole matter could be settled by arbitration at a conference of all the parties concerned. Sexton arrived on July 18, and agreed that the conference should be held on the 30th at the Irish Office in Westminster. Larkin did not attend this conference since the employers were not prepared to participate if he were present, and, therefore, he had nothing to do with the agreement arrived at in London. The most novel feature in the agreement was the arbitration clause, which was an enormous and unusual concession in those days of rough-and-tumble labour disputes. Both trade unionists and employers alike were wary about committing themselves to such a limited course of action, actuated as they were primarily by motives of mutual distrust. The agreements, though preserving the right of the men to combine, would strictly channel their efforts to bargain collectively through Sexton.[1] The crucial clauses in the London agreement were Four and Five. Clause Four removed Larkin as an effective force in local matters, since after dealing with the 'men concerned,' the employers would deal directly with Sexton in his capacity as General Secretary of the National Union. Significantly enough, when Sexton arrived in Dublin to explain the agreement to the men assembled in the Trade Hall, Larkin took the chair, and did not utter a word during the meeting. The men accepted the agreement and the meeting closed without any apparent display of enthusiasm.[2] Soon after, at a meeting of the Dublin Trades Council, Larkin complained that it was 'simply scandalous how some of the employers were going behind the settlements arrived at both in London and in Dublin.'[3] He emphasized, in a revealing *non-sequitor*, that though he had nothing himself to do with these agreements, 'the men were anxious not to precipitate a strike.'

In these months Larkin had been spending the greatest part of his time in Dublin. So much so that he decided to move his family over from Liverpool and set up his home there. As a result he naturally became more involved in local affairs. He was now in regular attendance at the fortnightly meetings of the Dublin Trades Council, where he was making every effort to get them to see the larger as well as the smaller view of the world. When, for example, there was a discussion about what action the Council should take with regard

[1] *Freeman's Journal*, August 3, 1908. [2] *Ibid.*, August 7, 1908.
[3] *Ibid.*, August 18, 1908. Dublin Trades Council.

to the closing of the newspaper reading rooms in the public libraries during the coming winter, Larkin proposed a resolution endorsing the Right to Work Bill then before the House of Commons. Larkin understood as well as any man that the closing of the reading rooms would be a great hardship on the poor and unemployed, who frequented the library chiefly to keep warm, but the unemployment problem was growing critical throughout Ireland as well as Great Britain, and something more than keeping reading rooms open would be necessary during the coming winter.[1] As a lifelong teetotaller, the temperance movement in Dublin also attracted Larkin's attention, and he was soon prominent in local affairs. In August he was the chief speaker at the celebration held in memory of Father Mathew, the Capuchin temperance priest of the 1840s. He managed to find some 400 temperate members in the Dublin branch, and, along with another 300 dockers down for the day from Dundalk, they paraded in the procession with banners flying. 'It was,' said Larkin on the occasion, 'with all the earnestness he could command, the duty of everyone who had at heart the welfare of Ireland to call upon the National representatives to put in the forefront of their programme legislation to crush the curse of intemperance.'[2] 'Such legislation,' he maintained, 'was logical. A man might have the right to get drunk, but he had no right by spending his means and his health upon drink, to cast upon the other citizens of the State the support of his wife and children.' In seconding Larkin, Alderman Sean T. O'Kelly added that 'Some years ago the Dockers' Union had a social club, and they could remember what sort of a social club it was. But since Mr. Larkin had turned up the state of things had altered, and was likely to remain altered so long as Mr. Larkin was there.'[3]

By this time branches had been organized by Larkin in all the major ports in Ireland, and only Cork remained outside the fold. Acting on information supplied by Sexton, Larkin, in August, 1908, sent James Fearon, who was then branch secretary of the Dundalk and Newry branches, to begin the work of organizing the port of Cork for the National Union of Dock Labourers.[4] Larkin had met Fearon in 1905 while trying to organize the iron-ore workers in Glasgow, and formed a good opinion of him and his abilities. Fearon

---

[1] *Freeman's Journal*, September 15, 1908.
[2] *Ibid.*, August 24, 1908.   [3] *Ibid.*
[4] *Cork Examiner*, September 17, 1909.

proved to be a capable organizer, for by November, 1908, he had organized some 800 men in Cork. In early November, Fearon felt the branch was strong enough to undertake a strike for an improvement in wages and conditions. He had requested in a series of letters to the employers, a rescheduling of wages, but the employers had ignored his communications. Conditions in Cork were much the same as elsewhere, in that the men were victimized for being members of the union and for demanding to see the bill of lading, particularly on the coal boats. The Cork employers, it seemed, had added a new turn to the screw, because the men were demanding 'the right to work a ship from start to finish, in preference to the old system of relief.' 'On all past occasions,' the men complained, 'we have only been able to get two or three hours labour, and then paid off, and fresh men taken on in our places.'[1] It was public knowledge in Cork that the dockers had not received an increase in wages for some twenty years, and that this was the first dispute in sixteen or seventeen years.[2]

On Monday morning, November 9, 1908, 150 men suddenly ceased work on the docks of the City of Cork Steam Packet Company. The strike spread rapidly to the other shipping companies, and soon there were clashes between the police and the men, with several injuries on both sides. The following day the places of some six to seven hundred men were filled by English and Scotch 'blacklegs' who arrived by boat-train from Holyhead. Larkin arrived on Wednesday and immediately branded as a lie the statement that the men were satisfied with the wages that had been paid for the past twenty years. He pointed out that the City of Cork Steam Packet Company were paying their men in Cork 19s. 11d. a week, while in Liverpool they were paying 30s. a week.[3] The next day, Thursday, a truce was arranged and it was agreed the issues involved were to be decided by arbitration early in December.[4] The agreement arrived at in December proved to be a very substantial victory for the men in that they received all they asked for with only some minor modifications.

Before the Cork dispute had come to a head, and with the Dublin coal men and dockers bound by the agreement ratified on August 7, Larkin began to agitate for a wage increase for the men in the carting trade. On September 30 he circularized the chief carting firms by

[1] *Cork Constitution*, November 10, 1908. [2] *Ibid.*, November 11, 1908.
[3] *Ibid.*, November 12, 1908. [4] *Ibid.*, November 13, 1908.

letter, requesting a readjustment in the wage scale.[1] On receiving no reply, he sent out a similar letter four weeks later, and again receiving no reply, he sent out another letter two weeks later demanding a definite answer. On Monday morning, November 16, some 150 carters of four firms struck work. Larkin, who was in Derry and had been ordered by the Executive of the National Union to proceed to Aberdeen, where there was some trouble, elected to return instead to Dublin. On Tuesday, Larkin reported 320 carters out, and asserted that by the next evening it was likely that 1,000 carters would be out. He was moderate in his language, but emphasized that there would only be one end to the strike, for their motto was 'No Compromise.'[2] That evening Larkin explained how the Union had waited patiently and long in the hope of avoiding a dispute, and then graphically sketched the wages and conditions of the Dublin carter:

> At present the men were paid not wages, but a pittance (hear, hear). A large number of the men in dispute were receiving wages by the ton. They were subject to be ordered off at certain hours in the morning, and some days men only earned 9d. He knew men to have been out a whole week, and only earning 9d. a day. That did not apply generally, but the case he had stated was by no means isolated. The men were subject to inclement weather; they had to look after a horse and cart; they had to carry heavy loads, pile them up to the slates, and when there was a rush of work they were expected to rush themselves to death (applause). One firm was working against another, and the employers took advantage of the competition to lessen the men's wages. Their Union was got up to protect the working man not from the honest, but from the unscrupulous employer, and to help the honest employer who was prepared to treat his men fairly (applause).[3]

'A carter in Dublin,' Larkin went on to point out, 'who did as much work in a day as a carter in Manchester or Liverpool would do in a week, and do a class of work—dragging loads—which the latter would not do, was lucky if he had £1 a week, as against 28s. and overtime paid to the English or Scotch carter.'

> In one of the affected firms in the city the men had sometimes to work 112 hours in the week, and they would be asked to work the whole 24 hours every day if the horse could hold out (applause). And often after finishing a hard day's work the carter was sent on a trip to May-

[1] *Freeman's Journal*, November 17, 1908.
[2] *Ibid.*, November 18, 1908.   [3] *Ibid.*

nooth to give him relish for his tea (laughter). They wanted higher wages to improve their conditions, and shorter hours to give other carters a job.

The following day, Wednesday, a visitor 'could not be blamed if he thought the city was in what is termed a state of siege,' as mounted police patrolled the streets, and lorries and vans were protected by police who prevented the carters' pickets from interfering with deliveries.[1] To add to the general excitement, 500 men in the Grand Canal Company picked this moment to strike for an increase in wages and an improvement in their really abominable working conditions. As in the case of the carters, the Union had long been in contact with the Company over the canalmen's grievances. Larkin, in addressing the men at a midday meeting in Bond Street, criticized the Company for having, on the average, eight or nine men, and sometimes as high as fifteen, sleeping in one room, with 'no sanitary accommodations.' The canal-boat men, he went on dryly, 'were often given a broken down horse, and if it collapsed on the way the unfortunate man was fined 10s., and the company bought a new horse with the money.' As with the carters, he declared there would be no settlement unless the terms of the men were met. He counciled the canalmen to talk to the 'blacklegs' as they went in, and reason with them. But in reply to a cry from the crowd for stronger measures, Larkin answered, amidst laughter, 'that "moral suasion" was the most effective weapon. They should not argue with a man and then knock him down.'[2]

On Thursday evening, November 19, I. H. Mitchell, representing the Board of Trade, met Larkin and the employers in separate and informal conferences at Dublin Castle. They agreed to meet again on Friday, but a hitch developed because the canalmen were not represented, and the negotiations were postponed until Saturday afternoon, when a provisional agreement was arrived at.[3] The night before, at a meeting of some 2,000 at the Custom House steps, Larkin said there would be no settlement unless the employers recognized the right of the men to combine. He denounced the 'low wages doctrine in Ireland' as an 'economic fallacy.' 'The secret of all the poverty and unemployment in Ireland,' he continued, 'was that Irishmen were willing to take 50 per cent less wages in Ireland than

---

[1] *Freeman's Journal*, November 19, 1908.
[2] *Ibid.*, November 20, 1908.
[3] *Ibid.*, November 23, 1908.

they would demand in England and Scotland.' This was pure selfishness, for 'men were so selfish here that they would work for low wages at long hours to do a brother out of a job.' He asked them to 'stand on a higher ethical plane than that, and look at the good of the whole. . . . The workers held out the hand of fellowship to every man in Ireland; but this was a class struggle; it was a bigger thing than a bob a day.'[1]

The carters and canalmen returned to work the following Monday morning, while the final terms of the agreement were to be worked out between representatives of the union and the employers. On Thursday, November 26, however, the Grand Canal Company broke off negotiations, declaring that there would be no compromise and they would abide by the port rules arrived at the previous July. The next day the Master Carriers' Association withdrew from the negotiations, saying, in a letter to Sir James Dougherty, the Under-Secretary for Ireland, that since the men refused to carry out the terms of the agreement, it would be fruitless to continue negotiations towards a permanent settlement. Sir James answered that though the complaint might be a legitimate subject for discussion, it did not furnish sufficient ground for breaking off the negotiations.[2] The Master Carriers curtly insisted on adhering 'to the decision announced in their first letter.' Larkin admitted that some carters refused to handle goods going to the Grand Canal Company, but added it was not serious, since it only involved a few loads, and the difficulty was soon straightened out.[3] Once again Larkin had 570 carters, 500 canalmen and 1,000 other men affected by the strike, on his hands. Since Sexton had just informed him that he was on his own as far as funds were concerned, Larkin was openly defiant in the face of his own executive and employers. He gave a 'final warning to the employers. They would crush the Carters' Association, or be crushed by it. . . . Let them now get the British army out as they did in Belfast. He hoped the day would arrive when these men would have to face a citizen army (applause).'[4]

Some days later, Larkin cooled down somewhat and gave a hesitant approval to a public proposal by William Partridge to allow the Lord Mayor and the two Archbishops of Dublin, Protestant and Catholic, to arbitrate the dispute. The negotiations proceeded quietly

[1] *Freeman's Journal*, November 21, 1908.
[2] *Ibid.*, November 28, 1908.
[3] *Ibid.*, November 30, 1908.   [4] *Ibid.*

enough for over a week, but on Friday, December 11, the negotiations were again broken off by the Master Carriers. Public opinion in Dublin had now come completely around to the side of the men. The *Freeman's Journal* summed up the general attitude in its editorial column when it said:

> It is extremely unlikely that the attitude adopted by the Master Carrier's Association will find many defenders among the general public. There is nothing in the letters of the employers that could not have been said when mediation was mooted, and had it been said, the Lord Mayor, and the two Archbishops would have realised the futility of intervention and would have been saved much time and trouble. No false hopes would have been created in the city.[1]

That same day Larkin's burden was further increased by a strike of the maltmen, those who prepared the hops for the local brewers, which added between 200 and 300 men to the strike benefit, now including some 2,500 men. A week later, with the strikers still holding out, the employers gave way in the face of a hostile Press, pulpit, and public opinion. On Sunday, December 21, a second truce was arranged, and the next morning the men went back to work as the issues were submitted to arbitration. The results were not published until the middle of February, 1909, and though Larkin was disappointed in the award, and bitterly critical of its schedule and terms, he abided by it, as he had agreed to do.[2]

Coming so soon after the upheaval in Belfast, Larkin's early achievements in Dublin have practically gone unnoticed. Conducting and winning three disputes during 1908 was no mean achievement. When it is understood they were won in the face of a severe economic depression, a serious unemployment situation, and a hostile Union Executive in the person of Sexton, the achievement was remarkable. Employers during these years were not easily persuaded, even when times were good, to narrow their profit margins by increasing wages, let alone to recognize combinations among their workers. They were even more difficult to convince with a vast army of unemployed available and only waiting to be called. Further, when the employers insisted on dealing with Sexton over Larkin's head, they were helping to create a very serious internal situation in

---

[1] *Freeman's Journal*, December 12, 1908.

[2] Arnold Wright, *Disturbed Dublin* (1914), pp. 303–11. See for text of the agreement.

the Union. There was, however, a wider and deeper significance to these disputes than may at first be apparent. Wider because these strikes were among the first successful attempts by the Board of Trade to introduce an effective arbitration machinery that eventually led to an intricate and workable system of collective bargaining in the British Isles. George Askwith, who had begun in Belfast what was to be a most successful career as an arbitrator of industrial disputes for the Board of Trade, made it a rule 'to receive the signature of the parties concerned of a permanent collective contract in such terms as would obviate future disputes.'[1] This policy was represented in the Dublin disputes by Askwith's very able colleague, I. H. Mitchell, and during the next fifteen years they painstakingly built up their system of collective bargaining contract by contract. The deeper significance of these early disputes, though no one realized it at the time, was that they were the beginnings of a truly revolutionary working-class movement in Ireland.

[1] Elie Halévy, *A History of the English People in the Nineteenth Century* (1952), Vol. VI, Bk. I, p. 265.

IV

CHAOS AND RECONSTRUCTION

BY 1906 the employers in Britain had been generally forced to concede the right of combination to the men employed in the transport trade. In Ireland, however, which was still twenty years behind in trade union organization, the employers usually ignored the unions among the dockers and carters, if, indeed, they did not actually condemn them. The basic right of combination had to be fought out in Ireland port by port. It had been Belfast in 1907, Dublin in 1908, and it would be Cork in 1909. Everywhere Larkin organized it was a bitter fight, which always involved serious, and often severe financial considerations. Sexton, it seemed, failed to realize that the Irish employers' attitude towards trade unions was primitive, and, if he did, he was not prepared in any case to empty the treasury of his British-based union in an attempt to organize Irish dockers and carters. On the other hand, Larkin was more than willing to levy an English or Scotch docker on his Irish brother's behalf, and, indeed, looked upon it as a moral obligation, if he thought the fight was necessary.

In the course of the Dublin carters' dispute, relations between Larkin and the Executive of his Union completely broke down. On December 7, 1908, Larkin was suspended by Sexton and informed that any further 'action taken by you will be on your own responsibility.'[1] Sexton, who dominated the Executive, never liked or trusted Larkin. Only Larkin's extraordinary ability, grudgingly admired even by Sexton, allowed him to gain a foothold in the

---

[1] *Cork Constitution*, September 6, 1909.

Union, and then attain his position as General Organizer. The mutual antipathy was buried for a time by Larkin's usefulness, but when it became apparent that their policies as well as their personalities were in conflict, a rupture was only a matter of time and circumstance.[1] When the carters' dispute began in the middle of November, 1908, Larkin's cup had already been filled to the brim by the Executive and Sexton. In October he had been reprimanded by the Executive and put on a leash in that he had to notify the Executive of any and all ports about to be visited. In the Cork dispute in November, Sexton answered Larkin's telegram appealing for help with a 'Can't accept responsibility' reply.[2] On November 28 he was informed that the Executive had voted Sexton the discretionary power of summarily suspending him.[3] Larkin openly defied Sexton and the Executive the next day and intimated that if he were pushed, the matter would not end with his suspension. 'There was a movement on foot,' he warned, 'for organizing the whole of unskilled labour in Ireland. He was in favour of the international federation of labour but it was a question whether the first step was not to organize the Irish workers as Irishmen, separately, and then to federate. He was seriously considering whether he should take up this project.'[4] Sexton's answer to this was to notify Larkin and all the Union branches of his suspension on December 7, 1908.

Larkin then founded the Irish Transport and General Workers' Union. In late December, in Dublin, a meeting was held 'of delegates representing the carters, dockers, and other trades of Dublin, Belfast, Dundalk, Cork, and Waterford for the purpose of forming a new Irish Trade Union for those engaged in the distributive trades.'[5] Larkin became the General Secretary of the new Union, and he carried the bulk of the Irish membership of the National Union with him. The National Union managed to hold its branches in Belfast, Derry, and Drogheda, though they rapidly declined in strength and numbers. The change-over was usually effected at a mass meeting of the men in the branch involved, with a simple show of hands to signify the men's approval. There is little doubt that the great majority of the men in the branches which joined the Trans-

---

[1] *Sinn Fein*, January 23, 1909.
[2] *Cork Examiner*, September 17, 1909.
[3] *Cork Constitution*, September 6, 1909.
[4] *Freeman's Journal*, December 1, 1908.
[5] *Irish Nation*, January 2, 1909.

port Union were in favour of doing so, but even so commendable a form of democracy seemed to have severe limitations as far as any minority point of view was concerned. As one Cork docker succinctly put it, when he did not put up his hand, he 'went very near not putting up his hand ever again, for he was nearly killed.'[1]

In launching his new union, Larkin also outlined a programme for Irish Labour in the preface to the Transport Union's *Rule Book*.[2] After announcing an end to the 'policy of grafting ourselves on the English Trades Union Movement,' denouncing the 'soulless, sordid, money-grubbing propensities' of the Irish capitalist class, and pointing out that the 'old system of sectional unions amongst unskilled workers is practically useless for modern conditions,' Larkin went on to advocate both a political and an economic plan of campaign. On the economic level he offered the Transport Workers' Union to the Irish worker as 'a medium whereby you may combine with your fellows to adjust wages, regulate hours, and conditions of labour, wherever and whenever possible and desirable by negotiation, arbitration, and if the conditions demand it, by withholding our labour. . . .' The political programme embodied a 'legal eight hours' day, provision of work for all unemployed, and pensions for all workers at 60 years of age. Compulsory Arbitration Courts, adult suffrage, nationalisation of canals, railways, and all the means of transport. The land of Ireland for the people of Ireland.' He proclaimed as the 'ultimate ideal, the realisation of an Industrial Commonwealth,' and wound up rhapsodically claiming that the completion of such a programme would 'obliterate poverty, and help to realise the glorious time spoken of and sung by Thinkers, Prophets, and Poets, when all children, all women, and all men shall work and rejoice in the deeds of their hands, and thereby become entitled to the fulness of the earth and the abundance thereof.'[3]

More people, however, than the employers and Sexton had been antagonized by Larkin since his arrival in Dublin. He had given the Irish Parliamentary Party, and its political machine, the United Irish League, serious cause for reflection when he re-established the Dublin branch of the Independant Labour Party early in 1908.[4]

---

[1] *Cork Constitution*, September 13, 1909.
[2] *Rules, Irish Transport and General Workers' Union, 1909*, Preface.
[3] *Ibid.*
[4] F. Cruise O'Brien, 'The Independent Labour Party in Dublin,' *Leader*, August 22, 1908.

Arthur Griffith, founder and editor of the Nationalist weekly, *Sinn Fein*, was bitterly critical of Larkin, and denounced him during the carters' dispute, as the representative of 'English Trades Unionism in Ireland.'[1] More important than either the Irish Party, or Griffith's denunciations, however, was the considerable body of potential support Larkin alienated among the Irish trade unionists by his break with Sexton and the National Union. Most of the criticism came from those trade unionists who were themselves members of amalgamateds, or British-based unions, with an Irish membership. They were mainly from the north of Ireland, where the fraternal and financial ties with the British-based parent bodies were highly valued. The effect of this point of view was immediately felt in Belfast, where Larkin and Sexton fought bitterly for control of the dockers and carters.[2] The Belfast correspondent of the *Forward* fairly pointed out that 'in the face of utterly contradictory statements, it is impossible for an outsider to get at the truth', and then critically noted that whatever the merits of the quarrel, Larkin had now become 'a party to sectional trades unionism, as if there were not more than enough unions catering for dockers [and] carters.'[3] Though Sexton was able to keep the Belfast men out of the Transport Union, he was not in the long run to keep them in the National Union, and the Belfast branch collapsed soon after.

After his pyrrhic victory in Belfast, Sexton pushed his advantage as he instigated Larkin's expulsion from the Parliamentary Committee of the Irish Trades Union Congress.[4] The Parliamentary Committee also decided against sending an invitation to the Irish Transport Workers' Union for the next annual Congress in Limerick. The battle was not so easily won by Sexton and his supporters, however, for Larkin carried the fight to the floor of the Congress, which met on May 31, 1909, in Limerick. While Larkin was a noisy spectator in the gallery, his friends stubbornly and resourcefully fought for the recognition and affiliation of the Transport Union.[5] When the vote was finally taken as to the recognition of Larkin and his Transport Union, the Larkinites lost 49 to 39. D. R. Campbell immediately moved the following resolution: 'That a Committee of

[1] *Sinn Fein*, November 28, 1908, December 5, 1908.
[2] *Freeman's Journal*, January 14 and 15, 1909.
[3] *Forward*, January 16, 1909.
[4] *Report of the Sixteenth Irish Trades Union Congress, 1909*, pp. 15–16.
[5] *Freeman's Journal*, June 1, 1909.

seven, consisting of three members of the Parliamentary Committee and four delegates be appointed to enquire into the cause and development of the dispute in the National Union of Dock Labourers, and the subsequent secession of a large number of members, and the formation of the Irish Transport Workers' Union.'[1] The resolution passed easily, and this clever manoeuvre made it certain that the matter would again be discussed at next year's Congress, and that Larkin's supporters would have a year in which to prepare the ground.

Hardly had he been expelled from the Irish Trades Union Congress, when circumstances again forced Larkin into a fight he was very reluctant to take up. Realizing that it was now a time for husbanding energy rather than expending it, he did all in his power to settle quickly the disastrous dispute that broke out in Cork early in June, 1909. After his quick victory over the Cork Shipping Companies in November, 1908, all was quiet until the following spring, when labour disputes grew very numerous in Cork. 'This revolt of labour' seemed to the *Cork Constitution* 'to be growing infectious,' since each 'successful strike seems to have the effect of encouraging similar revolts, and until unreasonable demands are met by stout and sustained resistance, there is reason to fear that such troubles are more likely to accumulate than diminish.'[2] When towards the end of May, a group of Cork employers, worried 'by the frequency of labour disturbances . . . came to the conclusion that, to maintain the commercial prosperity of the city, it was absolutely necessary that a Federation of Employers should be formed,' the stage was set.[3]

Most of the dockers and carters in Cork had been organized by the Transport Union, and when Joseph Harris, Irish organizer for the Workers' Union of Great Britain and Ireland, whose Liverpool branch Larkin had helped found some ten years before, began organizing in early June, there was a good deal of uneasiness among the Transport men. Harris had been advised at the Trades Union Congress meeting in Limerick by officials of the Cork Trades Council to stay out of Cork because the situation was extremely delicate.[4]

---

[1] *Freeman's Journal*, June 1, 1909, p. 42.   [2] *Cork Constitution*, May 5, 1909.

[3] *Ibid.*, August 10, 1909. See report of the 'committee in winding up of the Merchant's Committee and the completion of the formation of the Employers' Federation. . . .'

[4] *Cork Examiner*, June 22, 1909. See letter of Patrick Murphy, President of the Cork Trades and Labour Council, to the editor.

Harris, however, persisted in moving into what the Transport Union considered its preserve, and on June 10 a number of coal porters objected to working with members of the Workers' Union. Some days later, 140 Transport Union dockers struck work at the Cork Steam Packet Company because three Workers' Union men were employed.[1] The trouble spread rapidly, as several goods porters at the Great Southern and Western Railway, in sympathy with the dockers, refused to handle merchandise from the Cork Steam Packet Company, and were summarily suspended.[2] On the following day, Wednesday, 100 railwaymen struck work because the goods porters were suspended. The inevitable supply of 'blacklegs' was sent over by the Shipping Federation to replace the striking dockers, and the Great Southern and Western transferred men from other rail centres to replace the Cork men.[3] The carters, in an effort to block the effective use of the 'blacklegs,' struck in sympathy with the dockers and railwaymen the next day. On Friday the Cork Employers Federation Limited issued the following ultimatum:

> That we, the employers of Cork, hereby bind ourselves and the firms we represent as follows:
>
> (1) To immediately dismiss any employee who shall willfully disobey any lawful order out of sympathy with any strike or trade dispute.
>
> (2) That the vacancy so caused shall be filled forthwith by local labour if procurable, failing this that the vacancy be filled from any available source.
>
> (3) That any such employee discharged shall not be employed by any member of the Federation.[4]

By June 26 it was evident even to those who were the friends of labour that the 'strike was a most deplorable blunder on the part of the men. They came out without any resources either of money or otherwise.'[5] Larkin tried from the first to gain a settlement, but his appeals were ignored as the employers were determined to teach labour a lesson in Cork it would not soon forget. The Transport Union funds were soon exhausted, as were the funds of the Cork

---

[1] *Cork Constitution*, June 15, 1906.

[2] *Ibid.*, June 17, 1909.

[3] *Ibid.*, June 18, 1909.

[4] J. D. Clarkson, *Labour and Nationalism in Ireland* (1924), p. 225. See *Cork Constitution*, June 19, 1909.

[5] *Irish Nation*, June 26, 1909. 'In Cork.'

Trades Council. Help from the Dublin and Belfast Trades Council was nothing when compared to what was necessary. After four weeks the *Freeman's Journal* noted 'that no strike pay has been distributed, and now five to six thousand persons are involved in the strike. Subsistence is a mystery. Some trades have made levies, but many of them thrown idle by the strike . . . cannot further contribute. Collecting boxes marked "For the strikers' women and children" are carried through the streets, but they have not elicited a very hearty response.'[1] The recruiting sergeants were reported to 'have been very busy in the ranks of the strikers. And they have secured many candidates for military employment.'[2] On July 13 the carters returned to work after nearly a month's resistance without strike pay. They had suffered a severe defeat, as they 'simply agreed to perform whatever tasks they were called on to do in the ordinary discharge of their duty.'[3] The surrender of the carters was the beginning of the end for the other strikers, who also drifted back to work if, indeed, they were not victimized.

The strike was lost but, far worse, the labour movement in Cork was in a shambles. As a result of the strike there was a serious split in the Cork Trades Council. The skilled sections withdrew and formed the Cork District Trades Council because 'the mechanic, who has to learn a trade, and serve a number of years as an apprentice, is chafing at being led by the nose into labour disputes by quay labourers and others.'[4] To complete the chaos, Fearon and the executive of the Cork Trades Council quarrelled at a meeting some days after the split in the Council. Fearon, in a long letter to Larkin, reported that he 'was suddenly attacked . . . about the Transport Workers' Union as to its strength in Dublin, Dundalk, Belfast and Waterford . . . and the very poor response from all the would-be branches.'[5] A member of the executive actually charged that the Transport Union was not a trade union at all. In his letter to Larkin Fearon attributed the attack to panic, since the 'starting of the new Council has put them completely off their heads.'[6] Instead of at least being purified, if not strengthened, by the combined onslaught of the Employers' Federation, the Labour Movement in Cork was a

---

[1] *Freeman's Journal*, July 12, 1909.
[2] *Ibid.* See also *Cork Examiner*, July 15, 1909. Letter to editor from 'Saxon Shilling.'
[3] *Freeman's Journal*, July 14, 1909. [4] *Cork Constitution*, August 14, 1909.
[5] *Cork Examiner*, September 17, 1909. [6] *Ibid.*

wreck after the attack. The Movement was split into skilled and unskilled elements, the Transport Union branch expired by the end of the year, and it was not resurrected for nearly four years.

Troubles never seem to come in single numbers but in battalions. For Larkin the year 1909 resulted in one catastrophe following on another, and the worst was yet to come. On the evening of August 18, 1909, Larkin was arrested in Dublin on his way home from the Transport Union office in Beresford Place.[1] The next day he was taken to Cork where, along with Fearon and two other members of the Cork branch, he was formally charged before a magistrate with 'conspiracy to defraud.' After several days in jail, Larkin and the others were finally admitted to bail and released.[2] At the subsequent hearings, which lasted for nearly three weeks, they were accused of having taken sundry sums of money from the Cork dockers under false pretences and then having applied that money to their own use. The Cork Solicitor mentioned that the money collected in fees and dues from the Cork dockers had been obtained under false pretences since there had never been an officially established branch of the National Union of Dock Labourers in Cork. The substance of the Crown's case, therefore, pivoted on the crucial question of whether or not there was a 'properly constituted' Cork branch of the N.U.D.L. When Sexton testified that there 'was not, to his knowledge, in the month of August, 1908, or at any time since then, a branch of his society in Cork,' the whole matter became very serious for Larkin and his friends.[3] The second point in the charge was the alleged misapplication of the money collected from the Cork dockers. This arose out of the fact that the disowned Cork branch had sent some £147 to the Dublin carters in support of their strike in November and December of 1908. The Crown maintained that the money had not been contributed for that purpose and its application to such a purpose was contrary to statute.

Though much of the testimony taken at the hearings had little relevance to the charges made, it did shed much incidental light on matters that might never have been otherwise recorded. Sexton's testimony, for example, explained many things that could only have been inferred as regards the break between Larkin and himself. The letters made public from Fearon and Coveney to Larkin, which

[1] *Freeman's Journal*, August 20, 1909.
[2] *Ibid.*, August 24, 1909.
[3] *Cork Constitution*, September 6, 1909.

were found on Larkin at the time of his arrest, gave an intimate picture of the personalities and their bickerings which led to the disintegration and decline of the Cork Labour Movement. Coveney's letters, for example, while they showed the lack of confidence of the members of the Cork branch in Fearon, gave ample indication of the touching personal loyalty which the men had for Larkin himself. When it was evident to all concerned that the strike was lost, Coveney wrote Larkin:

> Sutton's and Whitehaven were to give in this week, but I am afraid it is all up now, and Harris will be whipping all our men into his union if you don't get here in all despatch, as the men will stick to you if you are here to advise them in time. I am doing my best until I see or hear from you. Come in God's name, and save the cause you have at heart. . . . Wire or write on return of post, for the men are going mad to see or hear from you. I wired you last night for to please the men, and they waited at my house until the reply came at twelve, midnight, and when they didn't hear from you they were very down hearted going away.[1]

The testimony of the Cork dockers, who appeared as Crown witnesses, though obviously one-sided, gave an interesting picture of Fearon's efforts to organize the Transport Union branch. Numerous witnesses testified to the intimidation, and strong-arm methods used to get them to join the Union. Most testified that they were told they 'would get no work' unless they joined, and one, amidst general laughter, said he 'was forced to join it by Mr. Fearon and three hundred more.'[2] One docker gave a pathetic picture of how he was run off the quays for two months and then brought before a mock court held by Fearon and fined ten shillings. He managed to get some work only when his wife scraped together a shilling to pay part of the fine.[3] Another instance, though more amusing, of the internal workings of the Union branch was given some time later by a Cork docker, who was a member of the branch committee. Under cross-examination he testified that 'they used to hold weekly meetings.'

> What business used you to do every week? If I were to answer that question I might shock the court (laughter.)
> Used you to ask any questions about the money of the society? No.

---

[1] *Cork Constitution*, September 16, 1909.

[2] *Ibid.*, September 13, 1909.

[3] *Ibid.*, September 16, 1909.

And what other work would you do? The other work was listening to Socialistic arguments (laughter).

They had no effect on you? That is a matter for myself (laughter).[1]

More light was shed on Fearon's personality and the rough-and-tumble conditions on the Cork quays when, in December, 1909, he was brought to trial for having caused a riot during the previous April.[2] A number of dockers who refused to join the Transport Union insulted Fearon on Patrick's Quay and threatened him with a knife. Incensed, Fearon returned to the Transport Union Office, where he gathered a number of supporters, returned to the quay, and a riot was the result. Even more interesting, however, was the testimony of the women who were involved in this free-for-all alongside their men.

> Mrs. Margaret Sullivan . . . stated she was on Patrick's Quay on the evening of the row. She went to her husband for his wages . . . and saw a crowd coming along the quay, with Fearon out in front of them, and . . . She saw a woman named Murphy kicked by Fearon . . . Fearon was throwing coal, and she saw Fearon hit one of the accused John Horgan—over the eye.
>
> Cross-examined by Mr. Reardon, she said she had on that evening an iron bolt in her hand, but she had taken it off one of the men in the crowd. She did not hit Daniel Burns with the bolt.
>
> Are you known as the 'Fighting women of the North West Ward?' No, sir.
>
> Did you get two months for striking a woman with a poker? She got two months for striking me (laughter) . . .
>
> You got two months for it? I did, and so did she. I didn't leave her go. I dragged her with me.
>
> Mrs. Kate Donoghue stated . . . She saw the crowd come down the quay, with whom was Fearon, stood by a heap of coal and fired it at the windows of the club room. Fearon called out to her—'Fire at the w—— at the door, and she can't tell anything.'[3]

Fearon received six months hard labour, and those arrested with him received anything from one to four months. Soon after beginning his sentence Fearon suffered a breakdown, and was removed to a mental institution.

In September, after being returned for trial at the Winter Assizes

---

[1] *Freeman's Journal*, June 17, 1910.
[2] *Cork Constitution*, December 18, 1909.
[3] *Ibid.*

in Cork, Larkin was again released on bail. Before the Winter Assizes, however, he asked for a postponement to the Spring Assizes so that he might apply for a change of *venue*, because he did not feel he could secure a fair trial in Cork.[1] The postponement was granted, and early in the new year the site for the trial was changed to Dublin.[2] At the Spring Assizes Larkin finally came to trial on an indictment that covered twenty-four counts. The counts ranged from 'criminal conspiracy' and 'false pretences' to 'having received and misappropriated certain sums of money.'[3] The trial covered much the same ground as the magisterial hearings in Cork, with Sexton and the Cork dockers again the chief witnesses for the Crown. When, after three days, the case went to the 'County Dublin common jury,' there was not much doubt as to what the verdict would be. A County Dublin common jury was always earnest evidence of the Crown's zeal to secure a conviction. When the jury found Larkin and Coveney guilty on all counts, therefore, the verdict surprised no one.[4] One Irish newspaper bluntly stated that 'Larkin was convicted by a packed jury which excluded Catholics and Nationalists.'[5] Since the verdict was a foregone conclusion, the only question of importance was what the sentence would be. When Mr. Justice Boyd began by remarking that he was not going 'to pass a heavy sentence by any means' because he thought that 'enthusiasm' led Larkin away, it was an ominous sign. At the end of the reassuring preface Larkin received a year's hard labour.[6]

The sentence was a stiff one and must have severely shocked Larkin,[7] yet, when Mr. Justice Boyd turned to sentence Coveney, who had been recommended by the jury to the consideration of the court, Larkin courageously interrupted on his fellow-prisoner's behalf. He said, 'Before you deal with Mr. Coveney, may I say a word. Mr. Coveney is an ordinary working man in Cork——'[8] Boyd broke

---

[1] *Cork Constitution*, December 8, 1909.

[2] *Freeman's Journal*, January 29, 1910.

[3] *Ibid.*, July 28, 1910. See indictment in application for a new trial.

[4] *Ibid.*, June 18, 1910.

[5] *Roscommon Herald*, quoted in the *Forward*, July 9, 1910. See also comment of *Donegal Vindicator*.

[6] *Freeman's Journal*, June 18, 1910.

[7] Daniel Corkery, 'Jim Larkin,' *Leader*, July 2, 1910. 'To say that the terrible sentence passed on him was unexpected by everyone that read through the case is entirely to understate the matter; it overwhelmed rather than surprised.'

[8] *Freeman's Journal*, June 18, 1910.

in by pointing out that he was 'going to consider very favourably the recommendation of the jury.' Larkin, who by this time had as little reason as anyone to be impressed by Mr. Justice Boyd's candid prefaces, again interrupted, 'Don't give him an hour. The man never received one penny of this money. Though things are put before the jury in a different position, Mr. Coveney had not had hand, act, or part in it, and to sentence this man would be a travesty of justice. He has a wife in Cork. I ask you to allow him to depart.' The Solicitor-General, who had nailed his man in Larkin, offered no objection, and Coveney was released. Larkin asked to be allowed to say a last word. He accused the prosecutor in Cork of being really 'the solicitor for the Shipping Federation.' 'I thank you, my lord,' he said, 'for the sentence, and I only ask my friends in the court to remain true to the Transport Union.'[1]

The year and a half that encompassed the founding of the Transport Union and his sentence to a year's hard labour, was a most difficult period for Larkin. He no sooner picked up the pieces of a disaster when a fresh one was upon him. Even before he had been convicted in late June, 1910, however, the tide had imperceptibly begun to turn. At its annual conference in Dundalk in May, the Irish Trades Union Congress voted, by almost two to one, to affiliate the Transport Union. Though Larkin because of a technicality could not be elected to the Parliamentary Committee of the Congress, the majority of those elected strongly supported his view that what Ireland needed was an independent and militant Labour Movement. In the long run the most significant event in the Irish Labour Movement in 1910 was the return to Ireland of James Connolly in the last week of July. Connolly had mellowed considerably during his seven years in the United States, and his friends were much impressed and pleased by his more temperate spirit.[2] Immediately he took up his appointment as national organizer of the Socialist Party of Ireland. After opening his organizing campaign in Dublin, he soon established branches of the Party in Belfast and Cork.

More conspicuously significant, however, was Larkin's release from prison after serving three months of his year's sentence. A few days after he had been sentenced the Dublin Trades Council rallied to his support. Joseph Clarke, who certainly was no supporter of Larkin's point of view in the Council, said, 'If Larkin had been a

[1] *Freeman's Journal*, June 18, 1910.   [2] *Harp*, January, 1910.

weaker man he would not have been attacked as he was. Any man who came in contact with Larkin, whether they agreed with him or not, should be impressed with his honesty.'[1] John Simmons, who had been a staunch supporter of Larkin, 'urged that a petition be presented to the Lord Lieutenant in the hope of having the sentence remitted. He was one of a deputation, which included Mr. Larkin, that waited upon the Lord Lieutenant in connection with a recent labour matter, and he knew that the Lord Lieutenant was not unimpressed by Larkin and if a moderate course was pursued he was sure it would have the desired result.'[2] A committee was appointed, and after Larkin lost his appeal a memorial was presented to Lord Aberdeen, who granted the petition, and announced that Larkin would be released on October 1, 1910.[3] The Labour Movement was jubilant, and the *Freeman's Journal* probably best expressed the general feeling:

> The circumstances under which Mr. Larkin was convicted and sentenced, in June last, are still fresh in the memory of that part of the public who take an interest in Labour disputes and their consequences, and the announcement that he will be released on October 1st causes no surprise because it was strongly felt by the public at the time of the trial that although technically he had broken the law he had been guilty of no moral turpitude, that the sentence was altogether disprotionate to the offence, and that, in fact, it ought not be allowed to stand.[4]

On the evening of his release a gigantic torchlight procession in his honour traced its way through the streets of Dublin. He climaxed the demonstration with a few words from the centre window of the union offices in Beresford Place. He thanked 'those who had participated in the welcome which had been given him. It was not him, however, they were honouring by their display, but the cause of Labour in Dublin. He was now once more amongst those he loved to work for, and who had worked so hard for him while he had been under the care of the British Government.'[5] While in prison, he reported, he had been well treated, working in the garden and the bakeshop, both being the lightest work possible for him under his 'hard labour' sentence. He also maintained the prison system was

<hr>

[1] *Freeman's Journal*, June 22, 1910. Dublin Trades Council.   [2] *Ibid.*

[3] *Ibid.*, September 15, 1910. See letter from the Lord Lieutenant to William O'Brien Hishon, who presented the memorial.

[4] *Ibid.*   [5] *Ibid.*, October 3, 1910.

'absolutely wrong,' because it was not reformative at all, but tended rather 'to deteriorate a man's character.'[1]

The next afternoon a mass meeting was held in Beresford Place, and the whole of the Labour Movement and its sympathizers turned out. The local trade unionists and city councillors vied with each other in eulogizing Larkin and expounding their faith in the eventual triumph of the cause of labour. Larkin himself was preceded by the Countess Markievicz, who announced that Larkin now 'recognised the doctrine that every Irishman ought to recognise that in regard to everything in Ireland, whether trade union or anything else, England was its foe.'[2] 'The great evil in this country,' continued the Countess, 'was English influence. In this fight of Irish labour against English labour Mr. Larkin ought to receive the support of every Nationalist minded person in Ireland, whether in the labour ranks or not.' Larkin opened his remarks by thanking 'the good women and the good men of this country,' and then, more pointedly, 'also across the Channel, who had done their utmost to prove the solidarity of the workers.' 'If all the men in Ireland,' he said, 'would think of that blessed word "toleration," and get it stamped on their minds and hearts, it would be a good day for Ireland.' He concluded by remarking that the Countess 'had blamed England. Let them put the blame on their own shoulders. It was they in Ireland who had to waken up.'[3]

Throughout 1910 Larkin's influence was slowly but surely growing among Irish trade unionists. By the spring of 1911 he and his friends were the paramount influence in the Dublin Trades Council and the Irish Trades Union Congress. The man that was most responsible, however, for the consolidation of the Larkinite point of view in the Council and in the Congress was William O'Brien, a young tailor of some thirty years of age. O'Brien, who had been in his teens when Connolly arrived in Dublin in 1896, became interested in Socialism because his two older brothers were in the Movement. He soon joined the Irish Socialist Republican Party, and he and Connolly became life-long friends. When Connolly's comrades in the Party argued that their tactics must be modified to suit Irish conditions, O'Brien took up his ground somewhere between Connolly and his critics. In a strongly worded letter to O'Brien, Connolly abused all those, including O'Brien, who criticized his leadership, and complained of their lack of faith in the cause and their want of

[1] *Freeman's Journal*, October 3, 1910.   [2] *Ibid.*   [3] *Ibid.*

loyalty to him.[1] The upshot of it all was that Connolly emigrated to America in disgust. Though there was an understandable coolness for a short time they continued to correspond. O'Brien soon noticed the new conditions encountered by Connolly in the United States resulted in a considerable change in his views on Socialism. Finally, it was mainly through O'Brien's efforts as Secretary of the Socialist Party of Ireland that Connolly was appointed national organizer of that organization.

There were, in effect, in these years two groups in the Dublin Trades Council. The Socialists and more advanced trade unionists made up the one, while the other, the majority, was merely anti-Socialist. The tactic which in the end broke the back of the anti-Socialist group was the proposal to form a municipal Labour Party. Smarting under the recent humiliation of having the Council's officially endorsed candidate ignominiously defeated, one of the stalwarts of the anti-Socialist group, actually proposed the establishment of a 'Labour Representation Committee with an independent Labour Policy.'[2] The anti-Socialists were then split because discussion arose between them as to whether political action was legitimate for trade unionists to indulge in. Though he could not quite articulate it, T. Milner came closest to sensing the real danger to the informal anti-Socialist alliance. He admitted that 'while he would like to see an independent party in the Corporation, he failed to see how they could have such a party without having in it men of Socialist tendencies, because all labour interests were more or less bound up with Socialism.'[3] Here was the real dilemma for the anti-Socialists. If they formed a Labour Party they would be honour bound to support their colleagues, Socialists or not, and more, since the Socialists and their friends had all the purpose, drive, and ability they would soon end up in control. The resolution passed easily, and the new Labour Representation Committee of eight members included Larkin and four of his supporters. Finally, in March, 1911, a Larkinite, Thomas Murphy, was elected Chairman of the Council, and more important, William O'Brien replaced for a time John Simmons, who was ill, in the crucial post of Secretary.

Larkin, O'Brien, and their supporters were all entrenched in the Council by May and were all prepared to launch a similar fight for

---

[1] William O'Brien, personal interview.
[2] *Freeman's Journal*, January 31, 1911. Dublin Trades Council.
[3] *Ibid.*

control of the Trades Union Congress which was to meet in June, 1911, in Galway. At the previous Congress in Dundalk, Larkin, it will be remembered, was not elected to the Parliamentary Committee because of a technicality. His point of view was well represented, however, for his supporters were in all the key positions of the nine-member Committee. The Chairman, D. R. Campbell, the Treasurer, M. J. O'Lehane, and the permanent Secretary, P. T. Daly, were all strong Larkinites. When the Congress met, in June, 1911, William O'Brien was once again quietly canvassing, manipulating, and trading in order to insure a Larkinite victory. O'Brien was fast becoming a past-master at the game of parliamentary manoeuvre. His first Congress had been at Limerick in 1909, but in Dundalk, in 1910, he showed his ability at getting out the vote. He gathered some 24 votes in an attempt to gain a seat on the Parliamentary Committee in this, his second year, when Larkin himself only polled 30.[1] In 1911, O'Brien was brilliant—of the eight elected members of the Parliamentary Committee, five were Dubliners and Larkinites, including Larkin and O'Brien, and one of the three others was the reliable D. R. Campbell.[2] It was a masterpiece of manipulation and electioneering, for it was all done in a Congress where O'Brien and the Larkinites on any straight vote would have been defeated, since they were in a slight minority. Though the Trades Union Congress had no funds to speak of, its leaders could claim to represent some 100,000 organized workers in Ireland.

Just before the Irish Trades Union Congress met in June, 1911, Larkin made his debut as editor of *The Irish Worker and People's Advocate*. Nothing like it has ever been seen since it was suppressed by the British Government in the early months of the First World War. This novel production was and remains unique in the history of working-class journalism. It was less a newspaper than the spirit of four glorious years. To read the *Irish Worker* of these years is to feel the quickening pulse of Dublin. Week after week the sordid tales of mischief, misery, jobbery, and injustice poured forth in a plaintive and never-ending painful dirge. Week after week, while working and waiting for the millennium, Larkin attacked with a monumental perseverance the sweating, exploiting employers and the corrupt, cynical politicians, who in his eyes were responsible for the reprehensible social condition of Dublin. He gave no quarter and

[1] *Report of the Seventeenth Irish Trades Union Congress, 1910*, p. 57.
[2] *Report of the Eighteenth Irish Trades Union Congress, 1911*, p. 42.

expected none as he villified any and all, high or low, who had the misfortune to come under the notice of his pen.

The idea of a Labour paper had long been on Larkin's mind. During the Belfast strike in 1907 he pleaded for a Labour paper for Ireland, and in the Dublin Trades Council in March, 1908 the subject was again brought up.[1] In the spring of 1908, however, it was the Cork Trades Council that brought out the *Cork Trade and Labour Journal*, which besides an ardent protectionist turn of mind had a peculiar anti-semitic twist.[2] In May, 1909, in imitation of their Cork brethren, the Dublin Trades Council produced the *Dublin Trade and Labour Journal*. The following month the title was changed to the *Irish Labour Journal*, which ran as a weekly until it collapsed in late September, 1909. On the whole the *Journal* was a sincere but mediocre effort. Written by trade unionists for trade unionists, it lacked any general perspective, colour, or intellectual stimulus.

Another attempt was made to launch a Labour paper some months later, when the *Harp*, a monthly, was transferred from New York to Dublin. The *Harp* had been edited and published by James Connolly in New York, and Larkin took over the sub-editorship in Dublin in January, 1910. Prior to its transfer to Dublin, the *Harp* was a tight and effectively written propaganda sheet for thinking Socialists of the Irish and Irish-American variety. That Larkin had other ideas as to what the style and tone of a labour paper should be no one had any doubts after his early editorials. He referred to the Nationalist Party and its leader, John Redmond, for example, as 'this ragged army, misnamed "A Nationalist Party," led by a Falstaffian Statesman who for the last thirteen years had continually been presuming and venturing to say, and desirous of pointing out, that in the not far distant day we shall have our own again. Oh what a burlesque!'[3] The Unionists were referred to as 'the sycophants, privilege mongers, place hunters, nation levellers, blood suckers, and carrion crows.' The 'ideal of the *Sinn Fein* Party,' he proclaimed, 'or at least a section who control the party, is to make cheap goods under sweating conditions by cheap Irish Labour . . . for imported foreign capitalists, such goods to be sold to any and every nation except England. That is retribution with a vengeance.'[4] When the paper went under in the

---

[1] *Freeman's Journal*, March 4, 1908.
[2] *Forward*, July 25, 1908. No file extant.
[3] *Harp*, February 1910.   [4] *Ibid.*

77

face of several libel actions inside a few months, it surprised no one. Before it did go under, however, Larkin did explain what he was trying to do. 'This paper,' he wrote, 'does not pretend to be a literary magazine. We desire to articulate working class opinion. What is wanted in Ireland, we are of the opinion, is a honest expression of dissatisfaction with the want of system in society—a statement of our principles, our ultimate aim.'[1]

The *Irish Worker* was an immediate and fantastic success.[2] In its first month, June, 1911, the circulation figure was 26,000. In July it was 64,500, in August, 74,750, and in September, 94,994. From this peak month it levelled off to something over 20,000 a week, which was an astonishing figure for an Irish weekly journal. *Sinn Fein*, the Nationalist weekly, for example, never went over 5,000 a week in the same period, and was closer to 2,000 throughout most of its subsidized existence.[3] There is not the slightest doubt that the success of the *Irish Worker* was due to Larkin's appointment of himself as keeper of the public conscience. Conscious of his own integrity, and comfortable in his own incorruptibility, Larkin exposed and denounced erring employers and corrupt public servants by name and number. As Larkin called the sinners to the paths of righteousness, his readers revelled in their secret hearts at seeing the men they called 'master' squirm. To understand the popularity of the *Irish Worker* is to realize that Dublin was a city of only 300,000, where everyone knew everybody of any social or financial consequence. Gossip in a closed community is not a thing to be underestimated, and with a people such as the Irish, it can reach sublime proportions. In the era before mass media, the *Irish Worker* provided enough food for talk for the whole week, and then some, for the indiscretions of friend or enemy always grew richer with the retelling.

Larkin set the pace in his first issue by announcing that a 'Legal Column' would be opened, where he promised 'ventilation will be given to any and every grievance.'[4] Since grievances were about the

---

[1] *Harp*, February 1910.

[2] W. P. Ryan, *The Irish Labour Movement* (1919), p. 197. See also Alfred Byrne in the Dublin Corporation, *Freeman's Journal*, January 23, 1912. The *Irish Worker* 'had an average circulation of 20,000.' See Larkin in the *Irish Worker*, October 21, 1911. 'Watchman! What of the Night?' The circulation figures for the first week were 5,000; second, 8,000; third, 15,000; and from then on about 20,000, 'and could sell double the quantity if we could print them.'

[3] Desmond Ryan, personal interview.

[4] *Irish Worker*, May 13, 1911.

only thing the Dublin workers had in common abundance, the paper never lacked for material. To give his readers encouragement and set the proper tone, Larkin, in the early issues, lampooned well-known Dublin personalities, and asked pointed and sometimes embarrassing questions of them. For example:

How much does ex-Alderman Irwin pay his work girls per week? How much per hour overtime? How much does he fine them per month? [1]

How much did Councillor Crozier pay for the last lot of house property he bought from the Corporation? [2]

Will Jamsey Fox, Councillor, P.L.G., election agent . . . ward heeler, etc. tell us how much the bhoys in the Corporation service collected for him. Jamsey, its a quare hole you could not get out of.[3]

Much of the material from the 'Legal Column' flowed over into the editorial columns, where Larkin himself took a personal hand in publicly chastising sweating employers. 'Another Sweating Den' was a typical example of Larkin's editorial technique in dealing with these unwholesome exploiters of the poor:

We have discovered another philanthropist. He has a drapery establishment in Earl street, and his name is Hickey. Now, Hickey is a tricky boy, and instead of paying his porters a reasonable wage, he gives them the magnificent sum of 9s. a week, and allows them to eat the scraps left over after the shop assistants have dined. Most of the men who work as drapers' porters are married and have families. Hickey's are no-exception, and some of his men have as many as five children. We would like to know does Mr. Hickey think it possible to support a family, buy clothes for them, and pay rent in Dublin out of this amount? If he will let us know how to do it we will be very thankful. Hickey knows it can't be done, but Hickey doesn't care.[4]

Week after week the pitiful tales poured in and were printed. A typical correspondent wrote:

Sir—Kindly allow me, through the columns of your much needed workers' journal, to call public attention to a barefaced system of white slavery which exists, and has existed, for some time in the paper sorting establishment of S. Irwin & Son, 121 Upper Abbey Street. The following are the facts which I can prove:—girls are paid in this

[1] *Irish Worker*, May 13, 1911.   [2] *Ibid.*
[3] *Ibid.*, June 3, 1911.   [4] *Ibid.*, June 24, 1911.

princely establishment at the rate of 2*s*. 6*d*. to 3*s*. per week from 8 o'clock in the morning until 7 at night, or often, if not enough work turned out, until 8 o'clock, and are not allowed out for dinner . . . the forewomen get up clubs to make money for themselves, all at the expense of the half-crown worker, and woe betide them if they do not join. If they do not they are marked for special tyranny, and all this is done with the knowledge of Mr. Irwin.

Another grave scandal is the system of letting the forewomen make tea, of the ounce to the gallon sort, and sell it to the workers for their dinner at ½*d*. per cup. One of the forewomen stands in the passage on Saturday evening when they are getting their handful of money and takes from them, in some cases sixpence and in more threepence.

I have known of girls, Mr. Editor, to walk home on Saturday with 1*s*. 6*d*. after a hard week's work.[1]

Larkin could only ask, 'Has Mr. Irwin anything to say? Our columns are open to him, and we are anxious to know how anyone in Ireland can manage to live on half-a-crown a week. Does Mr. Irwin know what low wages and hard, unhealthy work drive young girls to do? Does he care?'[2] Mr. Irwin did not reply.

It was no surprise that within a year 'no less than seven writs for libel were issued' against the *Irish Worker*.[3] None of them, however, were really successful. Most, like 'the great Mickey Swaine, boss of the United Irish League in Wood Quay Ward,' wrote Larkin, 'considered discretion the better part of valour and funked the starter.'[4] Larkin actually sued Swaine for failing to proceed with the libel action, and won a judgment and costs against him. When examined in court, Swaine's testimony gave an interesting insight into the character of the men who dominated local Dublin politics. Swaine was asked by Larkin's counsel:

Are you a bookmaker? I was, at one time; not now.

Witness further stated that he might win £100 one day and lose it another day. His wife was the general provider. What he won he generally paid for the rent. He was a member of the Dublin Corporation.

Who paid your expenses? My wife advanced it to me—about £50 or £60. . . .

When were you last fined? Around two years ago. I think the last time I was fined you were my counsel (laughter).[5]

---

[1] *Irish Worker*, July 1, 1911. [2] *Ibid.* [3] *Ibid.*, May 11, 1912.
[4] *Ibid.* [5] *Freeman's Journal*, December 10. 1912.

Another of those who sued Larkin for libel found himself in an even more unfortunate position. For, 'the Secretary of the Evicted Tenants Association, Mr. Dickson, the Tea Fraud,' wrote Larkin, 'the creature who robbed hundreds of working people of their hard earned money, he also wanted 1,000 pounds for defamation of character: well we got him nine months in a place where he will not be evicted.'[1] Larkin justified his exposures by pointing out that 'Thousands of working women and men have had the burden of late lightened owing to the *Irish Worker*. Light has been shed in dark places. The truth has been told for the first time about some of the hypocrites, who are trading under the cloak of religion, and hiding behind the mantle of Nationality, and untold benefits have accrued to the slaves who work for them.'[2]

The exposures and denunciations were for Larkin only the means to an end whatever they may have meant to his less inspired readers. He produced a popular paper and was a successful editor because he properly geared his efforts to his readers' abilities. That many of his readers mistakenly satiated themselves on the symptoms of a sick society was only a further indication of how really sick that society was. In the midst of all the exposures and denunciations Larkin never failed to call for something more than bread and butter. 'We are not going to be beasts any longer,' he proclaimed. 'We are going to *rouse the working* classes out of their slough of despond—out of the mire of poverty and misery—and lift them a plane higher. If it is good for the employer to have clean clothing and good food, and books and music, and pictures, so it is good that the people should have these things also—and that is the claim we are making to-day.'[3]

By the spring of 1911 Larkin had completed the journeyman phase of his career. In the Transport Workers' Union he had fashioned what would prove to be his masterpiece, and in the severe testing period during the next few months it would not be found wanting. The turn in Larkin's personal fortunes, and with them the fortunes of the Irish Labour Movement, was remarkable. Less than a year before he had seen his Transport Union at the edge of disaster, himself bankrupt, and facing a year at 'hard labour.' Now the Irish Labour Movement was his own. The Transport Union numbered over 5,000 strong, and the treasury showed a credit balance. With

---

[1] *Irish Worker*, May 11, 1912.
[2] *Ibid.* [3] *Ibid.*, July 29, 1911.

O'Brien's astute managing he dominated the Dublin Trades Council and the Parliamentary Committee of the Irish Trades Union Congress. Alone, he controlled the most effective propaganda sheet in Ireland, boasting a circulation of 20,000 a week. With trade conditions improving, and the worst of the unemployment crisis past, the times were ripe, indeed, for a forward movement.

PART THREE

Master, 1911–1914

V

SYNDICALISM AND THE 'ONE BIG UNION'

IN 1911 all Ireland basked in the warmth of a confident expectation. The Third Home Rule Bill would soon settle the national question which had occupied the thought and energies of the Irish people for over a century. The two general elections of 1910 had found the British electorate willing, though reluctant, and the Parliament Act of 1911 would soon limit the House of Lords to a mere suspensory veto. In three years, then, the last obstacle would be hurdled, and the Irish people were assured that a Parliament in College Green was now only a matter of time. All factious elements in Ireland ceased their carping criticism and silently waited for John Redmond and his Irish Party to deliver the goods. The Labour Movement in Ireland also began to glow in 1911, but it generated a warmth with a difference. Unlike the Nationalists, who were conscious of an historic mission about to be fulfilled, the Labour Movement became aware of an historic mission about to be begun. Even those who could not be numbered among the Socialists noticed prophetically that 'Labour has lost its old humility and its respectful finger touching its cap. It is one of the great powers of the world—the greatest almost now—certainly it is soon going to be the greatest. The child in the cradle to-day before it is a middle-aged man will see the hands of Labour in the reins of governments and the jaded beast called capital responding freely to the spur and whip.'[1]

[1] *Irish Homestead*, January 7, 1911.

Larkin was also very conscious that time was now on his side. On the masthead of the *Irish Worker* he asked and answered:

> Who is it speaks of defeat?
> I tell you a cause like ours,
> Is greater than defeat can know—
> It is the power of powers.
>
> As surely as the earth rolls round
> As surely as the glorious sun
> Brings the great world moon-wave,
> Must our cause be won.[1]

'We are living in stirring times,' he announced in August, 1911. 'Those of us who during the last years have been preaching the need of organisation in the industrial field have much to be thankful for. Many times have we had to pause and consider—Will anything come of our labours?'[2] In alluding to the long years in the wilderness, he asked the readers of the *Irish Worker* if they knew what it was 'to get up on a box or chair, physically and mentally tired ... amongst strangers ... and then suffering from lack of training, want of education, but filled with the spirit of a new gospel. . . . You try to impart to that unthinking mass the feeling which possesses yourself?'[3]

> The life all around seems to stagnate; everything seems miserable and depressing. Yet you want them to realise there is great hope for the future—that there is something worth working for, if the workers will only rouse themselves. You plead with them to cast their eyes upward to the stars, instead of grovelling in the slime of their own degradation; point out to them life's promised fulness and joy if they would only seek it. You appeal to their manhood, their love for their little ones, their race instinct, but all these appeals seem to fall on deaf ears; they turn away apparently utterly apathetic, and one tramps on to the next town or meeting, feeling it was hopeless to try and move them.[4]

Then, he continued, you 'creep into a hedgerow, pull out a cheap copy of "Morris's news from nowhere," ' . . . then forgetting the world, "and by the world forgot," one lives.' 'And then, suddenly, when things seem blackest, and dark night enshrouds abroad, lo!

---

[1] *Irish Worker*, May 27, 1911.
[2] *Ibid.*, August 12, 1911, 'Revolution.'
[3] *Ibid.* [4] *Ibid.*

The Sun, and lo! thereunder rises wrath and hope and wonder, and the worker comes marching on.'

Larkin's awareness of a brave new world to be won did not stem from the intuitional inner man alone. In 1911 the whole world of labour began to grow more militant. In France a revolutionary doctrine had been presented to the working classes under the name of syndicalism. This new gospel, given a kind of intellectual coherence by Georges Sorel, and in harmony with the new twist given to philosophy by Henri Bergson, was soon carried into Italy, Spain, and Portugal. In the United States, meanwhile, the Industrial Workers of the World had been developing similar ideas regarding the tactics to be pursued by the working classes in the struggle for their emancipation. These ideas were taken up in Great Britain and Ireland, and it is necessary to review briefly the nature and meaning of the term 'syndicalism' in France and in the United States before it can be understood as it applied in Britain and Ireland.

The French syndicalist movement was the intellectual parent of all syndicalism. Its chief influence was in the realm of ideas, for it gave syndicalism a theoretical basis, a working philosophy, and contributed most of the terminology that was to be so loosely applied in other countries. Syndicalism developed out of the important Proudhon–Bakunin quarrel with the Marxian dialectic. The supporters of the Marxist tradition held that the seizure of power in the capitalist state could best be achieved through the political action of the proletariat. A good many Marxists saw in democracy the natural implement by which to effect the socialist state. The syndicalists, on the other hand, saw in economic action the path to their brand of social salvation.[1] The *syndicat*, or trade union, was to be a tool in the education of the working class, and a weapon in the continual war on the capitalist state. Every strike was viewed as a step towards a syndicalist seizure of power, and the workers would take their last step the day they enforced *la grève générale*, or the general strike.[2] To over-simplify in order to draw a sharp distinction, the syndicalists made their stand on economic, or 'direct action,' as opposed to the Marxian concept of parliamentary, or 'indirect action.'

As syndicalism developed in other countries it was apparent that it would, as it had done in France, adapt itself to existing conditions

---

[1] Elie Halévy, *Histoire du Socialisme Européen* (1948), p. 288.
[2] *Ibid.*, pp. 232–33.

and base theory on practice. In any attempt to describe the French syndicalist movement, four points must be kept in mind. First, the insistence on 'direct action' as opposed to 'indirect action'; second, the belief in the necessity for a militant rank and file; third, the emphasis on localization as the basis of organization; and fourth, the acceptance of the principle of industrial unionism. There were many points of similarity between the several national syndicalist movements, but, more important, there were also sharp points of difference. Of the four features of French syndicalism mentioned above, only two found universal acceptance. These were the belief in a militant working class and the acceptance of industrial unionism. But, as was pointed out, industrial unionism seemed to be a qualified afterthought in France and not necessarily an integral part of French syndicalism. Actually, then, the real ground for an internationalist syndicalist understanding was a worldwide belief in the need for a genuinely militant working-class movement. It was on this tenet that syndicalism presented a common front, and it was this, probably more than anything else, that won for syndicalism the approbation 'revolutionary.'

The American movement evolved along different theoretical lines from the French movement, and developed a different organizational structure as well.[1] The emphasis in the French movement had been on localization, but in the American it was on centralization. The American syndicalists thought the only successful way to combat a heavily 'trustified' capitalist economy was to present an equally organized and centralized Labour Movement. The American syndicalists drew their inspiration for a centralized, industrial unionist structure from the defunct Knights of Labour, and the development of this idea was the original contribution of the American movement to world syndicalism. The main proponents of syndicalism in Great Britain drew their intellectual and practical stimulus from America rather than France.

Syndicalism in Great Britain was largely the result of the work of a handful of hardy, outspoken, and resourceful labour leaders who took full advantage of the fact that this was a period of declining real wages. Since 1900 real wages had been steadily reduced by the increasing cost of living. The great victory of the Liberal and Labour Parties in the general election of 1906 was followed by a severe trade

[1] P. F. Brissenden, *The I.W.W.: A Study of American Syndicalism* (1919), pp. 161–62.

depression and mass unemployment. The inability of the large Liberal majority and their Labour allies to cope with the decline in real wages and unemployment caused a widespread disillusionment among the working classes as to the effectiveness of political action. Since the two general elections of 1910 had more than satiated the political appetite of the working classes without improving their economic situation, they began to turn from political action to a more direct method for solving their problems. When trade began to improve in 1911, the working classes embarked on an odyssey of militancy that was to result in almost continual industrial unrest until the outbreak of the First World War in August, 1914.

As far as Ireland was concerned, the early Irish editions of the *Harp* indicated that Larkin and Connolly were remarkably in tune. Larkin had anticipated Connolly's ideas on the 'One Big Union' theme with the Irish Transport Workers' Union and was in full agreement as to the need for a militant and aggressive working-class movement with greater tolerance within the fold. It might be more correct to say that Connolly sharply articulated what had been on Larkin's mind for some time. Still, the ideas were in the air the world over and were not strange or alien as far as Irish labour conditions were concerned. In fact since the industrial side of the Irish Labour Movement had been in existence for so short a time, there was no traditional policy or interest to resist effectively the new currency in ideas, as was the case in the British Labour Movement. The British Labour Party and the powerful British craft unions, which put up a fierce resistance to the new ideas, found no parallel in Ireland. Ireland, therefore, became a fertile field for the sowing of the syndicalist seed, and, as everywhere else, the theory was conditioned to the facts.

The great wave of industrial unrest that broke in Britain in early summer, 1911, was not long in flowing over into Ireland. Two gigantic national strikes in Britain, the transport workers and the railwaymen, had a profound effect on the Labour Movement in Ireland. The first began with the seamen's and firemen's strike which broke out in Hull in the middle of June, 1911, and which by the end of the month had crippled every port in Britain. This was only the beginning of a sympathetic strike movement in the waterside trades. Dockers, coal-fillers, and carters were soon out in sympathy with the seamen and firemen, also demanding an improvement in their own wages and conditions. In Dublin the strike situation followed the same pattern. Dockers were soon refusing to unload ships from striking ports in Britain, claiming they would not work a ship manned by a 'blackleg' crew. Carters in turn would not handle goods consigned to ships that were manned by Shipping Federation crews. Larkin managed to keep the 'sympathetic strike' situation in Dublin under control, with no more than 300 dockers and carters out at any one time. When, however, in mid-July the Coal Merchants Association threatened to lock out all their coal-fillers and carters because the Transport Union men employed by one coal firm refused to unload a boat manned by an objectionable crew, Larkin's hand was forced.[1] On Friday, July 14, some 800 coal men were locked out, and over the weekend the total figure reached 2,000. Larkin supported the locked-out men and the dockers and carters who were out in sympathy with the seamen and firemen. The Shipping Federation's resistance crumbled before the concerted action of the waterside trades in Britain in late July, and peace was restored in Dublin as well. The men who came out in sympathy and who were locked out were all back at work by the end of the month, with an increase in wages for their trouble.[2] It was a stupendous victory for the waterside trades in Britain and a modest one for the Transport Workers' Union in Dublin. This was the first dispute of any importance that Larkin had won since 1908, and it did a great deal towards developing a confident and militant attitude among the transport workers in Dublin.

The second great national strike in Britain, which was to have serious repercussions in Ireland, was the railway strike called in August. The strike was called for the morning of August 18, and the railwaymen in Ireland, who were members of the British-based railway unions, loyally supported the strike call. The strike was effective in both Britain and Ireland, and a truce was reached through the intervention of the Government. Because of the disruption in rail service, however, the Dublin timber merchants locked out some 500 of their men on August 21. They offered to pay their men for the day lost, but the men, who were members of the Transport Union, demanded a two-shillings-per-week increase in their wages. The timber merchants refused, and the strike dragged on for nearly a month. On September 15 the Transport Union requested the goods

---

[1] *Freeman's Journal*, July 15, 1911.

[2] *Ibid.*, August 1, 1911. See T. Murphy in Dublin Trades Council, *ibid.*, August 15, 1911.

porters in the Great Southern and Western Railway in Dublin 'not to handle any timber from merchants who were involved in a dispute with their own men.'[1] The railway porters agreed to the request, and 400 executed a lightning strike in Dublin rather than handle the 'tainted' timber. The strikers informed the directors of the railway company by letter that they would continue to refuse to handle all freight from firms who had a dispute with their employees. The directors refused to recognize any such right on the part of the men and pointed out that the company was legally bound to accept the traffic tendered.

Tempers were short in these hectic days, and the representative of the men declared that 'the gage of battle was thrown down, and that the men accepted.'[2] He immediately appealed to the British Executive of his union for support. The Executive Committee of the Amalgamated Society of Railway Servants was not anxious to fight on the issue of a 'sympathetic strike,' because they knew it would seriously compromise the truce they had been party to since August. This attitude was apparent when J. E. Williams, General Secretary of the A.S.R.S., arrived in Dublin several days after the strike began and announced that the union was open to a settlement. The directors ignored him, and on September 21, he was forced to declare a national strike.[3] To the great disgust of the Irish members, however, it included only Ireland. They felt that since they had loyally supported the strike call in August, the least their British brethren could do was to call out the members in Britain.

More important was the refusal, however, of the Amalgamated Society of Locomotive Engineers and Firemen to strike, thus crippling the efforts of the A.S.R.S. to close down the Irish railways. By September 28, barely a week after the strike began, it was broken. Larkin agreed to stand aside and 'allow the railway companies and their employees to compose their differences.'[4] The settlement on the Great Southern and Western finally resulted in the company's agreeing to take back 90 per cent of the men immediately and the rest as vacancies occurred.[5] The other railway companies refused to guarantee any reinstatement, and the resulting victimization was cruel. Priests, parliamentarians, and the Press remonstrated with the directors, but to no avail. For the men the strike was more than a

---

[1] *Freeman's Journal*, September 16, 1911. See also September 28, 1911.
[2] *Ibid.*, September 18, 1911.   [3] *Ibid.*, September 22, 1911.
[4] *Ibid.*, September 28, 1911.   [5] *Ibid.*, October 4, 1911.

failure, it was ruin. The timber dispute, which was the beginning of it all, collapsed a week after the railway strike was broken, with a complete surrender on the part of the men.

Meanwhile at the end of August the Transport Union became involved in a dispute in Wexford.[1] The employees of Messrs. Pierce and Co., iron-founders, decided to join the Transport Union and formed a local branch. Messrs. Pierce refused to countenance any association of their employees with the Transport Union, though they said they did not object to the men forming an independent local union. Larkin saw this as another attempt on the part of employers to abridge the right of the men to combine.[2] Since Larkin was very busy in Dublin in August and September, P. T. Daly, who began the work of organizing the Wexford branch, took charge of the dispute. The resistance which the Transport Union met was nothing less than fierce. The Wexford employers locked out their men, poured police into the town, and imported 'blacklegs' to break the men's union. The ensuing struggle lasted nearly six months and was accompanied by a good deal of violence.[3] Clashes between the men and the police were frequent and bloody, and one of the workers was actually batoned to death by the police.[4] Daly did a good job in Wexford. He soon had the local men solidly organized for resistance and enlisted a good deal of local financial support and sympathy.[5] Daly directed the bitter struggle for over five months until he was arrested at the end of January, 1912, and deported to Waterford.[6]

Larkin immediately dispatched Connolly to Wexford, and he

---

[1] *Freeman's Journal*, August 29, 1911.

[2] *Ibid.*, September 12, 1911. See Larkin in the Dublin Trades Council.

[3] *Ibid.*, September 8, 1911.   [4] *Ibid.*, September 13, 1911.

[5] *Ibid.*, September 12, 1911. 'Enniscorthy Monday.' 'At a largely attended demonstration of the Irish Trade and Labour League, which is composed of agricultural labourers throughout the country, held in Oulart yesterday, the following resolution was carried unanimously: "That we express our sympathy with the men of Wexford in the manner in which they have been treated, and we hereby open a fund in their behalf." It was decided to hold a collection on Sunday week at every chapel gate throughout the country in aid of the men locked out. . . . The Chairman (Mr. J. Murphy, D.C.) said that it was admitted now that every section and class had a right to combine for their own protection. He asked what would have happened long ago if a tenant farmer was evicted because he joined the National League. The present lock-out in Wexford amounted to the same thing . . . Mr P. T. Daly . . . addressed the meeting. . . . The workingmen of Enniscorthy are also taking steps to have a collection made.'

[6] *Ibid.*, January 30, 1912.

negotiated a compromise early in February, 1912.[1] The terms of the settlement allowed the men to organize an Irish Foundry Workers' Union which was to be affiliated with the Transport Union. The substance of the victory was with the men, since the Foundry Workers' Union was for all practical purposes a branch of the Transport Union. In fact two years later it officially became the Wexford branch of the Transport Union. Larkin and the Transport Union claimed a great victory. In truth it was a significant victory, not so much for what the workers gained, but rather for what the employers were not allowed to do. Wexford did not become another Cork, though the employers did all and more than was done in Cork to crush the Union. The fight put up by the men was formidable, but in the end it was an outraged public opinion that won the day in Wexford, as it had lost it in Cork.

It would be a mistake to think that all these strikes and lockouts were confined to Dublin or those towns where Larkin and the Transport Union were in the ascendancy. The labour unrest was general throughout Ireland, and Larkin was again only a convenient focus for what was a national picture. Beginning in August, 1911, the workers from one end of Ireland to the other made demands on their employers. From Jacob's biscuit factory in Dublin to the bacon factories in Limerick, from the dock labourers in Belfast to the Urban Council employees in Cork, spontaneous demands were made and quickly conceded. Newsboys, clothing workers, golf caddies, tanners, maltsters, dairy workers, and tramwaymen all clamoured for an increase in wages. The *Freeman's Journal* had to open a special column for 'Irish Labour Troubles' in August to chronicle the sudden outburst of industrial unrest.[2] The Transport Union had more than enough to do in these busy months. Larkin and Partridge were in Dublin. Daly was in Wexford, M'Keown was in Dundalk, and Connolly was in Belfast. The general wave of strikes did not subside in Ireland until February of the following year.

The most novel feature in all these strikes in Great Britain and Ireland was their spontaneous and sympathetic nature. The victories won by the waterside trades and the railwaymen in the summer of 1911 were chiefly the result of the sympathetic and concerted action taken by all the men. In Ireland it was Larkin's use of the 'sympathetic strike' and his policy of refusing to handle 'tainted goods' that won for him, more than anything else, the reputation of being a

[1] *Freeman's Journal*, February 12, 1912.   [2] *Ibid.*, August 29, 1911.

93

revolutionary syndicalist. Yet he professed neither to believe in nor approve of strikes. In the course of a speech celebrating the victory of the dockers and coal men at the end of July, 1911, Larkin said, 'I have told them again and again [the employers] that I don't believe in strikes—never did I believe in strikes.'[1] A year later, in giving evidence before the Industrial Council, he was even more explicit when he said, 'I do not approve of strikes at all. I have been through too many. I have been through 33 of them both as a striker and a leader of strikers.'[2] How did this square with his approval and use of not only the strike but the 'sympathetic strike' and his policy of not touching 'tainted goods'? Essentially Larkin saw society in three stages—the present, the near future, and the millennium. Since even he admitted that 'some little time must elapse'[3] before the coming of the millennium, it was the present and near future that concerned him most.

As for the present, Larkin realized that in 1911 in the face of the exploiting employers the working classes had no defence except their trade union and no weapon in their armoury except the strike. What existed between capital and labour was actually a state of war, and what had happened in the summer of 1911 'was no more than an episode in battle.'[4] As regards the 'sympathetic strike,' Larkin explained, 'We believe that when one of our friends is attacked anywhere we are attacked. We follow the same lines of organization as the Shipping Federation. Wherever an individual shipowner is affected they are affected everywhere, and they take up the fight. When ever we find one of our friends attacked anywhere we take up the fight, too.'[5] As far as 'tainted goods' was concerned, 'The principle I have been working on always,' continued Larkin, 'is that when the cabinet workers are on strike I am on strike, and if that stuff is made under unfair conditions I have no right to handle it.'[6] In ustifying his use of the 'sympathetic strike' Larkin pointed out, 'If the organised employers are entitled to use the sympathetic lockout, then I say it must be available in logic that we should also use the sympathetic strike.'[7]

---

[1] *Irish Worker*, July 29, 1911.

[2] Report of the Industrial Council on Inquiry into Industrial Agreements, Minutes of Evidence, *Parliamentary Papers*, 1913, XXVIII (Cd. 6953), p. 248.

[3] *Ibid.*

[4] *Freeman's Journal*, October 10, 1911. Dublin Trades Council.

[5] Report of Industrial Council, Minutes of Evidence, *op. cit.*, p. 244.

[6] *Ibid.*, 245.   [7] *Ibid.*, p. 247.

But was this state of war to continue indefinitely until the social revolution brought the millennium in its wake and there would be no need for strikes because the working classes would finally be in the seats of power? No, according to Larkin, order was to be brought out of chaos in the near future by 'compulsory arbitration.' As early as 1909 Larkin advocated 'Compulsory Arbitration Courts,'[1] and later enlarged them to 'Compulsory Wages and Arbitration Boards.' In July, 1912, he made it clear he was in favour of compulsory arbitration and he would 'make' both employers and employees carry out their agreements under the penalty of 'either money or prison.'[2] Larkin was at the same time convinced that 'voluntary arbitrations are no use to anybody.' When a proposal was made in the Dublin Trades Council to establish a Conciliation Board, which was in effect to be voluntary, Larkin objected. 'They wanted,' he said, 'something that would remove the state of disease that existed. They did not want a Conciliation Board. . . . They wanted something that would prevent strikes.'[3]

On April 26, 1913, Larkin wrote an 'Open Letter to the People' in the *Irish Worker* on 'How to Stop Strikes.' In a remarkable preface to an even more remarkable arbitration scheme, Larkin wrote:

> FRIENDS, I appeal to you to read and study this letter impartially, not to be swayed by prejudice, personal antagonism, or false sentiment. My only reason for writing you is for the ultimate benefit of this nation. What is the problem? Allow me to state it as I see it. The employers desire to carry on industry and accumulate profits. The workers desire to live. The employers cannot carry on industry nor accumulate profits if they have not got the good will of the workers or their acquiescence in carrying on such industry. The workers must work to live; therefore it is to the interest of both parties that a mutual arrangement should be brought about. A mutual arrangement, I repeat, is the only satisfactory medium whereby the present system can be carried on with any degree of satisfaction, and in such an arrangement the employers have more to gain than the workers. I am, of course, aware that the ultimate solution is the ownership and control of the means of life by the whole of the people; but we are not at that stage of development as yet. Therefore it is essential that some

[1] Registry of Friendly Societies, Irish Transport and General Workers' Union, File 275, *Rules, In Force on and From January 1, 1909.*
[2] Report of Industrial Council, Minutes of Evidence, *op. cit.*, p. 244.
[3] *Irish Worker*, March 15, 1913. Dublin Trades Council.

means should be sought whereby the work of the nation may be carried on without constant yet at present necessary dislocation. The Strike is a damnable but necessary evil at present, and if it is possible to limit them in number, place and magnitude, all thinking people should assist to that desirable end. I therefore place before you in a general way a scheme which I have submitted to employers and workers upon a former occasion, and to use a formalism, anything not set down in this scheme can be added thereto, anything objectionable therein will be, I hope, worthy of discussion.[1]

In outlining his 'Wages Board' scheme, Larkin classified industry in Dublin in four distinct categories. Shipbuilding and engineering were classified under one heading, while building, transport, and distribution made up the other three. An equal number of representatives of the employers and the workers were to be elected from each of the above groups and form a Trade Wages Board. All demands made by the men were to be first presented to their individual employers. If no satisfactory arrangement could be come to, the matter was to be submitted to the Trade Wages Board, which had full power to act on behalf of their respective sections. If the Trade Wages Board failed to reach a decision the matter was to be then forwarded to a City Wages Board. The Board was to be composed of ten members, five representing the employers and five the men. If an employer or union flouted the decision of the Wages Board, Trade or City, they were to receive no help from their fellow employers or trade unionists.

What is there to be said about a scheme that was literally the antithesis of everything Larkin had been espousing for years? The inconsistencies are enormous, and they are inexplainable except as absolute contradictions. Larkin had advocated 'compulsory arbitration,' while this scheme does not even involve arbitration because there is no arbiter—only equal numbers of employers and trade unionists. He had definitely denounced 'voluntary associations,' while this scheme depended for its success on the faith and good will of the parties involved. He had advocated penalties of 'money or prison,' while this scheme involved no more than the ostracism of the erring employer or trade union. The scheme itself, on the face of and in the light of Larkin's own experience, was unworkable. For this mess of pottage, he was consciously aware, he was giving up the principle of the 'sympathetic strike,' since a dispute would have to run the whole gamut of Boards before a strike could be called. He

[1] *Irish Worker*, April 26, 1913.

even went further, as he set an abnormally high 80 per cent as the figure which would justify a union calling for a 'closed shop' in any trade. It is difficult to believe that Larkin was not wholly sincere in presenting this scheme for settling strikes, for his preface reads with a deep sincerity. Though naïve and incomplete, the scheme itself is a straightforward exposition and not the least bit muddled. The only conclusion that can be arrived at is that Larkin changed his mind about 'compulsory arbitration' some time between the end of July, 1912, when he gave evidence before the Industrial Council, and the publication of the 'Open Letter' in April, 1913. This is substantiated by the fact that when a new Transport Union Rulebook was issued in October, 1912, the only change in the re-written preface was that the 'Compulsory Arbitration Courts' was deleted.[1] What Larkin's reasons were for changing his mind are not known, since he never acknowledged that he had changed his mind.

Undoubtedly, the change in the position of his union and the influx of new ideas were the chief external reasons for the change in his thinking. When his union was weak, the chief problem facing Larkin was securing recognition from the employers. He was, therefore, in those days an advocate of 'compulsory arbitration,' which would assure him a position of equality with the employers in the councils of the state. As his union grew in strength, however, the principle of recognition did not loom so large. His union could now force the employers to recognize them without the aid of the state, and there was no longer any pressing need for the union to limit its freedom of action. Also, of course, the new syndicalist ideas were in theory opposed to all contracts and working agreements. No contract should be made for more than a year at the most because agreements tended to dilute the militancy of the working classes. 'Compulsory arbitration' was, therefore, in conflict with the temper of the times, and with the new positions of strength the unions found themselves in after so many years in the wilderness.

The question of whether James Larkin was a syndicalist or not must at this point come naturally to mind. Since it has been noted that syndicalism was more easily described than defined, and since this very lack of precision seemed to be an integral part of a period whose values were rapidly disintegrating, the answer cannot be simple or

[1] Registry of Friendly Societies, Irish Transport and General Workers' Union, File 275, *Rules, in Force from October 10, 1912.*

even complete. As far as Larkin himself was concerned, he was a Socialist. His friends, naturally enough, saw him in their own image and likeness, while his enemies viewed him as a dark spectre complete with horns and the cloven hoof. Time has mercifully blurred both the black and the white, and Larkin, in retrospect, seems to be more the unconscious eclectic, blending and borrowing what suited him and the moment best, in Socialism and in syndicalism.

In the popular mind of the time it was simply enough to be a 'political actionist' to be classified as a Socialist, and a 'direct actionist' to be categorized as a syndicalist. Vainly did Connolly protest that all that was meant by syndicalism was 'simply the discovery that the workers are strongest at the point of production, that they have no force available except economic force, and by linking the revolutionary movement with the daily fight of the workshop, mill, shipyard, and factory, the necessary economic force can be organized. Also that the revolutionary organization necessary for that purpose provides the framework of the Socialist Republic.'[1] Further, since 'as long as we agree on the essential point,' asked Connolly, striking at the heart of the matter, 'why cavil about others. And the essential point is a belief in the wisdom of organising the economic power of the workers for the revolutionary act.' Larkin himself never discounted 'political action.' 'I believe,' he said, 'that the workers should use every weapon against the entrenched powers of capitalism. I am an industrialist and at the same time appreciate the fact that Labour can accomplish a great deal through the intelligent use of the ballot. Why use one arm when we have two? Why not strike the enemy with both arms—the political and economic?'[2] As long as Larkin was directing the Irish Labour Movement, and Connolly providing the mental pabulum, there were no quarrels over sacrosanct principles in the syndicalist calendar of absolutes, for nothing was sacred. What was necessary would be done, and weapons that came to hand would be used. Circumstances beyond Larkin's control, however, weighted the scales in favour of syndicalist ideas, but never tipped them completely.

Paralleling the growth in 'direct action' and industrial unrest, which had begun in the early summer of 1911, was the increasing interest taken by Larkin and the Irish Labour Movement in 'political

---

[1] *Watchword of Labour*, October 30, 1920. Letter from James Connolly to Edward Lynch dated Belfast, May 23, 1912.

[2] New York *Call*, November 9, 1914.

action.' Thus did another of the major points in syndicalist theory fall before the tide of Irish circumstance. By the middle of 1912 the Dublin Labour Party and the Independent Labour Party of Ireland had been founded, and the necessary machinery for the launching of an Irish Labour Party had been approved by the Irish Trades Union Congress. This renewed interest in 'political action' began, it will be remembered, in late January, 1911, when the Dublin Trades Council appointed eight delegates to form a local Labour Representation Committee. Larkin and four supporters formed an absolute majority on the Committee. The Rules and Constitution were adopted on April 3, 1911, but nothing further was done until August, 1911, when the Committee elected its officers.[1] The four men elected were all staunch Larkinites and included William O'Brien, who was elected to the key position of Secretary of the Dublin Labour Party. In the meantime Larkin had indicated that he was anxious to enter the political arena. At the Dublin Trades Council, in May, he pointed out that it was useless to appeal to the Corporation on the matter of municipal contracts going to trade union firms, for they 'would never get Trade Union conditions from the Corporation until they put in their own men.'[2] His lead column in the first edition of the *Irish Worker* paid more attention to a political programme than an economic one.[3] In late May and June, Larkin actively supported those trade unionists who were seeking election as Poor Law Guardians. The four Labour men who went forward did well, for all were elected and two headed their polls by impressive margins.[4] In speaking for these Labour candidates, Larkin replied to those who condemned him for his Socialist opinions in a most interesting and oblique manner. What opinions he held, Larkin said, he 'owned freely and was not ashamed of. He was a Socialist, and he prayed for the day when they would all be Socialists.' 'Under Socialism,' he said, 'there would be no poverty, and no necessity to see that the children found in the streets would be properly baptised —because with society properly organised no children would be born in the streets, and there would be no homeless and no paupers (cheers).'[5]

With the approach of the Dublin Corporation elections in

[1] *Freeman's Journal*, August 25, 1911.
[2] *Ibid.*, May 23, 1911. Dublin Trades Council.
[3] *Irish Worker*, May 27, 1911. 'Our Platform and Our Principles.'
[4] *Ibid.*, June 3, 1911.   [5] *Ibid.*

January, 1912, when some 20 of the 80 seats fell vacant, the Dublin Labour Party began to prepare as early as late November, 1911. By December there was already trouble over discipline. One prospective Labour candidate, who was supporting a non-Labour man and thought that since Labour was not contesting the ward he could support whomever he liked, was himself stricken from the Council's list of candidates. Larkin, in saying he 'was not satisfied with the explanation,' went on to point out, 'If Mr. Lawlor was free to support one section, other members would be equally free to support other sections, and the organization would cease to exist as an independent party.'[1] On January 3, the Dublin Labour Party presented a list of seven candidates which included Larkin. Before election day, January 16, every means was taken to discredit Larkin and his followers. The *Irish Independent*, owned and controlled by William Martin Murphy, printed the most atrocious things. On election day there appeared in the *Independent* a list of purported reasons covered by the title 'Why oppose Socialism?'[2] The following are a few of the reasons presented by P. W. Collins, Secretary of the Electrical Workers' Brotherhood, and described by the *Independent* as 'clear cut, and worthy of study.'

1. Its philosophy as laid down in the Bible of Socialism (Karl Marx's *Capital*) is based on the materialistic conception of history, which is nothing less than Atheism.
2. Because the founder of that doctrine, Karl Marx, was an avowed Atheist, and bitterly opposed the teachings of Christ and His Church. . . .
6. Because Socialism would destroy the sancity of the family and the home, for which the Catholic Church has always stood. . . .
12. Because Socialism stands for Free Love, and derides marriage, calling it a Capitalistic institution and a tool for exploitation. . . .
15. Because Socialism justifies abortion, child murder, regulation of reproduction, prevention of conception, and its advocates proclaim it.
16. Because Socialists hate the Catholic Church and condemn it as an enemy of workers, whose friend it has been through the ages. . . .[3]

Since Larkin was an admitted Socialist, he was by implication an atheist, by insinuation an advocate of free love, and by innuendo an

[1] *Freeman's Journal*, December 12, 1911. For Programme and Pledge of Dublin Labour Party see *Irish Worker*, December 23, 1911.
[2] *Irish Independent*, January 15, 1912.   [3] *Ibid.*

abortionist. He was the enemy of God, man, and the nation, and so were his supporters for that matter. Still, he had little cause for complaint, because the victory was his. Five of the Labour candidates were returned in what was an enormous victory.[1] Larkin's own victory was a magnificent personal triumph. He polled over 1,200 votes to some 500 for his opponent. Though the Labour Party in the Corporation was infinitesimal when compared to the total number of seats (80), at least a beginning was made and a nucleus provided for an attempt to reform what was one of the world's most corrupt municipal bodies. In supporting another Labour candidate at a Corporation by-election some three weeks later, Councillor Larkin wanted to know 'was it only Lord Mayors that required salaries? Was no one to lift their voices on behalf of the downtrodden city toiler, whose whole life from the cradle to the grave was a never ending struggle to make ends meet?'[2] He pleaded, 'If their hearts were not made of stone, how could they calmly vote £3,600 odd to one man, to be used mostly in feeding the well-fed, while they all knew they had in their midst a vast mass of unemployed men with hungry women and children. The Dublin Labour Party would, at any rate, stretch a helping hand to lift their submerged brothers and sisters, and do what little they could to brighten their lives.' Larkin saw 'a great future . . . before the workers when they opened their eyes and realised their power. That they were beginning to do that was evident from the results of the recent elections.'[3] The Labour candidate, Thomas Farren, was returned, and the Party now mustered six strong in a body of eighty.

Another move in the direction of political action was made in the last week of May, 1912. The Irish Trades Union Congress, meeting at Clonmel, had approved a resolution that would provide machinery for an Irish Labour Party. With Home Rule a 'certainty,' Connolly had convinced even the most loyal adherents of the Irish Party among the trade unionists that the time was ripe for preparing the ground for Labour representation in the new Home Rule Parliament. The resolution was presented by Connolly. It was a cleverly worded affair in that it posed no threat to Home Rule itself by immediately demanding a national Labour Party, but it was evident that it would provide all the machinery necessary for Labour to contest seats in

[1] *Irish Worker*, January 20, 1912.
[2] *Freeman's Journal*, February 6, 1912.
[3] *Ibid.*

the first Home Rule Parliament. It may also be noted that this resolution has nothing whatever to do with Socialism.

> Resolved—that the independent representation of Labour upon all public boards be, and is hereby, included amongst the objects of this Congress; that one day at least be hereafter set apart at our annual gathering for the discussion of all questions pertaining thereto; that the affiliated bodies be asked to levy their members 1s. per annum for the necessary expenses, and that the Parliamentary Committee be instructed to take all possible action to give effect politically to this resolution.[1]

Larkin was the first on his feet supporting the resolution, saying, 'There was no argument against a policy such as was outlined in the resolution. In that resolution they had the lever to do their own work. They were not humbugged in the least by people who said that Home Rule meant the millennium, but they believed that Home Rule would give them an opportunity of expressing themselves physically and mentally. . . . They should remember that it would be too late to prepare when the battle-note was struck (applause).'[2] The opposition once again discredited itself by personal attacks on Larkin, and the resolution passed by a majority of almost three to one.

Councillor Larkin in the meantime had hardly lifted his victory draught when the cup was dashed from his lips. A month after his election Larkin was sued for his seat on the grounds that a convicted felon had no right to sit in the Corporation. Since his pardon from the Lord Lieutenant did not qualify as a free pardon, he was debarred from sitting for a period of five years. When the case came to court, Larkin's attorney applied for a postponement because his client was busy. In the course of the discussion, Larkin's attorney agreed that it was only proper that the *Irish Worker* should refrain from comment because it would be an 'act of gross disrespect to the Court.' But when he said 'From what I know of my client I believe he would be the last in the world to show any disrespect,' he was greeted with a great burst of laughter. The magistrate wryly, but aptly, remarked, 'that laughter shows public opinion on the subject.'[3]

Larkin loved to go to court; it was another platform on which to perform. His ready wit, repartee, and demagogic eloquence were always formidable and sometimes delightful, if not always relevant.

---

[1] *Report of the Nineteenth Irish Trades Union Congress, 1912*, pp. 12–13.
[2] *Ibid.*, p. 13.　　　　[3] *Freeman's Journal*, March 23, 1912.

When sued for libel in early 1913, for example, Larkin replied to the accusation that he was not slow in attacking other people by commenting, 'I never attacked anyone that did not deserve it.'[1] The attorney for the plaintiff, in trying to prejudice Larkin's case, pressed his point by asking, 'And you attacked Mr. Swifte, the magistrate?' Larkin blandly admitted that 'I wrote that article, and I take it that neither magistrate, judge, nor jury is above criticism—they are certainly not above mine (laughter).' Again Larkin was pressed— 'Did you in another case in which you were a party publish the names of the jury and addresses?' 'Yes,' Larkin replied readily, 'and so did the other papers. I took the names from a daily paper.' 'But did you publish something about each of them?' asked the attorney. 'Yes,' answered Larkin, looking significantly at the jury, 'and I may do so about another jury (laughter).' Eventually Larkin was debarred from sitting in the Corporation for a term of seven years when a petition to the Lord Lieutenant for a free pardon was refused.

This was a crucial turning point for Larkin and the Irish Labour Movement. By law he was now personally debarred for seven years from any political action. His enormous energy, therefore, would be devoted to his Union, and organizing the Irish working classes for 'direct action.' This short-sightedness on the part of Larkin's opponents in the hope of limiting his influence by doing him immediate harm, pushed him, in the long run, in a syndicalist direction. While it was very true that he warmly supported all the subsequent Labour candidates, both on the hustings and in the *Irish Worker*, the Labour Party in the Corporation was now without an effective leader. For Larkin—and it was as much a reservoir of his strength as it was a well of his weakness—was temperamentally one of those men who must be the prime and vital force in any movement.

Since the Clonmel Congress in May, William O'Brien had been working hard to get the Parliamentary Committee to implement Connolly's resolution. Larkin, who had been elected Chairman of the Parliamentary Committee, resigned in a huff at the initial meeting because the members of the Parliamentary Committee disagreed with a ruling he gave as Chairman.[2] He was adamant in his refusal to withdraw his resignation or to take the lead in forming the proposed Irish Labour Party. Though Larkin refused to chair a meeting in

---

[1] *Freeman's Journal*, January 23, 1913.

[2] *Ibid.*, August 6, 1912. See also *The Attempt to Smash the Irish Transport and General Workers' Union* (1924), p. 163.

September called by O'Brien, he did attend and speak.[1] What Larkin had to say was critical and pointless, and he was obviously upset. Whether this was owing to illness, as he said later,[2] or just that he did not get his own way, it is hard to say. Nothing more, however, was heard of this Irish Labour Party until the Irish Trades Union Congress met in 1914.

The political side of the Irish Labour Movement was actually in decline, just when its future seemed most bright. At the national level the difficulty was that Home Rule, with the suspensory veto of the House of Lords, would not finally pass through the House of Commons until 1914. In the meantime, the Irish Party claimed to be the official guardian of this guarantee of nationhood and disputed the right of any section of the Irish nation to contest for independent representation on a parliamentary level. The Labour Movement in Ireland could, therefore, do nothing before Home Rule became an actual fact in 1914, and two years was a long time to be doing nothing in Irish politics. Worse yet, on the local level, where Irish Labour might hope to keep the working-class voter politically conscious until the time was right for a venture into the national political arena, the Dublin Labour Party went into a decline. The new leader, Richard O'Carroll, was an able, honest, and energetic man, but he was not the man Larkin was. Then, too, the first flush of public enthusiasm, which always greets the party of reform, whether in Dublin or in New York, is a difficult thing to perpetuate into a political machine. As a rule, it is the reform parties that come and go, while the machine goes on for ever. In vain did the Labour Party protest they were only six, not sixty, in a body of eighty. In vain did they protest that their duties covered not only the Corporation, but the Poor Law Boards, the District Asylums, the Port and Docks Board. In vain did they protest that the whole machinery of an entrenched and kept bureaucracy was working against them. In vain did O'Carroll explain that the South Dublin Union, or poorhouse, was 'seething in corruption and debauchery.'[3] He and Councillor Lawlor did their best, 'but their protests were either ruled out of order or voted down by the corrupt gang who ruled that Board. They found that not alone were the Guardians opposed to them, but the majority of the officials, and even the inmates,

[1] *Freeman's Journal*, September 16, 1912.
[2] *Ibid.*, October 4, 1912.
[3] *Ibid.*, November 30, 1912.

conspired to prevent them exposing the abuses that cried out for redress in that institution.'[1] Once the public makes an effort, it seems, they no longer want to hear the same cries of vice, robbery, and corruption, for they voted to abolish those things last time out.

After Larkin had been ousted from the Corporation, in March, 1912, there was a by-election in June. Though the contest was won by the Labour Party's candidate, Peader Macken, a painter by trade and an avowed Socialist,[2] the local labour tide was sharply checked in October, 1912, when the Dublin Labour Party lost two crucial by-elections. In one the candidates tied at 820 votes each. On the recount the Labour candidate lost by five votes. In the other contest, W. P. Partridge lost in New Kilmainham Ward by 23 votes in a poll of nearly 900.[3] Both were cruel and disappointing defeats for Larkin. He had fought tooth and nail and made the issue a personal one. At the annual Corporation elections in January, 1913, Larkin was once again on the hustings, and the columns of the *Irish Worker* were more vitriolic than ever. In referring to one candidate, Larkin asked, 'And who are his backers?—John Saturnus Kelly, thief and blackmailer, liar and hypocrite; Bill Richardson, political corner boy and tool of Alfy Byrne, publican; and O'Hanlon, an alleged trade unionist.'[4] Of another candidate he wrote:

Here is a creature—Swaine—whose only prayer is a blasphemous obscene oath; a creature who is a byword and a reproach to all decent men; whose career has been one debauch of drunkenness, vice, and sin; whose very name breathes pestilence, standing as the champion of Religion and Nationality. . . . A creature of profligacy and vice, a creature who would have contaminated Sodom and Gomorrah if he had lived in those days. No deed too foul, no language obscene enough for Mickey. His very presence is an abomination and a disgrace to any city. And then his colleague Edelstein—a criminal lunatic, who has been found guilty of the most abominable offences; a creature who outraged and destroyed a little girl aged eight; this abominable beast is also a champion of Religion and Nationality. He is paid to try and influence the Jewish voters into voting for his Christian fellow-blackguard.[5]

[1] *Freeman's Journal*, November 30, 1912.
[2] *Ibid.*, June 27, 1912. The vote was 870 to 844.
[3] *Ibid.*, October 2, 1912. See *Irish Worker*, October 5, 1913.
[4] *Irish Worker*, January 11, 1913.
[5] *Ibid.*

The opposition had as much to say, if indeed, not more. John Saturnus Kelly wrote an election manifesto denouncing both Larkin and Partridge.

> In order to accomplish his hellish work he (Mr. Larkin) installed Mr. William P. Partridge as the caretaker or manager of his Socialistic or Anarchistic hall in Emmet road, Inchicore, to live on the hard earning of the quay labourers (earnings that should go to their wives and little children) to enable him (Mr. Larkin) to spread the Socialistic and anti-Christian doctrine of discontent amongst my fellow railway labourers. . . . I am quite confident that you will not sell Home Rule to the two howling wolves, viz.—Messrs. Larkin and Partridge for Socialism that I am out against at the cost of my life if necessary. They are thirsting for my destruction because I am their unflinching opponent against their vile and cruel intentions to injure or cause trouble in your great railway works, and subsequently starve your wives and children by sympathetic strikes in order that they (Larkin and Partridge) may live well. Also buy house property and get rich at the cost of your ruin by the smashing up of your stirring local industries. . . . I appeal to you men and women of the ward, in the name of Christianity and our dear motherland (Erin) not to give him (Partridge) an opportunity of selling the evil pest of Socialism that is the curse of our Christian country.[1]

In the libel action that followed, Kelly's attorney explained in an apology in open court, 'that they never meant any serious view should be taken.'[2] The Dublin Labour Party, however, won only two of the eight seats they contested, and now numbered only eight in eighty. Some solace could be taken in the fact that, since the Labour vote had been generally good, a politically conscious Labour nucleus was being formed. After the substantial victory of 1912, however, the gains of 1913 could not fail to come as an anti-climax.

One reason why there had been an increased interest in 'political action' in early 1912 was that the great wave of strikes that swept Ireland from the early summer of 1911 began to subside after six intensive months. Irish Labour had won over this period of unrest some rather substantial increases in wages. Employers generally gave way rather than jeopardize their chances of taking advantage of what were really the booming trade years of 1912 and 1913. Between February, 1912, and January, 1913, the industrial situation in Ireland was comparatively peaceful. This, coupled with Larkin's

[1] *Freeman's Journal*, February 11, 1913.   [2] *Ibid.*

exclusion from the Corporation in late March, caused him to turn his attention once again to his first love and his own creation, the Transport Workers' Union. He attempted to extend his union by including all those who had not been organized by an approved trade society. He had already, with the help of his sister Delia, begun to organize the Irish Women Workers' Union, whose sphere of operations was soon extended to Belfast.[1] Larkin also undertook to organize the port of Sligo in the west of Ireland, and arranged a working agreement with a local union in Limerick.[2] More interesting than all these efforts to spread his wings was the ambitious attempt he made to organize and control the whole of the port of Dublin.

Larkin realized that the key to the port of Dublin was in the hands of his dockers, the nucleus and backbone of his union. The dockers handled everything that moved in and out of Dublin. In that last analysis, since Dublin was a city that depended primarily on trade rather than industry, the subsidiary employments were all at the mercy of the men on the docks. The problem was that unemployment in Dublin in 1912 was still serious, though the problem had much improved in Britain. There were a large number of casuals, coming and going, who would never be satisfactory union members unless the employment situation on the docks could be stabilized. To remedy this situation, Larkin, in early June, 1912, decided to organize the stevedores, that is, those middlemen who contracted with the shipping firms to load and unload the vessels that came into the port of Dublin.[3]

At a meeting on June 10, in the Transport Union offices in Liberty Hall, Larkin suggested to the stevedores present that they form an association so that they would not be undercutting each other in an effort to secure contracts at each other's expense. He presented them with a printed set of rules, and coyly suggested that they might like to retire to consider the matter. In explaining his point of view Larkin said it was not so much an increase in wages the Union wanted, but 'larger gangs, increasing them to 15 and two boys and thus give more labour.'[4] He went on to point out to the stevedores

---

[1] *Irish Worker*, September 9, 1911. The I.W.W.U. was founded September 5, 1911.

[2] Report of the Industrial Council on Inquiry into Industrial Agreements, Minutes of Evidence, *Parliamentary Papers*, 1913, XXVIII (Cd. 6953), p. 242.

[3] *Freeman's Journal*, December 3, 1912. 'Long vs. Larkin.'

[4] *Ibid.*, December 4, 1912.

that 'Owing to the cutting down that had prevailed at the port four men were obliged to do the work of six at the holds, and two men instead of three at the trucks on the quay. The accidents minor and fatal, went up in five years from 330 by 50 per cent.'[1] Some ten days later, on June 20, the stevedores again met and approved the setting up of a Stevedores' Association and adopted Larkin's proposal for a new schedule of rates for the whole of the port of Dublin. Prices in the timber trade, for example, were nearly doubled.[2]

Larkin had clearly manoeuvred a significant victory for the Transport Union in Dublin. By persuading the stevedores to form an association he had detached them from the employers. Through their new combination the stevedores now enjoyed an independence of action they had never had before. The employer could no longer discard a stevedore if he were dissatisfied with him and employ another. Further, Larkin not only detached the stevedores from the employers, he bound them to himself and his Union. For now he was the only really effective agent for disciplining the individual stevedore who might rebel against the Association. Larkin could guarantee to chastise any wayward stevedore by refusing him dock labour. For all practical purposes Larkin was now master of the port of Dublin. The wages and conditions of dock labour were substantially improved, for the employers seem to have put up no general resistance to the new list of prices put forward by Larkin through the Stevedores' Association.

The reorganization of the port of Dublin increased the power of the Union, because more casual men were given steady employment and were better able, therefore, to pay their Union dues. Membership figures for the Transport Union are very difficult to assess. The figures given annually to the Registrar of Friendly Societies were not reliable because they included as a member of the Union anyone who paid the entrance fee and dues for a week. A man might, therefore, be a member for a week, or a month, and then drop out, and still be represented as a member on the books, which for all practical purposes he was not. The Registrar's figure for the Transport Union at the beginning of 1912 was 18,089, and the Union closed the year with 24,135, an increase of over 6,000 members.[3] The figures for union membership mentioned by Larkin or his representatives

---

[1] *Freeman's Journal*, December 4, 1912.   [2] *Ibid.*, December 3, 1912.

[3] Registry of Friendly Societies, Irish Transport and General Workers' Union, File 275, *Annual Return Prescribed by the Registar for a Registered Trade Union. Year Ending 31st December 1913.*

were also open to question because of their general nature and variance. When Larkin, for example, could not appear in court because of his union duties, his counsel pointed out he was the head of a Union with 15,000 members.[1] Some three months later in a petition to the Lord Lieutenant for a free pardon to enable him to take his seat in the Corporation, it was pointed out that Larkin headed a union 20,000 strong.[2] In giving evidence before the Industrial Council Larkin claimed to have 18,000 members.[3] Again there was not much use in these figures, except to show they were substantially less than those presented to the Registrar of Friendly Societies.

The best and perhaps the most accurate method for getting the Union membership figures was to examine the amount paid in Affiliation Fees to the Irish Trades Union Congress. The payment was based on membership, and if human nature counts for anything, it would mean that the figure would be underestimated. The figure for the spring of 1911 came to something less than 4,000; for 1912, something less than 8,000; for 1913, about 14,000.[4] These figures seem to be all the more reasonable when they are compared with the figure issued by the Insurance Commissioners who supervised the National Insurance Act. The Transport Union was listed as having 9,580 contributors in 1913 under the terms of the Act.[5] Since the contribution was a continuous and weekly affair, this figure gives the best indication of what the real strength of the Transport Union was during this period. Before the beginning of the industrial unrest in the early summer of 1911, the union membership did not come to over 5,000, and was probably closer to 3,000. With the unrest there came a startling increase in trade union membership. The National Union of Dock Labourers, for example, began 1911 with only 12,000 members and closed the year with over 50,000.[6] The field for recruiting was not so large in Ireland as in Britain, but a figure of 8,000 for the end of 1912 and 10,000 by the middle of 1913 seems to be a fair estimate.

Where did the bulk of these new members come from? The

---

[1] *Freeman's Journal*, March 23, 1912. [2] *Ibid.*, June 19, 1912.

[3] Report of Industrial Council, Minutes of Evidence, *op. cit.*, p. 242.

[4] *Reports of the Eighteenth, Nineteenth and Twentieth Irish Trades Union Congresses, 1911, 1912, 1913.* See Affiliation Fees.

[5] *Freeman's Journal*, July 5, 1913.

[6] *Ibid.*, May 21, 1912.

majority were recruited in Dublin, but important blocs of members were secured outside. In Belfast the beginnings of a branch were made while Larkin was in jail in the summer of 1910. When Connolly was appointed secretary of the Belfast branch in June, 1911, the branch reached its maximum strength during this period of between 600 and 800 members. The Belfast branch was composed chiefly of the men who worked the low, or deep-sea, docks, and they were nearly all of 'one-complexion' in that they were Catholics.[1] The Transport Union in Belfast made hardly any headway among the Protestant dockers and carters. Though the organization in Wexford was called the Irish Foundrymen's Union, it was to all intents and purposes a branch of the Transport Union, and by 1913 actually became such officially. The branch numbered between 500 and 1,000 strong.

When Larkin's sister Delia arrived in Dublin in the summer of 1911, the idea of founding an Irish Women Workers' Union was formulated.[2] The I.W.W.U., founded on September 5, 1911, with Larkin as President, was financed by the Transport Union.[3] In the spring of 1912 the Irish Women Workers' Union applied to the Trades Union Congress for affiliation and paid fees on some 1,000 members.[4] Connolly also helped found an Irish Textile Workers' Union in Belfast, and did his best, with the help of Mrs. Thomas Johnson, to organize the women workers in the linen industry.[5] When the National Seamen's and Firemen's Dublin branch went out on strike, in June, 1911, it was weak and financially vulnerable. Larkin reorganized the branch and financed it during the strike, and, like the Foundrymen's Union in Wexford, it became for all practical purposes a branch of the Transport Union.[6] A branch of the Transport Union was also organized in Kingstown, which was the Irish landing-stage for the important Dublin–Holyhead traffic. The branch was reported to be 'numerically fairly strong, but how its

[1] Report of Industrial Council, Minutes of Evidence, *op. cit.*, p. 409. See evidence of A. M'Dowell.

[2] *Irish Worker*, August 12, 1911, August 19, 1911.

[3] *Ibid.*, September 2, 1911, September 9, 1911.

[4] *Report of the Nineteenth Irish Trades Union Congress, 1912*. See Affiliation Fees.

[5] *Forward*, January 10, 1914. See James Connolly.

[6] London *Times*, November 24, 1913. J. H. Wilson said, 'Over two years the Sailors' and Fireman's Union—i.e., the Dublin branch—has been subject absolutely to the control of James Larkin.'

Jim Larkin at work at Liberty Hall.
From a drawing by Sir William Orpen, R.A.

In 1907 at Belfast

Jim Larkin (disguised)
following his arrest at
the Imperial Hotel
by Superintendent
Murphy of the D.M.P.
on Bloody Sunday.

finances stand is quite another question.'[1] The only other large acquisition of members outside Dublin in this period was in Sligo, which numbered between 500 and 1,000.[2]

After the strike wave petered out, in early February, 1912, Ireland was relatively quiet until the beginning of 1913. The employers, after the lean trade years between 1907 and 1910 and rocked by trade disputes for the greater part of 1911, were anxious to avoid trouble and drink deeply from the rising and rapidly flowing stream of trade. Larkin, for his part, was moderately satisfied during 1912 with his 'continuous and successful struggle to improve wages and conditions.'[3] Though only the lull before the storm, the reasonable spirit began also to permeate the Labour Movement. The newly elected president of the Dublin Trades Council as well as the retiring Thomas Murphy, a loyal Larkinite, urged 'the trade unions not to take extreme steps in labour disputes without having consulted the Council.'[4] Even Larkin went so far as to note that during the dislocation in the coal trade caused by the great Miners' Federation strike in Great Britain in early 1912, the principal Dublin coal merchants had treated their men with sympathy and generosity.[5] The coal merchants, almost to a man, had given their men coal and advanced them money to tide them over the trouble.[6]

Besides his attempt to reorganize the port in 1912, Larkin had begun to organize all the general and miscellaneous workers in Dublin who had never been catered to before. A small factory employing fifty men was a comparatively easy organizing task, for the small employer could not hope to cope with an organization as large as the Transport Union.[7] These small employers rapidly gave way in the face of having their businesses closed down, although they must have bitterly resented doing so. One manager of such a firm complained that after the Transport Union organized his employees they immediately presented a demand for an increase in wages. He

---

[1] *Freeman's Journal*, November 2, 1912. The Kingstown branch numbered about 250. See I.T.U.C., 1913, Affiliation Fees.

[2] *Report of the Twentieth Irish Trades Union Congress, 1913*. See Affiliation Fees.

[3] *Irish Worker*, January 4, 1913. See editorial, '1912–13.'

[4] *Freeman's Journal*, March 12, 1912. Dublin Trades Council.

[5] *Ibid.*, March 26, 1912.

[6] *Ibid.*, April 5, 1912.

[7] *Ibid.*, October 2, 1913. See T. M. Healy before 'Askwith Enquiry' on how Larkin organized the 'small and weak firms.'

pointed out how unfair the Union was because the firm had 'always dealt very fairly with its workers, but now it would appear that when, as a result of the Irish industrial revival, we have been doing an increased business the men think they can come in and say—"we must also have our share of the increased earning." ' Anyone could see, he continued, 'if that principle were accepted it would kill all industrial enterprise.'[1]

In building his 'One Big Union,' Larkin's inconsistencies and complete reversals of policy without so much as an acknowledgment were in complete harmony with the temper of the times. Between 1905 and 1914 there was an ever-widening and ever-deepening depreciation of reason. The result was an increasing militancy and a tendency to rely on force. This developing taste for violence was a worldwide phenomenon and permeated every branch of society. The growth of Syndicalist ideas everywhere was but a phase in the general picture. After 1911 the tempo increased as the whole world on all levels seemed intent on making one mad dash towards destruction. There developed everywhere a remarkable ability to articulate and remain at the same time basically incoherent. The First World War, in this context, was a supremely fitting conclusion to a period in which the rational was superseded by the intuitional. The personification of this tendency was James Larkin.

[1] *Freeman's Journal*, July 31, 1912.

VI

STRIKE

IN Britain, with the exception of the coal strike, 1912 was a comparatively quiet year when compared to 1911 or even 1910. The Labour Movement, however, was only pausing to catch its second wind, for the year 1913 opened with the proverbial bang. The renewed ferment in Britain was not long in flowing over into Ireland. In Dublin alone no less than thirty strikes took place between January and the middle of August. As a further indication of the increasingly militant and violent temper of the times, these strikes were accompanied by a good deal of disorder. Some forty-five people were prosecuted and convicted in Dublin.[1] As in 1911 the unrest was widespread, and very serious strikes took place in Galway and Sligo as well. These were also accompanied by a good deal of violence, which had not been generally the case in 1911. Further, these disputes were prolonged and deeply rooted, which again was not the case in 1911, except in Wexford. Though not directly involved in the Galway dispute, Larkin and the Transport Union extended their sympathy and their support. In Sligo the Transport Union branch was in the thick of the trouble, for the fight was as bitter as the one in Wexford had been. When the employers imported 'blacklegs' from Liverpool, the rioting was fierce.[2] The strikers actually swept the police from the streets, and in the savage fighting a striker was killed.[3] The Transport Union supported the men, eventually won the strike, and brooked no interference in managing the port,

[1] Report of the Dublin Disturbances Commission, *Parliamentary Papers*, 1914, XVIII (Cd. 7269), p. 2.
[2] *Freeman's Journal*, March 27, 1913.
[3] *Ibid.*, March 28, 1913.

as it eliminated the middlemen by taking over the services provided by the stevedores.[1]

The real strength of the Union was to be found in Dublin, however, and it was in Dublin that the 'One Big Union' was to stand or fall. At the end of January, 1913, a dispute began at the North Wall which resulted in Larkin becoming the virtual dictator of the port of Dublin. Since he had organized the dockers and detached the stevedores from the shipping companies, all that remained now was to bring the shipping companies around to his point of view. When the Transport Union men employed by the City of Dublin Steampacket Company walked off their jobs on January 30, 1913, the issue was joined. The nominal reason for the strike was that some five foremen refused to join the Union.[2] Though Larkin denied that this was the reason for the strike,[3] his inconsistency as regards the 'closed shop,' like his attitude on 'compulsory arbitration,' approached sheer opportunism. When he was weak he publicly stated that his members did not object to working with non-union men, though privately, undoubtedly, he was galled by having to make such an admission. When he was on his way to becoming a power he

[1] Irish State Paper Office, Green Carton, No. 51, Room VII, Chief Secretary's Office, Judicial Division. Intelligence Notes, 1913. Dublin Labour Troubles, pp. 19–21. James Larkin's Connection with Disputes in Belfast, Cork, Dublin, Wexford, Etc., p. 21. Courtesy of Eamon de Valera, then Prime Minister of the Irish Republic. 'On the 8th March, 1913, the crew of the s.s. Sligo belonging to the Sligo Steam Navigation Company deserted on the refusal of their demand for cattle money, i.e., money for attending to cattle in transit to Liverpool. The Company thereupon employed a non-Union crew, but on the return of the vessel to Sligo the dockers there (Transport Union men) refused to work with these men. This was followed by the Company's Mill hands going out on strike, and the dispute soon spread to carters and other labourers and developed into a trial of strength between the Employers and the Transport Union. Efforts were made by an official from the Board of Trade to effect a settlement, but without success. The demand of the Transport Union was that no free labour should be employed at the quay. The strike was finally settled in May and was a complete victory for the Irish Transport Union. All the non-Union Labourers except four and all the carters who worked during the strike were forced to submit to fines of £1 to £3 and had to join the Union. Larkin was represented by P. T. Daly during these labour troubles in Sligo. In consequence of some serious disorder on the quays. in which one life was lost, and of rioting throughout the town, a large force of extra police had to be drafted in for the preservation of the peace in the Borough.'

[2] *Freeman's Journal*, February 26, 1913.

[3] *Irish Worker*, February 8, 1913.

denied absolutely that he ever agreed to union men working with non-union men.[1]

Tactically, the City of Dublin Steampacket Company was a good choice for a stand-up fight. It was the oldest shipping company in Dublin, and its chairman, Sir Edward Watson, was much respected among the shipowners. The Company was vulnerable, and Larkin knew it, because it had the government mail contract,[2] and it was obliged to fulfil its contract or lose its lucrative and semi-official position. The fight was a long and costly one, extending over nearly three months. But in the end Larkin and his union were victorious.[3] The settlement resulted in the men gaining a very substantial increase in wages, with a full recognition of the Transport Union as the men's official bargaining agent. More important, however, the victory signified the beginning of the end of the resistance put up by the other shipping companies in the port of Dublin. On May 26, 1913, six of the most important shipping companies in Dublin signed an agreement with the Transport Union for a new schedule in wages.[4] The wage schedule gave the permanent men 30s. for a week of 60 hours, and the casual men 5s. for a 10-hour day. Dublin had finally, some twenty-five years after London, secured the 'docker's tanner.' It was a great victory for the men and their union, for recognition was now a matter of contract. Larkin did not get it all his own way, however, for he had, in effect, to give up the 'sympathetic strike.' There was to be no stoppage of work for any reason, since the Union had to submit its grievances in writing, and the agreement could only be terminated on a month's notice by either side. Still, the men were jubilant, and Larkin was master of the port.[5]

No sooner had Larkin settled with the shipping companies than

---

[1] Report of the Industrial Council on Inquiry into Industrial Agreements, Minutes of Evidence, *Parliamentary Papers*, 1913, XXVIII (Cd. 6953) p. 243. See also *Irish Worker*, November 25, 1911.

[2] *Ibid.*, p. 243.

[3] *Irish Worker*, February 8, 1913, April 5, 1913, and April 26, 1913.

[4] Arnold Wright, *Disturbed Dublin* (1914), pp. 307–8. See for full schedule of terms and agreement.

[5] *Freeman's Journal*, October 2, 1913. See Timothy Healy at 'Askwith Enquiry.' 'The result was that in the month of May last he had so organised the quay labourers of the city (where undoubtedly some grievances existed) that he reduced the port of Dublin to this condition that the masters and suffering owners surrendered to him.'

his restless energy found a new outlet. He began a campaign in early June to organize the most unorganizable workers of all—the agricultural labourers. Generally, the history of agricultural labour unions has been short and unhappy. The seasonal and uncertain nature of agricultural employment makes the agricultural labourer, almost of necessity, a migrant. Since he had no permanent stake in his employment, he consequently had no interest in expending his time or his money to protect it. The situation in County Dublin, where Larkin began his campaign, was somewhat different. The labourers, who worked the large farms around Dublin, were usually employed on a permanent basis. Further, they lived in village communities, which are really better described as rural slums, and were not, as were the other agricultural labourers in Ireland, isolated on a potato patch. Their class-consciousness and real sense of grievance, therefore, could be more easily organized. Also, though they were miserable in their poverty, the County Dublin labourers were somewhat better off than their brethren in the rest of Ireland. In 1907, for example, the wages around Dublin and Belfast were something over 13s. a week, while the Irish average was 11s. 3d.[1] The differences, incidentally, between agricultural wages in Great Britain and in Ireland were startling. The agricultural wage scale in 1907 for England was 18s. 4d. per week; Scotland, 19s. 7d.; and Wales 18s.[2] Every year, therefore, a large number of farm workers migrated from the West of Ireland to Great Britain for the harvest. Before 1907 the position of the Irish agricultural labourer had been much worse compared to his corresponding number in Great Britain.[3] For, between 1880 and 1907, agricultural wages in England and Wales rose by 10 per cent, by 17 per cent in Scotland, and by 24 per cent in Ireland.[4] In any case, in 1913, Larkin realized that the farm

[1] Report of an Inquiry by the Board of Trade into the Earnings and hours of Labour of Workpeople of the United Kingdom, V—Agriculture in 1907, *Parliamentary Papers*, 1910, LXXXIV (Cd. 5460), p. iii.

[2] *Ibid.*

[3] Report and Tables Relating to Irish Migratory Agricultural and other Labourers for the Year 1906, *Parliamentary Papers*, 1907, XCVII (Cd. 3481). See for: 1907–1908, CXXI (Cd. 4123); 1908–1909, CII (Cd. 4919); 1909–10–1910, CVIII (Cd. 5033); 1910–11–1913, CVI (Cd. 6019); 1911–1912, CVI (Cd. 6198); 1912–1913, LXXVI (Cd. 6928); 1913–1914, XCVIII (Cd. 7418). In comparing 1907 with 1913, it would seem that agricultural wages rose on the average throughout Ireland by about 1s. per week. In County Dublin wages were in 1907 between 10s. and 14s. per week, and 1913 between 12s. and 15s. per week.

[4] Report of an Inquiry by the Board of Trade, *op. cit.*, p. xv.

labourers of County Dublin were the readiest and best material to begin with.

Every Sunday the Transport Workers' Fife and Drum Band, together with its Irish pipers, accompanied by an odd array of wagonettes and jaunting cars, all with banners flying, made their way to Baldoyle, Clondalkin, Blanchardstown, Lucan, Fingal, or Swords. Larkin, Partridge, Thomas Lawlor, and Daly would all make speeches, and distribute leaflets and Union membership forms.[1] The campaign was very successful, for discontent was rife among the farm labourers. Larkin cleverly shaped his message to suit the Irish countrymen, who, even today, instinctively shrinks from the Dublin 'jackeen.' He told funny stories, like the one about the mule who kicked his stable down and when the farmer asked the mule what all the commotion was about, the mule replied that he was sick and tired of living in filth and dirt. The farmer was indignant, and he wanted to know why wasn't the stable that was good enough for the mule's father good enough for him. The mule simply replied that his father had been an ass. In a more serious vein Larkin told the County Dublin farm labourers that he came to organize them and get them better wages in order to stop them from flooding the city labour market and aggravating an already chronic unemployment situation.[2] By the middle of August, 1913, Larkin had organized enough of the County Dublin farm labourers to make a wage demand. The farmers, however, had by this time organized themselves in the County Dublin Farmers' Association.[3]

When the Farmers' Association refused to come to terms, a strike was called. The farmers were in an awkward position for resistance, since it was already late in August and with the variability of Irish weather they could easily lose their harvest. They surrendered on August 17, and it was an enormous victory for Larkin and his Transport Union. The wages for a 66-hour week were to be 17s., and to this should be added all the perquisites that were formerly granted. The increase in most cases amounted to about 3s., or a 20 per cent advance. The terms also included new wage scales for women, boys, and casuals, while the entire agreement was made retroactive to August 11. The Union, for its part, agreed to

[1] *Labour Leader*, August 28, 1913. See Shaw Desmond. 'A Revolution in Ireland.'
[2] *Irish Worker*, June 14, 1913.
[3] *Freeman's Journal*, August 13, 1913.

no stoppage of work until the matter under dispute was fully discussed.[1]

Larkin was now at the height of his power. He controlled almost all the unskilled labour in Dublin with the exception of the Corporation labourers and the builders' labourers, who were organized in their own unions. The leadership in both unions was somewhat hostile towards Larkin because of his attempts to organize in what they considered their private preserve. Now, only two large groups of workers remained unorganized in Dublin. One was Arthur Guinness' Sons, the famous makers of stout, and the other was the Dublin United Tramway Company. Guinness, which was directed by Lord Iveagh, the philanthropist, proved to be too much even for Larkin's organizing genius. The wages paid by Guinness were the best in Dublin, and Lord Iveagh treated his workers with a benevolent paternalism that was rare in his day. He provided houses at reasonable rates near the brewery, medical care, and all 'the eating and drinking' that was in a pint of the best Guinness 'XX.' Guinness proved to be impregnable because there was no discontent. The Dublin United Tramway Company was another matter entirely, for the problem was not discontent, which was plentiful, but merely how to organize it. The chairman of the Tramway Company was William Martin Murphy, who was the nearest thing Ireland had had to a multi-millionaire. Murphy owned or controlled the largest daily paper in Ireland, the largest department store, and the most prominent hotel in Dublin, besides railroad interests in Ireland and West Africa. He still retained large interests in the municipal electric tramway systems of many British cities, in whose construction he was the pioneer, as well as, of course, controlling interest in the Dublin United Tramway Company. Since Murphy's interests were so many and so varied, he could not be easily attacked even by so inclusive a weapon as the 'sympathetic strike.'

Larkin, however, was determined to organize the Tramway Company. He had made an attempt in the summer of 1911, but he did not have much luck.[2] Murphy had an employment system that defied trade union organization. In effect he kept two classes of men, permanent and casuals. The 'permanent' men lived a precarious life, with the casuals always at their backs and literally ready to step into their shoes. If a permanent man missed a day or even was late, his job was taken by the top man on the casual list. The unfortunate man

---

[1] *Freeman's Journal*, August 18, 1913.   [2] *Irish Worker*, August 26, 1911.

who was replaced had to take his turn at the end of the list, while the list was continually being infused with new blood from the country. A good many of these country men were only temporarily employed while waiting to be called up as police recruits for the Royal Irish Constabulary.[1] Larkin had a difficult time organizing the tramwaymen, for if a man was suspected of being a Larkinite and dismissed, he was replaced by a casual man who realized that his promotion was owing to the very fact that he was not a member of the Union.

To add to the difficulties, a bitter personal feud had been built up over the years in the columns of the *Worker* and the *Independent*, which was the paper controlled by Murphy.[2] Murphy was variously described in the *Worker* as the 'industrial octopus', the 'tramway tyrant,' a 'capitalist sweater,' a 'blood-sucking vampire,' or a 'whited sepulchre.' His *Evening Herald* was a 'vicious, immoral sheet . . . owned and controlled by a creature named William Martin Murphy, a creature who never hesitated to use the most foul and unscrupulous methods against any man, woman, or child who in the opinion of William Martin Murphy stood in William Martin Murphy's way, a soulless, money grubbing tyrant.'[3] The Christmas, 1912, number of the *Irish Worker* was a bit more charitable. It presented 'A Christmas Phantasy in Three Spasms,' entitled 'Ali Martin Baba and His Forty Thieves,' or, optimistically enough, 'The Victory of Shemus.'[4]

The Christmas spirit was short-lived, for Larkin, during the course of the City of Dublin Steampacket Company strike, referred to 'the most foul and vicious blackguard that ever polluted any country—William Martin Murphy—whose career has been one long series of degrading and destroying the characters of men who he was and is not fit to be a doormat for—a creature who is living on the sweated victims who are compelled to slave for this modern

---

[1] *Irish Worker*, September 9, 1911.

[2] *Leader*, September 27, 1913. Murphy 'had his knife' in Larkin, and Larkin 'had no love for Murphy.' 'Things might have jogged along, and the employers might have grinned and borne the occasional twitches of the sympathetic strike if Larkin had kept off the tram tracks. It is a pity that both Murphy and Larkin are not pugilists, as if they were they might have had it out on the stage of the Theatre Royal—tickets from one guinea upward, proceeds to go to a housing scheme. It is quite evident that both Larkin and Murphy were quite "mouldy" for a fight.'

[3] *Irish Worker*, September 7, 1912.

[4] *Ibid.*, Christmas number, 1912.

capitalistic vampire.'[1] Murphy was certainly not what Larkin pictured him to the Dublin working classes.[2] Among employers he was known as a hard man, but a fair one after his own lights. He worked hard and was a shrewd and able businessman who made his ventures pay handsomely. Like many another employer of his day, he considered himself the final arbiter in matters concerning his business, and would stand no interference. He did not like sweaters and did not suggest for a moment 'that the condition of the men, especially the unorganized men of this city is anything like what it ought to be.'[3] He charged that 'some employers in Dublin bred Larkinism by the neglect of their men, and then they continued to support him by not having the courage to stand up against him.' Murphy was not in business simply for the making of money, since he viewed high finance as an exhilarating game that made life worth living. To Murphy 'the making of profit had never been his leading idea. . . . To him and many others . . . the game of business . . . was more fascinating than any form of sport.'[4]

Forestalling the Transport Union's demand for an all-round increase in wages, the Tramway Company issued a statement that they would not recognize 'Larkin or his Union.' The Company then began to dismiss suspected Larkinites, and applied in the Dublin papers for non-Transport Union men to fill the places of the dismissed men.[5] The Company was swamped with applications for work. In anticipating a strike, the general opinion was that 'it will be no easily composed quarrel, for it is no secret that there are elements of bitterness in the contest that will not be easily appeased once the struggle is begun.'[6] Rumour was rampant that the strike was planned for Horse Show Week, the gala social event of the year in Dublin. The city would be crowded with visitors, and a tram strike

[1] *Irish Worker*, February 15, 1913.

[2] Appendices to the report of the Committee Appointed to Inquire into the Extension of Medical Benefits Under the National Insurance Act to Ireland, Minutes of Evidence, etc., *Parliamentary Papers*, 1913, XXXVII (Cd. 7039), p. 64. See William Martin Murphy's evidence. He was asked by J. Glynn, '2219. Therefore, don't you think that employers not as careful as you should be compelled to look after their employees?—I think if they don't they should be obliged to do it.'

[3] *Freeman's Journal*, September 2, 1913.

[4] *Ibid.*, January 2, 1915.

[5] *Ibid.*, August 18, 1913. See also *ibid.*, September 17, 1913.

[6] *Ibid.*, August 18, 1913.

would be no small inconvenience. Monday went by expectantly but quietly enough, and on Tuesday morning, August 26, at twenty minutes to ten, about 700 men walked off their trams, leaving them wherever they happened to be. Of the 1,700 tramwaymen, less than half were Transport Union members because of the recent victimization.[1] Larkin probably thought that his pickets would effectively curb the activity of those men who stayed in. With the aid of the police, however, the service was partially restored, and the strike was not nearly as effective as Larkin hoped.[2]

Some time before the tramway strike Larkin had been preparing his plan of campaign against Murphy. Early in August he had organized the dispatch boys in the distribution section of Murphy's paper, the *Irish Independent*. On hearing that Larkin had infiltrated this strategic section of his delivery unit Murphy had those who were members of the Transport Union locked out on August 15. In an attempt to bottle up Murphy, Larkin, through his pickets, persuaded a good many retailers to refuse to accept the *Independent* for sale. Larkin next approached Eason & Son, the largest newspaper distributor in Ireland and requested them to drop the *Independent* from their list. When Eason refused, Larkin called a strike in his firm.[3] Matters became even more complicated when the dockers on the quays refused to handle goods consigned to Eason from England.[4] The shipping companies complained that this was in contravention of the agreement signed on May 26, which had been in force since June 2. Larkin ordered the men back to work, but when the same thing happened two days later, the shipping companies called a meeting which Larkin attended. Larkin agreed that the contract should be carried out and again persuaded the dockers to return to work. Two days later Larkin 'intimated to the employers that he could not get his men to handle "tainted goods." ' The shipping companies were reported to have accused Larkin of bad faith, and he to have replied, 'When an army rebels, what is a commander to do?'[5] If this was true, then Larkin was certainly at fault. He signed the agreement

---

[1] *Freeman's Journal*, August 22, 1913.
[2] *Ibid.*, August 27, 1913.
[3] *Ibid.*, August 22, 1913.
[4] Wright, *op. cit.*, pp. 118–19. This account conveniently summarizes the statements and accusations levelled against Larking at the 'Askwith Enquiry' by the employers and their counsel, T. M. Healy. See for the employers' evidence and Healy's statement, *Freeman's Journal*, October 2 and 3, 1913.
[5] *Ibid.*, p. 119.

of May 26 and he was bound to fulfil its obligations. If he could not discipline the men he signed for he should have presented them with the alternative of his resignation. It is inconceivable, however, to suppose that Larkin could not have forced his men to handle the 'tainted goods' for his word was law on the docks, and though the men might demur, they would not be likely to rebel against such a commander.

Now, however, William Martin Murphy, took the offensive. On August 29, three days after the tram strike began, he called a meeting of the Employers' Federation Ltd.[1] The Federation had been formed in June, 1911, when the first wave of strikes broke on Ireland. It was modelled on the Cork Employers' Federation, which had crushed Larkin's union in Cork in the summer of 1909.[2] The meeting of the Dublin employers on the 29th decided to call a general meeting of the employers to deal with the Larkinite threat. After two preliminary meetings some 400 employers decided, on September 3, to lock out all their employees who were members of the Transport Workers' Union.[3] The day before the Coal Merchants[2] Association had locked their men out in an effort to break Larkin's union in the coal trade.[4] On September 4 it was reported that some 20,000 men were affected by the general lockout.[5] Further, on September 9, the Master Builders' Association locked out about 3,000 members of the Builders Labourers' Union for refusing to sign a pledge never to join the Transport Union.[6] Three days later the County Dublin Farmers' Association locked out 1,000 farm workers for being members of the Transport Union.[7] When the timber and cement merchants locked out their men on September 22, the total number of men affected was about 25,000.[8]

In the meantime Larkin was trying to hearten his supporters with brave words, and urging them to braver deeds. On the evening he called the tram strike Larkin, with O'Brien in the chair, spoke to a vast crowd in Beresford Place. 'Now I am always optimistic,' said Larkin, 'but my friend the Chairman is always pessimistic. O'Brien believes that the Tramway Company is the "Be-all" and the "Do-all" of Dublin industrial life, but I believe we can smash the Tramway

[1] Wright, *op. cit.*, p. 154.   [2] *Irish Worker*, July 29, 1911.
[3] Wright, *op. cit.*, p. 155. See also *Freeman's Journal*, September 4, 1913.
[4] *Freeman's Journal*, September 3, 1913.
[5] *Ibid.*, September 4, 1913.   [6] *Ibid.*, September 10, 1913.
[7] *Ibid.*, September 13, 1913.   [8] *Ibid.*, September 23, 1913.

Company in a few days, if the same determination and spirit exists as was seen today.'[1] 'They talk about victory and breaking Larkin,' he continued, but, 'Given the intelligence and discipline you ought to have, and taking the advice and leadership that I give you, I would wipe them off the face of the street in one hour, and they know that.' 'In Belfast, in 1907,' he reminisced romantically, 'all the forces had to keep their noses clean, and keep behind the four walls, and I promise that, living or dead, they will never break me, and dead I will be a greater force against them than alive.' 'My advice to you is,' he declared, 'if one of our class fall, then two of the others must fall for that one.' 'By the living God,' he concluded, 'if they want war they can have it.'[2] Larkin was followed by Partridge, who did not pour any oil on the troubled waters when he said:

In Ireland the old spirit is not dead yet, and there are men living to-day who do not fear to tread in the blood-stained footsteps of the past, and if William Martin Murphy defies Larkin, he will have to trample on our dead bodies. . . . The men behind Larkin are not only prepared to go to prison, but to lay down their lives to the cause. . . . There is no surrender in this fight, and no surrender means—no cars to-morrow. I will put it that no car can run on the streets of Dublin until the tramway men have got their terms.[3]

The next evening the Government issued a warrant for Larkin's arrest. On the following morning, Thursday, August 28, Larkin, O'Brien, Daly, Partridge, and Thomas Lawlor were all arrested for seditious libel and seditious conspiracy. They were released on bail, with the understanding that they would not break the law while awaiting trial.[4] The next evening Larkin gave another remarkable performance before some 10,000 people in Beresford Place. 'Before I go any further,' he began, 'with your permission I am going to burn the Proclamation of the King.'[5] 'People make Kings,'[5] he announced while burning the document, 'and people can unmake them.' 'I hope to hold a meeting in O'Connell Street,' he continued, 'and we will meet in O'Connell Street, and if the police and soldiers stop the meeting let them take the responsibility.' 'We want no men,' he warned, 'but men that will stand'. 'You have every right to hold a meeting,' declared Larkin characteristically, 'but you have been too

[1] Irish State Paper Office, Intelligence Notes, 1913, *op. cit.*, p. 3.
[2] *Ibid.*, p. 4.   [3] *Ibid.*   [4] *Freeman's Journal*, August 29, 1913.
[5] Irish State Paper Office, Intelligence Notes, 1913, *op. cit.*, p. 6.

supine and too cowardly in the past to hold the meetings . . . and if they want a revolution there that day, there will be a revolution.' 'I am a rebel,' he continued, 'and the son of a rebel.' 'I recognize no law but the people's law,' concluded Larkin. 'We are going to raise a new standard of discontent and a new battle-cry in Ireland.'[1]

The following afternoon, Saturday, August 30, Larkin was in Liberty Hall when O'Brien arrived and informed him there was another warrant out for his arrest.[2] Since Larkin had promised to speak in O'Connell Street the next day he was anxious to avoid arrest. O'Brien quietly got a cab and brought it to the back entrance to Liberty Hall to avoid the enthusiastic crowds that were waiting out front for a glimpse of Larkin. Larkin decided the safest place for him was the Countess Markievicz's house in Rathmines. Soon after Larkin's arrival the house was watched by detectives, who suspected he might have taken refuge there.[3] To throw the police off the track the Count and Countess decided to give a party, and sent out the invitations on short notice. As the guests arrived and the merry-making began, the police concluded they were on the wrong track and gave up their vigil.

The next morning the problem was how to get Larkin to his meeting in O'Connell Street from Rathmines. Since he would be instantly recognized a disguise was agreed on. He was dressed and made up to look like an elderly clergyman. His hair was powdered and he was provided with a crêpe hair beard. To shorten his rather prominent nose he put on a pair of spectacles. As the finishing touch, the Count, though no admirer of Larkin's, loaned him his frock coat and top hat. A carriage was called, and it was further agreed that since Larkin's Liverpool accent and his distressing habit of dropping his 'aitches were impossible to disguise, he should pretend to be stone deaf. He was to be accompanied by a young lady who was visiting the Countess and who was not known in Dublin. The young lady was to pose as his niece and was to answer all the necessary questions for her deaf uncle. About one-thirty on Sunday afternoon the carriage pulled up in front of the Imperial Hotel in O'Connell street,

[1] Irish State Paper Office, Intelligence Notes, 1913, *op. cit.*, p. 6.
[2] William O'Brien, personal interview. Mr. O'Brien heard the news of a warrant being out for Larkin from F. Sheehy Skeffington.
[3] John Brennan (Madame Czira), 'How the Countess Trained an Army,' *The Irish Digest*, December, 1951, pp. 61–62. Madame Czira was the 'niece,' and gives an eye-witness account.

the property, ironically enough, of William Martin Murphy. Larkin, aged and bent, was assisted from the carriage by his niece and wobbled towards the hotel entrance. Inside, he straightway made for the first floor, nonchalantly lighting a cigar as he went, sauntered into the dining-room, walked to the french windows overlooking O'Connell Street, stepped out on to the balcony, and began to speak.[1] The crowd gathered below did not recognize him for a moment, but after a few words they surged towards the hotel. Larkin had only uttered a few words when he was seized and arrested and led away between four policemen.[2]

The crowd was not a large one and made no attempt to interfere with the police. When, however, the police attempted to interfere with the carriage of the Countess, who was demanding three cheers for Larkin, there was a scuffle. When the officers in charge panicked and gave orders for a baton charge, the police fell on the people with a vengeance.[3] A good many of those who were batoned had just come from mass in the pro-Cathedral in Marlborough Street and were taking their Sunday afternoon stroll before going home. Since the police batoned indiscriminately, pandemonium was the result. One section of the unfortunate crowd fled up Prince's Street to escape and were unhappily met by a squad of police who had explicit orders to allow no one to pass. They thought the surging throng flying before the batons were rioters, and immediately began to baton right and left.[4] The headlines told the whole story the next day:

BLOODSHED IN DUBLIN

APPALLING SCENES IN THE CITY

FIERCE BATON CHARGES

HUNDREDS INJURED

TWO MEN DEAD

HOSPITALS OVERCROWDED

MR. LARKIN ARRESTED AT THE IMPERIAL HOTEL[5]

The brutality of the police was exceptional. There were several reasons alleged for it, but the most important was the trying time that the Transport Union pickets and their sympathizers had given them

[1] *Freeman's Journal*, September 1, 1913. See account by Handel Booth, a Liberal M.P., who was a guest at the Imperial that Sunday morning.
[2] Report of the Dublin Disturbances Commission, *op. cit.*, p. 5.
[3] *Ibid.* [4] *Ibid.*, p. 6. [5] *Freeman's Journal*, September 1, 1913.

125

the day and night before. The patience and endurance of the police had been thoroughly strained on Saturday afternoon and night. The attention of the strikers on Saturday was directed principally towards the trams. Several groups of men, often accompanied by women, in various parts of the city of Dublin attacked the trams and the 'scabs' who ran them. When the police interfered with the 'pickets' and protected the 'scabs' they very naturally received a good deal of attention themselves. After Larkin had been arrested in O'Connell Street on Sunday afternoon the riots grew more serious. The temper of the strikers had changed, however, for they seemed to be more interested in coming to grips with the police than in checking the operation of the trams. The rioting continued through Sunday night and the next day, when it subsided.[1] In all some 200 police were injured and countless numbers of citizens. Dublin was in an uproar, and a Commission was appointed to inquire into the conduct of the police. The report, which was presented some five months later, resulted in a complete whitewash of the police.[2]

When the riots had subsided another catastrophe shook Dublin. On the evening of September 2, two four-story tenement houses collapsed, killing seven and injuring many.[3] The collapse of these tenements were a frightful testimony to the pitiful conditions endured by the Dublin slum-dwellers. The very houses that collapsed had a short time before been inspected and passed by the municipal authorities as safe to live in. As usual a Commission was appointed. The only result, however, was another valuable historical document in the social history of Dublin. The day after the tenements collapsed, there was a gigantic funeral procession for one of the men killed in the riots on the previous Saturday. At the inquest the jury found that the injuries that led to the unfortunate man's death were caused by the blow of a baton. Though several eye-witnesses named and numbered the constable involved the jury thought the evidence too conflicting to say by whom the blow was administered.[4]

Little wonder that people were becoming exasperated. It was a gloomy procession that followed the hearse to Glasnevin as the band played a solemn funeral march. Keir Hardie, who had only just

[1] Report of the Dublin Disturbances Commission, *op. cit.*, p. 14.
[2] Report of the Committee of Inquiry on the Royal Irish Constabulary and the Dublin Metropolitan Police, *Parliamentary Papers*, 1914, XLIV (Cd. 7421).
[3] *Freeman's Journal*, September 3, 1913.
[4] *Ibid.*, September 6, 1913.

The scene in O'Connell Street on Bloody Sunday, 31st August, 1913, during the police baton charges.

TOO MUCH ROPE!

"SUNNY JIM:"

GRACE GIFFORD

THE OWNER OF THE "FIERY CROSS" THAT FIZZLED OUT.

From *Irish Life*, 12th December, 1913.

arrived, was conspicuous in the funeral cortège. That night, with Larkin in jail, Hardie was the main speaker in an attempt to raise the spirits of the locked-out men. Interpreting a remark made by Murphy to mean that he would starve the workers into submission, Hardie raised a wry laugh when he commented, 'Most of you have served too long an apprenticeship to starvation to be very much afraid of that.'[1] 'There will be no starvation,' promised Hardie. 'I know that the section of the movement with which I am most prominently identified in these past years—the Socialist side of the Labour Movement will stand by you solidly and firmly (cheers).' They must not be frightened, he continued, 'by hearing people say that Socialism was the worst enemy of the working classes. He was a firm believer in the Christian religion, and whether they were Roman Catholics or Protestants, they were all his comrades and members of his class, and he would say that they could never have God's Kingdom upon earth until Socialism had settled the working-class question (cheers).'

With Larkin, and Connolly who had also been arrested, in jail, O'Brien and Daly were running the lockout. They immediately dispatched Partridge, MacPartlin, and Lawlor to the British Trades Union Congress, which opened in Manchester on September 1. The appalling news from Dublin was published on the Monday morning the Congress opened, and after hearing the Irish delegates the Congress voted to send a committee to investigate the report.[2] The committee was headed by Arthur Henderson, M.P., who met the employers on September 5. The conference was enlarged on the 8th to include the representatives of the Dublin Lockout Committee, and broke up on the 12th, when the employers' representatives refused to give way in their effort to outlaw the Transport Union or to withdraw the 'yellow dog' contract they were asking the men to sign before they would take them back to work.[3] The committee reported that the locked-out men should be supported because the basic trade union principle of the right of combination was at stake. It was felt that if the Dublin employers were allowed the right to tell a man what union he could not belong to, they would be soon telling him what union he could join. On September 23, B.T.U.C. voted £5,000 and issued a call for more funds.[4] In early October the

[1] *Freeman's Journal*, September 4, 1913. [2] *Annual Register*, 1913, p. 200.
[3] *Freeman's Journal*, September 13, 1913.
[4] *Report of Proceedings at the 47th Annual Trades Union Congress, 1915*, p. 127.

Miners' Federation voted £1,000 a week, and various Labour news-papers opened subscription lists.[1] The Glasgow *Forward* alone raised £3,300 during the course of the lockout.[2] The B.T.U.C. raised the stupendous sum of £93,637-odd, or nearly half a million dollars.[3] William O'Brien, who was secretary of the Dublin Lockout Committee, said the total amount collected came to about £150,000.[4] It was truly a magnificent tribute to the spirit of solidarity in the Labour Movement.

The bulk of this support, however, began after September 23, and in the early days of the lockout the financial problem was acute. When Larkin was released from jail on September 12 on £100 bail he decided to leave immediately for England and Scotland to appeal for support.[5] Connolly, who was released after a week's hunger strike, took command of the situation in Dublin during Larkin's absence.[6] On Sunday, September 14, Larkin arrived in Manchester from Liverpool. He delivered a magnificent speech to a vast open-air meeting. 'I care for no man or men,' he began. 'I have got a divine mission, I believe, to make men and women discontented.'[7] 'I am out to do it,' he continued, 'and no Murphy or Aberdeen, nor other creatures of that type can stop me carrying on the work I was born for.' 'Hell has no terrors for me,' explained Larkin, 'I have lived there. Thirty-six years of hunger and poverty have been my portion. The mother that bore me had to starve and work and my father had to fight for a living. I knew what is was to work when I was nine years old. They cannot terrify me with hell.' 'Better to be in hell,' in any case, he declared, 'with Dante and Davitt than to be in heaven with Carson or Murphy.' 'I am out for revolution,' he concluded. 'What do I care? They can only kill me, and there are thousands more to come after me.'[8]

Though Larkin was back in Dublin the next day, he was soon on the road again and spoke to an enthusiastic audience in Glasgow on

---

[1] *Freeman's Journal*, October 8, 1913.

[2] *Forward*, February 28, 1914.

[3] Report, B.T.U.C., *loc. cit.*

[4] William O'Brien, personal interview. Mr. O'Brien retains the accounts of the Dublin Lockout Committee and the balance sheets, which he permitted me to peruse.

[5] *Freeman's Journal*, September 12, 1913.

[6] *Ibid.*, September 15, 1913.

[7] *Manchester Guardian*, September 15, 1913.

[8] *Ibid.*

September 21. The next day he was in London at a specially summoned private meeting of the National Transport Workers' Federation, which immediately called on its members to support the Dublin dispute.[1] That same day the British Trades Union Congress had voted £5,000 to the Dublin men. The initial contributions were spent on food, and four days later, on Saturday, the 27th, the foodship *Hare* arrived in Dublin. The food was unloaded and taken to Liberty Hall, where preparations were made for its distribution. Larkin, who supervised the unloading of the *Hare*, was careful to point out to the Dublin workers that the food was not charity, or even a gift. 'They did not thank,' he said, 'the British trade unionists for what they had done. A duty devolved upon the latter and they recognized it.'[2] On the following Saturday a second ship, the *Fraternity*, arrived with another cargo of food. Liberty Hall became one vast warehouse and welfare centre. Food packages were made up and food tickets were issued to the men when they collected their strike pay in accordance with the number of dependants they had. Clothes and underwear were also distributed to the needy. Soup kitchens were set up in the Hall and meals were served. Since many of the wives of the strikers stinted on their share to feed the men and children they were asked to take their meals in the Hall. Delia Larkin and the Countess Markievicz were in charge of the welfare operations in Liberty Hall during the lockout.

Appropriately enough Galsworthy's play, *Strife*, opened in Dublin in the middle of August, 1913. The reviewer in the *Irish Worker* wrote, 'It is not a play, as some of the Dublin critics have laboured to show, which points out the futility of industrial strife, but it points with scathing logic to the folly of Compromise.'[3] 'Labour and Capital,' he announced prophetically, 'have got to fight it out to the end some time and though Compromise may delay the final issue it will never prevent it.' By the middle of August, 1913, Larkin, too, had assumed a most uncompromising posture. His temper appeared to grow shorter as his power increased during 1913. The defeat of the City of Dublin Steampacket Company in April, the surrender of the cross-channel companies in May, and the triumph over the County Dublin Farmers' Association were all significant victories. As Larkin consolidated his position he seemed to grow more

---

[1] *Freeman's Journal*, September 24, 1913.
[2] *Ibid.*, September 29, 1913.
[3] *Irish Worker*, August 16, 1913.

inflexible, less conciliatory, and even more vitriolic than usual. Not only did Murphy and his 'scabs and Pimps' come in for Larkin's abuse in late July and August, but the Irish Party, the Ancient Order of Hibernians, and even the British Labour Party were reminded of their failings and called on to account for their sins.

VII

LOCKOUT

THE Government finally intervened on September 26, 1913. The Board of Trade, it was announced, would hold an official inquiry into the Dublin dispute. Sir George Askwith was appointed Chairman, and both parties to the dispute were required to attend and present their cases. The Court of Inquiry opened on September 29. Murphy was spokesman for the employers, while Harry Gosling of the National Transport Workers' Federation represented the Irish and British trade unionists. Larkin, it seemed, was taking a back seat for the moment. The employers were in favour of public hearings, but the representatives of the men thought an understanding could be better reached if the proceedings were private. From the tone and tenor of Gosling's remarks, it was evident that he was in an extra-conciliatory mood and anxious for a settlement.[1] Finally, it was decided that the hearings would be public, and they were to begin on Wednesday, October 1, 1913.

The employers arrived with a battery of first-class legal talent, but the men decided to present their own cases.[2] The employers' case was argued by T. M. Healy, K.C., who had long been a leading figure in Irish politics. His wit and bitter eloquence were well known at both the Irish and English bars, as well as in the House of Commons. Moreover, 'Thersites' Healy was a warm personal friend of William Martin Murphy. Since Healy had hardly more than a few days to master a rather complicated brief, his presentation of the employers' case was impressive. Healy shrewdly began by pointing out that 'during the past five years acts had been done which should make trade unionists ashamed, because they were in defiance of

---

[1] *Freeman's Journal*, September 30, 1913.   [2] *Ibid.*, October 2, 1913.

every trade union principle. The employers had been forced into a combination to preserve whatever little wreck was left of the trade and commerce of Dublin.' 'It was impossible,' said Healy, 'for the masters to bargain with the men, because they were not consulted by their leaders. Trades Unionism in the mouths of these men in Dublin was a mockery.' 'The present situation,' he continued, 'was the most finished system of tyranny that was ever started in any country, and the humble masters had worn out their marrow bones kneeling at the shrine of Jim Larkin.'[1] The substance of Healy's argument was that the 'sympathetic strike' made relations between capital and labour impossible. He wound up by citing numerous alleged instances of agreements being made and broken by Larkin.

The next day Healy called individual employers to substantiate and support the claim that it was impossible to carry on trade in the face of Larkin and his union, with their avowed policies of 'sympathetic strikes' and 'tainted goods.' Larkin took over as counsel for the men and subjected the individual employers to a rather severe cross-examination. As usual he indulged mainly in personalities and seldom kept to the point as he attempted to discredit the witnesses in the box. When Larkin cross-examined George N. Jacob, of Jacob's Biscuits Ltd., for example, he asked him for the scale of wages paid in his factory. Jacob refused to answer because he claimed it would give aid and comfort to his competitors. Larkin, exasperated, turned to the Court and denounced Jacob—'This man is ashamed of himself and his position. I have asked him and he has refused to answer. He refuses to state the wages paid by his firm; or what wages he pays for overtime, and what the conditions of work are. These are the people who cause disorder, turmoil, and trouble. They will not recognize trades unions. It is no use wasting time with men like him. He won't recognize a tribunal such as this.'[2]

The following day, October 3, Larkin and Murphy faced each other for the first time. A more incongruous picture was hardly possible. Murphy, a slight figure with unusually delicate and handsome features, looked anything but the wilful and stern paternalist he was. His white imperial and whiter hair belied the alert and intent searching glance of his grey eyes. As his voice was weak, he explained, he preferred to stand as Larkin cross-examined him. Larkin, with 'dark inchoate face' and large powerful body, also rose, and surprisingly enough he treated his antagonist with respect.

[1] *Freeman's Journal*, October 2, 1913.   [2] *Ibid.*, October 3, 1913.

He tried to discredit Murphy by gently raking up an old story about Murphy and Parnell. Murphy, although visibly upset, adroitly welcomed the chance to lay the vicious libel to rest, and Larkin did not press the point. He then asked Murphy, 'Did you ever get a report that I or any official of the Union went about your premises and interfered with your men?' Murphy sharply replied, 'I have no report. With regard to yourself personally, you are generally in a safe place.' Larkin was greeted with a great burst of laughter when he answered, 'Yes, you generally see that I am put there.'[1]

During the course of Larkin's cross-examination of Murphy, Healy continually sniped at Larkin. On one occasion when Larkin asked Murphy a question, Healy interjected with an inaudible Latin phrase. Larkin, nonplussed, turned to Healy and raised a laugh when he commented, 'We do not understand illegitimate Latin.'[2] Again, when Healy interrupted, Larkin replied, 'I am not in the box yet. I am entitled by the laws of evidence established by your trades unions (laughter) to put the question.' When Larkin wanted to read a letter from a former employee of Murphy's, Healy objected. Larkin said that since Mr. Murphy did not object, he did not see why Mr. Healy should. Larkin then added, amidst laughter, 'We are not getting a hundred guineas a day for attending here.' Healy then replied, 'I am obliged to Mr. Larkin for that suggestion (laughter). My solicitor will attend to it (laughter).'[3] The repartee was caustic and quick throughout. One observer wrote, after listening to Larkin's performance, 'There is no doubt about it he is glib in the tongue. He referred to his being at work at an age when Tim Healy was "wasting" his time at school. Of course Tim jumped up with the oft told tale that he left school at 13 years of age. This was one for Larkin, but Larkin, though he had implied that being at school was a waste of time, simply changed about and told Healy that he ought to go back to school.'[4]

The presentation of the men's case was made by Larkin. If Healy

---

[1] *Freeman's Journal*, October 4, 1913. John Eglington (W. K. Magee), *A Memoir of AE—George William Russell* (1937), p. 86. 'I looked in there one day, and a vivid recollection of the dark inchoate face of Larkin and of his tall ungainly figure, craning forward as he bellowed forth his arraignment; and opposite him the calm handsome face of Murphy, with trim white beard, speaking just above his breath and glancing occasionally at his angry foe: near him rose from time to time the robust form of his counsel, Thersites Healy, releasing effortlessly his biting speech.'

[2] *Ibid.*   [3] *Ibid.*   [4] *Leader*, October 11, 1913.

had been formidable in his presentation of the employers' case, Larkin was magnificent. Having the true dramatic instinct and realizing that this was one of the great moments in his life, he bent himself to his task with a will and produced an effort that was gargantuan in its proportions. It was an overwhelming experience for all who were present. Larkin began by denouncing the employers for the conditions of life and labour in Dublin:

> They take to themselves that they have all the rights that are given to men and to societies of men, but they deny the right of the men to claim that they also have a substantial claim on the share of the produce they produce, and they further say they want no third party interference. They want to deal with their workingmen individually. . . . It means that the men who hold the means of life control our lives, and, because we workingmen have tried to get some measure of justice, some measure of betterment, they deny the right of the human being to associate with his fellow. Why the very law of nature was mutual co-operation. Man must be associated with his fellows. The employers were not able to make their own case. Let him help them. . . . What was the position of affairs in connection with life in industrial Ireland? . . . There are 21,000 families—four and a half persons to a family—living in single rooms. Who are responsible? The gentlemen opposite to him would have to accept the responsibility. Of course they must. They said they control the means of life; then the responsibility rests upon them. Twenty-one thousand people multiplied by five, over a hundred thousand people huddled together in the putrid slums of Dublin.[1]

'We,' continued Larkin, 'are determined that this shall no longer go on; we are determined that the system shall stop; we are determined that Christ shall not be crucified in Dublin by these men.'

'Let the people who desired to know the truth,' declared Larkin, 'go to the factories and see the maimed girls, the weak and sickly, whose eyes are being put out and their bodies scarred and their souls seared.' And 'when they were no longer able to be useful enough to gain . . . whatever wage they earned,' he continued, they 'were thrown into the human scrap heap.' In referring to the evidence given by George Jacob, Larkin said that Jacob's 'had the worst sweating den in the four corners of Great Britain.' 'O'Connell street,' he added, 'was an abomination owing to the fact that girl wage slaves were driven on it under a terrible system.' 'Better for Ireland,' he

---

[1] *Freeman's Journal*, October 6, 1913.

wryly commented, 'that some of the industries we have got were destroyed and never started.' Turning to Healy, Larkin noted there was at least 'one industry—the lawyers and politicians—we could well do without (laughter). I came from Liverpool because I heard Mr. Healy was going over to London, and two great men could not be in the same country (loud laughter).'

Becoming more serious again after the moment of comic relief Larkin said, 'I believe in a co-operative Commonwealth. That is a long way ahead in Ireland. Why cannot I help as you can help in working the present system in a proper reasonable way, conducive to both sides, and I have suggested the machinery that may be put into operation.' Reminded of himself, Larkin asked:

> Can anyone say one word against me as a man? Can they make any disparagement of my character? Have I lessened the standard of life? Have I demoralised anyone? Is there anything in my private life or my public life of which I should be ashamed? These men denounced me from the pulpit, and say I am making £18 a week and that I have a mansion in Dublin. The men who are described as Larkin's dupes are asked to go back. All this is done two thousand years after Christ appeared in Galilee. Why, these men are making people atheists— they are making them godless. But we are going to stop that.[1]

'When the position of the workers was taken into consideration,' asked Larkin, 'was it any wonder that there was necessity for a Larkin to arise, and if there was one thing more than another in his life of which he would always be proud, it was the part he had taken in rescuing the workers of Dublin from the brutalising and degrading conditions under which they laboured.' 'We are out,' concluded Larkin, 'to break down racial and sectarian barriers. My suggestion to the employers is that if they want peace we are prepared to meet them, but if they want war, then war they will have.' Larkin's speech took nearly two hours to deliver, and he was followed by both Irish and British trade unionists. They all backed Larkin, and Gosling in particular pointed out that the employers would not be allowed to destroy the Transport Union as long as the British Trades Union movement existed.

The day after the hearings closed the Court of Inquiry submitted its Report. The Court had no power to impose its findings on either party to the dispute, but whichever way the Report fell it was bound to have an enormous influence on public opinion. Up to this point

[1] *Freeman's Journal*, October 6, 1913.

Larkin had public opinion on his side. The Report as presented, though fairly pointing out that 'No community could exist if resort to the "sympathetic" strike became the general policy of Trade Unions,' went on to say that the document which the men were asked to sign imposed 'upon the signatories conditions which are contrary to individual liberty, and which no workman or body of workmen could reasonably be expected to accept.'[1] Since Larkin and Connolly had intimated that they were willing to curtail their use of the 'sympathetic strike,' the onus of refusing to come to a settlement could only fall on the employers.

The same day the Report was submitted the employers refused to accept it as a basis for negotiation and backed out of the Inquiry. Public opinion now formed hard against them. The most conservative paper in Ireland, the *Irish Times*, printed AE's now famous 'Open Letter to the Dublin Employers.'

SIRS,—I address this warning to you, the aristocracy of industry in this city, because, like all aristocracies, you tend to grow blind in long authority, and to be unaware that you and your class and its every action are being considered and judged day by day by those who have power to shake or overturn the whole Social Order, and whose restlessness in poverty to-day is making our industrial civilisation stir like a quaking bog. . . .

Your insolence and ignorance of the rights conceded to workers universally in the modern world were incredible, and as great as your inhumanity. If you had between you collectively a portion of human soul as large as a three-penny bit, you would have sat night and day with the representatives of labour, trying this or that solution of the trouble, mindful of the women and children, who at least were innocent of wrong against you. But no! You reminded labour you could always have your three square meals a day while it went hungry. You went into conference again with representatives of the State, because, dull as you are, you know public opinion would not stand your holding out. You chose as your spokesman the bitterest tongue that ever wagged in this island, and then, when an award was made by men who have an experience in industrial matters a thousand times transcending yours, who have settled disputes in industries so great that the sum of your petty enterprises would not equal them, you withdraw again, and will not agree to accept their solution, and fall back again upon your devilish policy of starvation. Cry aloud to Heaven

[1] Eleventh Report by the Board of Trade of Proceedings Under the Conciliation Act, 1896, *Parliamentary Papers*, 1914. LXXXIX (89), p. 84.

for new souls! The souls you have got cast upon the screen of publicity appear like the horrid and writhing creatures enlarged from the insect world, and revealed to us by the cinematograph.

You may succeed in your policy and ensure your own damnation by your victory. The men whose manhood you have broken will loathe you, and will always be brooding and scheming to strike a fresh blow. The children will be taught to curse you. The infant being moulded in the womb will have breathed into its starved body the vitality of hate. It is not they—it is you who are blind Samsons pulling down the pillars of the social order. You are sounding the death knell of autocracy in industry. There was autocracy in political life, and it was superseded by democracy. So surely will democratic power wrest from you the control of industry. The fate of you, the aristocracy of industry, will be as the fate of the aristocracy of land if you do not show that you have some humanity still among you. Humanity abhors, above all things, a vacuum in itself, and your class will be cut off from humanity as the surgeon cuts the cancer and alien growth from the body. Be warned ere it is too late.—Yours, &c.,

DUBLIN, October 6th, 1913

AE.[1]

Even the London *Times*, on October 8, said it was about time the Dublin employers learned their lesson. The situation looked very promising for the men. The whole of public opinion in Great Britain and Ireland was behind them, and all the resources of the British trades union movement were pledged to their cause. They had only to sit back and wait for the good things to come. When the employers issued their official reply to the Askwith Report, it only seemed as if they were bent on hastening their end. They actually demanded that the Transport Union 'be reorganised on proper lines' and with 'new officials who have met with the approval of the British Joint Labour Board.'[2]

At this juncture, however, Larkin made a number of serious mistakes. He travelled to London and made a speech that was remarkable for its intemperateness. He made 'a violent attack on the Labour Party.'

They were the men, he said, who were standing in their road, and they would have to be pulled out of the road. They were about as useful as mummies in a museum. The weapon that was wanted was the sympathetic strike used in a scientific manner. There were hypocrites

[1] *Irish Times*, October 7, 1913.
[2] *Freeman's Journal*, October 15, 1913.

137

who told them they must not have sympathetic strikes because they caused inconvenience to the public. The officials of the Railwaymen's Union pleaded that there were agreements and contracts. To hell with contracts. The men were far in advance of the leaders, and they would tell their leaders to get in front or get out. . . . He had been told by a trade union leader to be careful what he was doing, because although the rank and file were with him the union leaders controlled the money. (Cries of 'Shame!') That was the sort of threat that was held over the man who belonged to the 'rebel' wing.[1]

Further, while Larkin was in London, it was suggested by Mrs. Dora B. Montefiori, a well-known social worker, that it would be a good idea to send some of the strikers' children to homes in England, where they would receive better care and attention than it was possible to give them in Dublin under the existing circumstances.[2] Larkin agreed, and Mrs. Montefiori, accompanied by an American, Lucille Rand, arrived in Dublin to give effect to their plans. The whole project was conceived in good faith, and it did not seem to these conscientious social workers that there could be any objection to this simple act of human kindness and Christian charity. When the project came to the ears of the Archbishop of Dublin, he condemned it outright. Archbishop Walsh, in a letter published in the Dublin daily papers on October 21, 1913, condemned root and branch the proposal to remove the children to foster homes in Britain. In a rather hysterical outburst he asked the mothers of the children if they had 'abandoned their faith.' He answered his rhetorical question with a 'surely not,' and claimed that 'they can no longer be held worthy of the name of Catholic mothers if they so forget that duty as to send away their children to be cared for in a strange land without security of any kind that those to whom the poor children are to be handed over are Catholics, or, indeed, are persons of any faith at all.'[3]

In vain did Mrs. Montefiori protest that the faith of the children would not be endangered, that in so far as it was possible they would be placed in Roman Catholic homes, and their religious instruction would be in Roman Catholic hands. It is perhaps the Irish penchant for alliteration that sees the Catholics converted and the Protestants proselytized, but Larkin and Mrs. Montefiori were actually accused by a number of the Roman Catholic clergy of con-

---

[1] London *Times*, October 11, 1913.

[2] *Ibid.*

[3] *Freeman's Journal*, October 21, 1913.

spiring to pervert the faith of the children under their care.[1] A goodly number of children had already been dispatched, but on the morning of October 22, the day after the Archbishop's letter appeared, a number of priests and friends prevented Mrs. Montefiori from departing with more of her charges. The priests actually invaded the Corporation Baths where the children, about fifty in number, were being scrubbed prior to their departure. Mrs. Montefiori managed to set off for Kingstown with some nineteen children, but the priests 'following in the track of the little voyagers, captured ten of the party before the landing stage was reached, and ultimately induced the remaining nine, after they had gone aboard, to come ashore.'[2]

Speaking that night from the window of Liberty Hall, Larkin did not hedge as he backed Mrs. Montefiori. He went on to say, 'I have tried to kill sectarianism, whether in Catholics or Protestants (cheers). I am against bigotry or intolerance on either side (cheers). Those who want to divide the workers have resorted to the foulest methods. . . . I have not read the evening papers, but I am informed vile things are stated in them. They have lit a fire in Ireland they will never put out (cheers). There will be a cry raised in England, Scotland, and Wales which will not be quietened for some time (cheers).'[3] Several days later Larkin was even more explicit when he said, 'I am not frightened by the Archbishop or the priests. No one ever heard me say one word against them, but I say the priest who says I would allow a child to be proselytized is a liar in his heart.'[4]

In the evening large numbers of Catholics, led by their priests, arrived at the North Wall to picket the boats embarking for England. When the last boat had left they marched along the quays singing 'Faith of Our Fathers' and other 'Catholic hymns and national airs.'[5] On October 24 Larkin's sister Delia, in place of Mrs. Montefiori and Mrs. Rand, who had been arrested on the grotesque charge of kidnapping, attempted to get a number of children off by rail for

---

[1] Arnold Wright, *Disturbed Dublin* (1914), p. 224. A Father Farrell of Donnybrook was reported as saying, 'this great demonstration was unorganized and unprepared. It shows the love you have for the Catholic children of this city. It is a magnificent protest against the proselytizing of our children in the Socialistic homes of England.' See *Irish Catholic*, November 1, 1913. 'We have very little doubt that most of the children rescued from the Socialists were the destined prey of the soupers to whom the miseries of the strike have simply brought grist to a clogged mill.'

[2] *Ibid.*, pp. 222–23.   [3] *Freeman's Journal*, October 27, 1913.

[4] *Ibid.*, October 27, 1913.   [5] *Leader*, November 1, 1913.

Belfast at the Amiens Street station. A group of priests, escorted by a band of young men, were something less than gentle as they prevented Miss Larkin from departing with her charges.[1] She was forced to retire to Liberty Hall, and no further attempts were made to place the children in foster homes.[2] The priests and their pickets continued their mass picketing of the quays each evening. The language and militancy of some of the clergy were hardly in keeping with their office. To plead that the clergy's motives were pure does not obviate the fact that their judgment was warped. Both Mrs. Montefiori and Mrs. Rand were eventually released on the undertaking they would give up their scheme.[3] Though the Larkinites had to abandon their 'Fight to Save the Kiddies,' they did have the satisfaction of seeing another pastoral letter published by the Archbishop in the daily Press. The letter called for the formation of a committee to provide food and clothing for those helpless victims of the strike, the children.[4] Two days later the Archbishop sent a circular letter to all his parish priests asking them to subscribe to the Dublin's Children's Distress Fund and making a point of the urgent need.[5] No one had the temerity to inquire why there was suddenly so urgent a need.[6]

Too much has been made of the deportation of the children as the factor that turned public opinion against Larkin and his followers. That it turned a segment of Catholic opinion against him, which might have remained neutral, there is no doubt. But as to how large or important the segment was, it is impossible to determine. Certainly the Dublin Press seemed to have taken the affair of the children in its stride and chalked it up as a tactical blunder on Larkin's part and not much more. The Dublin *Leader*, the organ of intelligent middle-class Catholicism, rebuked Larkin in the matter of the children but did not fundamentally change its position with regard to the lockout. The affair of the children was soon to be lost in a welter of other explosive problems.

[1] *Freeman's Journal*, October 15, 1913.

[2] For an amusing account of what happened when some of the children arrived in Liverpool see Fred Bower, *Rolling Stonemason* (1936), pp. 173–76.

[3] *Freeman's Journal*, October 30, 1913.

[4] *Ibid.*, October 27, 1913.

[5] *Ibid.*, October 29, 1913. See also *Leader*, November 29, 1913, February 7, 1913.

[6] Except W. P. Partridge, who commented, 'During all this time scarce a single Roman Catholic, cleric or lay, in Dublin displayed any concern for the wellbeing of these children.' *Irish Worker*, November 1, 1913.

Larkin soon had more pressing problems than the matter of the 'kiddies.' He was to go on trial on Monday, October 27, 1913, and he had to make preparations for his expected incarceration. In his farewell address to the men on Sunday afternoon in Phoenix Park he said he was prepared for anything from twelve months to two years. He was obviously worried about the lockout being settled to the men's disadvantage, and his advice was to 'guard yourselves.' After taking gratuitous note of those who interfered in the affair of the children, he went on to say that

> For years and years I have done the work I was born for. I have proved there were 21,000 families living five in a room in Dublin. Call that Catholicism, Christianity! It is something different. I have raised the morals and sobriety of the people. Even Murphy says Larkin has done good, but 'hands off the trams' (laughter). I have taken no man's honour or no woman's honour. I never stood in a public house bar and alcoholic drink never touched my lips. I am careful about my conduct because I know this cause requires clean men.[1]

He then announced that Connolly would succeed him as leader while he was in jail.

The following day he was sentenced to seven months without hard labour and was escorted to Mountjoy under an abnormally heavy police guard. On the following Sunday a gigantic meeting was arranged for the Albert Hall in London to protest Larkin's sentence. Delia Larkin, Connolly, Ben Tillett, George Russell (AE), George Bernard Shaw, Mrs. Montefiori, and George Lansbury all spoke. For a Fabian, Shaw was extremely militant, and his speech was an excellent example of the prevailing temper of the times.[2] Russell's rhetoric was brilliant as he castigated those who were responsible for the present situation in Dublin.[3] It was Connolly, however, who proposed the effective plan of campaign that was to bring about Larkin's eventual release. Connolly asked that everyone work and vote against the Liberal Government until Larkin was free. The radical Liberals and Labour men generally were very annoyed at the Government for arresting and sentencing Larkin on a charge of seditious libel, while Sir Edward Carson in Ulster was spouting treason, drilling men, and threatening to set up a provisional

---

[1] *Freeman's Journal*, October 27, 1913.   [2] London *Times*, November 3, 1913.

[3] AE's speech was not reported in the London *Times*. See *Freeman's Journal*, November 4, 1913. Also quoted in J. D. Clarkson, *Labour and Nationalism in Ireland* (1924), pp. 247–48.

government should the Home Rule Bill become law. The by-election results soon told the tale. At Reading, on November 9, a Unionist won the seat in a three-cornered fight from a Liberal. Some days previously the Liberal majority at the Linlithgow by-election had been heavily reduced. In referring to the by-election reverses at the National Liberal Club in London, Lloyd George admitted that 'there are explanations, the most prominent of which is, probably, Jim Larkin.'[1] Two days later Larkin was released after serving seventeen days of his seven-month sentence. Augustine Birrell, Chief Secretary for Ireland, offered some rather lame excuses to cover the Government's retreat, but it was manifest to all that British public opinion had opened the prison gates.[2]

Several important things happened while Larkin was in jail and Connolly in charge of the dispute. The important and influential Redmondite and Nationalist organ, the *Freeman's Journal*, dropped its neutrality as regards the lockout and denounced 'Syndicalism' in its editorial columns.[3] This was because Connolly appealed to the British working classes to vote against the Liberals even if it endangered Home Rule. This in turn produced dissension in the Irish Party. Stephen Gwynn, Member of Parliament for Galway City, dissociated himself from the *Freeman's Journal*'s editorial policy.[4] Several days later the employers began to import 'blacklegs' through the Shipping Federation to work the glutted quays.[5] As early as September 25 Connolly had remarked, on the rumour that the Shipping Federation was going to furnish 'blacklegs,' that 'if they bring that "scab" ship here . . . I know, you know, and God knows that the streets of Dublin will run red with the blood of the working classes.'[6] Connolly immediately issued a manifesto which called for mass picketing on the quays. When the mass picketing failed to produce the desired results, Connolly closed the port of Dublin.[7] This affected the City of Dublin Steampacket Company, the only cross-channel company operating between Dublin and the British ports. This was in direct violation of the agreement of May 26, 1913, but Larkin, on his release, backed Connolly publicly for the action taken.[8] The provocation was extreme, but tactically the move was a

[1] *Daily Citizen*, November 12, 1913.
[2] *Freeman's Journal*, November 18, 1913. T. P. O'Connor in Rochester.
[3] *Ibid.*, November 3, 1913.   [4] *Ibid.*, November 4, 1913.
[5] *Ibid.*, November 8, 1913.   [6] *Ibid.*, September 26, 1913.
[7] *Ibid.*, November 13, 1913.   [8] *Daily Citizen*, November 14, 1913.

blunder because it provided the employers with fresh ammunition. They renewed with vigour their cries of 'broken agreements,' and 'to hell with contracts.' Closing the port also affected those employers who had tried to keep clear of the dispute and were using the facilities of the Dublin Steampacket Company. Now all the employers were on the side of their class whether they wanted to be there or not.

About noon on the day of his release Larkin appeared at Liberty Hall and was reported as looking 'well and strong, but his voice did not carry as far as usual.' Larkin opened his remarks by pointing out 'his enemies wanted to get him out of Ireland. It would be a bad day for them when he did leave Ireland. He was going in a few hours to light a fiery cross in England, Scotland, and Wales . . . and he promised the employers of Dublin that they were going to sup sorrow with a long spoon.'[1] Connolly was even tougher as he boasted, 'We will carry on the fight until we have demonstrated that the Transport is going to rule the roost here in Dublin and throughout Ireland (cheers). . . . We have got our leader back, and you must now demonstrate and picket as you have never picketed before, and see if the police will clear us off the streets as they threatened. If they attempt to do so then the present strike in the port of Dublin will be nothing to what is to come.'[2] That night Connolly announced to a huge welcoming demonstration that Larkin was indisposed. The procession was an unusually noisy one. The women and the girls sang 'God Save Larkin,' 'Cheer Up Larkin,' 'We Are Going to Join Jim Larkin's Union,' and 'I Am One of Those Horrible Larkinites.' The last was the latest addition to the budget of strike songs.[3] Connolly wound up the proceedings in Beresford Place by calling for the formation of a Citizen Army. He said, 'They had proved by the release of Larkin that they were stronger than any Government. Every right had its duty, but when they were deprived of their rights, they owed no duty to anyone. That was what he meant by a state of

---

[1] *Freeman's Journal*, November 14, 1913.   [2] *Ibid.*
[3] *Ibid.* See also Desmond Ryan, *Remembering Sion* (1934), p. 168.

> 'In the streets the children sang:
> It's a wrong thing to crush the workers.
> It's a wrong thing to do.'

Or:

> 'Bring your own bread and butter,
> Bring your own tea and sugar,
> And join Jim Larkin's union.'

war.' 'Listen to me,' Connolly continued. 'I am going to talk sedition, the next time we are out for a march, I want to be accompanied by four battalions of trained men. I want them to come with their corporals, sergeants and people to form fours. Why should we not drill and train our men in Dublin as they are doing in Ulster? But I don't think you require any training (laughter).'[1]

The next day Larkin and Connolly issued a joint manifesto announcing that the port of Dublin was closed and appealing to British trade unionists to help keep it closed.[2] It was a very ambiguous document and it seemed to suggest far more than it said. The *Daily Citizen*, official organ of the British Labour Party, printed the manifesto and commented the next day in its editorial columns that 'In certain quarters a cry goes up for a general strike of British workers in aid of Dublin Labour. So far the proposal is urged in vague and superficial terms, and the details and consequences have clearly not been thought out.'[3] Larkin had, meanwhile, announced in Dublin that he would make a general policy speech in Manchester's Free Trade Hall on Sunday. It was a remarkable demonstration, for the huge hall was packed and 20,000 waited outside.

In Dublin men know that what I say is the truth. Do you think I dare come to a country like England, and to Lancashire, where at least one half of every four of you, or a little more, are Irish, and tell you a lie about my own country, a country I love as I love no other land and no other people? A man who won't love his own fireside can have no love for those outside. What I want to do is to lift up the class I belong to; I want to improve them physically and mentally, broaden their outlook as human beings, and because of this among the things said of me is that I live in a mansion and drive a motor-car. By God! if ever a man deserved a mansion or a motor-car that man stands here— Jim Larkin, the symbol and embodiment of the working classes in Ireland. (Loud cheers.) I speak to you here as their mouthpiece, the official mouthpiece, the ambassador from the working classes of Ireland, the Chairman of their Trade Union Congress. I do not come with any mandate from a clique, but from the whole working class population.[4]

[1] *Freeman's Journal*, November 14, 1913.
[2] *Daily Citizen*, November 14, 1913. The manifesto closed with 'We appeal to our brethren in Great Britain to second our efforts. We thank them for that cordial support which has made our blow so successful, and we counsel them to go ahead and strike while the iron of revolt is hot in our souls.'
[3] *Ibid.*   [4] London *Times*, November 12, 1913.

The substance of the speech, like the manifesto issued two days before, was ambiguous. Larkin did not want a general strike, but at the same time he did not want his English comrades to 'scab.' What did it all mean? Larkin also dropped some sarcastic references to the 'wise men from the East of England Trades Unionism.' Still there was nothing more in the speech than a remarkable demagogic effect, and it could not be taken as a personal attack on anybody. The great fault of the speech was that instead of settling anything it left everything precariously up in the air.

The following day, November 17, J. H. Thomas told a meeting of his railwaymen at Swindon that 'no trade union official, no matter how competent or able or influential, ought to have the sole power of telling men when they must cease work.'[1] The allusion to Larkin was too obvious to miss. The next day the Parliamentary Committee of the British Trades Union Congress met with Larkin and several delegates from the Dublin Trades Council. The Dublin men presented several proposals. They asked the B.T.U.C. to 'take steps to prevent the further importation of non-union labour into Dublin, and should also isolate the Dublin employers by holding up the transit of goods to that city.' The proposals were supposed to have met with a certain amount of support, but the majority of the Parliamentary Committee were reported as 'frankly opposed to any extension of the action beyond the support now being given to the Dublin strikers.'[2] The pressure from the rank and file of their membership, however, prevented the Parliamentary Committee from voting against the proposals. They decided instead to take the unprecedented step of calling a special session of the Trades Union Congress on December 9, or in three weeks' time. Larkin was supposed to have made it clear that he had 'no desire to usurp the place of the English Trade Union leaders in regard to their own members.' He further insisted that the reports of his 'fiery cross' speech in Dublin were misquoted.[3] The next evening Larkin was in London speaking at a meeting organized by the *Daily Herald* at the Albert Hall. George Lansbury, editor of the *Daily Herald*, Will Dyson, its trenchant cartoonist, and Cunningham-Grahame, the Scots Socialist, all denounced the Labour Party in particular and reactionary trade union officials in general. The *Herald* group were at this time the radical left wing of the Socialist Movement, and though they

[1] London *Times*, November 12, 1913.
[2] *Freeman's Journal*, November 19, 1918. Labour Press Agency.   [3] *Ibid.*

made a great deal of noise, their influence in the country was not very great. Larkin talked a great deal, as usual, but actually said nothing. He talked around the issues rather than at them. He did not denounce or attack anyone, and was obviously avoiding a wrangle over personalities.[1]

Sometime between that Wednesday evening and Saturday morning, Larkin made one of the most crucial decisions of his life. On Saturday, November 22, he published another manifesto. In this manifesto, which appeared in the *Daily Herald*, he made a definite appeal to the rank and file of the British Movement over the heads of their trade union officials. The manifesto said in part:

> Tell your leaders now and every day until December 9, and raise your voice upon that day to tell them that for the future they must stand for Trade Unionism, that they are not there as apologists for the short-comings of the Capitalist system, that they are not there to assist the employers in helping to defeat any section of workers striving to be free, nor to act as a brake upon the wheel of progress.[2]

The same day, Saturday, J. H. Wilson, head of the National Seamen's and Firemen's Union, issued a manifesto denouncing Larkin and the methods of the Transport Union in Dublin.[3] For the next few days Larkin was temperate. In Cardiff on Sunday, he did not indulge in personalities, and at Bristol on Monday, he confined himself to raking Augustine Birrell, Chief Secretary for Ireland and M.P. for Bristol, over the coals.

At Sheffield, on Tuesday, however, the proverbial roof came off. Larkin referred to J. H. Wilson and 'Jemmy' Thomas as being too 'big for their boots,' and specifically called Thomas 'a double-dyed traitor to his class.'[4] Robert Williams, General Secretary of the National Transport Workers Federation, who had been a strong supporter of Larkin throughout, cautioned Larkin in the *Daily Citizen* to remember 'this fight and its consequences are immeasurably bigger to us than fifty Larkins.'[5] This warning was timely as well as significant, for Larkin's vitriolic attacks were costing him influential support among even the more radical trade union officials. The *Daily Citizen*, official organ of the Labour Party, was in a

---

[1] *Freeman's Journal*, November 20, 1913.
[2] *Daily Herald*, November 22, 1913.
[3] *Freeman's Journal*, November 24, 1913.
[4] *Ibid.*, November 26, 1913.
[5] *Ibid.*, November 27, 1913.

difficult position. Its correspondent covering Larkin's 'fiery cross' was condemnatory. Of the Sheffield speech the *Citizen* correspondent referred to Larkin as a 'howling dervish,' and said his remarks about Thomas and Wilson were 'wild, illogical and untrue.'[1] The editorial columns were models of restraint. In handling Larkin's manifesto of the 21st, the editor of the *Citizen* calmly pointed out that while he understood Larkin's 'natural impatience' owing to the 'prolongation of the ordeal now being endured by the workers of Dublin . . . the reproaches which he directs against the responsible trade union leaders are not deserved.'[2] A few days later the editor of the *Citizen* temperately wrote that 'We do not suppose any argument will have much weight with Mr. Larkin in his present mood. For our part we have no end to serve except that of helping towards victory the locked out men and women of Dublin.'[3] A week later, Larkin referred to the *Daily Citizen* in Liverpool as 'that alleged Labour paper.'[4]

Larkin's attacks on the personalities in the British Labour Movement grew ever more violent. On Sunday, November 30, at a great meeting in London, in referring to Wilson and Philip Snowden, second only to James Ramsay MacDonald, leader of the Labour Party, Larkin said, 'I am not going to allow these serpents to raise their foul heads and spit out their poison any longer.' He had already denounced 'those Union leaders [who] had neither a soul to be saved nor a body to be kicked.'[5] Larkin continued his campaign of vituperation and vilification. In Leicester, Ramsay MacDonald's constituency, it was Williams who denounced the Labour Party in the persons of MacDonald and Snowden and was howled down. Larkin showed his courage as he faced the hostile crowd and in a few minutes had them cheering. He said anyone who objected to his speaking could object, as he did not want to apologize to anybody. He was going to say what he thought was true. 'If you don't like that,' he exclaimed, 'you can use any remedy you like to stop me (cheers). I am not concerned about men and women as men and women, but I am concerned with the principles that govern human life, and if you like to put up clay idols, then I have no more pleasure in life than in knocking them down (laughter and cheers).'[6]

The question now naturally arises, why did Larkin pursue such a

---

[1] *Freeman's Journal*, November 28, 1913.
[2] *Daily Citizen*, November 22, 1913.
[3] *Ibid.*, November 24, 1913.   [4] *Freeman's Journal*, December 2, 1913.
[5] *Ibid.*, December 1, 1913.   [6] *Ibid.*, December 4, 1913.

seemingly senseless course of action in denouncing British Labour leaders when his responsibilities were so great? Why did he literally bite the hand that was feeding him? The answer is much more involved than a bare examination of the narrative will reveal. It has to do with his personality, his social philosophy, and circumstance. Larkin's 'natural impatience' and his 'sense of mission' made a difficult man almost impossible. Still, his social philosophy was in complete harmony with the times, and as the temper of the times grew more violent he grew more militant. His early Socialism had long been tempered by the everyday necessity of trade union compromise. In time, however, there evolved in Ireland, under Larkin's leadership, a brand of revolutionary trade unionism often described as syndicalism. What was the nature of this revolutionary trade unionism in Ireland? To Larkin it simply meant that he would use the 'sympathetic strike' whenever he was able, and his members would not handle 'tainted goods.' Larkin maintained that these were basic and legitimate trade union principles. What then did the policy of the 'sympathetic strike' and 'tainted goods' actually involve? To Larkin, in practical terms they meant that no trade unionist could handle goods produced or worked under unfair conditions, and that no union man could cross a picket line. Larkin then logically maintained that no contract was valid that involved trade unionists in breaking legitimate trade union principles.

Today no trade unionist, and few employers, would deny that these are legitimate trade union principles. Those who translated or projected the 'sympathetic strike' into a 'general strike' did not give the same meaning to the term that Larkin did. To Larkin a 'sympathetic strike' simply meant that trade unionists were not willing to 'scab' on one another. That it could lead to widespread stoppages of work was owing not to how revolutionary were the aims of the men but rather to how reactionary were the views of the employers. In Ireland today no trade unionist will cross a picket line or handle 'tainted goods,' and no employer would be foolish enough to ask him to do so or dare to bring in 'scabs.' What was denounced as revolutionary syndicalism and Larkinism in 1913 has become commonplace trade union practice today.

Circumstances also conspired to cause Larkin to denounce the leaders of the British Labour Movement. It is not generally known that Larkin suffered a good deal of provocation before he attacked them. Early in the Dublin dispute a number of North-Western and

Lancashire and Yorkshire railwaymen in Liverpool, where Larkin's influence was still felt, declined to handle traffic from Dublin. They were immediately locked out, and the trouble spread to Birmingham, Crewe, Derby, Sheffield, and Leeds, 'but the men's union refused to support it and it was soon over.'[1] Hence Larkin's bitterness towards Thomas, who headed the railwaymen and refused to support the men. Some days before the railway trouble, the London *Morning Post*, the most rightwing of the London dailies, began a series of articles by four trade unionists on 'Do Strikes Pay?' One of the contributors was James Sexton, who though he had some nasty things to say about 'syndicalism,' did not mention Larkin or the Dublin dispute.[2]

When the series was finished, Philip Snowden, an influential member of the British Labour Party, wrote a letter denouncing the 'wild and revolutionary appeals of men like Mr. James Larkin and Mr. Ben Tillett.'[3] He went on to point out that 'the comparatively slight response to the appeal to the railwaymen to engage in a national strike in sympathy with the locked-out men in Dublin prove that, while there is still a noisy section of Trade Unionists who are undisciplined and dangerous, the great body of them are disposed to act only in a regular and disciplined way.' The next day J. H. Wilson contributed his share by commenting, 'The men often lose their heads, largely due to the fact that new teachers arrive on the scene, and they proceed to preach to their fellows that their old leaders are what sometimes is called back numbers. . . . The men who presume to be leaders have not felt the responsibility for office, consequently they can afford to give very cheap advice and in this way members of a Union are often led to get out of hand and make demands which it is impossible for the employers at that particular time to concede.'[4]

Snowden continued his attack in the editorial columns of the *Labour Leader* in a signed article. 'The old Trade Unionism,' wrote Snowden, 'looked facts in the face, and acted with regard to commonsense. The new Trade Unionism, call it what you will—Syndicalism, Carsonism, Larkinism, does neither.'[5] The following week Keir

---

[1] *Annual Register*, 1913, p. 203.
[2] *Morning Post* (London), September 16, 1913.
[3] *Ibid.*, September 20, 1913.
[4] *Ibid.*, September 22, 1913.
[5] *Labour Leader*, September 25, 1913.

Hardie wrote defending the strike weapon, the Dublin dispute, and Larkin.[1] Snowden made a rejoinder, and Hardie answered him effectively again. By this time the fat was in the fire, for Larkin had intimated that Snowden wrote to the London *Morning Post* out of 'mercenary motives.'[2] This was too much for Hardie, and he justly rebuked Larkin. In the course of his 'fiery cross' campaign Larkin confined his denunciations to Wilson and Thomas on the trade union level and to Snowden and MacDonald on the Parliamentary level. Larkin felt, and so did Hardie, that whatever the opinions of these men, the middle of a lockout was hardly the time to go into print with them. Especially since Larkin was doing his best, at the time the *Morning Post* published these articles, to get the British Trades Union Congress and the National Transport Workers Federation to back the Dublin dispute financially.

Back in Dublin Connolly, between running the lockout, editing the *Irish Worker*, speaking in Beresford Place, and recruiting for the newly organized Citizen Army, was having a busy time. He had anticipated Larkin's attack on the British trade unionists by announcing in Beresford Place that the 'labour leaders who were attacking them in England were only old fossils, and were willing to sell the pass any time.'[3] The same night, while Larkin was denouncing Wilson and Thomas in Sheffield, Connolly was attacking Wilson in Beresford Place and denying that the 'sympathetic strike' had 'been used recklessly in Dublin.'[4] To Connolly also fell the delicate task, in Larkin's absence, of negotiating for the Transport Union at the peace conference arranged by Archbishop Walsh. The conference opened on December 4, and some six clauses were agreed on as providing a basis for discussion. The men agreed to give up the 'sympathetic strike' but demanded in return that 'all men be reinstated.' The employers refused on the ground that it would be unfair to victimize the men who had been hired and, further, that the present stage of their business could not absorb all the men at once. The representatives of the men, fearing wholesale victimization of the most militant spirits among their members, could not possibly accept the employers' terms without some form of guarantee. The conference broke up on Sunday, December 7, over the question of reinstatement.[5]

[1] *Labour Leader*, October 2, 1913.   [2] *Ibid.*, October 23, 1913.
[3] *Freeman's Journal*, November 19, 1913.   [4] *Ibid.*, November 26, 1913.
[5] *Ibid.*, December 8, 1913. See also Wright, *op. cit.*, Appendix VI, pp. 313–16.

Finally, on December 9, the long-awaited event came to pass. The British Trades Union Congress met in Farringdon Hall in London. The Congress opened with a long report by Arthur Henderson on the negotiations between the Joint Board of Irish and British trade unionists and the Employers' Federation.[1] Henderson's chief complaint was, in effect, that the British trade union leaders were paying the piper and were not even allowed to request a tune. He adroitly avoided the personal issues, as did Harry Gosling, the Chairman, who followed him. Gosling was also conciliatory, but he asked the Dublin delegates to realize that the British delegates 'had got to have a word in as well as they.' Connolly answered for the Irish delegates, since Larkin had been on his 'fiery cross' tour during the negotiations.

Connolly accepted the substance of Henderson's report, and added that there had been 'too much recrimination on both sides.' He then skilfully pointed out that the negotiations with the Employers' Federation broke down, not because of the stubbornness or perversity of the Dublin men, but because the employers were willing to concede nothing on the vital question of reinstatement. He then read to the Congress the employers' proposal:

> The employers, whilst they cannot agree to dismiss men taken on who have been found suitable, will agree that as far as their business permits they will take on as many of their former employees as they can make room for, and in the operation of their business will make a bona fide effort to find employment for as many as possible as soon as they can.[2]

'Our attitude,' said Connolly, 'is that the conditions spoken of there are the conditions which exist where there is no trade union at all. If you had no trade union at all, that is what the employers do. They take on as many as they like to suit their own business, and are we to be told that the joint efforts of the trade unionists of Great Britain and Ireland can only succeed in getting terms that could be got by every individual if there was no trade union in the field at all?' The British delegates listened with attention and cheered loudly when Connolly made his crucial point. There was a stir, however, as

---

[1] *Freeman's Journal*, December 10, 1913. The *Freeman's Journal* carried a more complete account of the Special Congress than did the London *Times*. The following narrative and quotes are based on the *Freeman's Journal* account.

[2] *Ibid.*

he wound up his remarks by noting the 'Irish delegates were not withdrawing any criticism they had made. They were prepared to repeat it, but they were not going to allow their criticism of what had occurred, or the criticisms of them to draw them aside from the contemplation of the fact that they were that day fighting for liberty for at least 100,000 people in the city of Dublin (cheers).'

To the amazement of all present, Ben Tillett, then considered the most militant of British trade union leaders, closely associated with the radical *Daily Herald* group, and presumably pro-Larkin, moved the following resolution:

> That this Conference deplores and condemns the unfair attacks made by men inside the trade union movement upon British trade union officials; it affirms its confidence in those officials who have been so unjustly assailed, and its belief in their ability to negotiate an honourable settlement if assured of the effective support of all who are concerned in the Dublin dispute.[1]

This was most unfortunate, for now the issue of personalities, that up to then had been so carefully avoided, was to be discussed before the fundamental question of what was to be done about the Dublin dispute. It led only to more bitter recrimination as speaker after speaker condemned Larkin for his attacks on British Labour leaders. As each speaker mounted the rostrum the atmosphere grew more tense. One of Larkin's prime targets, the leader of the Railwaymen, J. H. Thomas, was greeted with a chorus of 'noes' when he asked the delegates, 'Were they to stand by and allow themselves to be libelled and slandered?' As for himself he said he 'was not going to for fifty Larkins.' Another of Larkin's favourite targets, J. H. Wilson, head of the Seamen's Union, did not even think it necessary to answer Larkin's charges. He added amidst laughter that he had come into the trade union movement thirty-six years before 'and was not kicked into it.' 'Mr. Larkin,' Wilson charged, 'had made great blunders from the very inception of the strike in Dublin. The state of affairs in Dublin would not have existed for twenty-four hours had he shown a little more common sense.'

When Larkin was eventually called by the Chair to reply, he opened his remarks with, 'Mr. Chairman and human beings.' This annoyed some of the delegates, but when Larkin went on to say,

[1] *Freeman's Journal*, December 10, 1913.

'He was not concerned whether they would let him go on or not,' and that 'He could deal with any or all of them at any place they liked to name,' there was an uproar. After the Chairman had restored order, Larkin created another uproar when he said, 'If they were not going to give him an opportunity of replying to the foul, lying statements which had been made it would only be what he expected from a good many of them.' When the Chairman managed to get some sort of order Larkin almost caused a riot by remarking, 'He did not suppose that, with the exception of a few trades, there was one man there who was elected.' Amidst all the noise the Chairman was heard to protest that the delegates had been elected according to the Standing Orders of the Congress.

When the delegates quieted down again Larkin went on to denounce Wilson, Sexton, Henderson, and Thomas. Throughout he was continually interrupted and heckled. At one point he again created an uproar when he told the delegates, 'You are afraid to hear the truth. Accept the guilt if you are guilty, and don't make lying statements about me.' When the disorder subsided Larkin exclaimed, 'I am not responsible for your intelligence.' This was too much for the delegates, and he was 'greeted with a hurricane of denunciation.' The Chairman was not able to quell the uproar as Larkin 'faced the storm and glared wildly at the assemblage, his face bathed in perspiration.' Larkin continued to fight a running battle with his hecklers, and then dramatically and defiantly he told the delegates:

> Neither you nor these gentlemen on the platform can settle this Dublin dispute. I challenge you to try it. I know, however, that the rank and file of the British trade unionists will support the Dublin men in their battle, and if we do not get that support we will do what we have done before—fight it out (cheers). This is a game of war; it is not a game of beggar-my-neighbour. I know the men we have to deal with. All they want to do is to delay the negotiations in order that they may weed the men out. The ban against the union has not been withdrawn. The employers of Dublin are neither truthful nor honest, and the only way to deal with them is to deal with them with a strong hand. We have always been able to do that. Take away your scabs, out of Dublin; take away the men who are organized scabs, who are acting worse than the imported scabs. The men of Dublin will never handle 'tainted' goods as long as I am an official (cheers).[1]

[1] *Freeman's Journal*, December 10, 1913.

153

He seemed to soften for a minute as he admitted 'He had said hard things, and they had said harder and more bitter things against him. He had done according to his lights.' He closed on a note of defiance, however, as he proclaimed, 'Larkin will go down fighting. They were not going to be beaten by the force of capitalists in that country or the men who were not out to fight capitalism in this country.'

In the afternoon session after an adjournment for lunch, Tillett's untimely resolution passed almost unanimously. Then the real issue was discussed. What was to be done about Dublin? John Ward, M.P., proposed a resolution thanking the British leaders for their generous support during the lockout and pledging their continued support until the Dublin dispute was brought to a successful conclusion. Both Ward and Ben Turner, who seconded the resolution, pointed out that the issue at stake was the right of combination in Dublin, and not a quarrel over personalities. The resolution passed unanimously. Then the crucial resolution as to what was to be done about bringing the Dublin lockout to a successful end was proposed by J. W. Kelly. He asked that another attempt by the Joint Board of British and Irish delegates be made to settle the dispute through negotiation.

This meant asking the Employers' Federation to reopen negotiations and tacitly implied the willingness of the men to ask for terms. In supporting the resolution, George Roberts, M.P., pointed out that the financial support could not go on for ever. Jack Jones, of the Gasworkers, a supporter of Larkin's, proposed an amendment to the resolution. He asked those unions in the transport trade to announce that they would not handle Dublin traffic after a certain specified date, and called for a monthly levy to be voted by the British unions to support the Dublin workers. After several other speeches the amendment was put to a card vote, and the result was an overwhelming defeat for the Larkinites. The vote was 203,000 for the amendment, and 2,280,000 against. The original resolution was then put and passed easily. To Connolly fell the unhappy task of answering for the Dublin delegates. After thanking the Congress for the financial support so generously given, he added that, while he realized the decision of the Congress could not be altered, 'there were some proposals they would not necessarily accept.'[1]

A great deal had been expected of this first special Trades Union Congress ever to be called in Great Britain. Yet, when it was all over,

[1] *Freeman's Journal*, December 10, 1913.

the general feeling seemed to be that 'it would have been better had it never been held.'[1] To talk about the failure of the Congress being due to those who had the responsibility for framing the agenda, and placing Tillett's resolution before the vital issue of what was to be done about Dublin, was to beg the main question.[2] The main question faced by the British trade union movement, and made amply clear at the Congress, was what was to be done on the industrial level now that Labour was organized on mass lines? Labour disputes were yearly increasing in number and magnitude. On the industrial side Labour was obviously on the move, but where was it going? What was to be done about this great mass of energy expended every year in strikes and lockouts? Could the organized trade union movement harness and channel this enormous energy and use it to advance the cause of the working classes? Since the Congress made no attempt to answer any of these questions, and gave no official indication of any lead for the future, it can safely be termed a proper failure.[3]

A week after the special Trades Union Congress had rejected Larkin's demand for sympathetic strike action, negotiations with the Dublin employers were once again resumed. Henderson led the British delegates and Larkin the Irish. It was suggested in the Dublin papers that a good deal of pressure was put on Larkin by both the British and Irish delegates 'to give a more or less willing assent to the terms of settlement.'[4] The Labour representatives proposed that the employers withdraw their ban on the Transport Union, and the Union in turn would give up the 'sympathetic strike,' pending the setting up of a Wages and Conditions Board by March 17, 1914. The crux of the whole matter, however, was the proposal that 'no member of any trade union shall be refused employment on the grounds of his or her association with the dispute, and that no new employees shall be engaged until all the old workers have been reinstated.'[5] The employers rejected the reinstatement proposals and reiterated their stand of December 7, when they said they would

[1] *Justice* (London), December 13, 1913.

[2] A. Fenner Brockway, 'British Trade Unionists and Dublin,' *Labour Leader*, December 11, 1913.

[3] The single exception was Robert Smillie's speech. In it was the germinal proposal for joint action in the future by the miners, railwaymen, and transport workers that led to the formation of the Triple Industrial Alliance.

[4] *Freeman's Journal*, December 10, 1913. Labour Press Agency.

[5] Wright, *op. cit.*, p. 317.

take back as many as they were able. The Conference broke up on Saturday, December 20, and no more negotiations for a settlement were undertaken.

The employers were aware of the difficulties confronting the men.[1] Larkin had alienated British support by his 'fiery cross' campaign, and on that support the dispute in Dublin must stand or fall. After the Trades Union Congress rejected Larkin's proposals on December 9, it was evident to all that it was only a matter of time before the dispute would collapse. Larkin might hurl defiance and announce to the Dublin workers that they would get along on their own, but supporting 20,000 men and their families was impossible on the slender resources of the Irish trade union movement.

As the funds from the Parliamentary Committee of the B.T.U.C. began to decline and the subscription lists in the Labour papers dwindled, the men in Dublin began to drift back to work. At a closed meeting of the Transport Union members of January 18, 1914, the advice given the men was to go back if they were not asked to sign the 'document,' and between January 20 and January 26 large numbers of the men applied for work.[2] On January 30 Larkin himself publically admitted, 'We are beaten, we will make no bones about it; but we are not too badly beaten still to fight (cheers). . . . Will our men sign the document? No! (cheers).'[3] The death knell for the locked-out men sounded when the Builders Labourers Union, 3,000 strong, agreed, on February 1, to a humiliating surrender. 'The Union agreed that none of its members should remain or become in the future, a member of the Irish Transport Workers' Union. Its members will not take part in or support any form of sympathetic strike; they will handle all materials, and carry out all instructions, given them in the course of their employment. Further, they will work amicably with all employees, whether they be unionists or non-unionists.'[4] When, on February 11, 1914, C. W. Bowerman announced that the Dublin Relief Fund, sponsored by the B.T.U.C., was officially closed, the lockout was in fact over.[5] Connolly was bitter when he wrote, 'And so we Irish workers must again go down into Hell, bow our backs to the lash of the slave driver, let our hearts

[1] *Forward*, March 14, 1914. Connolly wrote: 'At the next Peace Conference in Dublin the employers would not even look at the joint proposals unanimously agreed to by the representatives of the English and Irish Trade Unions.'

[2] *Freeman's Journal*, January 20–26, 1914.   [3] *Ibid.*, January 31, 1914.

[4] *Irish Times*, February 3, 1914.   [5] *Daily Express*, February 11, 1914.

be seared by the iron of his hatred, and instead of the sacramental wafer of brotherhood and common sacrifice, eat the dust of defeat and betrayal. Dublin is isolated.'[1]

But, if the men lost, what did the employers gain? Connolly later commented that the 'battle was a drawn battle.'[2] Yet it was the *Irish Times*, strangely enough, that clearly saw the handwriting on the wall—

> The settlement of the strike has, in fact, settled nothing. The very necessary business of 'smashing Larkin' is successfully accomplished; but that is very far from being the same thing as 'smashing Larkinism'. There is no security whatever that the men who are now going about their work brooding over the bitterness of defeat will not endeavour to reorganise their broken forces, and, given another leader and another opportunity, strike a further and a more desperate blow at the economic life of Dublin.[3]

Since the lockout was lost because the British Labour Movement refused to continue to support the Dublin men, the fundamental question is why did they refuse that support. At first glance the answer seems simple enough. Larkin alienated them by his abuse. In fact, however, Larkin's abuse was more the excuse rather than the cause of their refusal to continue their support. What has generally been overlooked is that whether Larkin had denounced them or not, they could not have agreed to his demand for sympathetic action in support of the Dublin men because it would have involved them in a general industrial war in Britain. This the British labour leaders were not willing to undertake. Indeed, in 1911 they had reacted precisely the same way to the same situation on a smaller scale, when they refused to call out their British members in support of the National railway strike they had themselves declared in Ireland. In 1913 the British labour leaders knew only too well their own organizational weaknesses, and they rightly suspected that the British worker would not respond to a declaration of industrial war, especially if the issue was purely Irish. In any case the leadership was certainly divided, and even the most militant were hesitant, maintaining the moment was not ripe for a forward movement. There was also the long political tradition that social and economic

---

[1] *Forward*, February 7, 1914.
[2] *Irish Worker*, November 28, 1914. Quoted in W. P. Ryan, *op. cit.*, p. 234.
[3] *Irish Times*, February 3, 1914.

grievances could be successfully resolved within the Parliamentary system, and it was far from played out either in the minds of the Labour leadership or among the working classes, who for the most part, still voted Liberal rather than Labour. Larkin's fatal mistake, in antagonizing the British labour leaders, was not so much that he denounced them, but rather that he asked them to do the impossible —to declare for a means that could well take them outside the constitutional framework.

Why then did Larkin ask them to do the impossible, especially when his own responsibilities were so heavy? He did it because in the seven years since he had come to Ireland he had become an Irishman, and was acting in 1913 out of an Irish rather than a British frame of reference. The problem that confronted the Irish Labour Movement in 1911, and again in 1913, was simply the problem that had confronted the British and Irish nations for centuries. The fundamental needs of the Irish and British nations has always been and still were different in both time and place, and it was out of these essentially different needs that their national mentalities were shaped and the two nations made. Unlike Britain, where the political pendulum in the nineteenth century swung between two parties devoted to playing the game outlined in the Constitution, the pendulum in Ireland inscribed an arc between the Party of the Constitution and the Party of the Revolution. To the Irish, and to Larkin, Revolution was still a legitimate mode of political action, for in his mind the conviction was steadily growing that nothing less than a Revolution was necessary to build a new social order in Ireland. To the British, and to their labour leaders, such a course for them would be simply suicide, for they realized that if even they were willing to take a step in the direction of Revolution, their followers were not. In the last analysis then the quarrel between Larkin and the British labour leaders had much more to do with the fundamental need of each to maintain and retain the confidence of their respective followers than with personalities. The choice came down to Reform or Revolution, and it was not to be the last time that Larkin declared for the Revolutionary way. The confrontation of British and Irish Labour in 1913 was the sad prelude to the final confrontation of the British and Irish nations some few years later.

VIII

THE CHIEF

THE political history of modern Ireland is largely a study in biography. Ireland's long struggle for national freedom, with each generation needing new and fresh inspirational symbols, has seen the cult of hero worship become a national pastime. Why should the the Irish be so prone to follow the leader? Was George Russell, the poet AE, close to the truth when he wrote, 'the one political institution we have to our credit is the clan chief: and the genius of personality has always swayed us more than a love of abstract ideas of principles?'[1] There is pregnant significance in the fact that Parnell was referred to as the 'Chief,' and that even today de Valera is referred to in the same way by his colleagues. By 1913 Larkin, in the eyes of his followers, had also ascended to the level of a 'Chief.' In one of the huge processions during the lockout, the principal 'feature of interest . . . was a large portrait in oils of Mr. Jim Larkin,' over which was the inscription:

> The chief who raised the red hand up
> Until it paled the sun.
> And shed such glory o'er our cause
> As never chief has done.[2]

Larkin had not only convinced himself that his true vocation was to preach the gospel of divine discontent, he had convinced his followers. William P. Partridge, his most loyal and faithful lieutenant, stated that he believed Jim Larkin was sent by God to save the

[1] *Irish Homestead*, July 10, 1909.
[2] *Freeman's Journal*, October 17, 1913. From 'Shane's Head,' by John Savage.

working classes of Dublin.[1] Words are almost impossible to find to describe Larkin's ascendancy over the workers in this period.

There is always great difficulty in accounting rationally for the irrational. Faith and devotion are the words that explain the cult of the hero, not reason.

Yet an attempt must be made, for feelings are often rooted in something very real. The reasons for the hero worship of Larkin by the Dublin working class are a combination of the historical, personal, and psychological. The psychological need of the inarticulate masses to express themselves is not a new idea. The Dublin masses found their instrument in James Larkin. Larkin's ability to identify himself with the masses, to be only one of themselves yet something more than each, was the basis of his power. He said as much when he told the Dublin workers:

> Don't bother about cheering Larkin—he is but one of yourselves. It is you that want the cheers, and it is you that deserve them. It is you and the class from which I come—*the down trodden class*—that should get the cheers, and all the good things that follow the cheers. I don't recognize myself—a mean soul like myself in a mean body— as being the movement. You are the movement and for the time being I have been elected as your spokesman.[2]

Those who listened were heartened, for in cheering Larkin they were cheering themselves.

When an acute observer described one of Larkin's meetings as 'a cross between a Welsh Revivalist gathering and a Continental Anarchist Conference,'[3] he was more than half right. The chastisement and castigation of the congregation was not a new technique in Ireland. Daniel Corkery noted of Larkin as early as 1910, 'I regard him as one earnest to a fault, for I never heard him speak to the class for which he stood that he did not half offend them by dwelling on the failings which kept them powerless and timid.'[4] Countess Markievicz perhaps summed it all up when she wrote:

> Sitting there, listening to Larkin, I realised that I was in the presence of something that I had never come across before, some great primeval force rather than a man. A tornado, a storm-driven wave, the rush into

---

[1] *Irish Worker*, June 27, 1914. P. W. Partridge said 'He believed that Larkin was designed by God to perform the social work in which he was engaged.'

[2] *Ibid.*, July 29, 1911.

[3] Arnold Wright, *Disturbed Dublin* (1914), p. 237.

[4] *Leader*, July 2, 1910.

life of spring, and the blasting breath of autumn, all seemed to emanate from the power that spoke. It seemed as if his personality caught up, assimilated, and threw back to the vast crowd that surrounded him every emotion that swayed them, every pain and joy that they had ever felt made articulate and sanctified. Only the great elemental force that is in all crowds had passed into his nature for ever.[1]

By 1913 Larkin had convinced the Dublin working classes that he was their instrument, working only in their interest and for their welfare. His honesty, integrity, and sincerity of purpose in these years is unquestioned. 'He had no property except three sons and a wife, and some sticks of furniture not worth £5.'[2] He took £2 10s. a week in salary, which he turned over to his wife. They lived in a little house in Auburn Street for which he paid 9s. a week. He could never run his union on a businesslike basis, for he was ever reaching in his pocket for those who wanted a 'hand-out.' His devotion to the cause of temperance won him the loyalty of the workers' wives.[3] Many of the Dublin workers were heavy drinkers, and alcohol was the greatest drain on the weekly earnings of the family. The women would often come to Larkin and complain about their husbands' drinking. Larkin would see to it that the wives and children received first consideration, and after that the men could do what they liked. More than one drunken docker went head first down the steps of Liberty Hall with Larkin the propelling force. He was usually looked upon by those he chastised, when they sobered up, as 'only talking right,' and 'being for their own good.'[4] Larkin became their moral policeman.

In these years Larkin made his union something more than an instrument of industrial advance. He made it a vehicle for social and cultural advancement as well. He was strongly influenced in this direction by his own early experiences in Liverpool with the Clarion Fellowship promoted by Robert Blatchford. When the Transport Union acquired Liberty Hall early in 1912, a centre was founded for the social activities of the Union.[5] Before this time the union socials consisted mainly of the joint annual outing organized by the Transport and the Women Workers' Union, which had been founded in September, 1911. A good part of the social programme work was taken over by Larkin's sister Delia. In March, 1912, Delia organized

---

[1] *Eire*, June 16, 1924. This is the Countess Markievicz's account of her first meeting with Larkin in October, 1910, on his release from prison.
[2] *Irish Worker*, August 23, 1913.   [3] Barney Conway, personal interview.
[4] *Ibid.*   [5] *Daily Herald*, October 20, 1913.

the 'Irish Workers' Choir,' and rehearsals were announced for 'Juvenile and Adult Dancers' at the Irish Women Workers' Hall.[1] When Liberty Hall was acquired, along with the choir and dancing classes,[2] an Irish language class was formed, and in June Delia founded the Irish Workers' Dramatic Company.[3] At Christmas, 1912, the company, with Delia as star, did four one-act plays two nights running. On St. Patrick's Day, 1913, the company performed again for two successive nights, presenting three one-act plays. In the meantime, Sunday-evening socials, with a lecture and a concert, became a standard feature at Liberty Hall at only nominal charge to union members and their families.[4] Larkin had early organized a fife-and-drum band, and in June, 1913, an Irish pipers' band.[5] Every Christmas there was a party for the workers' children, with presents and ice-cream for all.[6]

The crowning achievement of Larkin's social programme, however, was the rental of a house and three acres in Clontarf as a recreational centre for the union members.[7] On Sunday, August 3, 1913, Croydon Park was officially opened with a 'Grand Temperance Fête and Children's Carnival.' There was dancing and singing and games for the children as the band played all day.[8] Croydon Park and Liberty Hall continued to function socially in a limited way during the lockout. Of necessity Liberty Hall, the Headquarters of the Union, became the centre for the distribution of food and clothing for the victims of the lockout. At the Hall, one observer wrote:

> The work has grown to such proportions that five rooms in Liberty Hall are set aside for the various activities in connection with the administration of the Fund. . . .
>
> In one room women are working sewing machines making up serge and flannellette into warm clothing; another room is arranged as a warehouse, with wires stretched across the ceiling, from which hang the boots and clothes ready to be distributed every morning after the children had their breakfast.
>
> I saw the piles of excellent whole meal bread, which with butter and cocoa, forms the children's breakfast. . . .[9]

[1] *Irish Worker*, March 2, 1912.   [2] *Ibid.*, May 11, 1912.
[3] *Ibid.*, June 8, 1912.   [4] *Ibid.*, November 2, 1912.
[5] *Ibid.*, June 21, 1913.   [6] *Ibid.*, December 30, 1911.
[7] *Ibid.*, August 2, 1913.
[8] *Ibid.*, August 9, 1913. See EUCHAN, 'The Jovial Revolution.'
[9] *Daily Herald*, December 24, 1913.

At Croydon Park the same observer saw the 'surprises that Santa Claus is preparing for the kiddies who are to have a Christmas. . . . Three large marquees are to be pitched close to the house in Croydon Park, and in these 5,000 children are to be fed and entertained. A Christmas tree is rearing its bravery of light and colour in the conservatory of the fine old house. . . .' Larkin wrote a Liverpool seed merchant that 'I want to interest our people in the culture of vegetables and flowers and window-box displays. . . . The gardens have been neglected for some years. We have vines and hot houses. I myself have not had the experience I would like in these matters. . . . I want to get good results, so as to encourage our people.'[1] He also bought a cow and a calf to familiarize the Dublin slum-dweller with another side of Irish life. In addition, two football teams and a boxing team were organized for the sports enthusiasts in the Transport Union.[2]

These were the reasons why Larkin was the idol of the Dublin working classes. He gave them more of his time, his energy, and himself than anyone had ever given them before. Were they to believe that the man who gave their children a smile at Christmas was an enemy of the family and an atheist to boot? Was the man who gave them a social life besides the public house and the tenement stoop or window an enemy of God and a foe to nationality? Larkin and his sister brought a measure of hope and happiness into the narrow lives of those who were interested, by providing them with new outlets. The achievement was modest, for the resources were slender. After all, Liberty Hall was comparatively small, and Croydon Park could only accommodate a limited number of workers and their families. Still, a great deal was done with very little where nothing had ever been done before.

Larkin did not lose the support of his followers with the defeat of the Transport Union. Instead they were sullenly convinced that they had been betrayed and that the English labour leaders were the arch villains.[3] The municipal elections in January, 1914, indicated that Larkin still wielded considerable influence with the Dublin workers. Larkin fought the local elections with even more than his accustomed vigour since he knew they would be interpreted as a barometer of his personal influence among the workers. The contests

---

[1] *The Attempt to Smash the Irish Transport and General Workers' Union* (1924), p. 133.

[2] *Irish Worker*, May 2, 1914.   [3] *Leader*, February 7, 1914.

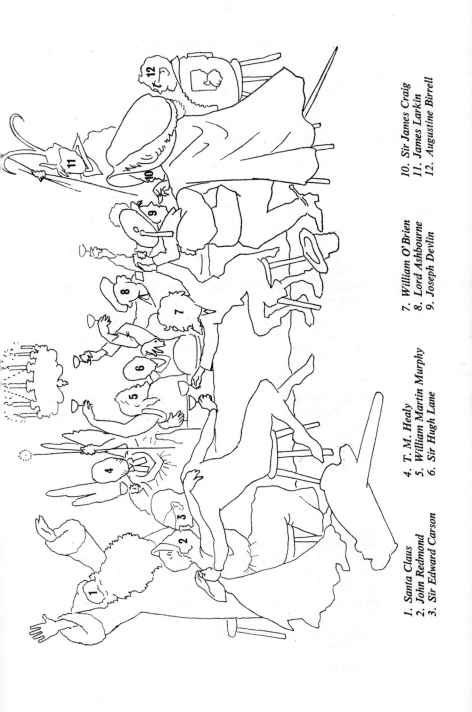

1. Santa Claus
2. John Redmond
3. Sir Edward Carson
4. T. M. Healy
5. William Martin Murphy
6. Sir Hugh Lane
7. William O'Brien
8. Lord Ashbourne
9. Joseph Devlin
10. Sir James Craig
11. James Larkin
12. Augustine Birrell

were far more bitter than in any previous year. The Larkinites were easily the more justified in name-calling because the men they were fighting were, as usual, the worst types in a corrupt municipal body. Larkin and his associates were denounced as Socialists and therefore enemies of God, family, and the nation. The *Irish Independent* published a letter from 'Anti-Socialist' who claimed to be quoting the Irish-American Archbishop of New York:

The Socialists have in this city schools to which they send their children. They have catechisms of their own, with questions and answers gotten up in practically the same way as our own, but far different texts:

'Who made you?—I grew up; my father and mother made me.'
'Who is God?—There is no God.'
'Who is Christ?—He was an imposter.'
'What is sin?—There is no such thing as sin.'
'Does marriage bind and bond?—None whatever; you can leave it whenever you want to.'

These are the doctrines of Socialists. Now, what is your duty in face of all that? I say it is the duty of every person in the city, whatever his creed or his nationality, to form a determination to do what he may to combat this great plague, seeking to devour the very best and oldest of our doctrines.[1]

'Anti-Socialist' then went on to say, 'The above warning and advice of our exalted fellow-countryman should be taken to heart by people here at home. The same danger exists in Ireland as in America as is evident from the recent upheaval in Dublin.' Larkin countered with a special election edition:

Priest and parson, politician and . . . press, and police authorities have admitted that there is a condition of things here in Dublin which is unequalled in Western Europe. Poverty stalks in your midst; disease is rampant; vice lifts its foul head naked, unashamed; sweating and overworking are ever present; underfeeding is plain to anyone with eyes to see; dirt, disease and death caused by the exploitation of the dispossessed worker by the unscrupulous unchristian employer; children rot and die in the slums; women are broken-hearted and degraded; men are dispirited and debauched owing to the wretched conditions of life. . . . The only cure is clean honest administration of the city's affairs by clean, honest, intelligent men and women. Therefore, to you is given the duty to return such men.[2]

[1] *Irish Independent*, January 3, 1914. [2] *Irish Worker*, January 14, 1914.

Labour contested 13 seats and won only two. Several contests were close. South Dock was lost by 13 votes, and a number of others by less than 200 votes. Larkin's opponents polled 14,978 in the 13 contests, while the Larkinites polled 10,377 votes. Those who ran on a Nationalist-Labour ticket but were not endorsed by the Dublin Labour Party polled 1,649. The gain in seats was small, but the Labour vote, overall, was very strong, and indicated that the Larkinites were gaining strength, if not seats.[1]

After his defeat at the British Trades Union Congress in early December it was obvious even to Larkin that the 'fiery cross' had fizzled out. 'The chief who raised the red hand up' now needed another and more positive slogan with which to hearten his followers. He found his new slogan in the 'Co-operative Commonwealth.' At the Askwith inquiry in October, 1913, it will be recalled, Larkin announced that he believed the problems of the working classes would only be solved when the 'Co-operative Commonwealth' was established. By the middle of December Larkin was back in Britain trying to raise funds for a 'Co-operative Commonwealth' for Ireland. The man who undoubtedly influenced Larkin most in this direction was George Russell (AE). Russell was the editor of the *Irish Homestead*, a Co-operative weekly subsidized by Sir Horace Plunkett. Every week in the *Homestead* Russell propounded his ideas on art, poetry, literature, history, philosophy, and economics. Every week he was scintillating as he tilted with his readers, provoked their imaginations, and argued and questioned to the point of exasperation.

In the early days of the Dublin struggle when AE was critical of Larkin and Irish Labour's lack of a programme, he wrote with telling insight that 'They are not even socialist or syndicalist, nor do they seem to have any idea of the future. Certainly they do not hint at any future culmination of organised labour in guilds of workers such as the intellectuals of labour in England have been expounding in the *New Age*.'[2] AE also wrote W. P. Ryan, the assistant editor of the *Daily Herald*, early in September, 1913, that 'It would be worth while to read all the articles on the wage system and on Guild Socialism and the Railway Guild articles carefully and have them all in your mind. They are the best thinking on Labour and its future in England, and if you popularise them without having

[1] *Irish Worker*, January 14, 1914. [2] *Irish Homestead*, September 6, 1913.

the rather bitter tone of the *New Age* you may become a great power.'[1] Larkin became very much interested in Guild Socialism himself, as expounded by A. R. Orage and S. G. Hobson in the *New Age*.[2] The central idea of the Guild Socialists was the organization of industry into National Guilds which would be taken over and operated by the workers themselves. This was not very different from Connolly's ideas on the 'Workers' Republic,' with which Larkin had been familiar for some years.

When the struggle in Dublin was about over Larkin launched his programme for a 'Co-operative Commonwealth.' His ideas were unique in that he outlined a plan for a producers' co-operative rather than the usual consumer and distributor co-operative. The plan was to start slowly and simply and then build up:

> How are we to begin? By taking up those industries or occupations that are simple in their operations for a beginning, especially those things we can supply ourselves, and which are consumed and used by our own class. This means that the loyalty exemplified by the Dublin working class during the late prolonged dispute must be utilised in a sane business-like way. We all eat bread so we must develop the cooperative bread production and distribution. We all wear clothes. We must make and sell our own boots. We must import our own coals. . . . We have the men, we have the women, and we must get the necessary fluid capital in the shape of money to start. . . .[3]

AE was quick to notice the new plan of campaign. In the *Homestead* he wrote 'A Word of Warning to Labour,' in which he pointed out that the real history of producers' co-operatives was notoriously sad. The proper way to make a beginning, he advised, was to concentrate on the distributive aspect and organize a market for the product.[4] Still, it was here that one noted the basic difference between AE's brand of co-operation and Larkin's. It was the difference between those who were not Socialists and those who were. For the Socialist control of production was the means to the end, while to the co-operator the means to the end had to do with the elimination of the middleman by controlling distribution. Larkin's ideas on producers'

---

[1] MS., Letter, Russell to Ryan (September 6, 1913), *loc. cit.*

[2] Wright, *op. cit.*, p. 260. See interview with Larkin.

[3] *Irish Worker*, February 14, 1914, 'Our New Campaign.' See 'Shellback,' *ibid.*, February 28, 1914.

[4] *Irish Homestead*, February 28, 1914.

co-operatives, like most of his constructive ideas, were not expressed in a clear or coherent manner. The 'Co-operative Commonwealth' unfortunately came to be no more than a still-born hope.

In order to finance the programme for producers' co-operatives in Dublin Larkin undertook extensive speaking engagements in Britain. All of February and most of March was spent in a vain attempt to fill an empty Transport Union treasury.[1] The tour's real significance, however, was not in how much money it brought in but rather in how conscious it made the British trade unionists of Industrial Unionism. In Britain Larkin soon came to be recognized, after Tom Mann, as the outstanding advocate of the new revolutionary trade unionism. He helped popularize the idea of the general strike through his insistence that the 'sympathetic strike' and the policy of not handling 'tainted goods' were legitimate trade union principles. If he did not convince the British working classes or their trade union leaders, he certainly made them aware of his proposed line of action.

Before Larkin began his campaign for 'sympathetic strike' action on the part of British trade unionists in November, 1913, there had been a good deal of talk in Britain about concerted action by the big three of the trade union world—the miners, the railwaymen, and the transport workers. In the summer of 1911 many miners were left idle at the pits because of the general strike in the transport trade. When the miners struck, in early 1912, many transport workers found themselves with no work on the docks. When the various railway unions amalgamated in the National Union of Railwaymen in early 1913, the time seemed ripe for common action. This question of united action arose again when the Dublin dispute posed the vexing problem of how far trade unionists were willing to go in protecting the general interests of the trade union movement. The special Trades Union Congress decided that as far as Dublin was concerned, they would support the struggle financially but would not engage in any sympathetic strike action that might lead to a general strike. It was Bob Smillie, representing some 800,000 trade unionists in the Miners' Federation, who made the most important speech at the special Congress. Smillie said in part, 'he thought sympathetic action between Trade Unions would certainly come in the future, but the knitting together of organisations such as the Transport workers

---

[1] *Freeman's Journal*, February 11, 1914. See Mr. M'Keown's letter in the Glasgow *Forward*, June 13, 1914.

and the Miners must not be accomplished in a moment of pressure, but with deliberation and care.'[1]

What Smillie actually said was that there was nothing wrong with what Larkin proposed as far as sympathetic action was concerned but that the time was not yet ripe for such a move. This was most unfortunate for Larkin and the Dublin workers, because Smillie's 800,000 votes were cast against them. For the whole of the first half of 1914 negotiations went on between the miners, railwaymen, and transport workers. In June an Advisory Council was set up with authority to declare three simultaneous strikes if their demands were not met.[2] If, on December 1, 1914, the railwaymen did not get what they wanted from the railway companies Britain would be faced with a general strike involving some 8,000,000 workers who made up the Triple Industrial Alliance. What the outcome would have been will never be known, for the First World War broke out in early August, 1914. Less than six months after the Dublin dispute, then, the Triple Industrial Alliance officially adopted a policy for which Larkin had been denounced as a revolutionary syndicalist.

The British tour was not a financial success, and the situation in Dublin was very discouraging. The Transport Union was shrunken in numbers and the treasury was practically empty. Now that the lockout was over and there was no longer any pressing need to preserve the solid phalanx of Labour opinion, some latent criticism of Larkin began to be heard. Most of it was oblique in nature and had more to do with Larkin's autocratic manner and his apparent inability to husband money than with any difference over principle. With the catastrophic losses the lockout entailed, it was only natural that Larkin's infallibility as a leader should be questioned. A man more politic and tactful would have realized that this was not the time to antagonize critical supporters by acting like an arbitrary tribal chieftain.

The 1914 meeting of the Irish Trades Union Congress demonstrated more than anything else the great gifts and the real faults of James Larkin. He was Chairman of the Congress, and his presidential address was perhaps the finest of his many remarkable

---

[1] A. Fenner Brockway, 'British Trade Unionists and Dublin,' *Labour Leader*, December 11, 1913.

[2] Elie Halévy, *History of the English People in the Nineteenth Century* (1952), VI, p. 486.

extemporaneous efforts. He began: 'Comrades—We are living in momentous times.'[1] 'We are now,' he continued amidst cheers, 'on the threshold of a newer movement, with a newer hope and a new inspiration. The best thanks we could offer those who went before and raised the Irish working class from their knees was to press forward with determination and enthusiasm towards the ultimate goal of their efforts . . . a "Co-operative Commonwealth for Ireland." ' Larkin then denounced the bigotry and intolerance that was dividing the country north and south. 'The question of religion,' he maintained, 'was a matter for each individual's conscience, and in a great many cases was the outcome of birth or residence in a certain geographical area.' 'Claiming for ourselves liberty of conscience, liberty to worship,' he continued, 'we shall see to it that every other individual enjoys the same right.' 'Intolerance,' he noted, 'has been the curse of our country. It is for us to preach the gospel of tolerance and comradeship for all women and men.' 'There must be freedom for all to live, to think, to worship,' he added amidst cheers and applause, 'no book, no avenue must be closed. By God's help, and the intelligent use of their own strong right arms they could accomplish great things.'[2]

Turning to the lockout, Larkin denounced it as a 'deliberate attempt to starve them into submission, and met with well deserved failure.' 'The workers,' he maintained, 'emerged from that struggle purified and strengthened, with a fierce determination and a fixed purpose.' 'The employers attitude,' continued Larkin, 'was a direct attack on the principles of trade unionism. The outcome of the attack had been the initiating of a new principle of solidarity inside the union, and for the first time in the history of the world of labour the beautiful and more human principle had received universal recognition. . . . "An Injury to One is the Concern of All." '[3] If 'solidarity' was their watchword, he added, a few years only would be necessary to regain 'the liberties curtailed by the most unscrupulous and most vindictive capitalist class that any country was ever cursed with.' Reminded of his standing enemies, Larkin began to castigate them all—'Police, politicians, the Press, and the judges on the bench were simply the tools of the employing class. No city in the world had a more useless or vicious capitalist class than that of Dublin.'[4]

[1] *Report of the Twenty-First Irish Trades Union Congress*, 1914, p. 32.
[2] *Ibid.*, pp. 32–33.　　　[3] *Ibid.*, p. 33.　　　[4] *Ibid.*, p. 35.

171

As an example of what he was talking about Larkin asked the delegates to

> Think of the treatment meted out to the soldiers in the industrial army by judges appointed for their political views (hear, hear). One of these judges gave two years hard labour to our comrade, Tom Daly, for a common assault on a scab; and the same judge in the same court gave a degenerate who ruined a child of seven years old a sentence of three months. That was the class war they had to submit to. The foul, putrid Press who told of the alleged attack by Daly published not a word about the foul creature who ruined a beautiful flower of womanhood in the Christian city (shame). Condemnation and calumny had been poured out upon the heads of the leaders of the working class. I, too, received more than my share. The agitator had been denounced by Press and pulpit, but thank God, the agitator was the salt of the earth (cheers).[1]

After an impassioned appeal for the support of the One Big Union, the Co-operative Commonwealth, and the newly formed Irish Labour Party, Larkin, winding up his address, said:

> I hope we will see the day when we will take full advantage of our opportunities, cry 'finis' to our differences, and obliterate all the jealousies from our ranks. Be truly Irish of the Irish. Give ear to all men who do worthy work (applause). Ireland must no longer be Niobe but Mercury amongst the Nations. Let us be comrades in the true sense of the word, and join with our brothers the world over to advance the cause of the class to which we belong. On that day we will put upon our escutcheon a mark worthy of the trust reposed upon us twenty-one years ago. We are entering upon a new era to do work worthy of the cause to which we are attached (hear, hear). Cathlin ni Houlihan calls upon us to abolish old jealousies, old intolerances that she may sit enthroned in the midst of the Western Sea (applause). I claim we have an opportunity given us of achieving much in the near future in our beloved country, to work for, and if needs be die, to win back, in the words of Erin's greatest living poet, for Cathlin ni Houlihan her four beautiful fields (loud and prolonged cheering).[2]

Both friend and foe at the Congress were impressed. In seconding the vote of thanks, one delegate remarked he 'had attended a few Congresses, both in England and Ireland, and that was the most remarkable address he had ever heard; it came from a remarkable

[1] *Report of the Twenty-First Irish Trades Union Congress*, 1914, p. 35.
[2] *Ibid.*, p. 38.

man.'[1] Thomas Johnson added 'the address would mark the Congress as historic. They had all been inspired by the idealistic fervour and the sound common sense.'[2] Larkin, with his characteristic abruptness, said, 'the best thanks was to get on with the work.'[3]

The sessions were stormy, and Larkin as Chairman was no mollifying factor. He interrupted on every issue and was seldom mindful of the impartiality of the chair. He berated the delegates for wasting too much time, and continually interrupted others himself. Connolly, O'Brien, and Johnson all became involved in wrangles with the chair. The attitude of the delegates was best expressed at the close of the Congress when the usual vote of thanks was proposed to the Chairman. Mr. Cassidy, in proposing the vote of thanks, noted that the 'manner' in which the Chairman carried on the work of the Congress 'had been unique.' Mr. Cassidy had only one objection, and that was the Chairman 'arrogated too much of the time. But all would confess that Mr. Larkin was an impartial Chairman. He had no respect for what delegate he sat upon.'[4] Another delegate from the Limerick Trades Council, in seconding the vote, described how his apprehensions about sitting 'under' Larkin had been dispelled, for he had 'found him a lamb.'[5]

O'Brien, who had crossed swords with Larkin several times in the course of the Congress, desired to be associated with the vote of thanks, and wryly commented that Larkin 'had certainly proved a remarkable Chairman, indeed a unique Chairman. He had made them revise all their dictionaries and all books written on rules of order. But they had put him in the chair, not because they thought he would make an ideal Chairman, but to honour him for his work for the Trades Union movement.'[6] Larkin, unabashed by all the criticism, remarked that he 'was glad someone had added salt to the soup. He did not thank them for eulogy; he was more used to other sorts of flattery. He was a strong man with any amount of confidence. He would love his enemies and beat his friends into doing things. All he thought of was principle, and when he took a line of action nothing would stop him.'[7]

The fact was that Larkin's confidence had been severely shaken. In the face of the responsibilities imposed by the losses in the lockout and his inability to recoup the losses by his personal tours in Britain, his optimistic buoyancy was a good deal less than it had

[1] *Report of the Twenty-First Irish Trades Union Congress*, 1914, p. 38.
[2] *Ibid.* [3] *Ibid.* [4] *Ibid.*, p. 104. [5] *Ibid.* [6] *Ibid.* [7] *Ibid.*

been. At the Congress Larkin was impossible, but the weight of the responsibilities over the previous eight months had frayed his nerves and warped his judgment. He came to see every legitimate criticism as a personal affront. The petty conflicts that in another day might have been seen in their proper perspective were all out of focus. A crisis was finally reached in the middle of June, 1914, when he resigned as General Secretary of the Transport Union and made plans to return to Liverpool.[1] A meeting of the Executive Committee of No. 1 Branch of the Union was called by Thomas Foran, the General President, to consider the resignation. They decided to call a general meeting of the membership and asked Larkin to present his resignation to them and explain his reasons for doing so.[2] At the general meeting in the Antient Concert Rooms in Dublin Larkin announced that:

> He was prepared to accept the verdict of the meeting as to what was going to take place in the future. There was a certain amount of discipline, honesty and loyalty wanting in their ranks. Those men who were the shouters at meetings and who cheered the loudest were some of those who had sold them in the past. He had not, however, contemplated resigning because of the existence of traitors like these, for they were not worthy of consideration. The Great Omnipotent chose twelve and one of the twelve betrayed Him. It would be too much to expect that an humble man like himself should not find a Judas in the ranks.[3]

'The whole history of this country in the past,' he went on to say, 'had taught him that what they greatly loved was to place a man high upon a pinnacle and then pull him down and destroy him.' At Croydon Park, Larkin continued, 'he had intended to start an open-air school for defective children and to establish a general clinic in Liberty Hall. The premises lately occupied by the Clyde Shipping Co. was to be converted into a dental surgery. They would then be in a position to minister to the health of the workers' families. It was proposed to have a nurse in attendance who could be sent into the working people's homes.' Larkin maintained he 'had given much attention to this scheme, and he had been promised the active cooperation from those from whom he had expected much, whilst the Committee of the Union were actually interfering with him and preventing his proposals from being carried out (Shame).' 'This

[1] *The Attempt to Smash, op. cit.*, Appendix IX, p. 131.
[2] *Ibid.*   [3] *Irish Worker*, June 27, 1914.

Committee,' he claimed, 'was penny-wise in regard to funds. Forgetting that all of these schemes was an essential part of their work, they disapproved of certain things he suggested because they failed to grasp the spirit of the work.'

> He now wanted their mandate approving of his work, and their declaration that he was the man in charge of their union (Loud Cheers); that no matter what forces were opposed to them he and their sons would work together from this onward (applause). He would forgive those members of the Union who had forgotten their positions, and he would appeal to the strong to let him deal fairly and leniently by the weak. . . . Let them remember the traditions of their race—how their fathers had gone forth wherever Cathlin ni Houlihan gave the call. . . . The working class had never betrayed her. All her ills and sorrows were the outcome of middle and so-called upper class treachery. They, the workers must realise themselves and rise to their responsibilities.[1]

Larkin was followed by Foran, who said he 'was proud to have been Larkin's servant and apprentice during the last seven years, and he had never betrayed his leader. On behalf of the Committee he wished to say . . . they were prepared to co-operate with him in the future in any scheme he took up (cheers).' The resignation was then burned 'amidst an indescribable scene of enthusiasm.' Larkin's position had never been threatened. As Connolly pointed out, in swearing his allegiance after Foran:

> If there were any friction it meant that the men to whom Larkin had given new power and dignity were taking active interest in every detail of the Union's work instead of leaving him to carry it all on his own shoulders. The price Jim had paid was that he had broken down physically, run down mentally, and almost worn out. Hence he did not realise himself that what he needed was a rest. Overstrained by anxiety, he perhaps saw opposition where there was only an anxious desire to help him.[2]

Connolly was right, and it was Larkin's desire to prove to himsel that he was still needed that led to his resignation. His depleted confidence needed this fresh avowal of loyalty on the part of his colleagues and followers.

Not only was Larkin's confidence in himself severely shaken during this period but his Socialist faith was put to the stiffest of tests in a

---

[1] *Irish Worker*, June 27, 1914.   [2] *Forward*, June 27, 1914.

most interesting and oblique way. The developing crisis over Home Rule resulted in a militant Nationalism putting every other idea and theme in Ireland in its awful shade. For some years past the legislative measure that was expected to solve all of Ireland's political, social, and economic problems was the Third Home Rule Bill. This faith in Home Rule was an accepted fact in Nationalist Ireland. Remove England's infectious hand and Ireland would flourish. All else must wait then, until the great political question as to who should govern Ireland be settled. In the spring of 1912 the Third Home Rule Bill was passed in the Commons and defeated in the Lords. The Bill was passed again in 1913 and again defeated in the Lords. In the summer of 1914 it was to be passed for the last time in the Commons, for the Parliament Act of 1911 had reduced the power of the House of Lords to a mere three-year suspensory veto. The Home Rule Bill was a modest recognition of Ireland's national aspirations. The proposed Irish Parliament was severely limited in matters concerning finance, religion, foreign affairs, and police power. The advantages were summed up in the guarantee of the Imperial Exchequer to make up the deficit in the Irish budget indefinitely if necessary. Because of the limitations imposed on the Irish Parliament Imperial representation would be reduced at Westminster. Instead of 103 seats, as formerly, the Irish would now have only 42. On the whole the proposed constitution gave Ireland a modest measure of local government.

It was surprising in fact that the Nationalists, and with them the Irish people, were willing to accept so modest a solution for so serious a problem. The moderate stand taken by the Nationalists was not appreciated by their Unionist fellow-countrymen. John Redmond, the Nationalist leader, who had finally persuaded the Irish people to unreservedly play the game of parliamentary politics and subordinate themselves to the law,[1] now found that the men who had for a lifetime been calling him a revolutionary were themselves now in the position of the pot calling the kettle black. The accredited leaders of the Unionist Party, Carson, Londonderry, Craig, and

---

[1] *Leader*, September 8, 1913. 'You cannot debase the currency in the matter of political ethics without doing hurt to the body politic. In England the militant and property-destroying Suffragettes quoted Carson, Larkin quoted Carson. Poor Carson is not a very helpful quotation, for Carson should have been disowned long ago by every respecter of constitutionalism and law and order.'

F. E. Smith, when faced with the probability of Home Rule, all began to spout revolution as the best way in which to express their loyalty to Crown and Empire. They maintained they would resist Home Rule by force if necessary. They went so far as to raise an army of Ulster Volunteers numbering 100,000 besides setting up a provisional government, which was to come into force the day Home Rule became law.

This turnabout would have been ludicrous if it had not been so serious. The whole situation presaged a civil war by 1914. For in answer to the Ulster Volunteers Redmond had taken over a Nationalist force raised in the South called the Irish Volunteers. Once again North and South, Protestant and Catholic, Unionist and Nationalist faced each other in uncompromising posture. The situation deteriorated rapidly in the early months of 1914. In March General Gough and a majority of his officers at the Curragh, a military camp in Kildare, took the unprecedented action of threatening to resign their commissions rather than receive orders to march against the Ulster Volunteers. The 'Curragh Mutiny' was still another anarchic sign of the times.[1] The following month the Ulster Volunteers succeeded in landing 40,000 German Mausers and a million rounds of ammunition despite a royal proclamation forbidding the importation of arms into Ireland. In the face of Unionist militancy the Liberal Government tried desperately to find a compromise solution. On March 9, 1914, the Prime Minister, Herbert Asquith, announced in the House of Commons that he would introduce an Amending Bill when the Home Rule Bill was read for the third and last time before becoming law. Redmond and the Irish Party were persuaded by Lloyd George to accept the compromise. Once again the Nationalists managed to keep Ireland quiet in the face of this proposal, which would, in effect, partition Ireland, in that Ulster could opt out for a period of six years.

Both Larkin and Connolly had welcomed Home Rule in 1912, but with qualifications. Larkin felt that under Home Rule Labour in Ireland would at last have a real chance. He thought sectarian intolerance would be dealt a final blow and the real issues involving social and economic reform would no longer be overshadowed by the national question. As the Bill progressed in Parliament Larkin was often critical but never condemnatory. His attitude from 1912 to 1914 was that Home Rule was the necessary beginning and certainly

[1] A. P. Ryan, *The Curragh Mutiny* (1956).

177

not the end.[1] The greatest bone of contention the Labour Movement had to pick with the Irish Party over the Home Rule Bill was the scheduling of seats in the proposed Irish Parliament. The schedule gave only 34 out of 164 seats to urban areas. This was only some 20 per cent of the total seats, while the portion of the population that was urban approached some 30 per cent of the total in Ireland. Larkin demanded a more equal distribution of seats and presented a revised schedule that would allow 51 urban seats rather than only 34. Since this amounted to about 30 per cent of the seats it was a much fairer distribution than the original schedule.[2]

In March, 1914, when Asquith had announced that he was considering, with Redmond's approval, the alternative of opting Ulster out of the Home Rule Bill for six years, the Irish Labour Movement protested vehemently. The Parliamentary Committee of the Irish Trades Union Congress, of which Larkin was Chairman, placed 'on record its emphatic protest against the suggested exclusion of any portion of Ireland, whether temporary or permanent, from the provisions of the Home Rule Bill, as we consider such exclusion would be a national disgrace. . . .' Further, the Parliamentary Committee, in denouncing the 'Curragh Mutiny,' remarked 'that in strongly and emphatically protesting against the recent attempt of certain military officers to utilize the armed forces in this country for the purpose of furthering the interests of their class, we desire to impress on the workers the necessity for learning aright and fully digesting the full significance of this action, and in future apply it in a similar manner in the interests of their own class.'[3]

In vain did Irish Labour appeal to their comrades in the British Labour Party. Relations between Irish and British Labour had been strained long before the Dublin lockout and Larkin's 'fiery cross' campaign. The trouble had sprung from the tendency of the Labour Party to take its lead on Irish matters from the Nationalist Party at Westminster. Larkin had personally protested in July, 1913, in London in the presence of Keir Hardie, Ramsay MacDonald,

[1] *Irish Worker*, April 13, 1912. 'Shall the Bill be a Final Settlement?' See also April 20, 1912; April 27, 1912. For more detailed criticism by Larkin see the *Irish Worker*, July 20, 1912. For Connolly's view see *The Workers' Republic; a selection from the writings of James Connolly* (1951), edited by Desmond Ryan, introduction by William McMullen, p. 98.

[2] *Report of the Twenty-First Irish Trades Union Congress*, 1914, pp. 1–2. For schedule see pp. 27–30.

[3] *Ibid.*, p. 18.

Henderson, and Roberts. He fulminated against their 'taking counsel with the Irish National Party on Labour matters or on questions affecting the workers in Ireland over the heads of the representatives of the Irish Trades Union Congress.'[1] Relations did not of course improve during the lockout, and most of the British labour leaders, especially Henderson, had little liking for the strong Nationalist point of view of the Irish labour leaders. He thought they should have a more international turn of mind, and was particularly anxious to define the relationship that would exist between the British Labour Party and the newly formed Irish Labour Party.[2]

Henderson was in fact trying to reduce the Irish Labour Party to a tail of the British Labour Party. The Irish labour leaders refused to countenance this and emphatically said so. It soon became evident that the British labour leaders had no intention of taking their lead from Irish Labour on Irish affairs at Westminster. When Connolly, in the columns of the Glasgow *Forward*, made some very pertinent remarks about the attitude of the British Labour Party towards the exclusion of Ulster and its travelling in the wake of the Irish Party, George Barnes answered him bluntly enough. Barnes admitted, 'I have taken my line, along with my colleagues, from the Irish Nationalists.' As to the proposed exclusion of Ulster, he remarked without a blush that 'It was a sheer waste of fact arguing about it. Nobody defends it on its merits. It is put forward as the price of peace. If peace is not bought by it, then it goes by the board.'[3] Chamberlain was no more explicit about Munich.

Larkin, however, did not see the danger of Ulster's exclusion as early or as clearly as did Connolly.[4] When one Ulster delegate to the June, 1914, Irish Trades Union Congress said it was a 'waste of time in making preparations for a Parliament to sit in Dublin, which Ulster would not have,' Larkin sarcastically asked, 'Who said Ulster men did not have a sense of humour?'[5] When another delegate suggested that civil war might be too high a price for a united Ireland, Larkin answered, 'It was the law of the world that those in power shall carry out the law, and that those who suffer should

---

[1] *Report of the Twenty-First Irish Trades Union Congress*, 1914, p. 2.
[2] *Ibid.*, pp. 4–10.
[3] *Socialism and Nationalism: a selection from the writings of James Connolly* (1948), edited with an introduction and notes by Desmond Ryan, p. 124.
[4] *Ibid.*, p. 109. See Connolly's articles in the *Forward* from March 21, 1914 on.
[5] Report I.T.U.C., 1914, *op. cit.*, p. 62.

break it. The cowardliness of the Government was responsible for the trouble in Ulster. He was an Ulsterman and he would put down civil war in an hour. They were determined that Ireland should not be dismembered.'[1] When, in the following month of July, it was announced that the Irish Party had accepted in effect the principle of partition, Larkin, who did not think such a thing was in the realm of possibility, nearly lost his reason. In an editorial in the *Irish Worker*, headed 'The Home Rule Betrayal,' he wrote:

> Ireland one and indivisible. That is the maxim of the Irish worker. Ireland one and indivisible is supposed to be the abiding principle of the Irish Parliamentary Party. . . . When the exclusion of Ulster was first mooted they expressed their determination that they would not abate one jot of their demands. They are in as strong a position now as they were then. But nevertheless it is practically agreed that they will now accept the Bill as bad as it was, with the exclusion of Ulster for a period. But what is not understood is, that if any part of Ulster votes itself out of the Bill that part can only come with the consent of the Imperial Parliament with a smaller Irish representation. . . .[2]

Larkin closed this editorial with a romantically ominous threat, 'We can only say that if the workers of Ireland stand idly by whilst they are being betrayed, they get what they deserve, and only that. Our fathers died that we might be free men. Are we going to allow their life sacrifice to be as naught? Or are we going to follow in their footsteps at the Rising of the Moon?'[3] Some weeks later Larkin's threat became less romantic and more ominous. 'What an awakening,' he wrote, 'some poor witless creatures who still believe in political action have received . . . constitutional law is a myth—the old law of the jungle still prevails! Force is still the remedy! The justice of a cause is a very nice thing to talk about and sing about! But the power to act and the courage to act gives one a right to shout.'[4]

The quarrel over partition was at this juncture overshadowed by an even greater calamity as far as Irish Labour was concerned. On August 4, 1914, Britain declared war on Germany. Redmond spontaneously announced in the House of Commons that Ireland stood solidly beside Britain in that momentous crisis. The Irish people fully approved of Redmond's action in committing them to support the war. Though all Ireland was in Redmond's arms Larkin did not

[1] Report I.T.U.C., 1914, *op. cit.*, p. 73. [2] *Irish Worker*, July 11, 1914.
[3] *Ibid.* [4] *Ibid.*, July 25, 1914.

waver an instant. He denounced the war and denounced, still more, Ireland's participation in it. 'Oh Irishmen, dear countrymen,' he pleaded, 'take heed of what we say, for if you do England's dirty work you will surely rue the day.' His advice was to 'Stop at home. Arm for Ireland. Fight for Ireland and no other land.'[1] That Larkin had other ideas as to what the war might mean to Ireland's future was evident when he asked his countrymen to realize 'that England's need is Ireland's opportunity.'[2]

The stand against the war took a great deal of courage, for the opponents of the war were indeed a lonely minority. The war mania was running high in the early days as Larkin remarked, 'One could not recognize this country at present as Ireland.'[3] Again and again, week in and week out, Larkin pleaded with his countrymen in the name of Ireland. 'Let the political compromisers and the hireling press,' he wrote, 'sell themselves for thirty pieces of silver. It is for you to remember the great Queen who has drunk the waters of bitterness for eight hundred years! Surely you will not disgrace the fathers that bore you? They suffered and died that she "Our Dark Rosaleen," might enter into her inheritance.'[4]

Larkin, however, was no pacifist. He was aware, as he said himself, that 'there were times when war was essential—times when a man must defend himself.' 'Such a time, however,' he added, 'had not yet arisen in Ireland.'[5] After the initial shock had passed Larkin did not slacken his pace. His *Irish Worker* was a *mélange* of anti-war propaganda and denunciations of the Irish Party. He organized gigantic anti-war demonstrations in Dublin and made anti-war speeches at every opportunity. When Redmond began to urge Irishmen to enlist in the British Army this was too much for Larkin. 'England might pass Conscription Acts,' he declared, confusing things a little, 'but not all her fleet would take him.'[6] In identifying himself with the nation and denouncing the Irish Party Larkin said, 'Ireland had always been the Ishmael of the nations—always betrayed by her own sons.'[7] As Redmond pushed the recruiting campaign in Ireland Larkin frantically denounced him as the 'Irish Judas.' 'Are we to be sold like dumb driven dogs?' he asked. 'Is this to be another garden of Gethsemani?' 'With this difference,' he

---

[1] *Irish Worker*, August 8, 1914. [2] *Ibid.*
[3] *Ibid.*, August 22, 1914. [4] *Ibid.*, August 15, 1914.
[5] *Ibid.*, August 22, 1914. [6] *Ibid.*, August 29, 1914.
[7] *Ibid.*, August 22, 1914.

answered, 'instead of Christ betrayed, a nation betrayed. Is there no man to provide a rope and a tree for this twentieth century Judas?'[1] When Larkin finally closed his comments on the 'Irish Judas' it was with a treatise entitled 'Redmond Eats His Own Vomit.'[2]

For a long while Larkin had been moving towards 'direct action.' The defeat of the Transport Union, the proposed partition of Ireland, the coming of the war, and Ireland's participation in it resulted in Larkin losing faith in constitutional methods, and he became more and more outspoken on the side of physical force. He began by pointing out that Ireland 'had now the finest chance she had for centuries.'[3] In a speech before 7,000 people in O'Connell Street he announced that the Transport Union was prepared to do all it could to facilitate the landing of rifles in Ireland.[4] He wound up the meeting by asking 'all who are going to take part in the coming fight—our fight—to hold up their hands.'[5] In appealing for recruits for his Citizen Army Larkin made Ireland the new mystical body, as he warned, 'You may have to seal your faith, love and loyalty for her in your blood.' 'Remember,' he asked, quoting Macaulay of all people—

How can man die better than facing fearful odds,
For the ashes of his fathers and the Temples of his Gods.

Larkin closed this 'hymn' by reminding his listeners, 'To enlist for Catlin-Ni-Houlihan may mean a dark and narrow cell for your body, but think of the great joy it will bring to your soul.'[6]

Catlin-Ni-Houlihan had, indeed, replaced Christ as a devotional symbol. But more important still was the fact that for Larkin she had now replaced the working classes, who had always stood highest on his altar. This shift in emphasis in Larkin's point of view was subtle, and undoubtedly he was unaware of it himself. Still it was

---

[1] *Irish Worker*, September 27, 1914.   [2] *Ibid.*, October 17, 1914.
[3] *Ibid.*, August 29, 1914.
[4] Fred Bower, *Rolling Stonemason* (1936), p. 218. 'Some time before he went to America, Jim had sent me an address in Liverpool where I was to call for six guns and ship them to Ireland. Being by now in a small tombstone business, I took a crate to the place and packed the guns carefully in the case, which I addressed on my business cards showing a tombstone printed on them, and labelled the crate "Tombstone, With Care." In the bottom of the crate was laid a slab of stone one inch thick, then the guns, then another slab an inch thick. This crate was handled at the Dublin docks by the men of Jim's union. . . .'
[5] *Irish Worker*, September 5, 1914.   [6] *Ibid.*, October 10, 1914.

no longer the working classes, the class from which he had sprung, that gave all the meaning to his life and his work. For now he wrote, 'one thought only should inspire that work—namely that the results of my efforts and labour during life . . . in every field of activity, should have for its object the advancement of Ireland. . . .'[1] Indicative of this unconscious change in Larkin's thinking was his new arrangement of national heroes. No longer were the social revolutionaries Lalor and Davitt the first off his lips or his pen but rather the heroes of national resistance and insurrection—Wolfe Tone, Emmet, and Dwyer. In asking, 'Emmet or Redmond, Which the Traitor?' Larkin readily answered, 'Emmet, in life, in death, we are one with you.'[2] In an appeal to history a week later Larkin rolled out the whole catalogue, 'Let your answer ring in no uncertain tone, let it vibrate throughout the universe. Throw the lie back in Redmond's throat; tell Asquith what Red Hugh told Perrot; what Owen Roe told Munroe; what Emmet told Norbury; tell him what Michael Dwyer told the hired assassins when called on to surrender, "Never; we defy you in the name of Ireland." '[3] Larkin, too, had finally been swallowed by the National Being, but the great question remained—would he prove digestible?

This ascendancy of Nationalism for a time over Socialism in Larkin's mind is important in understanding how he was able to claim to be at one and the same time a Nationalist, a Socialist, and a Catholic. How, indeed, could a man harmonize the three most dissonant themes of his day and yet remain over the long run true to himself? The answer of course is that Larkin would never have allowed the assumption that there was any necessary conflict between these ideas. Was he simply deluding himself then? No, for Larkin was doing what Irishmen had been doing for over a century with regard to Nationalism and Catholicism. Out of a very respectable historical tradition, he maintained that there was no necessary contradiction, and then merely added another dimension—Socialism. Further, like a good many other men of action, he had a habit of compartmentalizing his ideas and therefore never was bothered about the rather subtle and complex relationships that may exist between things.

All this of course does not obviate the basic question of whether

[1] *Irish Worker*, September 5, 1914.
[2] *Ibid.*, September 19, 1914.
[3] *Ibid.*, September 26, 1914.

or not Nationalism, Socialism, and Catholicism were mutually contradictory. All it does explain is that Larkin took up his ground on a very real historical tradition and struck a mental attitude that might have been legitimate, even if limited. Suffice it to say, if the relative harmony that exists in Great Britain, Ireland, and most Western European countries today between these three themes is any indication, then Larkin, Connolly, and generations of Irishmen have been historically, if not logically justified. When Larkin left Ireland for the United States in late 1914, however, for a speaking tour to raise funds for his Transport Union and the Irish Labour Movement, he found that his Nationalism, Socialism, and Catholicism did not harmonize nearly as well in an American atmosphere as it had in an Irish one.

PART FOUR

Bolshevik, 1914–1923

IX

THE WAR

WHEN he arrived in America Larkin expected to stay only long enough to complete a lecture tour yet he remained nearly eight and a half years. What happened to him over this period significantly enough is what happened to a large part of the world Socialist Movement. The failure of Socialists everywhere in August, 1914, to do anything to prevent the war was a demoralizing blow to the international Socialist Movement. Not only did their failure reveal that the Movement was merely a giant with feet of clay, but more— that the faithful were weak in their faith. They had failed in the moment of crisis to meet the ascendent heresy, Nationalism. The shame was not so much that the working classes the world over could be duped into making unnatural war on each other, but rather that Socialists could be found everywhere urging them to it. Those Socialists who opposed the war held to their faith with an obstinacy that was compelling. In their dwindling numbers, in the face of a patriotic persecution, they were determined to hold to their faith, confident of better days.

The unexpected success of the Bolsheviki in the November Revolution in Russia in 1917 was more to these beleaguered Socialists than the triumph of the Social Revolution and the ushering in of the millennium. To them it was more than an historical justification; it was deeply personal as well. The historical justification they had been sure of, for that was the basis of their faith, but that it should come precisely in their time of trial and vindicate them in their hour of need, was more than they had ever expected or even hoped. When, however, those who had been blind refused to see the light and only redoubled their fury against those who had revealed the truth the disappointment was cruel. Still, confident in their convictions, and clothed in the garment of the whole truth, these Socialists met the new persecution with a renewed vigour and offered up their martyrs with a sublime trust in the triumph of their truth. Larkin was one among the many who fought the good fight and suffered in the name of the cause in these years. For the four years that the war continued he agitated and worked against it. The price he paid was poverty, loneliness, and persecution. But it was a small equivalent to him when the faith was put in the balance. Larkin embraced the idea of the Bolshevik Revolution with a fervour that would have made St. Paul tremble with ecstasy. For this the price he paid was almost three years in prison on top of the poverty and loneliness. Again he paid the price without regret or complaint.

When Larkin arrived in New York in early November, 1914, he was already comparatively well known to the American public. His activities in Dublin during the lockout of the preceding year had been well reported in America as well as in Europe. American journals and newspapers, ranging from the radical and near revolutionary *International Socialist Review* published in Chicago, to the more sober and respectable *New York Times* had given Larkin and his activities a surprising amount of coverage. During the Dublin lockout Larkin had emerged as an outstanding personality in the Labour world with an international reputation.[1]

On his arrival he pleased almost all varieties and shades of American Socialist opinion by his violent and vehement denunciations of the war then raging in Europe. These Socialists viewed the war simply as a jingo-imperialist venture engineered by a capitalist clique to the shame of the international Socialist Movement. Larkin's appeal to Americans to stay out of the war also pleased both the Irish- and German-Americans. These hyphenated groups applauded Larkin's stand on the war, but each in its own interest. To the Irish England's difficulty was ever Ireland's opportunity while to the Germans it was a matter of *sub rosa* nationalism. Thus the Irish and

---

[1] *International Socialist Review*, William E. Bonn, 'Home Despotism in Ireland,' November, 1913; Caroline Nelson, 'Jim Larkin,' December, 1913; William E. Bonn, 'The Fiery Cross in Ireland and England,' January, 1914; William D. Haywood, 'Jim Larkin's Call for Solidarity,' February, 1914. *New York Times*, September 19; October 3; November 10, 13, 14, 15, 17, 20, 23, and 24; December 25, 26, 27, 29, and 31. *New York Tribune*, September 19, 1913. *New York Sun*, November 20, 1913. *The Masses*, 'Larkinism,' January, 1914.

the Germans in America as well as the Socialists agreed that the
United States should stay out of the war.

Larkin wasted no time in getting his views on the war on record.
Soon after his arrival he gave an exclusive interview to the New York
Call, a Socialist daily.[1] 'We realize in Ireland,' said Larkin, edi-
torializing freely, 'that this war is only the outcome of capitalistic
aggression, and the desire to capture home and foreign markets.
Behind the gods of militarism is a foul, grasping and vicious and
inhuman power, the god of Mammon.' He went on to 'hope' that
his 'American brothers' realized that 'though not actively engaged
in the field of battle they are affected in their economic life and that
England's two thousand millions of capital, which is operating to
the detriment of the American workers has a strangle-hold on the
economic life of this great continent. We in the British Isles realize
that the greatest factor for peace and the betterment of human
society will be an intelligent protest by the American working class.'
In closing the interview Larkin offered a potpourri of recently
acquired American quotations to emphasize his point. 'Sherman's
word has proven true—all war is hell.' 'We have got to realize the
truth of Lowell's statement right here and now, that "He who takes
a sword and draws it and goes sticks a feller through—government
ain't goin ter pay for it—God'll send the bill to you." '

Several days later before some 15,000 Socialists and sympathizers
gathered in Madison Square Garden to celebrate the victory of
Meyer London, Socialist Congressman—elect from New York City,
Larkin was among the notables who paid vocal tribute. On rising to
speak, he was given a great ovation. 'Women and men of the City
of New York,' he began, 'I want to congratulate the Comrades on
the work they have done. Remember Comrades, this is only an
entering wedge. The citadel of capitalism still remains. The task
before you is great. You must realize the great responsibility that
faces you. It takes great men and women to stand up and say "We're
Socialists." We are fighting to abolish this system of exploitation.
You have the power within yourselves to make Socialists of the
people who have the right to vote.'[2] He then turned quickly to the
subject of the war and told the gigantic meeting that 'there is no real
labor movement in Great Britain, now that the Labor unionists
have become staunch supporters of the war.' He castigated those
labour leaders in Britain who were 'on the platform advising the

[1] *New York Call*, November 7, 1914.   [2] *Ibid.*, November 9, 1914.

workers to enlist in the army to become cannon fodder.' 'My God,' exclaimed Larkin, 'what a crime! We Socialists are against war on the field of battle. We are also against a more brutal war, the war of capital against the men who are oppressed and who have only their labor power to sell.' 'We Socialists,' he closed exultingly, 'want more than a dollar increase for the workers. We want the earth.'

Among the Irish-Americans Larkin also opposed the war, but his change in emphasis was obvious. In the year preceding his American tour, and especially since the outbreak of the war, it has already been noticed that Nationalism was the idea to which Larkin seemed most attached. His violent espousal of revolutionary Nationalism in Ireland had won for him the approval of Thomas J. Clarke, head of the secret, oath-bound Irish Republican Brotherhood, and the man most responsible for the coming Easter Rising in Dublin in 1916. Larkin had received a note from Clarke introducing him to John Devoy, who edited the *Gaelic American*, a New York weekly. Devoy controlled the *Clan-na-Gael*, the front organization for the Brotherhood in the United States. The note simply asked Devoy to do all he could for Larkin. Devoy responded immediately in the *Gaelic American* by announcing, 'no man in Ireland had been more abused or misrepresented by the capitalists and their friends for his advocacy of the workers' cause than Jim Larkin, and nobody connected with the labor movement there has done as much to improve the condition of the men who toil as he has.'[1]

Devoy invited Larkin to address a meeting in honour of the Manchester Martyrs for the Irish Volunteer Fund Committee. The proceeds of the meeting were to be used to buy arms for the Irish Volunteers in Ireland, a para-military organization actually controlled by Clarke and the I.R.B. The Manchester Martyrs, Allen, Larkin, and O'Brien, had been hanged in 1867 for their part in rescuing two Fenian prisoners, in the act of which a police sergeant was accidentally shot and killed. The speech was another of Larkin's remarkable extemporaneous efforts and is quoted from at length because it was typical of his approach to the Irish-Americans during this period.

I call to your memories tonight the three men who died in Manchester prison on that dark and gloomy morning in 1867—Allen, Larkin and O'Brien. They came from a class of men who have always been true

---

[1] *Gaelic American*, November 14, 1914.

to Ireland and who never failed her yet—the men of the working class. There is one grand, glorious page in Irish history that has never yet been turned down or besmirched, and that is the page that records in undying words the fact that the Irish working class never deserted her or betrayed her. . . .

It takes great strength, great courage to be a man, and those men were born of a race that never lacked in courage. We make mistakes, we have our faults, and God knows some of us have more than our share, but when danger threatens and duty calls, we go smiling to our own funeral. . . .

Larkin, Allen and O'Brien are dead—so they say. It is not true. Larkin, Allen and O'Brien live, and not only in the spirit, but in the flesh, because of you who are here to-night. While there is one man left in Ireland who defied the British Government, Ireland is not conquered, and Allen, Larkin and O'Brien are not dead. True there are some, a few, a very few, Irishmen who would sell their birthright—aye, and they would sell the mother who bore them—but, thank God, the heart of Ireland is true and strong. She still breeds men determined some day to break the shackles and stand erect as free-born men. . . .

Speaking generally of the country, I assure you that the workers of Ireland are on the side of the dear, dark-haired mother, whose call they never failed to answer yet.

We have altogether about 5,000 rifles. We have few bayonets. We have little ammunition; that is the only difficulty we have. We have got the men. Believe me, and I would not deceive you, the men who are in our movement in Ireland—the men who are the backbone of any movement—are solid and united and are only waiting for a defeat of some magnitude when the word will go out again; again will the call ring out over hill and dale to the men who always answered the call of Caithlin-ni-Houlihan.

Are we not worthy of our fathers? The purpose of this meeting to-night is not merely to listen to the singing, which has been very beautiful and very stimulating. You have come here to-night whole-heartedly and earnestly, determined to fight and work, and sometimes it is harder to work than to fight. My appeal to you is: Give us money or give us guns, and by the Living God who gave us life we'll not fail you and we'll not fail the mother of our race, I plead with you. You do not know the times you are living in.

For seven hundred long and weary years, we have waited for this hour. The flowing tide is with us and we deserve to be relegated to oblivion if we are not ready for the 'Rising of the Moon'.[1]

---

[1] *Gaelic American*, November 21, 1914.

This speech made an enormous impression, and Devoy immediately invited Larkin to speak for the *Clan-na-Gael* in Philadelphia in honour of the Manchester Martyrs. The meeting was to be unique in that representatives of the German-American National Alliance were to speak along with the Irish. Larkin covered much the same ground as he had in New York, but was much more pointed in his remarks about Britain:

> Why should Ireland fight for Britain in this war? What has Britain ever done for our people? Whatever we got from her we wrested with struggle and sacrifice. No, men and women of the Irish race, we shall not fight for England. We shall fight for the destruction of the British Empire and the construction of an Irish republic. We shall not fight for the preservation of the enemy, which has laid waste with death and desolation the fields and hills of Ireland for 700 years. We will fight to free Ireland from the grasp of that vile carcase called England.[1]

At this critical moment 'Larkin, bitter, acrid, quivering with emotion finished his plea . . . the curtains rolled back and the audience leaped to its feet with cheers at the spectacle. A company of Irish Volunteers, with guns at present arms faced a company of German Uhlans with drawn swords.'[2]

The attempt to maintain a position in two camps so utterly divergent in their basic views as the Socialists and the hyphenated Americans would have been near impossible for a man with far greater tact and patience than Larkin. In no time he found that in pleasing everyone he ended by pleasing no one. Among the Socialists he found it necessary to defend himself against the pro-German label that was being applied to him. Some two months after his arrival he had to assure a large gathering of Socialists that, 'I have been accused of being pro-German, but I am not for the Kaiser any more than I am for George Wettin of England.'[3] 'I am,' he continued, 'for the working classes of every country. The English working class is as dear to me as that of my own country or any other, but the Government of England is the vilest thing on the face of the earth.'

Still, the grounds for the pro-German label were better than even the Socialists knew. Not only did Larkin associate and speak from the same platform with prominent German-Americans and well-known German agents in this country, but he was acquainted on

[1] W. E. Walling, *The Socialists and the War* (New York, 1915), p. 339.
[2] *Gaelic American*, December 5, 1914.   [3] *Call*, January 8, 1915.

an intimate level with the negotiations going on between the Imperial German Government and Sir Roger Casement on behalf of the Irish Republic, 'now virtually established.' Larkin and Devoy were at Judge Daniel F. Cohalan's house the night Professor Kuno Meyer, the noted German Celtic scholar, arrived from Germany with Casement's initial message.[1] Moreover, at the Manchester Martyrs meeting in Philadelphia in late November, 1914, when Irish- and German-Americans spoke from the same platform, Larkin was introduced to the German and Austrian consuls.[2] Immediately on his return to New York he was contacted by Captains Von Papen and Boy-ed, military attachés assigned to the German Embassy. In a long private conversation with Captain Boy-ed Larkin was informed that an alliance existed between the Irish-Americans and the Germans, which operated under three main headings—open propaganda in the interests of the Central Powers, joint political pressure in Washington through Irish- and German-American political organizations, and 'a special secret department charged with hindering or interfering with the transportation of supplies.'[3] Boy-ed explained he was not yet at liberty to reveal the extent of his plans because he understood that Larkin was not subject to the discipline of the Irish revolutionary organization, and the Irish leaders therefore refused to take any responsibility for his actions. However Boy-ed expected a freer hand as soon as new instructions, personnel, and credit arrived from Germany. In the meantime he offered to put Larkin on the payroll at $200 per week, but Larkin refused.

Shortly before Christmas, 1914, Larkin was again contacted by Boy-ed who proposed without much ado that he engage in sabotage

[1] MS., Letter from John Devoy to Frank Robbins, September 21, 1923, *National Library of Ireland*, 2112. Courtesy of William O'Brien.

[2] MS., 'Affidavit of Mr. James Larkin, No. 990—A, dated January 22, 1934, 24 pages,' R.G. 76, *Record of Boundary and Claims Commissions and Arbitrations*, National Archives, Department of State, Washington, D.C., p. 2. Hereafter referred to as 'Affidavit.' Larkin made this affidavit at the request of John J. McCloy, who represented the United States in a suit against the German Government before the Mixed Claims Commission in 1936, involving some $40,000,000 in claims for damages for alleged German sabotage during the First World War. See *New York Times*, March 1, 1936. The 'Affidavit,' which has never been made public, is an account of Larkin's association with German agents in the United States and Mexico between 1914 and the end of 1917. The 'Affidavit' is corroborated by what independent evidence is available, and is generally accurate considering the interval of sixteen years.

[3] *Ibid.*, pp. 2–3.

for the Germans on the waterfront. Larkin explained that he was already engaged in organizing stoppages in key industries through the trade unions and his newly organized Four Winds Fellowship. The latter was an organization which had recently been founded by Larkin and open only to trade unionists and Socialists born in the British Empire, who pledged themselves to oppose the British Government during the war. Boy-ed continued to press for sabotage, and Larkin explained that his views would not allow him to have hand or part in the destruction of human life in this way. He further explained that he only assisted the Germans to the extent that a German military victory would contribute to Irish independence. 'My object,' said Larkin, 'was to see a deadlock arrived at, hoping that the workers would revolt in the several countries.'[1]

If Larkin's differences with the American Socialists had been limited to his supposed pro-German sympathies there would have been little difficulty. A good many American Socialists, it seems, could not understand how Larkin could be at one and the same time a professed Catholic and a practising Socialist. This difference, involving Larkin's religious convictions, pre-dated his arrival in the United States. During the 'fiery cross' campaign in Britain Larkin refused to speak at a Socialist rally because he objected to the chairman. The story that made the rounds in America was that Larkin refused to speak because the man in question was divorced. Larkin did not dignify the *canard* with a reply but later explained the incident to a close friend.[2] The reason he had refused to speak, Larkin explained, was not that the man was divorced, but rather that he had treated his wife in a most shameful fashion that was unworthy of a Socialist. Upton Sinclair, novelist, poet, and Socialist, wrote a long letter to the *New York Times* protesting that Larkin's seemingly narrow and parochial views on marriage were not representative of the Socialist Movement.[3] Despite his 'bad press' on this issue, Larkin at one of his first meetings in New York, 'shocked a Socialist audience by unbuttoning his shirt and producing a golden cross. Holding the cross before him he shouted at the audience, the large majority of whom were not Irish and decidedly atheistic, "There is no antagonism between the cross and Socialism. A man can pray to Jesus and be a better militant Socialist for it. There is no conflict between the

[1] *Ibid.*, p. 5.
[2] Jack Carney, personal interview.
[3] *New York Times*, December 31, 1913.

religion of the Catholic Church and Marxism. I stand by the cross and Marx. I belong to the Catholic Church. In Ireland that is not held against a Socialist. I defy any man to challenge my standing as a socialist and a revolutionist!" ' [1]

That Larkin's Catholicism was not much appreciated by the American Socialists was made amply clear when he felt called upon to defend himself some months after his arrival. He protested that:

> In fact I have never found more bigotry and intolerance than I have found among a certain wing of the Socialist party. I know whereof I speak for I have been made to suffer for this intolerance as an Irishman and a Catholic, but as I understand it, it is impossible to believe in the economic doctrine of Socialism and still worship what God or gods one pleases where and how one pleases.
>
> There are Jews, Protestants, agnostics and secularists, sectarians of all kinds within the ranks of the party. If we are to have a real international movement, there must be room in it for the Catholic worker too. A short time ago, I asked a man here, a Socialist, why something was not done about organizing the subway workers, and he replied it was useless since they were Irish and Catholic. Well on investigation, it turns out they are 16 per cent Jewish, 20 per cent Italian, 40 per cent Irish and the rest American Born. But suppose they were all Irish and Catholic? Aren't you going to organize them? Are the Capitalists losing any chance of getting these people? I deny that it is any harder to organize Irish Catholics than any other people, and I know because that has been my work. [2]

As if Larkin's Irish Nationalism, which was too easily translated into a pro-Germanism, and his open profession of Catholicism were not enough, he succeeded now in antagonizing the very powerful right wing of the American Socialist Party. The Executive Committee of the New York City Socialist Party stated in answer to Larkin that the truth was that the Socialist Party could not organize Catholics, not that they would not. 'The fact is,' said the Committee, 'that we have found it extremely difficult to organize Catholic workmen owing to the strong anti-socialist attitude of the Catholic Clergy.' [3] Probably more important than the influence of the Clergy

---

[1] Benjamin Gitlow, *The Whole of Their Lives* (1948), pp. 38–39.

[2] *Call*, January 18, 1915.

[3] Executive Committee, *New York City Socialist Party*, Minutes, January 25, 1915, p. 83 (The Tamiment Institute Library, New York City). I am obliged to Melvyn Dubofksy, University of Rochester, for calling this to my attention.

was the fact that the Irish in New York had very effective representation in the Democratic Party. In any case the section that controlled the Socialist Party in 1914 did not look with favour on syndicalist ideas on 'direct action' at the expense of 'political action.' When he arrived Larkin was shrewd enough not to be drawn into the doctrinaire wrangle on 'direct' and 'indirect action.' He took the commonsense view that the course of action in a given situation depended on the terrain. 'Political action,' he announced in his initial *Call* interview, 'while an important working class weapon, and to be used whenever possible will not avail the Irish workers much. . . .'[1] At the Madison Square Garden meeting, a few days later, he said, 'I believe that the workers should use every weapon against the entrenched powers of capitalism. I am an industrialist and at the same time appreciate the fact that labor can accomplish great things through the intelligent use of the ballot. Why use one arm when you have two? Why not strike the enemy with both arms—the political and the economic?'[2]

Still, Larkin's reputation as a revolutionary syndicalist had preceded him, and his close associations and contacts among the most militant section of the American Labour Movement, the Industrial Workers of the World (I.W.W.), did not endear him to the right wing. Larkin seemed to have been aware that on entering the American arena there would be factions vying for his favour. In an effort to line up speaking engagements before his arrival, Larkin wrote Con Lehane that, 'I am not going to speak for any Section; I am prepared to speak to any Section.'[3] Through chance more than design Larkin's chief personal contacts in the United States were of the militant variety closely associated with I.W.W. Through Connolly Larkin contacted Patrick L. Quinlan.[4] Quinlan and Connolly had founded the Irish Socialist Federation some years before Connolly returned to Ireland in 1910. By 1914 Quinlan was prominent as a labour agitator and strike organizer. When Larkin arrived he was out on bail awaiting a decision on his appeal to the New Jersey

[1] *Call*, November, 7 1914.

[2] *Ibid.*, November 9, 1914.

[3] *The Attempt to Smash the Irish Transport and General Workers' Union* (1924), Appendix P, p. 165. Letter from James Larken to Con Lehane, July 1, 1914. For short biography of Lehane see *Sunday Call*, October 4, 1914. Edmond McKenna, 'A new Spirit in Old Ireland.'

[4] *Ibid.*, p. 166. Letter from James Larkin to Patrick L. Quinlan, August 12, 1914.

State Supreme Court. He had received a two to seven year sentence
the previous year for his part in the Paterson silk strike.[1]

Connolly had also given Larkin the address of the Flynns in the
Bronx. Thomas Flynn's daughter, Elizabeth Gurley Flynn, though
still in her early twenties, had already made a national reputation as a
strike organizer. She had come into prominence in the Lawrence
mill strike of 1912, and had been arrested with Quinlan in the Paterson strike in 1913 but had not been prosecuted.[2] Larkin frequently
visited the Flynn home and often stayed for tea. Catherine, Elizabeth's sister, tells how Larkin was shocked when they smoked
cigarettes after tea on one of his first visits and later cautioned
Mrs. Flynn about allowing her daughters such 'free ways.'[3] Larkin
was also known to be a close friend of 'Big Bill' Haywood, the one-
eyed and one-time organizer of the Western Federation of Miners
and outstanding personality in the I.W.W.[4] They had met in England
while Larkin was on his 'fiery cross' campaign. Haywood had been
in France inspecting the French syndicalist movement and had
hurried across the channel with a donation of 1,000 francs from the
syndicalist controlled *Confédération Générale du Travail* to the
locked-out workers of Dublin.

To add to the company he kept, Larkin had the misfortune a few
weeks after his arrival to attend a meeting of the I.W.W. and make
a speech that was almost criminally misquoted in the *New York
Tribune*. He attended the meeting primarily out of curiosity and
had no intention of making a speech. He was immediately recognized
and asked to speak. Though he demurred at first he was finally
persuaded. A reporter for the *Tribune* made it appear from his report
of Larkin's speech that he was nothing less than an out-and-out,
bomb-throwing anarchist. As an appetizer Larkin was reported to
have advocated bomb-throwing as a prime method of settling
industrial disputes. He was then represented as offering for the main
course the project of burning New York City to the ground. Dessert

---

[1] *Call*, January 25, March 15, 1915. Quinlan had to serve a two to seven year
sentence. Elizabeth Gurley Flynn and 'Big Bill' Haywood were also indicted with
Quinlan, but Miss Flynn's jury disagreed, and the charge against Haywood was
dropped.

[2] Elizabeth Gurley Flynn, *I Speak my Own Piece* (1955), p. 173.

[3] Catherine Gurley Flynn. Telephone interview.

[4] William D. Haywood, *Bill Haywood's Book* (1929). See also his article
'Jim Larkin's Call for Labor Solidarity,' *International Socialist Review*, February,
1914.

appeared in the form of his having allegedly insulted the American flag by referring to it as 'that rag.' In a letter to the *Tribune* Larkin denied categorically the allegations made and demanded that the reports of his alleged speech be corrected:

I do not object to honest criticism of myself as a factor in public life.

I do very strenuously protest against deliberate lies manufactured to place me in a false position before the American public. I did not say as the Tribune reported me as saying last Friday at a meeting in Manhattan Lyceum, that the whole of New York ought to be burnt up. . . .

I may be considered a crank or a faddist, but I am not prepared to assume responsibility for the vivid imagination of your reporter. My reference to 'that rag' applied to the Union Jack and dealt with the crimes of bloodlust and race destruction perpetuated by its up-holders.

No working-class organization or propagandists ever advocated bomb-throwing as a remedy for the evils of capitalism; on the contrary, I pointed out that in the European holocaust the bomb thrower who, from his aviation machine, destroyed human life or property was considered a hero and decorated with Victoria or Iron Crosses by the capitalist Governments engaged in the war. . . .

In conclusion, I expect this correction and repudiation to receive the same publicity as the report of my alleged speech.[1]

This original *Tribune* report was widely circulated and, needless to say, the adverse publicity did not endear him to his new-found American friends, Socialist or Irish. The Socialist New York *Call* studiously ignored the whole affair, trusting, it may be supposed, that the faithful were too loyal to read anything else. Gradually announcements of Larkin's speaking engagements became fewer in the *Call*, even when the *Gaelic American* was still carrying notices and reports of what were Socialist meetings rather than Irish.[2] To Devoy's credit the *Gaelic American* did the best it could to curb the effect of the *Tribune*'s reporting. In his editorial columns Devoy levelled the most damning accusation possible by an Irishman against the *Tribune*. He accused that paper of being, 'since this war began . . . simply an English hireling.'[3]

Despite Devoy's efforts, however, the fat was in the fire, for John T. Keating wrote to Devoy from Chicago that the 'Larkin slander was damaging, and it is so hard to overtake such. It was in every news-

[1] *Gaelic American*, December 5, 1914.
[2] *Ibid.*, January 30, February 6, 1915.
[3] *Ibid.*, December 5, 1914.

paper here.'[1] Larkin further narrowed his opportunities to speak under *Clan-na-Gael* auspices by alienating a good many local Clans when he did speak. Years later Devoy complained in a private letter:

> We recommended our friends everywhere to support him and in most places they did, but at a very early stage, he turned them against him by making public attacks on the *Clan-na-Cael* because of yarns given to him by some local Socialists who had personal grudges. Without making the slightest examination, he assumed that the stories were true and at once made the attacks. We ignored all this and treated him well to the best of our ability.[2]

Devoy, though a fanatic on the subject of Irish independence, was not narrow or parochial in other ways. In his youth he had joined the French Foreign Legion to gain the necessary military experience which he hoped to put to good use in Ireland against the British. In 1865 he had been arrested in Dublin for his part in the Fenian conspiracy to establish an Irish Republic, transported, and after a general amnesty in 1870, settled in New York. In the ensuing years he devoted himself selflessly to the cause of making Ireland a nation.[3] Though he had been a member of the Executive of the International Workingmen's Association, or the First International, when it was transferred to New York in the early seventies, Devoy was never a Socialist.[4] He had spent a lifetime devoted to an unpopular cause, and it would have been almost unnatural if he did not sympathize with those in the same position. During Larkin's eight and a half years in the United States Devoy remained friendly, and this was no mean achievement. When the *Freeman's Journal* and the *Irish Independent*, two of the chief Dublin dailies, gleefully announced a disagreement between Larkin and himself Devoy countered with a warm appreciation of Larkin in the *Gaelic American* even though there was some justification for the reports of friction between them:

> Our readers need not be told that the story of a row between James Larkin and the *Clan-na-Gael* is a lie made out of whole cloth. The

---

[1] William O'Brien and Desmond Ryan, eds., *Devoy's Post Bag* (1953), II, 471. Letter from John T. Keating to John Devoy, no date; about December, 1914.

[2] MS., Letter from John Devoy to Frank Robbins, June 14, 1923, National Library of Ireland, 2112. Courtesy of William O'Brien.

[3] John Devoy, *Recollections of an Irish Rebel* (1928).

[4] *Devoy's Post Bag, op. cit.*, I.

best proof of this consists in the fact that he is on the best of terms with the editor of *The Gaelic American*, that this state of feeling has continued uninterruptedly since the day that Larkin landed in America, that he visits the office of the paper constantly while in New York, was here on the day this article was written, the day before, and the day previous to that, and we have no doubt this friendship will continue as long as he remains in America and after he returns to Ireland.[1]

In December, 1914, Larkin had announced in the *Call* that the National Socialist Party was making arrangements for a projected lecture tour and asked all Socialists and locals to get in touch with party headquarters in Chicago.[2] There did not seem to be much response since Larkin was still reported to be in New York in early February.[3] A notice of a meeting in Pittsburgh for Sunday, February 14, 1915, appeared in the *Gaelic American*, but the fact that the lecture was to 'be free,' and 'Larkin will remain in Pittsburgh for the week following the lecture so that any Irish society that wants to hear him can secure his services at a nominal cost,' was not encouraging.[4] The enormous first impression made by Larkin on all sides did not survive the test of time. By the end of January, 1915, the aura of good feeling generated among the Socialists and the hyphenated Americans by his anti-war stand had evaporated. It is useless to plead that with a little more tact and more circumspection he could have made his road that much easier, for then we would not be discussing Larkin.

That he was in straitened financial circumstances was obvious from the way he lived. 'He was very poor,' wrote Elizabeth Gurley Flynn in her memoirs, 'and while in New York, he lived in one room in a small alley in Greenwich Village, called Milligan Place. . . . His ways of life were frugal and austere.'[5] 'Here,' reminisced Benjamin Gitlow, then a left-wing Socialist of the carnivorous variety, 'the towering man held court. On the small gas stove, tea was usually brewing, a dark concoction which Larkin drank by the bucketful. . . . His was an informal court. The haughty Larkin did not insist on ceremony, but he did insist on dominating the scene.'[6] In these lean months Larkin continued to speak and agitate. He was often to be found on the New York waterfront under the green banner of the

[1] *Gaelic American*, April 17, 1915.
[2] *Call*, December 16, 1914.
[3] *Ibid.*, February 2, 1915.
[4] *Gaelic American*, February 6, 1915.
[5] Elizabeth Gurley Flynn, *op. cit.*
[6] Benjamin Gitlow, *op. cit.*, p. 39.

Irish Socialist Federation, preserved in the years since Connolly's departure by Mrs. Flynn, talking and organizing among the long-shoremen.[1]

His loneliness, disappointments, and homesickness resulted naturally enough in his asking his wife in April, 1915, to make arrangements to join him in America. That Mrs. Larkin had to ask the Executive of the Transport Union in Dublin for travelling expenses was only a further indication of the difficult financial circumstances her husband found himself in.[2] Larkin was still attempting to arrange a lecture tour when he was very nearly asphyxiated by a faulty gas stove in his room.[3] It was almost a month before he was well since he was reported to have given 'a stirring and exceedingly interesting talk on the "New Unionism" in Great Britain and elsewhere, to the New York Chapter of the Intercollegiate Socialist Society.'[4] He finally managed to make arrangements for a lecture tour on the west coast and spent the greater part of the summer and fall of 1915 in California and Montana.

Larkin began his tour of the west coast in San Francisco during the second week of July, 1915. In his lectures he managed to be less diffuse than usual, and with a certain amount of mental discipline he reduced what was generally chaos to a simple disorder. He concentrated on three subjects, the War, Industrial Unionism, and Ireland, which he linked up in his own unique way. The war of course was a distressing proof of Labour's weakness, while its remedy was to be found only in industrial organization, and Ireland, with her Labour Movement militantly opposed to the war and organized on industrial lines in the Transport Workers' Union, was an excellent example of what could be done if Labour were properly organized. This simple rationalization of the things that were closest to Larkin's heart is an indication of a shift in his opinions on the relative merits of direct and indirect action. The syndicalist reliance on direct action was getting the upper hand. This is quite understandable in Larkin and those militant trade union Socialists who thought like him. For, as the war continued and in its increasing magnitude became more appalling, the 1914 failure of the Socialist parties to attempt to prevent the war seemed even more criminal. Further, it became obvious that the worker was much less vulnerable at the point of

---

[1] Elizabeth Gurley Flynn, *loc. cit.*
[2] *Attempt to Smash, op. cit.*, p. 128.
[3] *Ibid.*   [4] *Call*, May 23, 1915.

production than on the political platform, for a nation at war can easily do without politics, but not without production.

Except for an initial lapse when interviewed by one of the local San Francisco papers Larkin hewed pretty much to the above line. In this early interview he pronounced on all and sundry, and even indulged himself in prophecy. While admitting he did not know how long the war would last, he believed 'it would finally end in a deadlock. Afterwards there would be great social and economic and industrial changes, all for the good, creating a more democratic order. . . .'[1] After discussing the struggle for power between Kitchener and French in the British High Command Larkin noticed that Winston Churchill 'was finished.' 'Though he was only in the early forties,' commented Larkin, 'he had burned himself out by over work. It was curious that his career should be repeating his father's experience.' 'The Marlboroughs,' he concluded, 'had a weakness for petering out.' 'Here, however,' the reporter who was interviewing him noted, 'Larkin made no allowance for the American strain in Churchill.'

While in San Francisco the Building Trades Council invited Larkin to address a meeting in the Dreamland Rink. The meeting was well advertised and reported in several of the local papers.[2] The following week he moved on to Los Angeles and after seeing the sights visited the 'Llano del Rio Colony for the purpose of studying the scheme of co-operative enterprise established by Job Harriman.'[3] Later in the week at the Court House Park in Fresno Larkin addressed a meeting that was described as 'a memorable event in the history of the Raisin City.'[4] 'Even today,' lamented Larkin in Fresno, 'we hear of the out-of-work dubbed as lazy indolent loafer. Many persons fail to realize that economic determinism and the machinations of that law determine our whole existence.'[5]

> The real curse of our society is not this presumably indolent fellow. The real curse lies in the poverty caused by the right of the master class to take away the surplus wealth produced by the working class.
>
> We have no enemy save the capitalist class. Let us get down to first

[1] *Workers' Republic* (Dublin), August 14, 1915.

[2] *San Francisco Chronicle*, July 11, 1915; *San Francisco Call*, July 13, 1915; *San Francisco Daily News*, July 15, 1915.

[3] *Citizen*, July 30, 1915. Larkin arrived in Los Angeles on July 23, 1915.

[4] *Ibid.*   [5] *Ibid.*

principles and assume the offensive rather than the defensive, as here-
tofore, and carry the war into the enemy's camp.

The working class functions in the mines, on the dock, in the
factory—that is, at the point of production. The proper method of
organizing the working class is on the industrial field.[1]

'Get off your brothers' backs,' begged Larkin, 'and take them by the
hand, and they will respond to you.' Who was responsible for the
crimes against the Labour Movement? 'You and I,' answered
Larkin, 'the working class and its leaders.' And why? 'Because
solidarity did not exist.' The greatest crime committed against the
working classes by the capitalists was the present war. 'It is a pity,'
said Larkin, 'that the workers now fighting in the trenches do not
remember and heed the advice of George Bernard Shaw, "Shoot
your officers and come home."' In a final burst Larkin prophesied,
'In this country, there have been two wars for freedom, one to throw
off monarchical tyranny, the other to establish wage slavery in place
of chattel slavery. The next struggle will be for humanity.'[2] Larkin
returned to Los Angeles for several speaking engagements, and then
visited San Pedro to give a talk on 'The Relation of the Working
Classes to the War in Europe.'[3] His performance resulted in 'one of
the most remarkable meetings ever held in San Pedro,' and Larkin
was described as having 'held the close attention of 1,000 people for
two hours. . . .' 'He is,' said the San Pedro News Pilot, 'one of the
greatest Labor Leaders in the world, and to hear him is to be convinced that his power to lead comes from a firm conviction working
heart and soul in an unselfish cause'[4] Larkin had certainly not lost
his touch.

Though he remained in California until the end of August his
speaking engagements became fewer and fewer, and he was reported
to have been 'much hampered by want of funds.'[5] Since his career as
a lecturer was not a resounding financial success, Larkin naturally
turned to what he knew best. He undertook an organizing campaign
for the Western Federation of Miners.[6] After a few weeks learning

[1] *Citizen*, July 30, 1915.   [2] *Ibid.*
[3] *San Pedro News Pilot*, August 3, 1915. Quoted in *Workers' Republic*, September 4, 1915, erroneously as 'San Pedro Daily Pilot.'
[4] *Ibid.*
[5] William O'Brien and Desmond Ryan, eds., *Devoy's Post Bag* (1953), II, 475,
Letter from Kuno Meyer to John Devoy, September 2, 1915.
[6] 'Affidavit,' *op. cit.*, p. 1.

the fundamentals in Tucson and Phoenix he descended on the toughest mining town in America, Butte, Montana. There was no place in the United States where one's place in the community was so simply determined—you were either Anaconda Copper Mining Company or you were Miners' Union. In 1913 the miners had succeeded in electing a Socialist Mayor, and in 1914 had secured a majority of one on the City Council. In June, 1914, however, the Labour Movement in Butte had split wide open over differences between the 8,000 miners and the leadership of their union, the Western Federation. The miners had revolted against the union, and a riot ensued between the miners and some 250 union officials and their followers. The miners destroyed their union hall, and the Socialist Mayor had refused to allow the police, in an attempt to restore order, to fire on the rioters. The Governor of the State then declared martial law, suspended the Mayor, and sent in the State militia. Under martial law the President and Secretary of the Industrial Workers of the World Propaganda League were arrested and sent to jail on charges of inciting to riot, while the editors of the *Butte Socialist* and *Montana Socialist* were intimidated with threats of imprisonment if they offered the miners any encouragement in resisting the militia. Twenty-three teachers were dismissed by the Board of Education for alleged Socialist sympathies but were reinstated after a popular outcry. Martial Law was then lifted and the local government was put into the hands of an acting Mayor, Michael Daniel O'Connell. Such was the explosive situation when Larkin arrived in Butte in the middle of September, 1915, to try and persuade the miners to rejoin the Western Federation.[1]

On his arrival he introduced himself with an article in the *Montana Socialist* on 'The Friends of Small Nationalities.'[2] The burden of the article was an acid criticism of both Russia and Britain for 'standing solidly together in favor of small nationalities everywhere except in the countries now under Russian and British rule.' On his first Sunday evening in Butte, which had a large Irish population, he gave a talk in the public Auditorium on 'Ireland and her People.'[3] Presumably nearly all the Irish in Butte were in attendance, for Larkin, in warming them up, noted that 'England's standard and ideals are commercial,' while the 'Irish people have all the idealism,

---

[1] *Worker's Republic*, November 13, 1915.
[2] *Montana Socialist*, September 18, 1915.
[3] *Ibid.*, September 25, 1915.

the poetry, the ethical and social vision which the English people lack.' Then Larkin characteristically proceeded to contradict himself by denouncing the Irish in Butte for allowing themselves to be exploited by the powerful Anaconda Copper Mining Company interests. The duty of every immigrant he pointed out, was 'to give the best that his race has to offer and by remaining true to the traditions of his country to make it count in the final product.'

> It is the sort of educational work that is sadly needed in Butte as elsewhere, this frank and open statement of our frailities. It is time we outgrew the miserable and petty narrowness that resents criticism, no matter how kindly it is offered. The nation, the community, the individual that cannot accept and profit by suggestions for betterment of its actions is hopelessly damned. We need more of sanity and less of vain and ignorant pride, as a nation and as a community.[1]

The following Sunday, it was announced, Larkin would hold a meeting for the miners of Butte in the public Auditorium. The subject would be the 'genesis, development, and achievements' of the Miners' Union of Great Britain with special reference 'to the chaotic condition of Miners in this vicinity and suggest a remedy.'[2] The acting Mayor of Butte, Michael Daniel O'Connell, forbade Larkin the use of the public Auditorium, and when Larkin tried to hold an open-air meeting the police interfered.[3] Larkin then asked those assembled to follow him to the Carpenters' Hall, the use of which he had been promised earlier, but when they arrived the caretaker informed him the trustees had reversed their decision. Finally Larkin managed to hold a meeting in the Finlander Hall, the property of the Finnish workers of Butte. By this time, needless to say, Larkin was in a fierce mood and his speech was ferocious.[4] 'My friend and Comrade, Duncan, has spoken to you of the gospel of love,' he began. 'I bring you the gospel of hate; hatred of tyranny and tyrants; hatred of traitors to the cause of freedom; hatred of all modern Judases who . . . are willing to betray into the hands of their exploiters the cause of organized labor which alone has won for you miners of Butte what little advantages you have.'

> I am an Irishman. I love my native land and I love my race, but when I see some of the Irish politicians and place-hunters you have in Butte, my face crimsons with shame, and I am glad they did not remain in

---

[1] *Montana Socialist*, September 25, 1915.
[2] *Ibid.*
[3] *Ibid.*, October 2, 1915.
[4] *Ibid.*, October 9, 1915.

Ireland. Born and nurtured in hate of oppression and all oppressors, and bearing good Irish names, they have come to this country and have become the slaves of the oppressors, the dirty instruments of oppression and even to defend and lend themselves to the abrogation of the hard-won right of free speech—the right for which thousands of heroic men, Irishmen among them, have shed their very life-blood. I tell you the Irish champions of freedom—Emmet, Mitchel, Tone and the rest—whose names these contemptible traders in Irish patriotism take on their lips for their own selfish purposes, would spit in the faces of these renegade shoneen Irish of Butte.[1]

Larkin, 'with withering scorn and a flood of invective, then paid his respects' to 'Mr. Michael Daniel O'Connell.' 'Yes,' said Larkin, 'the voice is the voice of Jacob, but the hand is the hand of Esau (the A.C.M. Co.).' Next came the 'immortal ten'—the democratic aldermen who confirmed the action of the acting Mayor with regard to the use of the Auditorium. Finally, Larkin got down to the difficult and dangerous business of trying to persuade the Butte miners to go back into the Western Federation of Miners, even though they detested its leadership. He asked them to forget personalities and stand by the principle of organization. 'Never mind Moyer,' advised Larkin referring to the Federation President. 'You can take care of him afterwards. He is not and should not be made the issue. The issue is organization. You have got to have organization to accomplish anything.'[2]

Larkin's Montana visit was interrupted by an invitation to come to Washington by Dr. Dernburg, the German Minister, for an interview.[3] In the late spring or early summer of 1915 when he had been in serious financial difficulties, Larkin, through John Devoy, had contacted the Germans. Devoy described the interview years later in a private letter to a friend:

Later on he made arrangements with other people and they insisted that I must be the medium of transmitting the money to him. I did not want this, but I was forced to let it stand, and I gave him the money according as I got it. It was not possible to keep records, and I cannot go into the matter now. All I had to do with the matter was to introduce him to a certain man who could only transmit his offer (which came from himself) to the chief parties and could make no decisions himself. He asked Jim how much he thought the work would cost and

[1] *Montana Socialist*, October 9, 1915.
[2] *Ibid.* [3] 'Affidavit,' *op. cit.*, p. 6.

he said ten or twelve thousand dollars. The man said, 'I think that is a reasonable amount.' L. from that time on insisted that was a bargain and that I was a party to it. . . .[1]

Why did Larkin ask Devoy to arrange a meeting that he could have easily arranged himself? Larkin was shrewd enough in this instance to protect himself. He wanted a witness, and one that was incapable of being refuted, as to exactly what kind of a deal he was making with the Germans. It seems obvious that Larkin was trying to avoid being committed to sabotage, while accepting German money for helping to frustrate efforts to aid the Allies in this country through the organizing of labour troubles.

In Washington, Dernburg, in the presence of James K. Maguire, a close associate of Devoy's, pressed Larkin 'to undertake the work of supervising Port Groups who were charged with destructive sabotage.'[2] Once again Larkin refused, and then 'they asked me regarding my success along my own lines.' Larkin submitted a verbal report of his activities and returned to New York, where he made arrangements for his wife and two youngest sons to come to the United States. Some months later, when in New York on a flying visit from Chicago where he had set up a permanent headquarters, Larkin was pressed by Captain Boy-ed's successor, Wolf Von Igel, to take charge of all German sabotage operations on the East Coast.[3] In an attempt to persuade Larkin as to the efficiency and seriousness of the operations Von Igel took him to Hoboken, where he showed him the whole German technical apparatus for conducting sabotage. The main item of interest was a certain 'liquid fire,' which was phosphorus reduced to liquid, and put up in vials that could be carried in one's watch pocket. Demonstrated also were contraptions

[1] Devoy to Robbins, *op. cit.*, June 14, 1923.

[2] 'Affidavit,' *loc. cit.* See also *Call*, December 6, 1915, Department of Justice 'Claim' that Captain Boy-ed of German Embassy Staff paid $150,000 to Labour Leaders to conduct German propaganda.

[3] *Ibid.*, p. 8. See also in Larkin file in National Archives, Department of State, letter from Thomas I. Tunney, then in charge (1915–16) of Bomb Squad, New York Police Department, to John J. McCloy, February 13, 1934. 'Robert Foy, a German agent, who I arrested for making mines, to be attached to the rudders of ships in New York Harbor, for the purpose of blowing them up at sea after their departure from our ports, told me that he made frequent visits to Captain Von Papen previous to his arrest.' See also depositions from F. Von Papen (May 16, 1934, Berlin), B. Derburg (April 16, 1934, Berlin), and W. Von Igel (April 16, 1934, Berlin) in which they all denied having anything to do with sabotage.

and gadgets for wrecking the steering mechanisms and propellers of ships to make them easy prey for German submarines after leaving American ports. Though he still would not commit himself to sabotage Larkin continued to keep in touch with Von Igel. In fact he had an appointment with him the very day American secret servicemen raided his offices in New York. On entering the building Larkin noticed the place was swarming with Federal men and hurriedly caught the next train to Chicago.

What had brought Larkin to Chicago originally in November, 1915, was the funeral of Joe Hill.[1] Hill was an I.W.W. organizer and poet who had been executed before a Utah firing squad for an alleged murder in Salt Lake City. He pathetically protested his innocence to the last:

> The main and only fact worth considering, however, is this: I never killed Morrison and do not know a thing about it. . . . Shortly before my arrest, I came down from Park City, where I was working in the mines. Owing to the prominence of Mr. Morrison, there had to be a 'goat', and the undersigned being, as they thought, a friendless tramp, a Swede and, worst of all, an I.W.W., had no right to live anyway, and was therefore duly selected to be the 'goat.' . . .
>
> In spite of all the hideous pictures and all the bad things said and printed about me, I had only been arrested once before in my life, and that was in San Pedro, Cal. At the time of the stevedores' and dock workers' strike. I was secretary of the strike committee, and I suppose I was a little too active to suit the chief of that Burg, so he arrested me and gave me thirty days in the city jail for 'vagrancy'—and there you have the full extent of my 'criminal record.'
>
> I have always worked hard for a living and paid for everything I got, and my spare time I spend by painting pictures, writing songs and composing music.
>
> Now if the people of the State of Utah want to shoot me without giving me half a chance to state my side of the case, then bring on your firing squads—I am ready for you.
>
> I have lived like an artist and I shall die like an artist.[2]

His funeral in Chicago was a rallying point for Socialists of extreme views. 'Big Bill' Haywood and Larkin spoke in English as 5,000 mourners listened to speakers in ten different languages.[3] 'Joe Hill's

---

[1] *Call*, November 25, 1915.

[2] Joseph Hillstrom, 'Joe Hill to the People of Utah,' *International Socialist Review*, November, 1915.

[3] *Ibid.*, January, 1916.

last words were,' said Larkin, ' "Don't mourn for me: organize!" The I.W.W. movement has been sealed in the sweet blood of the poet radical. His callous, cold-blooded murder will do more to solidify the sentiment of the workers of the world than any other crime of the master class.'[1] Larkin was deeply affected by the execution of Hill, for he wrote in an article, 'Murder Most Foul,' in the *International Socialist Review*:

> Joseph Hillstrom, one of the Ishmaelites of the industrial world, was to hand and they 'shot him to death' because he was a rebel, one of the disinherited, because he was the voice of the inarticulate downtrodden; they crucified him on their cross of gold, spilled his blood on the altar of their God—Profit. . . .
>
> Therefore, Comrades, over the great heart of Joe Hill, now stilled in death, let us take up his burden, rededicate ourselves to the cause that knows no failure, and for which Joseph Hillstrom cheerfully gave his all, his valuable life. Though dead in flesh, he liveth amongst us, and cries out:

> Arouse! Arouse! Ye sons of toil from
>   Every rank of Labor,
> Not to strife of leaping lead, of bayonet or of saber.
> Ye are not murderers such as they who
>   Break ye day and hour!
> Arouse! Unite! win back your world
>   With a whirlwind stroke of power![2]

The Hill funeral and his own recent experience in the United States had led Larkin to a broader and deeper appreciation of the I.W.W. 'Maybe I, like many others of its critics,' wrote Larkin, 'lack the intelligence and requisite courage to fit me for membership in the organization which in its brief life has displayed more real revolutionary spirit, greater self-sacrifice, than any other movement the world of labor has produced. . . .'[3] 'Never at any time or place under the most adverse conditions,' continued Larkin, 'can it be charged with having obscured the issue or with ever having preached permanent peace with, or given recognition to, the capitalist system.' 'No! but true to its mission as the pioneer movement of the

---

[1] *Chicago Tribune*, November 25, 1915. Quoted in *Workers' Republic*, December 25, 1915.

[2] James Larkin, 'Murder Most Foul,' *International Socialist Review*, December, 1916.

[3] *Ibid.*

newer time,' declared Larkin, 'it advocated perpetual war on, and the total abolition of the system of wage slavery that blights humanity. . . .' Larkin was facing left.

Events in Ireland, in the meantime, were proceeding towards a revolutionary climax. As early as August, 1914, shortly after the war began, the Supreme Council of the Irish Republican Brotherhood decided to stage an insurrection in Ireland before the war was over.[1] The Brotherhood, through Sir Roger Casement and its own secret agents, had been in touch with the Imperial German Government in both Berlin and New York.[2] The situation in Ireland was, of course, extremely delicate since the great majority of the Irish people felt themselves committed to the war. The Supreme Council passed most of the year 1915 in intricate manoeuvring in an effort to gather into their own hands all the threads of organization available to the revolutionary movement in Ireland. In January, 1916, the Supreme Council decided to have an insurrection on Easter Sunday, April 23, 1916.[3] John Devoy and the *Clan-na-Gael* were informed in February and negotiations were undertaken once again with the Germans, who were asked to send arms, and if possible, military personnel to Ireland to give direct aid to the insurrection.[4]

James Connolly, who since Larkin's departure was not only in charge of the Transport Union but Commander-in-Chief of the Citizen Army, decided to throw in his lot with the extreme Nationalists and committed the Citizen Army to the Rising. In fact Connolly had been so forward and militant in his newspaper, *The Workers' Republic*, that the Supreme Council was forced to explain their plans to him in order to prevent him from precipitating a rebellion before they were ready for it themselves.[5] Connolly was co-opted to a seat on the new revolutionary directorate, the Military Council, and contributed materially to the plans laid for the Easter Rising in 1916.[6]

Larkin had, of course, been aware, through his Irish and German contacts, that preparations were being made for a rising. He was

[1] P. S. O'Hegarty, *A History of Ireland Under the Union, 1801–1922* (London: 1952), p. 697.

[2] Desmond Ryan, *The Rising* (Dublin, 1949), pp. 14–29.

[3] *Ibid.*, p. 47.

[4] O'Brien and Ryan, eds., *op. cit.*, II, 485–89.

[5] Ryan, *op. cit.*, pp. 47–50.

[6] *Ibid.*, p. 61.

advised of Casement's unsuccessful attempt to recruit an Irish Brigade from the Irish prisoners captured by the Germans. In fact in April, 1915, Larkin claimed, the Germans tried to persuade him to go to Germany *via* Spain to aid Casement, but after several unsuccessful attempts to get away he suggested a trusted friend, Captain Robert Montieth, who arrived in Germany in the fall of 1915.[1] Larkin met Kuno Meyer, the German Celtic scholar, again in California in early September, 1915, and they exchanged notes on the situation in Ireland, for Meyer wrote Devoy, 'As for Cathleen (Ireland), the psychological moment has hardly arrived but everything should be prepared for it, and from all I can gather from your letter and from what our friend J.L. . . . told me here, the other day, the preparations are on the whole all that can be expected.'[2]

When however news of the Easter Rising reached Larkin he was completely stunned. He could not be contacted for several days, and when he was finally reached at home by telephone his only comment was, 'I have nothing to say on the Irish question.'[3] All further efforts to question him were useless. Though the evidence is slim there is little doubt that Larkin had serious reservations about Connolly's committing the Citizen Army to the insurrection. This is complicated by the fact that Larkin had different reasons for his reservations both before and after the Easter Rising. Before the rising, in late 1915 or early 1916, Larkin actually sent specific instructions to Connolly telling him 'not to move.'[4]

Why Larkin should have done this raises some interesting questions. His whole line when the war began, both in Ireland and soon after his arrival in the United States, was an espousal of the idea of an armed insurrection in Ireland. How then does one explain that in something less than a year, he sent a message to Connolly telling him 'not to move'? In the first place, the emotionally charged atmosphere of Ireland and the New York and Philadelphia meetings dominated by Irish Americans more radically bent than even Irishmen, was diluted both by distance and a variety of new experiences.

[1] 'Affidavit,' p. 6. See Robert Monteith, *Casement's Last Adventure* (Chicago, (1932). There is no awareness on Monteith's part that Larkin might have had a hand in his assignment.

[2] O'Brien and Ryan, *op. cit.*, II, 475. Letter from Kuno Meyer to John Devoy, September 2, 1915.

[3] *New York Times*, April 29, 1916.

[4] *Attempt to Smash, op. cit.*, p. 135. Letter from James Larkin to Thomas Foran, January 22, 1917.

Safer and saner second thoughts about the feasibility of a successful insurrection and its terrible cost had more room for play than was allowed for them in the narrower Irish circles. Also, as the war progressed and his Irish contacts became fewer, the horrors and casualties gave ample evidence of the seriousness and ruthlessness of the combatants, so that Larkin came to see the hopelessness of a successful revolution in Ireland until such time as either England was defeated by Germany or a stalemate finally resulted in one or more of the major powers being overthrown through internal revolution. Further, considering Larkin's nature, it is inconceivable that he would have approved of any insurrection on the part of Labour in Ireland that he was not to lead himself. Both his personality and his dramatic instinct would not allow for it; one of the great actors on the Irish stage could hardly have been expected voluntarily to vacate that stage at so great a moment in Irish history.

In saner surroundings Larkin's mind, undoubtedly, turned on the question of the success or failure of the proposed insurrection, and this was certainly more a matter of tactics than of principle. He could continue to be devoted to the idea of a revolution in Ireland and still be doubtful about when it should take place. Knowing Larkin it should cause no surprise that he thought himself a better judge than even the men on the spot. The men who planned the Easter Rising in Dublin, however, were under no illusions about the success of the insurrection or their treatment when it should fail. If these men had hoped for or promised a successful revolution then they should be properly denounced as lunatics or worse. They had something else in mind other than their success or failure, however, for they wanted to prove to themselves, to their people, and to the world that the party of the Revolution in Ireland was not dead. They wanted to make it self-evident to all that there was still enough in the idea of Ireland as a nation to cause good men to offer up their lives. No one expressed it better than Patrick Pearse, Commander-in-Chief of the Republican forces and President of the Provisional Government, when he said at his court-martial:

> I have helped to organize, to arm, to train, and to discipline my fellow countrymen to the sole end that when the time came, they might fight for Irish freedom. The time, as it seemed to me, did come. We seem to have lost, we have not lost. To refuse to fight would have been to lose, to fight is to win, we have kept faith with the past, and handed a tradition to the future. . . . You cannot conquer Ireland; you can-

not extinguish the Irish passion for freedom; if our deed has not been sufficient to win freedom, then our children will win it by a better deed.[1]

Pearse was executed with Thomas J. Clarke and Thomas Mac-Donagh by a firing squad the next morning.[2] Within ten days fourteen men were executed after summary court-martials. On May 12 James Connolly, who had been wounded in the fighting and was unable to stand, was executed while tied sitting in a chair.[3] Thus the British Government resurrected what had been dead and buried in Ireland for two generations, the party of the Revolution. The whole temper of the Irish people changed after the executions. The man who had been the strongest supporter of the British connection in Ireland, for example, the Most Rev. Dr. O'Dwyer, the Roman Catholic Bishop of Limerick, and an anathema to all shades of Irish Nationalists, said in September, 1916, 'The very Government against which they rose, and which killed them so mercilessly, has proclaimed its own condemnation. What is that ghost of Home Rule which they keep safe in lavender on the Statute Book but a confession of the wrong of England's rule in Ireland? *Sinn Fein* is, in my judgement, the true principle, an alliance with English politicians is like the alliance of the lamb with the wolf.'[4]

'Though fate,' wrote Larkin a short time after the rising, 'denied some of us the opportunity of striking a blow for human freedom, we live in hopes that we, too, will be given the opportunity.'[5] Deep as his disappointment was over the rising, soon after the news of the executions Larkin roused himself and organized a mass meeting in support of the insurrectionists in the Grand Opera House in Chicago on May 21, 1916. Larkin's nerves were in a desperate state for when a man in the audience in an emotional outburst denounced the 'murder' of the executed men, Larkin misunderstood him, 'leaped from the stage,' 'smothered' his further remarks 'by a flying tackle,' 'choked the offender,' 'shook him till his hair was awry and his collar loose,' and 'hustled' him out of the meeting.[6] Despite the momentary lapse, despite his own deep disappointment, and in the face of his own complex personality, Larkin did understand, in the deepest sense, what the rising meant. Speaking for himself as well as many more, Larkin wrote, 'It is possible amongst your readers there are

[1] Ryan, *op. cit.*, Appendix I, p. 260.   [2] *Ibid.*, Appendix III, p. 264.   [3] *Ibid.*
[4] *Ibid.*   [5] James Larkin, 'The Irish Rebellion,' *The Masses*, July, 1916.
[6] *New York Herald*, May 22, 1916.

men and women who may, though thinking the rebellion an unwise one, cherish the ideals these men and women lived and died for, and it must be admitted that the most glorious thing that has happened during this carnival of blood-lust in Europe was the self-sacrifice and devotion of these men to a cause which they believed in.'[1]

A few weeks after the Chicago meeting Larkin left for San Francisco where he had an interview with the German Consul, Von Bopp, who asked him how his work was proceeding.[2] While in San Francisco Larkin was 'visited nearly every day by Tom Mooney,'[3] who would be soon tried, convicted, and sentenced to be executed for the San Francisco Preparedness Day Parade Bomb Plot of July 16, 1916, in which a number of people were killed. Von Bopp later told Larkin that Mooney had been 'railroaded,' though he did admit that Mooney had been active along the same lines as Larkin in strikes and stoppages to slow up the American effort to aid the Allies.[4] When Larkin arrived back in Chicago he found a note from John Devoy asking him to come to New York. He had only been in New York a few days when the 'Black Tom' explosion took place, and after taking note of all the places and people he had seen that evening he returned immediately to Chicago. Larkin was in an extremely dangerous circumstantial position. He had been in San Francisco only a short time before the Preparedness Day Plot and in close contact with the man who had been arrested for it, and now had been in New York when the largest single piece of sabotage in the whole war was carried out. On returning to Chicago he found out through James K. Maguire that the Germans wanted to see him again in Washington. They asked him to proceed to Mexico City where he would be interviewed by some high German officials who did not dare come to the United States. Larkin crossed the border at Laredo, Texas, with the help of a very efficient German secret service system, and arrived in Mexico City about the middle of September, 1916. He went to the German Embassy where he received a letter of apology from the German minister, Herr Von Eckhardt, for not being able to keep the personal appointment. It was explained to Larkin that the situation in Mexico was extremely delicate because the British Government was putting a great deal of

[1] Larkin, *loc. cit.*   [2] 'Affidavit,' *op. cit.*, p. 11.
[3] *Naval Intelligence Bureau, Office of Naval Censor, San Francisco*, October 29, 1917. This is a report of an agent of the Naval Intelligence Bureau, Larkin File, National Archives, Department of State, Washington, D.C.
[4] 'Affidavit,' *op. cit.*, p. 13.

pressure on the Mexicans for allowing the Germans to operate so freely against the Allies on what was professedly neutral territory. Von Eckhardt requested Larkin to proceed to San Francisco where he would receive further instructions from their Consul there, Von Bopp. When Larkin arrived in San Francisco he had to keep under cover because Mooney was in serious jeopardy. Von Bopp was very upset at the way things were going. He had found out that most of the Irish- and German-Americans were simply, as he expressed it to Larkin, 'hot-air merchants,' and he needed good men. A large part of his espionage and sabotage apparatus had been broken up because of the infiltration of Federal agents and he asked Larkin to take over the direction of West Coast operations from Vancouver to Guatemala. Larkin declined the offer and returned to Chicago.[1]

In Chicago Larkin decided to bring out an American edition of the *Irish Worker* with the help of Jack Carney.[2] Carney, who had only recently arrived in the United States, had been converted to Socialism in Widnes, near Liverpool, by Larkin in 1906, and had been associated with him during the lockout in Dublin in 1913. He was now in Chicago trying to earn a living as a free-lance lecturer and journalist. There are no surviving copies of the *Irish Worker*, but Carney has described it as consisting of '16 pages in small 8 point type'—

The first page was a cartoon drawn by one L. S. Chumley, who was then drawing for Solidarity, the official organ of the I.W.W. I combed the British and Irish newspapers for news of Ireland, while Jim would dictate the main story. I would sit at the typewriter and he would dictate until all hours of the morning. We had 4,000 readers, mostly subscribers. We had to type the wrappers for subscribers in addition to the preparation of the material for the paper and also arrange its make-up. As soon as we had carried the bags of mail to the post office, we would be starting the next issue. Jim wrote as if he were in Dublin and offended many Irish-Americans. He singled out the late John McCormack, the singer, for attack for attending an Allied Bazaar in Chicago and other pro-Ally Irish and Irish-Americans.[3]

In the six months between his return from Mexico City in early October, 1916, and America's entry into the war in April, 1917,

---

[1] 'Affidavit,' *op. cit.*, pp. 13–15.

[2] MS., 'Jack Carney on James Larkin,' p. 8. This is a nineteen-page typewritten memoir by Jack Carney written at my request in May 1953. Hereafter referred to as 'Carney Memoir.'   [3] *Ibid.*

Larkin's activities were still governed by his violent antipathy to the war. In the Presidential election of 1916 he and Carney were in Terre Haute, speaking for Eugene Debs, Socialist candidate for Congress, whose anti-war attitude was as uncompromising as any expressed in the United States.[1] Larkin's opposition to the war was not just talk, for the Chicago Intelligence Office later reported to the War Department:

> In 1917, the British Embassy sent a communication to our State Department, alleging that a movement had been instituted in this country against the British Government, the plan of the conspirators being to obstruct the manufacture of war material, etc., and to use as confederates persons of German extraction and Irishmen belonging to the Sinn Fein faction.
>
> *James Larkin* was especially active in this movement which seemed to center about the Sherman House in Chicago, Ill.[2]

Carney has also related how Larkin 'would call a meeting of the *Clan-na-Gael*. I was the messenger. I would meet a certain person, at this time one of the heads of the Chicago police, and hand him a note with instructions. I saw the men arrive for the meetings and checked on their numbers. Larkin knew how many would attend and who would attend.'[3]

Just before America entered the war in April, 1917, Larkin decided to try to get to the Socialist Peace Conference called for that summer in Stockholm by the International Socialist Bureau. In fact, he received $2,000 from John Devoy out of *Clan-na-Gael* funds to pay his expenses.[4] When America entered the war, Larkin's chances of getting out of the country were considerably reduced. There was no change in his attitude towards the war, however, which he made amply clear in an interview with John Reed for the *New York Evening Mail*.[5] Reed was also trying to get to Stockholm for the Peace Conference and to Russia. He was more fortunate than Larkin in getting away and finally arrived in Petrograd for the Bolshevik Revolution in November, 1917, where he was an eye-witness to his

[1] *Terre Haute Star*, November 5, 1916.

[2] MS., Department of Intelligence Office, Chicago, Illinois, *Report*, December 8, 1919. Information taken from D.I.O. files 540, 5496, 5508/56, 7818, 6536, 7743, Larkin File, National Archives, Department of State, Washington, D.C.

[3] 'Carney Memoir,' *loc. cit.*

[4] MS., Letter from John Devoy to Frank Robbins, September 21, 1923, National Library of Ireland, 2112. Courtesy of William O'Brien.

[5] *Evening Mail*, June 6, 1917.

'Ten Days that Shook the World.'[1] A few weeks after the *Mail* interview Larkin was arrested for making a speech at a Socialist meeting in which he was alleged to have advised against registering for conscription.[2] Larkin was reported by the police as having said, 'Soldiers are hired assassins. I don't tell you not to obey the conscription, but I'll not submit to conscription.' 'If you want to go to war,' continued Larkin, 'you can go to hell.' 'There are not,' he summed up, 'enough soldiers in New York State to make me go to war.'[3] In magistrate's court Larkin denied the statements attributed to him were in their proper context, and the charges against him were dismissed. When, in cross-examination, the Assistant District Attorney asked him if he were a graduate of Dublin College, Larkin replied haughtily, 'I am a graduate of the school of adversity.'[4]

He was still trying to get away in August when a message arrived from Von Bopp asking him to go 'to Mexico City because of complications arising out of the military situation.'[5] When Larkin arrived in San Antonio at the beginning of September German agents informed him the machinery for getting him into Mexico had been destroyed, and their fake passport bureau had been discovered. They advised him to try *via* California and asked him to deliver some letters to their agents in Mexico. Larkin refused, but on receiving a letter from James K. Maguire asking him to do what the Germans asked, even at the risk of his life, he consented. He then made his way to San Francisco where he contacted a German agent, Carl Witzke, who was looking for agents 'to send to Australia and especially to Russia.'[6] Witzke later testified that 'Larkin got me several men . . . Leveskovski and McIntyre, both of them labor agitators and radicals. As far as I know, both of these men went to Vladivostok. The main idea of going to Vladivostok was to spread

---

[1] Granville Hicks, *John Reed* (New York, 1936), p. 250.

[2] *New York Times*, June 24, 1917.

[3] *New York Sun*, June 24, 1917.

[4] *Call*, June 29, 1917.

[5] 'Affidavit,' *op. cit.*, p. 17.

[6] MS., Deposition by John J. McCloy (Exhibit 'C'), Larkin File, National Archives, Department of State, Washington, D.C. 'The following references to Larkin . . . are found in Captain Tunney's interviews with Witzke at Fort Sam Houston in September, 1929. In the interview held on September 17, Witzke in telling about his connection with the I.W.W., Socialists, Anarchists and other radicals, said that he was organising a mission to Australia and Vladivostok.' See also 'Affidavit,' *op. cit.*, p. 23. Larkin admitted meeting Witzke in Los Angeles in October, 1917.

radical propaganda . . . and incidentally to blow up the munitions stores.'[1] Larkin then moved down to San Diego and crossed the Mexican border at Tia Juana, and delivered the entrusted letters to German agents in Ensenada. The Mexican Governor of Lower California arranged for transportation to La Paz, and Larkin crossed by motor launch to Guaymass on the mainland. After waiting several days he was contacted by German agents who told him a revolution had broken out in the Tepiz province and all railways and bridges were down. They suggested that he go farther down the coast by boat and then cut back across country to Mexico City. He finally arrived in Mexico City about the middle of October,[2] where he was interviewed by the German Minister, Von Eckhardt and his staff. Von Eckhardt explained that the military situation was becoming desperate. If the Allies were not halted Germany must soon negotiate for peace. The situation in Mexico was also awkward, for President Carranza had sold the Germans out and gone pro-British. Their greatest need, Von Eckhardt explained, was trustworthy and loyal men. The Germans then brought out maps, on which Larkin noted, 'was marked every oil field, railway junction, and to my knowledge, the majority of ammunition and steel plants in the United States and port terminals.'[3] They claimed that the 'Black Tom' had been their greatest success, and then asked Larkin to undertake sabotage for them in the United States. When he refused their hitherto friendly demeanour changed and the interview was quickly brought to a close. The next day his wallet was stolen and the following day his suitcase was gone. He was then presented with a substantial hotel bill and with his last few pesos he wired both San Francisco and New York for money.[4] After much delay the money arrived and Larkin made his way back to New York, his adventurous career as a German agent coming to an abrupt end.

[1] *Ibid.*

[2] 'Affidavit,' *op. cit.*, p. 18. Larkin thought he arrived in September, 1917, but a photostat of Hotel Iturbide's Register, shows his signature on October 15, 1917.

[3] *Ibid.*, p. 20. See also deposition from H. Von Eckhardt (April 16, 1934, Berlin), which specifically denies Larkin's charges but admits meeting him in Mexico City.

[4] *Ibid.*, p. 22. See Larkin File for two cables from Mexico City signed 'James Larkin,' and dated October 17 and 26, 1917, asking the proprietor of the Hotel Fresno in San Francisco to forward money and letters. See also J. Dempsey to John Devoy, July 28, 1923, reprinted in *Irish Worker*, September 8, 1923. 'I know Clan-na-Gael men who helped Larkin to get back from Mexico when he was stranded there after a silly attempt to go to Russia.'

X

THE REVOLUTIONARY
WAY

WHILE Larkin was slowly making his way back from Mexico great events were taking place in Russia. On the night of November 6–7, the Bolsheviki led by Lenin and Trotsky, seized power from the tottering Kerensky régime in Petrograd. In the ensuing ten days the radical left won the first successful Socialist revolution in the most backward country in Western Europe. Socialists of all shades of opinion were everywhere electrified by the inspiring news. Many pacifists and liberals were also attracted by the Bolshevik battle-cry of 'Peace, Bread, Land, and All Power to the Soviets.' The pacifists applauded the immediate and uncompromising demand for peace, while the liberals interpreted rule by the Soviets as another extention of democracy and representative government.

Meanwhile, at the other end of Europe, events were also proceeding in a revolutionary direction. Eamon de Valera, the only surviving commandant of the Easter Rising in 1916 and now President of the *Sinn Fein* had openly declared for an Irish Republic while coolly advising his partially-armed Volunteers to be ready for the call to arms when the time came. A crisis was reached in early April, 1918, when the British Prime Minister, Lloyd George, decided to apply the Conscription Act to Ireland. All Ireland vowed resistance if the Act was enforced, and the deadly serious, earnest, and unexcited nature of the opposition resulted in the Government, after a long second thought, allowing the Act to become a dead letter in Ireland. The successful resistance to conscription increased the prestige of *Sinn Fein* and considerably strengthened the hand of the party of Revolution throughout the country.

219

Radical opinion in the United States was also moving to the left. American Socialists, pacifists, and liberals, and to some extent the Irish, all found a common ground in the prevailing enthusiasm for the Bolsheviki in the months following the November Revolution. The very names of the speakers announced at the first meetings called by the various committees and groups in New York and Boston in support of the Russian Revolution were evidence enough of the varied political convictions and interests of the people involved. They range from what were to be some of the biggest names in the early Communist Party, such as Louis C. Fraina, Santeri Nuorteva, and Ella Reeve Bloor, through the Socialist centre with men such as Alexander Trachtenberg and Ludwig Lore, to the Socialist right with James Oneal, and wind up with what might be best termed the liberal 'libertines,' Frank Harris and Hutchins Hapgood.[1]

When one of these early groups, the Friends of New Russia, which had quickly succeeded the Friends of the Russian Revolution, held a meeting at Carnegie Hall on December 21, 1917, another dimension, the Irish, was added to a picture that was already somewhat complicated.[2] At the meeting, which called for an immediate Armistice and American recognition of the Soviet régime, a resolution was introduced in the name of the Irish Progressive League, which demanded that Ireland be recognized at the Peace Conference. The League had been formed by those Irish in New York whose Socialist sympathies, presumably, were second only to their concept of Ireland as a nation. Several members of the committee of the Friends of New Russia were also prominent in the affairs of the Irish Progressive League, while the speaker who introduced the resolution at the Carnegie Hall meeting was Patrick L. Quinlan, who was well known and respected in the extreme wings of both the Irish and Socialist Movements.[3] It seemed as if an effective bridge between the Irish and Socialists had been established through the League, but whether the traffic was to be both ways was another question.

When Larkin arrived back in New York in early 1918 he found a good many changes in the Irish and Socialist movements, and they were not all to his liking. He noticed with a jealous eye and a private

[1] *Call*, December 3 and 21, 1917; January 8, 1918.
[2] *Ibid.*, December 21, 1917.
[3] December 3, 1917. See for names of Committee. James J. Bagley, Dr. Gertrude B. Kelly, and Vida Milholland were listed, and were also prominent in Irish Progressive League.

pen the continued success of the Sinn Fein among the American-Irish at the expense of the Socialist and Labour Movements. He wrote Thomas Foran, General President of the Irish Transport Workers' Union, that:

> The Sinn Fein movement here is anti-labor and for the Socialists they think they are anti-Christs. They have tried to impress the American public that the Revolution was a Catholic revolution, in fact they have done the cause incalculable harm. They are the most violent American jingoes always boasting how loyal they are too and how many Irish have fought and died for this Free Republic. Moryah! They make me sick to the soul. They held a meeting in Chicago sometime back and they spent 2,600 dollars on the meeting, 1,700 dollars to erect a special star spangled flag, electrically arrayed which flashed all thru the meeting. They are in a word super-fine patriots and the most consummate tricksters of politicians. This applies to all of them without exception and the crowd that have lately come over are no better.[1]

These Irish who had recently crossed the Atlantic to help raise money and interest for Ireland fared no better in Larkin's private letters. Most prominent among these were Mrs. Hannah Sheehy Skeffington, whose husband was shot and killed out of hand by a British officer during the Easter Rising, Nora Connolly, the eldest daughter of James Connolly, and Dr. Patrick McCartan, the unofficial Sinn Fein ambassador to the United States. Larkin wrote Foran in early May:

> I must again call attention to the fact that Mrs. S— is just an apologist for the Sinn Fein crowd. She never speaks of the Labour movement nor of the Socialist Party. She leaves the impression that Skeffy and herself were members of the Sinn Fein movement at home. Nora C follows the same lines . . . McCartan is a rank reactionary; struts about like a stage hero. We here cannot afford to expose them at present. They make out Arthur G [Griffith] as a God-given saint and statesman; nobody in Ireland done anything but Sinn Fein. Connolly and the other boys all recanted Socialism and Labour, and were good Sinn Feiners. My God it is sickening. Let ye over there insist upon respect. I may manage to cross. I am going to get home if it is at all possible.[2]

---

[1] M.S., Letter from James Larkin to Thomas Foran, no date (about May, 1918). Courtesy of William O'Brien.

[2] *The Attempt to Smash the Irish Transport and General Workers Union* (Dublin, 1924), p. 169. Letter from James Larkin to Thomas Foran, no date.

Larkin was also very much worried about the Sinn Fein Movement seizing the initiative from Labour in Ireland. 'What are O'Brien and the rest doing in allowing the Griffith gang to monopolize all the credit for the effort,' wrote Larkin to Foran in the late spring of 1918.[1] 'I wish O'Brien and the others would declare themselves,' he continued. 'Are they all turned Sinn Fein? ... Have our Section any representation on the alleged *Provisional Government*? *This is important*.' At the end of 1918 Larkin was still earnestly advising—

Don't be led astray by the ephemeral political movements of a moment. Our work is fundamental. Not only do we want an independent Ireland, but we demand a free Ireland of free men and women. I realize the tortuous paths you and your colleagues must walk. Certain forces in Eire seem to have exploited the struggle for their own ends. Don't be in any way deterred: hew straight to the line, let the chips fall where they may. Be assured we are on the side that must ultimately prevail. Leaders, moryah! and parties rise up and pass away in a night but men live on forever and principles are permanent.[2]

Not only was Larkin dissatisfied with the bulk of American-Irish opinion, and the trend of events in Ireland, he was also very critical of the Socialist Party's attitude towards the recruiting of the Irish in America. At an early meeting of Mrs. Skeffington's in New York, where she spoke on 'The Labour Movement in Ireland,' under the auspices of the Socialist Party, Larkin made an uninvited speech from the floor, in which he declared that the Irish, 'although a revolutionary people, are not in the Socialist Party in this country because the party's attitude is hostile and uninviting.'[3] He was immediately contradicted 'in an earnest and impassioned reply,' by Edward F. Cassidy, who presided—a Socialist and prominent in the affairs of the Irish Progressive League. If the American-Irish were all that Larkin said they were in private, they would be the last group he would tolerate within the Party, yet he publicly berated the Party for doing nothing to incorporate them. This curious ambivalence is partially explained by the fact that Larkin was an extreme romantic who always had difficulty in appreciating things up close. He could love humanity but he had difficulty loving Tom, Dick, and Harry.

[1] *The Attempt to Smash, op. cit.*, p. 167. Larkin to Foran, no date.
[2] *Ibid.*, p. 169. Larkin to Foran, no date.   [3] *Call*, February 20, 1918.

His criticism, however, did result in greater activity by the New York Socialists among the American-Irish. On St. Patrick's Day, March 17, 1918, a large rally was announced to be 'the first concerted effort by the Party in this city to get together the fast rising ride of Socialist sentiment among the Irish.'[1] Announced also was the formation of the James Connolly Socialist Club with offices at 43 West 29 Street.[2] Larkin soon dominated the affairs of the Club, which rapidly became the centre of left-wing activities among the Irish Socialists in New York.[3] Why, it might well be asked, did Larkin ignore the Irish Progressive League and virtually create another organization to bridge the gap between the Irish and the Socialists? Part of the answer was that, though he had many good friends in the League, he did not care for many of those who were playing a leading part in its affairs such as Mrs. Skeffington and Nora Connolly. Further, most of the Socialists connected with the League, except for Quinlan and a few others, were of the right-wing variety for whom Larkin had only contempt. Finally, and most important, the League was mainly concerned with interesting Socialists in the Irish question and not with making Socialists out of the Irish. Personality, politics, and principle all resulted in Larkin throwing himself into the work of the Connolly Club, but whether it was to be any more effective than the League had been in converting the American-Irish to Socialism was again another question.

Soon after his return from Mexico, then, Larkin sized up the situation among the Irish at home and abroad and decided where he stood. The American-Irish must be converted and the Movement in Ireland must not allow itself to be swamped by bourgeois Nationalists. The balance had come down firmly on the side of Socialism. Defining his relationship to the American Socialist Party which he had joined before his trip to Mexico, however, caused him greater difficulties. The problem was not his alone, but actually the dilemma of the whole of the American Socialist left. The left-wing Socialists, as they came to style themselves, had long been looking for a focal point and had now found it in their common appreciation

[1] *Call*, March 17, 1918. See also *Call*, May 12, 1918, 'Bronx Socialist Meeting for Irish.'

[2] *Ibid.*

[3] *Voice of Labour*, May 16, 1925. See long letter from John J. Lyng. See also *Irish Worker*, September 8, 1922, for J. Dempsey to John Devoy, July 28, 1923, for Larkin and Connolly Club. Both letters are violently anti-Larkin.

of the Bolshevik Revolution. Yet, while the left-wing had begun to focus in early 1918, it had not begun to crystallize. The burst of enthusiasm that greeted the November Revolution in December and January died down, and was not revived until John Reed returned from Russia at the end of April with his eye-witness account of the ten days that shook the world and the confident conviction that the 'Bolshevik Victory is Assured.'[1] Larkin had missed the first wave, but it was not long before he was riding the crest of the second wave created by Reed. A few weeks after his arrival Reed spoke before the Connolly Club, and he made an extremely important convert in his friend Larkin.[2] For, a short time later, Larkin was the main speaker at a rally called for the recognition of the Bolsheviki by the four Russian branches of the Socialist Party.[3] In his usually grandiloquent way Larkin announced that 'the Russians must not fear being left friendless,' for 'the Irish are with the Russians.'[4] 'There is no man in Europe, in Asia, in South America, or on the face of this great continent,' said Larkin, 'who has yet given a reason or argument why the Soviet government of Russia should not be recognized.' In an effort to counter the argument that the rule of law did not prevail in Russia, and therefore, should not be recognized, Larkin declared, 'There is less disorder in Russia today after the country has passed through two stirring revolutions in one year, and after it is in the throes of this great war, than there is today in peaceful Mexico.' Driving the analogy home Larkin pointed out, 'There are places in Mexico where the common law is not recognized and the people are still fighting amongst themselves. Russia, on the other hand, is today the most peaceful and orderly country in the world. Yet Mexico is a recognized government, while great, free and democratic Russia is an outcast among nations.' Amidst wild applause, he concluded, 'The recognition of the great and newest Republic of Europe means the Socialist salvation of the entire world. It means democracy for humanity.'[5] Though he had little knowledge or understanding of what was happening in Russia there is no doubt that Larkin's imagination was captured by the idea of the Bolshevik Revolution.

This enthusiasm created by Reed for the Bolshevik Revolution was general among Socialists. Right and left wings applauded Reed

---

[1] *Call*, April 30, 1918.
[2] Granville Hicks, *John Reed* (New York, 1936), p. 305.
[3] *Call*, June 6, 1918.   [4] *Ibid.*   [5] *Ibid.*

as the bandwagon began to roll to the tune of 'Recognize Soviets.'[1] Though Larkin was somewhat premature in his performance before the Russian branches, the 'Russian Soviet Recognition League,' under the chairmanship of Alexander Trachtenberg, soon picked up the refrain. Fifteen thousand heard Norman Thomas in Madison Square Garden on June 11, 1918, demand American recognition for the Soviets,[2] while two weeks later Scott Nearing and Irwin St. John Tucker added their voices to the growing chorus at Hunt's Point Palace.[3] How much depended on Reed's magnetic, first-hand account of what had happened in Russia was quickly demonstrated when he left the New York area for a tour of the mid-west. The bottom practically fell out of the left-wing platform, and it was obvious, once again, that though the left wing could focus, it still was not able to crystallize.

This was not all the fault of the Socialists in the extreme wing of the Party. The difficulty of forming a left-wing nucleus on the Bolshevik model when no one really knew what the Bolsheviki, beyond their immediate and very pragmatic programme, actually did stand for, was impossible. Larkin had given an excellent example of the prevailing vagueness when he spoke before the Russian branches, for he had no more to offer really than a naïve faith in the goodness of the Russian Revolution. Though Reed clarified the issues to the extent that he maintained the Bolsheviki were not only in power, but more than likely to remain there, his message still had more of the millennial about it than the immediate. Larkin's own conversion to Bolshevism and his impression of the Russian Revolution is an excellent example of the type of impact Reed had. More important, however, than even the ignorance of what the Bolsheviki were trying to do, in explaining the inability of the American left to come together, was the simple fact that the United States was still at war. Reed, for example, was faced with three separate indictments soon after his return, and some one hundred I.W.W.s were at the same time being tried *en masse* in Chicago.[4] Socialists were every day being arrested on charges that ranged from obstructing the draft to treason, while Eugene V. Debs, the most human and greatest of all the personalities in the American Socialist Movement, and four times

[1] *Call*, June 4, 1918. See announcement for June 11, meeting of 'Russian Soviet Recognition League,' with Alexander Trachtenberg as temporary Chairman.
[2] *Ibid.*, June 12, 1918. [3] *Ibid.*, June 25, 1918. [4] Hicks, *op. cit.*, pp. 311, 315.

Socialist candidate for the Presidency, fell before the Espionage and Sedition Acts in late June, 1918.[1]

Much of Larkin's energy while the war continued, went into attempts to raise money for the 'foolishly honest' I.W.W.s on trial in Chicago, and for the relief of their wives and children.[2] He himself went as far as it was possible to go in his opposition to the war without being jailed and 'was merciless in his denunciation of what he termed the "so-called International Socialists" here as elsewhere for their war attitude and defined his attitude to be with the Socialists and workers of America who remained true to the "real internationalism of labor".'[3] This veiled reporting of his speech by the Socialist New York *Call* was another tribute to the effective wartime censorship imposed by the Government. It was difficult enough for radical papers to survive in this atmosphere, let alone to allow for the establishing of a militant left-wing journal. Still, a newspaper was an absolute necessity if the left wing was to find itself.

When Reed returned to New York in August, 1918, after being away nearly two months, the Bolshevik bandwagon again began to roll, but the tune as well as the personnel had changed. A meeting was called for August 23, 1918, which was announced to be 'the first step in a campaign of national scope to express the sentiments of the American people on Russian affairs.'[4] The speakers were to be Reed, Nearing, Fraina, Nuorteva, now official representative of the People's Republic of Finland, and Emmett O'Reilly, a lieutenant of Larkin's and prominent in the affairs of the Connolly Club. Surprisingly enough it was also announced that money "has been contributed very generously and is still coming in to the secretary of the Local New York Committee, J. L. Manning.' Manning was also a close friend of Larkin's and a member of the Connolly Club.[5] The meetings of the group were limited to New York and Boston in September and October of 1918. Unfortunately there is no record or report of what was said, but the subjects of the speakers in the

[1] Ray Ginger, *The Bending Cross* (New Brunswick, 1949), p. 359.

[2] *Call*, May 5, 1918, 'Police break up Labor Defense Rally in Brooklyn.' 'Jim Larkin not allowed to speak in Lyceum, but shifts to clubhouse.' 'Larkin evidently won the goodwill of the Irish policemen who faced him all evening, for they were in good spirits at the close of the meeting, everything ending well.'

[3] *Ibid.*, May 14, 1918.   [4] *Ibid.*, August 20, 1918.

[5] John J. Lyng, 'How Larkin Acted the Parasite in America,' *Voice of Labour*, May 18, 1925.

announcements obviously reflect some new directions in their thinking. Nearly always the general title had to do with a discussion of the 'Situation in Russia' or with 'Russian Affairs,' while speakers such as Fraina were even more pointed with 'Socialism and the Soviet Republic' and 'The Task of Socialism.'[1] The great days of the November Revolution were passed and the time had come to examine the implications and lessons of the historic upheaval. Now that the Bolsheviki were in power, what did they stand for and what did it mean to the rest of the world? Larkin was now found most often on the platform with Reed, Fraina, Nuorteva, Sen Katayama, pioneer Japanese Socialist, Gregory Weinstein, and Nicholas I. Hourwich, editor and sub-editor, respectively, of the Russian language newspaper *Novy Mir*.[2] All of these were soon to be the big names in the Communist Movement, and the liberals, pacifists, and right-wing Socialists were now conspicuous by their absence. The left wing had finally found itself.

Five days after the war ended the left wing began the publication of the *Revolutionary Age*. The first number was published on November 16, 1918, in Boston under the editorship of Louis C. Fraina. The associate editor was Eadmonn MacAlpine, another close friend of Larkin's, and also a stalwart in the Connolly Club.[3] The early issues of the bi-weekly were devoted to European events with Fraina concentrating on Germany and MacAlpine on Ireland. Reed, Katayama, Weinstein, and N. I. Hourwich were all contributing editors. Revolution appeared to be sweeping Europe, and the *Revolutionary Age* was swept up in the tide of European events. Everywhere the parties of the left were gaining in strength, as strikes and violence became the order of the day. Germany, Austria, and Hungary all seemed to be on the verge of going Bolshevik. Lloyd George summed it all up in March, 1918, when writing Clemenceau a secret memorandum a few days after Bela Kun had set up a Soviet Republic in Hungary. 'The whole of Europe is filled with the spirit of Revolution. There is a deep sense not only of discontent but of anger and revolt amongst the workmen against pre-war conditions. The whole existing order in its political, social, and economic

---

[1] *Call*, September 21, 27, 29, and 30; October 15, 1918.   [2] *Ibid*.

[3] Lyng, *loc. cit.* See also Eadmonn MacAlpine, 'Can Lloyd-George's Conference help the people of Ireland?' *Call*, July 22, 1917, for Larkin eulogy. Also MacAlpine, 'Sinn Fein and the New Struggle,' *Revolutionary Age*, November 27, 1918, quotes Larkin.

aspects is questioned by the masses of the population from one end of Europe to the other.'[1] The early numbers of the *Revolutionary Age*, consequently, paid no attention to what was happening in the United States. Therefore, the problem that the left wing had partially solved just before the end of the war in its attempt to cut through the glamour of the Russian Revolution and reduce it from an end to a means was made more difficult by the continuing success of the revolutionary elements in Europe.

Early in 1919 Larkin too was still much affected by the heady wine of Revolution in far away places. At the climax of 'Red Week' in Boston on February 2, 1919, at the Grand Opera House and in the company of Ludwig Lore, N. I. Hourwich, and MacAlpine, Larkin was the main speaker at a memorial meeting for the German Communists Karl Liebknecht and Rosa Luxemburg, who had been 'shot while trying to escape' during the recent Spartacist rising in Berlin.[2] A Russian Soviet banner was displayed and most of those present wore red carnations, as Larkin charged that 'organized agents of a bourgeois Government were responsible for the deaths of Karl Liebknecht and Rosa Luxemburg.'[3] He then boldly stated that 'Russia is the only place where men and women can be free.' The *New York Times*, obviously exasperated, commented the next day:

> When a man speaking in an American city excites the applause of numerous auditors by telling them that 'Russia is the only place where men and women can be free,' the fact raises a good many rather serious questions.
>
> The first of them—Why did he make a statement at once so stupid and so false?—is easily answered. The speaker was *James Larkin*, who is himself as much a Bolshevik as he can find time to be in the moments when he does not have to be a Sinn Feiner and an exponent of what in this country is the I.W.W. But this statement was made in Boston, and it is difficult to understand there of more than a small handful of out-and-out lunatics that are desirous of having the only sort of freedom now existing in Russia. It is the freedom of a small class to kill and steal, and the freedom of everybody else to be murdered and robbed.
>
> Of course Mr. *Larkin* would not put the case exactly that way, but no other way suggested itself to him, so he abstained from what he knew or felt would be the dangers of definition. Mr. Larkin has been

---

[1] Quoted in E. H. Carr, *The Bolshevik Revolution, 1917–1923* (London, 1953), III, 128.

[2] *New York Times*, February 3, 1919.   [3] *Ibid.*

credited with ability of a kind and with moving eloquence. That is what makes him dangerous, but one observes that he prefers America to Russia as a place in which to do his preaching.[1]

As the Bolsheviki strengthened their position in Russia, Larkin's opinions, along with those of the entire left wing, hardened with regard to the revolutionary value of the Second International. It will be remembered Larkin had spent the whole spring and summer of 1917 in a frantic effort to get to the Stockholm Peace Conference, which was organized by Camille Huysmans, Secretary of the International Socialist Bureau. By the late spring of 1918 Larkin was somewhat less open-minded on the subject of International Socialists other than those approved by the Bolsheviki. 'You are aware,' he wrote Foran, General President of the Transport Union in Dublin, 'that I have notified our comrades in Russia not to accept any delegates or agents pending advice from your side. My instructions will have reached Petrograd ere this.'[2] 'I hope they acted,' he continued, referring to the official Irish Labour Movement, 'on my urgent representations in my last communications to elect delegates to act as agents in Russia, Stockholm, or any part of Europe they may be able to reach.' His instructions had been acted on, for William O'Brien and David R. Campbell, representing the Irish Trades Union Congress and Labour Party, interviewed Maxim Litvinoff, official Soviet representative in Britain, early in 1918 in London.[3] Litvinoff had promised Russia's full support for Ireland's admission to the International as a nation. Soon after the invitations went out from Moscow in January, 1919, for the First Congress of the Third International, Larkin wrote Foran, 'Our advice to you and those to be relied on is no conciliation with the Huysmans gang. We have opened up negotiations with Moscow officially.'[4] The Third International, as far as Larkin was concerned, was the only *bona fide* organization for International Socialists.

Soon after the war was over the struggle for power between the right and left wings of the American Socialist Party was on, and

[1] *New York Times*, February 4, 1919.

[2] *The Attempt to Smash*, *op. cit.*, p. 167. Letter from James Larkin to Thomas Foran, no date.

[3] *Report, Irish Labour Party and Trades Union Congress*, Waterford, August 5–7, 1918, pp. 48–49.

[4] MS., Larkin to Foran, no date. Courtesy of William O'Brien.

Larkin was in the middle of it.[1] As early as November 30, 1918, the left-wing central committee of the very powerful Boston local of the Socialist Party was calling for 'an immediate emergency National Convention,' while the left wing in Chicago had already organized the Communist Propaganda League. In early January, at a meeting of the central committee of all the locals of the Socialist Party in the New York area, the left wing made a stand.[2] This meeting was called to consider the action of the Socialist Aldermen who, in the spring of 1918, had endorsed the fourth Liberty Loan, and who, in the fall, had added insult to injury by voting approval for a Victory Arch at Fifth Avenue and Madison Square. Larkin was one among the many in the Socialist Party who were incensed, and he later declared, 'As Socialists and members of our Party you have no right to play that kind of game.' 'You go there,' said Larkin referring to City Hall, 'and pass a vote for $80,000 for a Victory Arch and upon that Victory Arch you put the name of Murmansk to the honor of the American Army, and at the same time you go on public platforms and . . . say you . . . believe in the Soviet Government.'[3]

The right-wing chairman of that meeting so exasperated the left-wing members present with his delaying tactics that they walked out and held a meeting of their own.[4] A City Committee of fourteen was appointed to draft a manifesto and appeal to the rank and file of the Party. This City Committee next met on February 2, 1919, the same day Larkin was in Boston putting the finishing touches to 'Red Week' with the Liebknecht–Luxemburg meeting. The Committee took the momentous step of deciding to set up a Party within a Party. County organizers and a speakers' committee were appointed, membership cards were to be issued, and ten cents a month in dues were to be collected. Larkin, though absent, was elected with Rose Pastor Stokes, Hourwich, and Reed to serve on the International Bureau of the Left Wing.[5] Moreover, a 'Manifesto and Program'

---

[1] *Minutes, Left Wing Section Socialist Party*, February 2, 1919–June 2, 1919. Larkin was very prominent and important as these Minutes demonstrate. Photostatic copy—Courtesy of Theodore Draper. Originals are in Lusk Committee Files, New York State Library, Manuscript Division, Albany, New York. See Theodore Draper, *The Roots of American Communism* (New York, 1957), p. 422, n. 41.

[2] Draper, *op. cit.*, p. 144.

[3] *People* vs. *Larkin*, *op. cit.*, p. 739.

[4] Draper, *op. cit.*, p. 145.

[5] *Minutes, Left Wing*, *op. cit.*, February 8, 1919.

was drawn up by John Reed and Bertram Wolfe, which was later revised by Louis C. Fraina. That Larkin approved of this left-wing call to arms was obvious when two weeks later, on February 15, 1919, at Odd Fellows Hall, St. Mark's Place, in Manhattan, he was elected to serve on the nine-man Executive Committee of the Left Wing Section of the Greater New York Locals of the Socialist Party.[1] The City Committee was enlarged to fifteen, with Larkin a member, and the 'Manifesto and Program' was adopted. By March 8 the *Revolutionary Age* was even more insistent—'We must have a National Emergency Convention.' Ever more conscious of its gathering strength, with local after local affiliating, the Left Wing demanded the transfer of the *Revolutionary Age* from Boston, and when this was refused, they founded the *New York Communist*, with John Reed as editor and Eadmonn MacAlpine coming back from Boston as associate editor.[2]

The right wing in the Socialist Party who still controlled the offices, committees, and finances of the organization, though obviously and rapidly becoming a numerical minority, quickly declared preventative war on the Left Wing for attempting to set up a Party within a Party. The New York State Committee of the Socialist Party met in Albany on April 13 and voted 24 to 17 with 2 abstentions to revoke the charter of any local that affiliated with the Left Wing. When the National Executive Committee of the Socialist Party met in Chicago on May 24 some 20,000 members were either suspended or expelled during its four-day session, and an emergency National Convention of the Party was called for August 30, 1919, in Chicago. By the beginning of July, however, two-thirds of the Party, which in January, 1919, numbered 110,000 members had been suspended or expelled.[3]

The Left Wing, meanwhile, had issued a call for a National Left Wing Conference in New York on June 21, 1919. Some ninety-four delegates, including Larkin, met at the Manhattan Lyceum for the three-day Conference. Almost immediately a discussion arose over whether, in view of the expulsions and suspensions, it might not be best to form a Communist Party right away, or to wait for the Socialist Party Convention in Chicago on August 30 to try to capture the Party machinery and finances intact. MacAlpine moved

[1] *Minutes, Left Wing, op. cit.,* February 15, 1919.
[2] *New York Communist,* April 19, 1919.
[3] Draper, *op. cit.,* pp. 156–58.

and Fraina seconded a motion that the rules be suspended so this important question could be discussed. Larkin rose to amend the motion, adding 'that Hourwich, representing those favoring an immediate Communist Party, and C. E. Ruthenberg, representing those favoring the other view, be empowered to draw up a joint resolution around which the discussion should center.'[1] The amendment was accepted, but the attempt on Larkin's part to remove the contentious issue from the floor of the Conference to the more peaceful province of a two-man committee availed nothing. When the discussion was resumed those who favoured the immediate formation of a Communist Party went down to defeat 55 to 38. When Hourwich, who was spokesman for the numerically very powerful foreign language federations, failed to secure the representation on the proposed National Council of the Left Wing that would give the federations control, he and some thirty others walked out. Larkin was then elected to the nine-man National Council which was instructed by the Conference to prepare for a Convention in Chicago on September 1, 1919, at which, presumably, they would found a Communist Party if, by that time, they had not succeeded in capturing the Socialist Party. The *Revolutionary Age* was to be moved to New York and incorporate the *New York Communist*. A Manifesto which was to have enormous consequences for Larkin was drawn up by Fraina and published in the *Revolutionary Age* on July 5, 1919. Larkin's name, along with the other eight members of the National Council, appeared on the masthead.

The walkout of Hourwich was much more serious than was indicated by the thirty-odd delegates he brought out of the Left Wing Conference with him. The bulk of the 70,000 members expelled or suspended by the Socialist Party were in the foreign language federations, and Hourwich and his group represented about two-thirds of this dispossessed membership. While among the various federations the Russian federation now dominated the others because of its numerical preponderance, and the almost mystical prestige generated in its favour by the Bolshevik Revolution. In early July the Hourwich group, who set up the National Organization Committee, began to publish *The Communist*, and called for a Convention on September 1, 1919, in Chicago to form a Communist Party. They had effectively stolen the thunder of the National Council of the Left Wing. By July 28 the nerve of the majority of the National Council

[1] *Revolutionary Age*, July 5, 1919, 'The National Left Wing Conference.'

broke, and they caved in to the Hourwich group. The National Council decided by a vote of 5 to 2 to reverse their decision about attempting to capture the Socialist Party and simply form a Communist Party on September 1 with the Hourwich group. Larkin refused to give way and he found himself with Benjamin Gitlow in a minority of two on the nine-man Council. Two of the members of the National Council, Fraina and MacAlpine, did not vote because they were on the *Revolutionary Age*, but Fraina sided with the majority and MacAlpine with the minority.[1]

Though outvoted the minority was adamant, and with the backing of Reed, they began to publish the *Voice of Labor* on August 15, 1919. They decided to continue the plan to capture the Socialist Party, or failing in this, to set up another Party. Reed and Gitlow arrived in Chicago, and on August 30 were forcibly ejected by the police from the Socialist Party Convention along with some fifty other delegates. The next evening eighty-two delegates from twenty-three states came together for a three-day conference that resulted in the founding of the Communist Labor Party. In the offices of the Russian language federation in Chicago, meanwhile, the Communist Party was founded by the Hourwich group and the majority section of the National Council. The Communist Party was now the largest with a membership of about 60,000, while the Socialist Party counted nearly 40,000, and the Communist Labor Party mustered less than 10,000. Larkin did not attend the Chicago Conventions, and it is difficult to say exactly why. He was at this time making every attempt to get back to Ireland and was probably unwilling to undertake the responsibility that would go with attending the Conventions.[2]

How the Left Wing split into a Communist Party and a Communist Labor Party is obvious enough, but why they split is much less clear. In attempting to explain why Larkin ended up in the Communist Labor Party, a good deal is learned about the differences among the Left Wing and the lack of homogeneity in the Communist

---

[1] *The Communist*, October 18, 1919, 'Communist Party and Left Wing,' see for account and justification of 5 to 2 vote on July 28, 1919. Draper, *op. cit.*, p. 175.

[2] *Workers' World* (Kansas City), October 17, 1919. See cable from Larkin 'To the Old Guard of the I.T.W.U. Stand fast, I am returning. . . .' See also *Watchword of Labour* (Dublin), October 11, 1919, for E. MacAlpine bringing to attention of Dublin Trades Council the fact that Larkin was being denied a passport. See also *People* vs. *Larkin, op. cit.*, p. 456. (Exhibit 31). When Larkin was arrested he had a faked passport in his possession.

Labor Party itself. First and foremost in the struggle for power, who was to control the Left Wing, the Russians in their domination of the language federations or the Americans? To Larkin, as an Irishman, and in light of his own practical experience as a propagandist and a trade unionist, there was no room for doubt. When the mill strike broke out in Lawrence, Massachusetts, in March, 1919, Larkin went up and 'saw 28 different groups with no common medium of conversation of carrying business,' and he 'went in amongst them and told them what they ought to do, to get Americans to take charge of their business.'[1] When asked to take charge Larkin said, 'No, I am not an American. I am not going to give these people any right to interfere on the ground that their leader is not an American.'

Besides the obvious impracticality of a Russian leadership Larkin shared, along with Reed and Gitlow, a strong dislike of the abstract theorizing of the self-appointed interpreters of the Marxist holy writ. He 'denounced the Communist Party because of the love of its leaders for long words and abstract reasoning which went over the brows of the masses.'[2] 'Their talk,' said Larkin revealingly, 'is full of stuff against "Parliamentary Government." The people can't understand them. We can't accomplish anything until we get the intellectuals out of the movement.'[3] Larkin always had a bad habit of equating and therefore confusing intellectuals with theoreticians. Moreover, to Larkin the propagandist the communication of ideas always took precedence over the creation of ideas. All his life, he explained, he had been trying 'to simplify terms, to get men to understand if they can't understand a five syllable word, to get it into a word of two syllables. That is more important than making yourself a theoretician and giving yourself great credit as a literary person. Get the truth and put in language so that all men can understand it.'[4] The day of the Prophets and the Master was done, for the Disciples had come into their own.

[1] *People* vs. *Larkin*, pp. 751–52. See also for Lawrence Strike, *New England Leader*, March 1, 1919.

[2] *New York Times*, November 11, 1919.   [3] *Ibid.*

[4] *People* vs. *Larkin*, *op. cit.*, p. 745. See also p. 127. 'I held to the language of the man in the street as much more useful until the time they reached a better level, until he becomes more class conscious.' With him in this section were, Larkin claimed, Reed, MacAlpine, Gitlow, Carney, and Wagenknecht. See also 'Carney Memoir,' *op. cit.*, p. 18. 'He [Larkin] was in constant argument with the intellectuals, whose leader was Louis Fraina. . . . There were arguments as to

On top of his dislike of Russian domination and his obvious dis-
taste for theorists and their terminology, Larkin disagreed also with
some of his Left Wing comrades on the place of trade unions in the
revolutionary movement. The question posed here was one of
emphasis rather than of difference. It was certainly no accident that
the Communist Labor Party should choose to dilute its title with
the word labor. The old DeLeonite Socialist Labor Party and
Syndicalist tradition was still strong among the Left Wing, especially
among those western delegates who came out of and leaned heavily
on a revolutionary trade union background.[1] Needless to point out,
Larkin's own experience in the Irish Movement and the turn of his
thoughts in more recent years in America were largely Syndicalist in
nature. Larkin and those who thought like him placed a high value
on trade unions as revolutionary instruments, while others thought
of trade unions as merely a conservative force.[2] Though Larkin
despised Samuel Gompers and his American Federation of Labor,
he advised his friends 'to go into labor unions and try to revolu-
tionize them.'[3] He did not accept the dual unionist idea, inherited

[1] *Workers' World*, August 22, 1919. The Larkin, Gitlow, Reed Group 'decided
to publish a paper for the workers to be called The Voice of Labor, whose policy
is to explain and advocate Industrial Unionism and control by the rank and file
through the shop committee system. Simple language, plenty of illustrations and
cartoons, detailed and attractively written accounts of new developments in the
labor movement feature the paper.'

[2] *The Communist*, October 4, 1919. See article by J. T. Murphy, 'Industrial
Unionism and the Revolution,' this is reprinted from 'The Workers' Dread-
nought' in England. 'A year of revolution will teach the masses more of industrial
organization than fifty years of propaganda.' See *Ibid.*, April, 1921, 'The International and Unionism,' by Louis C. Fraina.

[3] *New York Times*, February 3, 1919.

the name of the organ of the Left Wing. Jim was annoyed when they rejected his
suggestion of calling it the Worker. They never did reach agreement and it was
called the Revolutionary Age. They feared the influence of Jim so they ran it from
Boston.' See also Hicks, *op. cit.*, p. 232, for Reed's attitude towards intellectuals,
though of a different variety. See also the *Workers' World*, August 22, 1919.
'There has been for a long time a wide-spread recognition of the need for Socialist
propaganda for the working masses, reducing the statements of theory to the
simplest possible language and having for its primary purpose the unification of
the labor movement under the control of the rank and file. This doesn't mean that
we should dispense with theoretical literature, but that we departmentalize our
propaganda, thereby greatly increasing the efficiency of the movement.' This
paper was a weekly published in Kansas City and edited by Earl R. Browder and
James P. Cannon, who supported the Communist Labor Party.

from the Knights of Labor and typified by the I.W.W., that the revolutionary workers should organize in separate industrial unions while maintaining their membership in their craft unions. This concept did not appeal very much to Larkin since he came out of a British trade union tradition that was hostile to dual unionism.

It is now obvious, in the light of Larkin's attitude towards 'intellectuals' and the place of trade unions in the revolutionary Socialist Movement, that any characterization of the Left Wing split as simply a struggle for power between the 'Russians' and the 'Americans' will not do. Another question arises, however, when Larkin's importance in the early Communist Movement is considered—how American were the 'Americans'? If Larkin were the only Irishman in the movement he might be passed over as simply an aberration. Such was not the case for Irishmen were both numerous and significant. Eadmonn MacAlpine and Jack Carney, for example, were Irish, intimate personal friends of Larkin's, who unhesitatingly followed him into the Communist Labor Party. MacAlpine was associate editor of the *Revolutionary Age*, the *New York Communist*, and the *Voice of Labor* in that order, while Carney was the editor of the Communist Labor Party organ *Truth* in Duluth, and as violent an opponent of the Communist Party as Larkin. It would then be more correct to refer to the 'English speaking' opposition to the 'Russians' in the early Communist Movement than to the 'American'. The significant point, however, is that an important section of the so-called 'Americans' were Irish, and that their roots were as deeply struck in European Socialism as those of the 'Russians,' though it was in the British Socialist tradition rather than the continental tradition.[1] How much the American Communist Movement owes to this bastard Irish strain of British Socialism is, no doubt, difficult to assess, but it would be a mistake to overlook it.

While the Socialist Movement in the United States was fragmenting into a collection of impotent sects in 1919, the national scene appeared to be ripening for revolution. During 1919 the nation was rocked by the most serious wave of strikes in its history. This series of strikes, which began with the Seattle General Strike in February and culminated in the gigantic steel and coal strikes in the fall, indicated a deep dissatisfaction with the post-war economic order in

---

[1] *People* vs. *Larkin*, *op. cit.*, p. 130. 'You know,' said Larkin, 'I belong to the British school of Socialism.' MacAlpine was born in Belfast, Carney in Liverpool as was Larkin, but they all considered themselves as being Irish.

the United States as well as in Europe. Though these strikes had little or no political significance the cry of Bolshevik plot, early and often, produced a profound state of national hysteria. The 100 per cent Americans in their 100 per cent American organizations such as the American Defense Society, the Klu Klux Klan, and the American Legion all rallied to slay the Bolshevik dragon. Senatorial Committees on the federal and state levels, such as the Overman Committee and the Lusk Committee in New York, respectively, were empowered to investigate the extent of Bolshevik penetration and influence, while the Congress armed the Justice Department with an appropriation of $500,000 to secure the nation against anarchist bomb plots. American society was in the throes of what has been aptly described as the 'Red Scare.'[1]

On November 7, 1919, the second anniversary of the Bolshevik Revolution, A. Mitchell Palmer, Attorney-General of the United States, ordered that the offices of the Union of Russian Workers be raided simultaneously in twelve cities. The main blow fell in New York as some 200 members of the U.R.W. were arrested at the Russian People's House, 133 East 15 Street. The next evening the Lusk Committee raided seventy-three radical centres in New York City and arrested some 500 persons. Among these were Larkin and Benjamin Gitlow.[2] Along with thirty-three others they were charged with violating the New York State statute on criminal anarchy, which had been passed twenty years before after President McKinley was assassinated in Buffalo. At the time of his arrest Larkin was described 'as one of the most dangerous of the agitators in this country.'[3] On Monday morning, November 10, 1919, Larkin and Gitlow, after spending the weekend in the Tombs, were charged before Chief City Magistrate McAdoo with violating the statute on criminal anarchy by publishing the 'Left Wing Manifesto' in the *Revolutionary Age*, some four months before on July 5, 1919, and were held in $15,000 bail each.

In an attempt to have what was an enormous bail reduced a few days later, their attorney Charles Recht argued 'that these articles were not incitations to the violent overthrow of the United States Government, but peaceful writings containing abstract reasoning.'[4] He maintained that 'the Government was trying to make a crime of

[1] Robert K. Murray, *Red Scare* (Minneapolis, 1955).
[2] *New York Times*, November 9, 1919.   [3] *Ibid.*
[4] *Ibid.*, November 14, 1919.

socialism and to punish men who were holding views which failed to agree with those of the majority.' Recht summed up by referring to Larkin and Gitlow as 'pioneers in a movement for a better day.' The Assistant District Attorney, Alexander I. Rorke, on the other hand, argued that Larkin and Gitlow had 'played a part in preparing the violent manifestos, as well as printing them.'[1] 'This manifesto,' he declared, 'runs afoul of our statutes on criminal anarchy, and it advocates the overthrow of the Government by violent force and unlawful means.' 'It means,' he summed up, 'the conquest of the Government by bullets rather than ballots.' The next day Magistrate McAdoo refused to reduce the $15,000 bail, stating, incidentally, 'that every member of the Communist Party in this State, numbering 75,000 or more, was guilty of criminal anarchy in becoming a member of the party.'[2] When City Magistrates feel called upon to declare on the legality of political parties, there is, undoubtedly, a fever in the body politic.

There was some difficulty in raising the bail, but between John Devoy, the Irish Provisional Government, local Socialists and Communists, and a national and international appeal, the $15,000 was posted and Larkin was released on November 20, 1919, twelve days after his arrest.[3] Though out on bail Larkin and Gitlow appeared at a meeting of their sympathizers where 'more than 500 men and women rose to their feet and took the Communist oath,' administered by Larkin, 'to fight for and remain true to the party's tenets.'[4] In the course of his remarks Larkin referred to Senator Lusk and his Committee as the 'microbes of society', 'men with the minds of an amœba,' and, for good measure, 'a body with the vile odor of the skunk in and about them.' 'We had in Russia the Black Hundred, the Lusk Committee of Russia,' Larkin continued. 'The people of Russia rose in their might and took them and they went out of history.' In dismissing the Government's assertion that they had found explosives in the raid on the offices of the Union of Russian Workers Larkin wondered, 'if the police thought the American people were so stupid as to believe the combustibles were really there as claimed.' 'We don't use such weapons,' Larkin declared. 'We use mental bombs to blow the new idea, a new ideal, into life.' In closing, he urged 'the workers to spread the tidings of Communism.'[5]

[1] *New York Times*, November 14, 1919.
[2] *Ibid.*, November 15, 1919.
[3] *Ibid.*, November 20, 1919.
[4] *Ibid.*, November 29, 1919.
[5] *Ibid.*

Meanwhile, three others besides Larkin and Gitlow, Harry Winitsky, Isaac F. Ferguson, and Charles A. Ruthenberg were also indicted, but all were to be tried individually. Gitlow was first and his trial began on January 30, 1920.[1] He was defended by Clarence Darrow, the greatest trial lawyer of his day, but after Darrow's summation to the jury Gitlow insisted on thanking Darrow but explained to the jury that he was a Bolshevik and would always be a Bolshevik.

> My whole life [said Gitlow] has been dedicated to the movement which I am in. No jails will change my opinion in that respect. I ask no clemency. I realize that as an individual I have a perfect right to my opinions, that I would be false to myself if I tried to evade that which I supported. Regardless of your verdict, I maintain that the principles of the Left-Wing Manifesto and Program on the whole are correct, that capitalism is in a state of collapse.[2]

Alexander I. Rorke, the Assistant District Attorney who prosecuted the case, remarked later that he thought Darrow had won over the jury until Gitlow insisted on destroying the effect with his *beau geste*.[3] The jury took Gitlow at his word and found him guilty, and a few days later he received a sentence of five to ten years in Sing Sing. Harry Winitsky was tried six weeks later and was defended by William Fallon, 'The Great Mouthpiece,' perhaps the outstanding criminal lawyer in the country after Darrow, but the precedent of Gitlow and the rising hysterical tide contributed to by a second series of 'Palmer Raids' in early January, 1919, were too much for even the best of legal talent. Winitsky was also found guilty, and he received a five-to-ten-year sentence as well.[4]

Since the best in legal talent was obviously of no avail Larkin decided to save the fees and defend himself. He was, however, privately advised by Jeremiah O'Leary, who had just been acquitted himself in a celebrated treason trial. His trial opened on April 16, 1920, and with the stage entirely to himself Larkin gave one of the finest of those remarkable virtuoso performances of which he was so capable. No one would ever argue that Larkin was profound, but he had when necessary a sound grasp of fundamentals, which, coupled with a stubborn sincerity and a remarkable ability to articulate, made

---

[1] *New York Times*, November 29, 1919.
[2] *Communist Labor*, February 25, 1920.
[3] Alexander I. Rorke, personal interview.
[4] *New York Times*, March 21, 1920.

him formidable under any circumstances. Larkin had not only the ability to recognize and to respond to a challenge but also to emerge at the moment of crisis fully convinced that he was Everyman. The trial took ten days and the transcript ran to nearly 250,000 words. Since Larkin called no witnesses, except himself of course, the burden of his defence and the high point in the trial lay in his three-and-a-half-hour summation to the jury. To characterize this effort would be to characterize Larkin. He was, at one and the same time, proud and humble, arrogant and defiant, articulate and incoherent, sincere and affected, naïve and shrewd, maudlin and magnanimous. The total effect was overwhelming and the examination of the parts does not do him justice. The summation was a seamless garment and nowhere and in nothing was Larkin seen more whole or more constant.

After some perfunctory and complimentary remarks to the jury Larkin reminded them in the third person that it was no crime of violence that he was charged with.

> The defendent claims here now that he is not getting tried for any overt act; he is not getting tried for any intent to commit an overt act, he is getting tried for within his mind focusing the ideas of the centuries, and trying to bring knowledge into a co-ordinate form that he might assist and develop and beautify life. That is the charge against the defendent—that he preached a doctrine of humanity against inhumanity; that he preached the doctrine of order against disorder; that he preached the doctrine of brotherhood as against that mischievous hellish thing of National and brute, unheard hatred.[1]

'Some people have suggested the Socialist Movement I belong to is religion,' Larkin went on to say, 'inasmuch as religion seems—I think the definition is admitted by everybody—a reaching up to the higher things of life, doing something or leaving something that is greater than yourself.'[2] If that is the case, Larkin maintained, then the Socialists are the only people in the world who are practising their religion.

'The question,' said Larkin, 'has been raised as to the defendant having advocated force, violence and unlawful means to overthrow the Government.' Though he denied the charge Larkin asked, 'Do the People of the State of New York say that you have not the right to overthrow organized Government?' 'This country,' said Larkin, quoting Abraham Lincoln, 'with its institutions, belongs to the

---

[1] *People* vs. *Larkin, op. cit.*, pp. 690–91.   [2] *Ibid.*, p. 694.

people who inhabit it. Whenever they shall grow weary of the existing government, they can exercise their constitutional right of amending it, or their revolutionary right to dismember and overthrow it.'[1] Drifting into the relationship between 'economic determinism' and justice Larkin maintained that all abstract principles, such as justice, have concrete roots in the prevailing economic conditions and 'if the conditions are not such that justice itself can have voice and being, there can be no justice.' The present economic system could only result, then, in Larkin's opinion, in the subversion of justice.

After discussing the appalling social condition of Liverpool that he saw in his youth and early manhood, which led him to embrace Socialism, Larkin explained that he, too, had an American heritage: 'How did I get the love of comrades, only by reading Whitman? How did I get this love of humanity except by understanding men like Thoreau and Emerson and the greatest man of all next to Whitman—Mark Twain? Those are the men I have lived with, the real Americans.'[2] Woodrow Wilson also helped Larkin find his way along life's long road, and he quoted passages from the President's *New Freedom* that declared, 'Our Government has been for years under the control of heads of great allied corporations with special interests.' 'That is not the Communist Manifesto,' said Larkin, 'that is an American with a long tradition, the Revolutionary tradition.' Reflecting on the rights of a minority in a democracy Larkin again quoted Lincoln—'If by mere force of numbers a majority should deprive a minority of any clearly written constitutional right it might in a moral point of view justify revolution.' 'Gentlemen,' said Larkin solemnly, 'I warn you, you twelve men, it may be that you are going to justify revolution, a revolution that is not even thought of yet.' Worse than that, said Larkin, where was this all to end? 'Sh! He is a dangerous man. He is trying to overthrow the government. Put him in the darkness. And then they take the next man, and that man he isn't so dangerous, and so finally they come to you.' 'I suggest to you,' said Larkin, 'the time to stop this manifestation of brutality and force and passion is right now.'[3]

Though he did not stand for the 'terminology' in the Manifesto in the *Revolutionary Age* Larkin defended the Manifesto as a point of view. First, he argued at great length that the Manifesto and the ideas expressed in it could not be understood without a thorough

---

[1] *People* v. *Larkin*, *op. cit.*, p. 709.
[2] *Ibid.*, pp. 722–23. [3] *Ibid.*, p. 746.

grounding in the writing of Karl Marx and Frederick Engels. Whose word are we to take? An Assistant District Attorney 'who never read . . . an economic treatise in his life' or Socialists who have devoted their lives to study and to the cause. Even after acquiring an authoritative understanding of the Marxian dialectic what about the interpretation of the specific phrases in the Manifesto? What about, for example, the phrase 'final act,' which the District Attorney made much of in the course of the trial? 'There can be no final act, gentlemen,' declared Larkin. 'Anyone who knows life knows there is no final act. Death itself is not final, and yet you go and sentence a man for five or ten years on the phrase "the final act." '

What does all this mean for the freedom of thought and inquiry? asked Larkin. Why 'Einstein and men like him would not be allowed to function, would not be allowed to think. You would have no field of activity either in religion, in art or in science.' State functionaries are going 'to put a steel cap on the minds of the people of this country and they are going to screw it down until they make you all one type,' Larkin warned.[1] 'I have been a man who has always abhorred violence,' he said, 'because I have been brutally abused by this organized force.' 'Who used force and violence?' Larkin asked. 'Is it the strong that use force? Is it the strong that use violence?' 'It is always the weak, the cowardly, those who can only live by conservatism and force and violence.' 'It has always been down the ages the weak, the bigoted, those who want [lack] knowledge, that have always used force and violence against the advancement of knowledge,' and Larkin observed pointedly, 'It comes with ill grace from the constituted authorities of America. . . .'[2]

'Gentlemen,' said Larkin, beginning the end of his summation, 'some day you in America will be told the truth. In the meantime we who have been on the housetops telling the truth have to suffer. We have to go down the dark days and the dark nights, but we go there with the truth in our eyes and our hearts, and no lie upon our lips. . . .' 'I have read Wendell Phillips since I was a boy. Wendell Phillips says,' said Larkin quoting, ' "Government exists to protect the rights of minorities. The loved and the rich need no protection—they have many friends and few enemies. We have praised our Union for seventy years. [Speaking of 1860.] This is the first time it is tested. Has it educated men who know their rights and dare

[1] *People* v. *Larkin, op. cit.*, p. 767.
[2] *Ibid.*, p. 770.

to maintain them?" '[1] 'The ways of the broad highways have been my ways,' said Larkin concluding, 'and I have never been encompassed by walls, and so it may be tomorrow—you may decide . . . that in the interest of this great Republic of 110,000,000 people, this individual will have to be put away for five or ten years.'

> I do not object to your doing it. I say you have a right in honor and truth, if you believe this man has ever been guilty of any crime against your country, stand by your country, live by its people, live always in its interest. I have always done that with my country, and that is the reason I stand practically without anybody of my own people standing with me except the poor and unfortunate. I have got Irishmen, and Irishmen in this country, who believe in me and who will see to it that I have got a decent chance; and to those who belong to me at home they have always known me, always known what I stood for, and my wife and children will be looked after.
>
> And so I thank you.[2]

When the case went to the jury there was 'a belief among the lawyers and spectators that a feeling of sympathy might result in a disagreement.'[3] The jury, however, returned a verdict of guilty after 'considering the evidence not more than an hour.' On May 3, 1920, Larkin received a sentence of five to ten years and was removed immediately to Sing Sing.[4]

There was much commiseration and many demands for his release on both sides of the Atlantic. The Socialist New York *Call* carried a very sympathetic article by Agnes Smedley the day after his sentence.[5] The Communist Labor Party *Voice of Labor* denounced the 'Brutal Sentence on Larkin,' while his wife announced that the United States Government had refused a visa to their eldest son and thus prevented the boy from visiting his father whom he had not seen in nearly six years.[6] In Boston his friends held a mass meeting demanding his release, while in Dublin 2,000 of his faithful dockers struck work for two hours and proposed a memorial asking for his release.[7] The Socialist Party of New York State incorporated a demand for his release in their platform and the Irish Labour Party and Trades

---

[1] *People* v. *Larkin, op. cit.*, pp. 797–98.   [2] *Ibid.*, p. 799.
[3] *New York Times*, April 28, 1920.   [4] *Ibid.*, May 4, 1920.
[5] *Call*, May 4, 1920.
[6] *Watchword of Labour* (Dublin), May 15 and June 26, 1920.
[7] *New York Times*, June 31 and July 7, 1920.

Union Congress protested his sentence and imprisonment.[1] The Connolly Clubs organized in New York, Boston, Philadelphia, and Butte were somewhat more practical and retained Frank P. Walsh, a celebrated labour lawyer and liberal, as chief counsel to handle the appeal of his case.[2] In Chicago a Larkin Defense Committee was organized by his old friend John Fitzpatrick of the Chicago Federation of Labor.[3]

Not long after his arrival in Sing Sing, Larkin, with Gitlow and Winitsky, was quietly shifted to Clinton prison in Dannemora.[4] The new accommodations, though in the heart of the Adirondacks, did not offer the many amenities that were provided in Sing Sing. Money allowances, food packages, mail, visiting privileges, prison discipline, and regimen were all more restricted than they were in the sociological showplace Sing Sing had become under Warden Lawes. The prisoners in Dannemora were of a different type also, more dangerous, and generally serving longer terms.[5] Agnes Smedley, the *Call* reporter, managed a visit to Clinton prison and wrote that Larkin was ageing fast in cruel Dannemora.[6] Rumour that he was suffering from tuberculosis reached Britain and resulted in a motion in the House of Commons asking that he be released for treatment.[7] The adverse publicity had its effect, for Larkin, Gitlow, and Winitsky were all transferred back to Sing Sing in November, 1920.[8]

While in Sing Sing Larkin worked in the bootery, manufacturing and repairing shoes. He received many visitors, and his friends and the Larkin Defense Committee kept him supplied with enough money to meet his needs.[9] His spirit was certainly not broken by

[1] *New York Times*, July 5, 1920. *Watchword of Labour*, August 14, 1920.

[2] *Watchword of Labour*, September 11, 1920. See letter from Michael T. Berry, August 10, 1920.

[3] *New York Times*, October 11, 1920. See 'Convict No. 50943.' A booklet of 30 pages prepared by the 'Larkin Defense Committee.' See p. 23 for picture of John Fitzpatrick. This booklet is at Tamiment Institute Library, 7 East 15 Street, New York 3, N.Y.

[4] Benjamin Gitlow, *I Confess* (New York, 1939), p. 95.

[5] *Ibid.*, pp. 95 ff.

[6] *Call*, July 25, 1920. See Gitlow, *op. cit.*, pp. 116–17.

[7] *New York Times*, October 22, 1920.

[8] *Ibid.*, November 28, 1920.

[9] Frank Harris, *Contemporary Portraits* (London, 1924), Fourth Series. See Chapters IV, 'Charlie Chaplin, and a Visit to Sing Sing,' and XXI 'Jim Larkin.' See also 'Carney Memoir,' *op. cit.*, pp. 8–9. See also *Voice of Labour* (Dublin), December 3, 1921—'A visit to Jim Larkin.'

prison life and he appeared to take it all, on the whole, pretty much in his stride. On his first St. Patrick's Day in Sing Sing, for example, he was invited to address the prisoners at their annual celebration. In those days many of the prisoners were either Irish or Irish-American, and perhaps an even greater percentage of the prison guards were also of Irish background. Larkin opened his remarks by recalling the ancient legend about how St. Patrick had chased all the snakes out of Ireland and remarked that he had never really believed the myth until the present moment. To the great delight of his fellow prisoners Larkin blandly looked at rows of guards and explained that the snakes had really come to America and become 'screws' and 'warders.'[1] Things were made even easier for him when he was shifted to Comstock, which was an open prison with little supervision and the prisoners engaged mainly in farm work.

The Larkin Defense Committee meanwhile continued its work in conjunction with the newly formed Irish American Labor League, 'which was little more than the Connolly Club . . . directing the activities of those subscribing to Larkin's defense.'[2] When the leading lights in the Labor League, T. J. O'Flaherty, brother of the novelist Liam O'Flaherty, and Emmett O'Reilly quarrelled for one of those reasons Irishmen know best and both resigned in a huff, the task of carrying on the attempt to secure his release fell to Mina Carney, the wife of Jack Carney.[3] Mrs. Carney approached Governor Miller in the fall of 1922 after Larkin had served over two years and asked him for a free pardon for Larkin. The Governor countered with a suggestion that she secure the signatures of ten important and representative people in the community, and he promised he would do what he could. Mrs. Carney, with the help of Jeremiah O'Leary and Dr. Gertrude Kelly, began to collect the signatures. The celebrated Father Duffy, chaplain of the 'Fighting 69th,' Monsignor James Power, prominent in Irish-American affairs, and William P. Larkin, a namesake and head of the Knights of Columbus, all signed the petition. Mrs. Carney also interviewed Cardinal Hayes, then Archbishop of New York, who did not sign the petition but promised to write to the Governor on Larkin's behalf.[4] When, however, Frank P. Walsh entered an appeal without Larkin's knowledge the

[1] Benjamin Gitlow, personal interview. Flynn, *op. cit.*, p. 262.
[2] Lyng, *loc. cit.*
[3] 'Carney Memoir,' *op. cit.*, p. 9.
[4] Mina Carney, personal interview.

petition was automatically disqualified and Governor Miller's hands were legally tied.

Prior to this in March, 1922, Governor Miller had been asked to consider a pardon, and even though Alexander I. Rorke, the Assistant District Attorney, who prosecuted Larkin recommended leniency in view of the action taken in other states on similar sentences, the Governor had decided against granting the pardon.[1] Larkin had then applied for his release on a certificate of reasonable doubt since his case was pending before the State Court of Appeals. He was released on May 6, 1922, and immediately rearrested on another charge of criminal anarchy.[2] The authorities threatened to arrest him again as soon as he delivered bail, and two more warrants were reported to have been issued. The next day he was released from the Tombs, but the police did not rearrest him. Among the greetings he received after his release was the following cablegram:

Moscow, May 27, 1922

To Jim Larkin:

   The Communist International sends its warmest greeting to the undaunted fighter released from the 'democratic' prisons.

ZINOVIEV.

President of the Communist International.[3]

The State Court of Appeals, however, upheld his conviction in July, and he returned to Sing Sing to finish his five-to-ten-year sentence.[4]

In November, 1922, Alfred E. Smith won the election for Governor in New York and was inaugurated on January 1, 1923. A few days later the Governor granted a public hearing for an application for a pardon for Larkin on January 9, 1923.[5] At the hearing representatives of various patriotic American and Irish organizations explained why they thought he should be released. The Rev. John H. Dooley, speaking on behalf of the American Association for the Recognition of the Irish Republic, said Larkin was 'not an anarchist.' 'His Irish nature and his Catholic training preclude that,' explained Father Dooley. 'He is the victim of the hysterical times.'[6] Representing the Daughters of the American Revolution Mrs. Malcolm Duncan asserted, surprisingly enough, that 'If the Constitution of the

[1] *New York Times*, March 28, 1922.   [2] *Ibid.*, May 2, 1922.
[3] *Workers' Republic* (Dublin), June 10, 1922.
[4] *New York Times*, July 13, 1922.   [5] *Ibid.*, January 10, 1923.   [6] *Ibid.*

United States were strictly enforced there would be no political prisoners in this country.'[1] The Speakers Bureau for American Independence and the Irish Progressive League also sent representatives to plead for Larkin's release.

Eight days later, on January 17, Governor Smith granted Larkin a free pardon. 'The great public interest aroused by this case,' wrote Governor Smith, 'prompts me to state my reasons.'[2] The reasons are not only a warm tribute to the memory of Al Smith, but if Liberty is to be maintained through democracy this is the manner in which the majority must respect the rights of the minority, and the strong must protect the weak:

> The statute upon which Larkin was convicted defines criminal anarchy as the doctrine 'that organized government should be overthrown by force or violence *** or by an unlawful means.' It provides that whoever advocated such a doctrine is guilty of a felony. What Larkin did was to join in issuing the manifesto of the so-called 'Left-Wing' of the Socialist Party. That manifesto counsels a change in our form of government to what is described as the 'dictatorship of the proletariat,' and that this change should be accomplished by strikes called to affect the political action of the electorate.
>
> My present action in no way involves the slightest agreement with this manifesto. I condemn the dictatorship of 'the proletariat,' of the farmers, of the capitalists, of the merchants or of any other section of the community. In a free democracy we know no dictatorships and we endure none. No group has any legal, social or moral right to impose by dictatorship its views or interests on any other group. Likewise I condemn the project to coerce political action by any such method as the calling of general strikes. Labor has the right to strike for the purpose of securing reasonable improvement of its own conditions, but not for the purpose of driving other groups into the acceptance of a proposed political dictatorship. I disapprove such a project just as I would disapprove a combination of capitalists or of manufacturers to constrain political action of the laborers or the farmers by withholding from them the means of procuring the necessaries of life.
>
> I pardon Larkin, therefore, not because of agreement with his views, but despite my disagreement with them.
>
> Moreover, I believe, that the safety of the State is affirmatively impaired by the imposition of such a sentence for such a cause.
>
> Political progress results from the clash of conflicting opinions. The public assertion of an erroneous doctrine is perhaps the surest way to

[1] *New York Times*, January 10, 1923.   [2] *Ibid.*, January 18, 1923.

disclose the error and make it evidence to the electorate. And it is a distinct disservice of the State to impose, for the utterance of a misguided opinion, such extreme punishment as may tend to deter, in proper cases, that full and free discussion of political issues which is a fundamental of democracy.

Stripped of its legalistic aspects, this, to my mind is a political case where a man has been punished for the statement of his beliefs. From the legal point of view it is a case where a man has received, during the period of unusual popular excitement following the close of the war, too severe a sentence for a crime involving no moral turpitude. One of the prevailing opinions in the Court of Appeals stated that the judge of that court recognized that 'the sentence may have been too heavy for the offence.' He has already served over two years in prison. This, in my judgement, fully expiates his offense. The State of New York does not ask vengeance and the ends of justice have already been amply met.[1]

On his release from Sing Sing in January Larkin did not immediately make arrangements to return to Ireland. Instead he tried to implement an idea that had first occurred to him the previous June when he had been released on a certificate of reasonable doubt. The newspapers had reported that Belfast had been reduced to almost famine conditions because of the fratricidal strife then raging between Nationalists and Unionists in Ireland. No doubt with the Dublin lockout of 1913 in mind, he had conceived the dramatic idea of fitting out a relief food ship. 'Send us $20,000,' he had imperiously cabled Foran, the President of the Transport Union, 'to furnish ship. Our Volunteer crew and loaders ready. Will get food cargo here.'[2] The idea of a foodship had not slipped his mind, and soon after his release he again took up the project. In the company of Mrs. Hannah Sheehy Skeffington, and with Jack Carney as Chairman, he held a meeting in Chicago, and raised some $1,500. He and Carney then 'inspected some ships on Long Island. They were good ships with new Scotch boilers. They could have been had for $15,000. It was then that Jim cabled the Union for money.'[3] A series of cables ended with the following message from Foran on April 9, 1923—'Executive cannot sanction application for five thousand pounds. Executive request reply . . . as to date of your return.'[4]

Larkin, accompanied by Carney, then went to Washington 'for

---

[1] *New York Times*, January 18, 1923.   [2] *Attempt to Smash, op. cit.*, p. 142.
[3] 'Carney Memoir,' *loc. cit.*   [4] *Attempt to Smash, loc. cit.*

the *sole* purpose of forcing the Government to deport him.'[1] 'We met,' Carney wrote years later, 'the then Secretary of Labor, Mr. Davis, who was amazed at the forceful manner in which Jim asked to be allowed to go home. Within 24 hours he was arrested and placed on Ellis Island.'[2] At police headquarters, after his arrest, Larkin laughed and chatted with the detectives and on leaving shook hands all around saying, 'Well, I guess its back to the old country this time all right, and I'm glad of it. If you ever come to Ireland, look me up. You'll find me at Liberty Hall in Dublin.'[3] Carney, meanwhile, had signed on the S.S. *Majestic* as a French chef, the ship on which Larkin was to be deported. They did not mind so much his not being French, but when they found out he was not even a chef, they were outraged and put him to work stoking the boilers.[4]

[1] 'Carney Memoir,' *loc. cit.*
[2] *Ibid.* The Secretary of Labor was James J. Davis.
[3] *New York Times*, April 20, 1923.
[4] 'Carney Memoir,' *loc. cit.*

PART FIVE

Ishmael, 1923–1947

XI

HOMECOMING

A LITTLE after five on Monday evening, April 30, 1923, the mail-boat from Holyhead in Wales steamed alongside Carlisle pier at Kingstown, the port terminus for Dublin. Larkin in his black broad-brimmed hat stood on the boat deck, 'his hands thrust deep in the pockets of his black overcoat. A grim-faced, dour looking man of middle age, he seemed wholly unconscious of the excitement which his coming appeared to evoke.'[1] He had been away for nearly eight and a half years. When he left Ireland in late 1914 she was already involved in the beginning of the First World War. Now he returned to find her in the last stages of a disastrous civil war. Some fifty followers had made the ten-mile journey from Dublin to greet their returning Chief, but they were prevented from getting on to the pier by five or six armed sentries.[2] With the other passengers, Larkin 'had to submit to a cursory search of his clothing.' 'I haven't got a gun yet, anyhow,' he was heard to remark gruffly to the official who 'frisked' him.[3]

When his train pulled into Dublin's Westland Row station Larkin was greeted by nearly five thousand enthusiastic admirers. With great difficulty he made his way to a waiting brake, behind which the crowd followed in procession through Brunswick Street and Tara Street into Beresford Place, while music was provided by the O'Connell fife and drum band.[4] A halt was called in Beresford Place and Larkin, as in the old days, made a speech from an upper story window in Liberty Hall. 'Comrades,' his voice rang out clearly, 'this was a meeting of the old guard and the new guard, and they all

[1] *Irish Times*, May 1, 1923.   [2] *Ibid.*   [3] *Ibid.*
[4] *Freeman's Journal*, May 1, 1923.

knew the old rule of the Transport and General Workers' Union: "Each for all and all for each." [1] 'Unity was strength,' continued Larkin, 'but there had been a lack of faith and a limitation of vision. Those who had founded that hall had dreamed great dreams and were going to realise them.' Since he had come back, he noticed, 'the rich were now richer and the poor were poorer.' 'There were many ways to win freedom and liberty,' said Larkin amidst cheers, and they had not tried them all yet. He advised that the three important things for them 'were unity, solidarity and charity.' Larkin then touched upon the burning issue of the day—the civil war. 'It was a bitter truth,' he lamented, that they, 'who should love each other, they who were the Gael, were seeking by every means in their power to destroy the Gael. . . .' He now suggested 'the time had arrived when peace should be their motto, and peace should be their work, and peace would come in their time.' 'Any section,' he concluded amidst cheers, 'that continued the strife would be remembered as traitors to the nation and renegades to their God.'

In justice, however, Larkin must be asked to bear some measure of the responsibility for the civil war in Ireland. The tortuous years between 1918 and 1923 in Ireland are the most painful in her exciting history. Irishmen contended in these years not only with each other but with those fundamental ideas that cause all men to search their souls. The frame of reference provided by the ideal of Ireland a nation, which had served Irishmen for over a century, was broken by the civil war. The eternal questions of ends and means, principle or survival, conscience, justice, power, the lesser of two evils or the greater good, caused even those who were pygmies among their fellows to pause for reflection. The horrors and honours of a national war waged against the British and won against terrible odds was soon forgotten when the country found itself in the dreadful maw of civil war. The redeeming feature of the civil war, paradoxically enough, was that it was complete. It permeated the roots of Irish society, for no section, class, or family had a monopoly on a point of view. The grievous wounds inflicted on pride and person in the name of principle will happily pass with that generation of individuals who were so deeply concerned and affected.

Soon after the end of the First World War in November, 1918, Sinn Fein declared for an Irish Republic. There followed a guerilla war, which continued for nearly three years until October, 1921,

[1] *Freeman's Journal*, May 1, 1923.

when Lloyd George, the British Prime Minister, and Eamon de Valera, President of the Irish Republic, 'now virtually established,' agreed to negotiate the Irish Question. What emerged from a conference held in London, which de Valera did not attend in person, was the offer of 'dominion status' on the Canadian model for Ireland. The 'Articles of Agreement,' or as it was popularly called, the 'Treaty,' was agreed to and signed on December 6, 1921, by the Irish representatives, who then returned to Ireland to submit their work to the Dail, or Irish Parliament, for ratification. De Valera immediately declared his opposition to the 'Treaty' on the grounds that it completely subverted the idea of a Republic. On the other hand it was argued by Arthur Griffith, one of the representatives to the London conference, that 'dominion status' was a good and legitimate beginning towards any end the Irish people might desire in a form of government, whether it be an Irish Free State or an Irish Republic. When the 'Treaty' was submitted to the Dail on January 7, 1922, it was approved by a vote of 64 to 57. De Valera resigned as President, and a motion that he be re-elected was defeated by a majority of two, 60 to 58. Arthur Griffith was then elected President and formed an Executive to implement the 'Treaty,' but the opposition led by de Valera ominously walked out of the Dail as the Roll was being called. Several days later Griffith summoned the Dail, but the Republican deputies refused to attend. The Dail, the Army, and the people were split from top to bottom and right down the middle. The nation had begun to drift towards a terrible point of no return.[1]

In America, meanwhile, Larkin, though in jail, issued a manifesto on December 10, 1921, four days after the 'Treaty' was signed in London. In throwing his weight to the Republican side Larkin was as intemperate in his language as he was intransigent in his opinions. To Larkin, when the issues were stripped bare, the 'Treaty' merely posed a naked question of principle. 'We pledge ourselves,' he wrote, 'now and in the future, to destroy this plan of a nation's destruction. We propose carrying on the fight until we make the land of Erin a land fit for men and women—a Workers' Republic or Death.'[2] In the course of his manifesto Larkin cast serious doubts on the integrity of those who signed the 'Treaty.' 'It was born in dishonour

[1] Dorothy McArdle, *The Irish Republic* (Dublin, 1951), pp. 532–648. This is the best available account, but is heavily weighted in de Valera's favour.
[2] *Voice of Labour* (Dublin), January 7, 1922.

and shame,' wrote Larkin. 'It was drafted and signed by creatures for their own aggrandizement—or because of ambition, and due to their lack of courage, signed this unholy compact under duress.' The editor of the *Voice of Labour*, in which the manifesto was published in Ireland, dissented and commented, 'bare justice to even our political and social opponents compels us to dissociate this Union and this journal from these charges.'[1] Larkin's bitter antipathy towards the 'Treaty' was seconded only by his intense dislike of the chief supporter and architect of the document, Arthur Griffith.[2] This coupled with his warm admiration and respect for Eamon de Valera, though they differed on social questions, cemented his stand on the Republican side.[3] Still to Larkin the end remained a Workers' Republic, and Labour was the force which would regenerate the nation.

An uneasy truce followed the ratification of the 'Treaty' in January and continued through the general elections in June of 1922. The Irish Labour Party decided to contest the election and Larkin was nominated for North Dublin.[4] When the news reached Larkin, however, he cabled Foran—'Decline emphatically. Charge you and all comrades to remember purposes of Union—"an injury to one" etcetera. What of Ulster? Damn politics, politicians, especially carellists [careerists?]. Let them clean up mess.'[5] The Labour Party withdrew Larkin's name, but undaunted put forward eighteen candidates, seventeen of whom were elected. The Party had taken no official stand on the 'Treaty,' but the Labour candidates were popularly rated as pro-Treaty.[6] The elections which were held on June 16, though limited by pre-election panel arrangements by the pro- and anti-Treaty parties, were an indication that the Irish people were for the 'Treaty,' if the alternative was continuing the national struggle against the British. The party of the revolution and the Republic no longer had the confidence of the people.

Meanwhile the party of the constitution and compromise was galvanized into action by the assassination in London on June 22, of Sir Henry Wilson, commander of the constabulary in Ulster by two

[1] *Voice of Labour* (Dublin), January 7, 1922.

[2] *Workers' Republic* (Dublin), June 3, 1922. See Letter from Larkin to A. J. Dooney for vicious criticism of Arthur Griffith.

[3] *Irish Worker* (Dublin), September 15, 1923. See for a warm appreciation of Eamon de Valera.

[4] *Voice of Labour*, April 1, 1922.   [5] *Ibid.*, June 10, 1922.

[6] J. D. Clarkson, *Labour and Nationalism in Ireland* (New York, 1924), p. 458.

Irishmen. The British Government in the person of Winston Churchill reminded the provisional government in Ireland that the 'presence in Dublin of a band of men styling themselves the Headquarters of the Republican Executive is a gross breach and defiance of the Treaty.'[1] On the morning of June 28, 1922, the provisional government demanded the surrender of these 'irregular' Republican troops, who had occupied and set up their headquarters several months before in the Four Courts buildings in Dublin. The 'irregulars' refused to surrender and were shelled into submission by the artillery loaned to the government troops by the British for the occasion. The Army split widened as the issues were submitted to the dreadful arbitrament of force. The die was cast when de Valera, the leader of the Republican opposition in the Dail, reported to his old unit, the Third Dublin Brigade, and was attached to its Headquarters Staff.[2]

The civil war continued through December of 1922 when it became evident that the Republican forces could not maintain themselves in the field. A ruinous guerilla war was continued by the 'irregular' die-hards from January to April of 1923, but the feeling was growing among the more responsible Republican leaders that the continuance of the struggle was useless. When the leader of the irreconcilable element, General Liam Lynch, Chief of Staff of the Republican forces was killed in action on April 10, 1923, the way was opened for a formal cessation of hostilities. On April 27, 1923, Eamon de Valera, President of the revolutionary Republican Government, and Frank Aiken on behalf of the Irish Republican Army ordered 'the suspension of all offensive operations' from noon on April 30, 1923. This was qualified, however, by the instruction to individual commanding officers that—'all units will take adequate measure to protect themselves and their munitions.'[3] The Republican Army was looking for terms but were not ready to surrender their arms.

Five hours after the cease fire Larkin landed in Ireland and called for peace. In the difficult days that followed he continued to call for peace and love, concord and charity, justice and mercy. In a general message to the membership of the Transport Union, several days after his return, he again turned to the problem of the civil war. 'Now in the crisis confronting the nation,' he wrote, 'we again speak with no uncertain voice'—

[1] Quoted in McArdle, *op. cit.*, p. 741.   [2] *Ibid.*, p. 747.   [3] *Ibid.*, p. 848.

'Peace, reconstruction, charity to all,' is the demand we make and to you this charge is given, unto each and every man, member of Rank and File or Officer entrusted with duties, perfect your organization. Solidarity the keynote, Get ready, be prepared to enforce peace, to carry out construction measures, and live true to the motto of this Pioneer Union. 'Each for All, and all for Each,' steady and be ready![1]

The day after this appeared, Sunday, a gigantic Labour Day celebration was arranged by the Transport Union in Croke Park in Dublin. After the festivities, which included a sports meeting and a concert by the three bands sponsored by the Union, Larkin addressed the vast assemblage. 'It was easy,' he began, 'to preach hate and destruction, and they would always get men who would sell themselves for a price to preach hate.'[2] 'For the sake of the new race,' the children, he pleaded, we have 'got to have peace and concord, charity and forgiveness of wrong to all men. . . .' 'Two armies were contending for power in the nation,' he declared, 'but he was speaking to the greatest army of all of them, and it was the working classes who were going to bring peace.' Larkin then asked, since Irishmen had a great responsibility, 'would they be true to that responsibility?' And when he was answered with cries of 'Yes,' he asked, 'Would they pledge themselves to work for peace as a first measure, and understanding, fellowship, friendship and charity to all men as a second measure?' Again he was answered in chorus with cries of 'We will.' A show of hands indicated there was a 'unanimous response' in support of his proposals. 'I am glad,' concluded Larkin, 'to see a man in uniform in the crowd raised his hand in favour of peace. Now let us march forward with peace on our banners and victory in our hearts.'[3]

The same evening at the Theatre Royal, after the scheduled Connolly Commemoration concert, Larkin maintained that 'it was about time that the common people of Ireland who had been so long silent and inarticulate, who comprised 82 per cent of the population, should speak out.'[4] The questions of the day should be argued 'with reason and logic,' he said, 'for the sword, the bayonet, and the rifle never proved to be anything but brutality. Force meant that might was right. . . .' 'A Labour Government,' he announced, 'would not allow this state of things [to] last an hour, for the Labour

[1] *Voice of Labour*, May 5, 1923.   [2] *Freeman's Journal*, May 7, 1923.
[3] *Ibid.*   [4] *Ibid.*

Party lived for peace.' 'Everybody,' he complained, 'was sitting down like cowards afraid to speak. People thought it was courageous to take a gun or a mine and use it, but it required more courage to speak the truth. They had assassination by word and by deed, and the worst form of it was moral assassination. They would have to get rid of this curse which was bringing their country into the contempt of the world.' Larkin then asked 'all those who desired peace to rise.' The audience then rose. When they were seated Larkin said, 'I now ask all who believe in a continuance of this fratricidal strife to rise.' No one moved, but when a Republican shouted from the dress circle, 'We are for peace with honour,' there was loud cheering. Larkin tartly answered—'There can never be dishonour in peace.'

The following Sunday, May 13, 1923, at a meeting commemorating the seventh anniversary of the execution of James Connolly, Larkin made a heroic decision. He asked the Republicans to give up the armed struggle and take up the constitutional struggle. Only a man with a profound sense of duty and enormous moral courage could have burdened himself with so thankless a responsibility. Larkin was so affected by what he was going to say that he took the un-precedented action of sitting up 'during the previous night *preparing his speech.*'[1] It was an unruly crowd with many Republicans present. They had interrupted and heckled the speakers before Larkin, though when he rose to speak there were loud cheers on every side. He began in his characteristic way by admonishing them. He said he was sorry that they were not engaged in trying to 'discipline them-selves,' and 'regretted that emotionalism had run riot.'[2] 'Surely,' he continued, 'if James Connolly was not with them that day, James Larkin was with them to fulfil his promises.' When he first at-tempted, Larkin explained, 'to try and find a common denominator to bring peace into the land he was told that it was a dangerous doctrine.' 'Give up your arms,' he advised, for there was no disgrace in laying down your arms when the forces opposed to you were over-whelming. Do not mind, he concluded, 'words about allegiance, and giving up guns' so long as you do not give up 'the principles of Ireland a nation, one and indivisible.'

A week after this speech Larkin began a two-week tour of Trans-port Union branches in the south of Ireland in an effort to become acquainted with the membership after his long absence. Some of the local branches declared the day of his intended visit a general holiday,

[1] 'Carney Memoir,' *op cit.*, p. 9.   [2] *Irish Times*, May 14, 1923.

while the local papers gave his visit 'half a page, and sometimes half the paper.'[1] Overflow meetings and official welcomes from Mayors and Urban Councils were the order of the day. In short his was 'a triumphal march.'[2] Everywhere his message was 'Peace by understanding.' 'We must have peace immediately. We must have peace by understanding. Peace. Somebody said with honour to me the other day. There can never be dishonour with peace. It is only a change of tactics, a change of methods.' 'If Connolly and Pearse and Clarke and the others who formed the galaxy of Irish heroes of 1916,' said Larkin, 'were big enough to give up their arms for a time and give them up in the face of known death, I say to you . . . that there can be no dishonour in giving up arms.'[3]

Ten days after Larkin's call to the Republicans to give up their arms in Dublin at the Connolly memorial meeting, the Chief of Staff of the Irish Republican Army ordered his troops to 'cease fire' and 'dump arms.'[4] Accompanying the order was a personal message from de Valera—

> Soldiers of the Republic, Legion of the Rearguard: The Republic can no longer be successfully defended by your arms. . . . The sufferings which you must now face unarmed you will bear in a manner worthy of men who were ready to give their lives for their cause. The thought that you have still to suffer for your devotion will lighten your present sorrow and what you endure will keep you in communion with your dead comrades who gave their lives, and all these lives promised, for Ireland.[5]

The Republicans had not surrendered their arms but concealed them. Unarmed they were now arrested in large numbers and interned in prison camps without trial. They would not come into the nation because if the Republic did not exist in fact it was there, all the same, in their mind's eye. The Republican deputies refused to take their seats in the Dail because, under the terms of the Free State Constitution, they would be required to take an oath of allegiance to the King, which they maintained would violate their conscience. The Free State Government insisted on the oath if the Republicans were to take their seats as a loyal opposition. The result was peace, but there was no understanding. Larkin continued to be explicit—'The Premier of the Free State Government had laid

---

[1] *Voice of Labour*, May 19 and 26, 1923.   [2] *Ibid.*, May 26, 1923.
[3] *Ibid.*, June 2, 1923.   [4] McArdle, *op. cit.*, p. 857.   [5] *Ibid.*, p. 858.

down certain conditions and had said to the Republicans: "You must accept them." [1] 'Accept them,' said Larkin. 'The whole nation would rise up and take those men to its heart,' he prophesied, 'and in less than one year there would not be a member of the Free State Government who were now abusing their power sitting in the Dail (cheers).' [2] The whole of this dramatic struggle was thus reduced to a moral dilemma pivoting on the question of tender conscience.

Still, while Larkin would not admit that it was a principle he was sacrificing but only a question of a change in tactics, there are other questions that remain to be answered. How did he account for his apparent change of mind between his manifesto issued after the signing of the 'Treaty,' in which he called for a 'Workers' Republic or Death,' and his more recent exhortations to 'Peace by understanding'? As was usual with him he did not account for it and has left the thankless task to others. When Larkin called for a 'Workers' Republic or Death,' he clearly envisaged the 'Death' portion of it to be at the hands of the British. When the civil war broke out and completely altered the situation Larkin called for peace as the first consideration above all others. To him the greatest evil was that Irishmen should raise their hands against Irishmen, and not that Ireland was not yet a Republic. The latter would be remedied in time, while the former was nothing less than a monstrous anomaly.

While Larkin was unsuccessfully attempting to persuade the Republicans to come into the nation there was developing within the Transport Union a quarrel which was to rend the Irish Labour Movement from top to bottom. The seeds of dissension were stirring even before Larkin left for America. When Larkin left for America in late 1914, it will be remembered, he left Connolly in charge of the Union and the Citizen Army, while P. T. Daly was to be in charge of the Insurance Section. Before Larkin left there had also been problems of a minor order between his sister Delia and officials of the Union. [3] After his departure the friction continued until Delia left for England. When Connolly committed the Citizen Army to the Easter Rising and was executed the difficult task of

---

[1] *Freeman's Journal*, June 25, 1923.

[2] *Ibid.* See also July 9, 1923. Larkin said, 'Everybody knew he was against the Free State. He did not deny it. He was for a Republic, but he recognised that the Government of this country was the Free State Government, and he was prepared to argue the question as between it and a Republican Government.'

[3] *Attempt to Smash the Irish Transport and General Workers' Union* (Dublin, 1924), p. 132.

picking up the broken pieces of the Union fell to Thomas Foran, the General President. Though he had been President since the Union was founded Foran had little chance to exercise any real authority in the face of such formidable personalities as Larkin and Connolly.

When the disaster of Easter Week resulted in the entire burden of reorganizing the Union being thrown on him, he naturally sought the aid of someone with more administrative experience. He turned to William O'Brien, whose close friendship with Connolly made him intimate with the Transport Union's affairs and whose knowledge and influence in the Irish Labour Movement was wider and deeper than that of anyone else in Ireland. After their release from a British internment camp in the fall of 1916, Foran and O'Brien applied themselves to their broken machine, the Transport Union. In a little over a year they had increased the membership from 5,000 to 14,000 and the branches from 10 to 40. During 1918 the growth of the Union was phenomenal, mainly because of general wage demand movement throughout Britain and Ireland. By the end of the year the membership numbered nearly 68,000 in 210 branches, and the treasury boasted a credit balance of some £19,000. When Larkin returned in April, 1923, the Union totalled 100,000 members in 350 branches with a balance of £140,000. Foran and O'Brien could look at their achievement with understandable pride.[1]

Meanwhile within the Union the chorus of dissent had been growing as O'Brien began to increase his power and consolidate his position. P. T. Daly, the disappointed heir-apparent of Larkin in 1914, became the leader of the opposition. As early as January, 1917, they were appealing to Larkin over Foran's head. In exasperation, Larkin wrote Foran—'tell Daly from me to turn in and do his work properly. . . . It is useless—them writing to me, whoever they are—asking me to come home. Surely they know that if facilities offered—of any sort—I would be with them long ere this.'[2] The opposition was reinforced by the return of Delia Larkin to Dublin in 1918, but Daly was defeated by O'Brien in a contest for the office of General Treasurer of the Transport Union in January, 1919. He was further humiliated when he was removed as head of the Insurance Section by the annual delegate conference of the Union a

---

[1] *Attempt to Smash the Irish Transport and General Workers' Union* (Dublin, 1924), p. xxiii.

[2] *Ibid.*, p. 135. Letter dated January 22, 1917.

few months later.[1] Finally, at the annual Irish Trades Union Congress and Labour Party meeting in Waterford in August, Daly's cup was filled to the brim when he was defeated by O'Brien for the office of Secretary to the Congress, a position he had held for eight years, by the narrow margin of 114 to 109.

The lines of battle had hardened before this, however, since the opposition, who now termed themselves 'Larkinites,'[2] began to publish a weekly newspaper, *The Red Hand*, in early July under the editorship of Delia Larkin.[3] When Larkin heard about the extension of the quarrel he was furious. He wrote Foran, 'I desire you to come to your senses at once. . . . This quarrel must cease—a truce must be carried out between both parties until I land, which may be sooner than you or some folks welcome.'[4] He ordered *The Red Hand* to cease publication or he would denounce it, and the *Voice of Labour*, the official Transport Union organ, was to give no more publicity to the quarrel. Both sides complied, but in its minutes the Executive Committee of the Union complained about the 'tone' of Larkin's letter to Foran and further denied 'the right of an official of the Union to reverse a decision arrived at by the duly elected representatives of the members.'[5] The removal of Daly as an official of the Union was sustained by the Executive Committee. Larkin insisted on the last word, however, as he cabled—To The Old Guard of the I.T.W.U.: 'Stand fast. I am returning. Take no side in this fratricidal strife going on in the Union. You and I will settle the matter as we solved more serious problems in the past. . . .'[6]

Matters were made worse by the infant Communist Party in Ireland when they freely used Larkin's name in their attacks on the Transport Union. 'Jim Larkin,' they declared in their official organ, *Workers' Republic*, 'has seen through the sorry pretence and camouflage of O'Brien, Foran, and O'Shannon posing as revolutionaries. The clear out is coming.'[7] Relations were further strained, just

---

[1] MSS., Letter from Jack Carney to Thomas Foran, July 9, 1919. Carney wrote that Larkin 'has absolute faith in the actions of the Union and regards most unfavourably the attempt of Daly *et al.* to cause strife within the Union.' Courtesy of William O'Brien.   [2] *The Red Hand* (Dublin), July 19, 1919.

[3] *Ibid.*, July 12, 1919.   [4] *Attempt to Smash, op. cit.*, p. 136.   [5] *Ibid.*, p. 137.

[6] Quoted in *The Workers' World* (Kansas City), October 17, 1919.

[7] *Workers' Republic*, June 3, 1922. See also *ibid.*, March 31, 1923. 'The advent of Jim means, without any doubt, that we will get another chance of organising ourselves into a body capable of fighting the Bosses with some chance of success. Let us see that we don't miss it this time.' When Larkin arrived in Dublin,

before Larkin returned, by the exchange of cables over the Executive Committee's refusal to send the £5,000 for the purchase of a 'food ship.' In one cable Larkin had wired, 'Suggest money withheld, you, O'Neill and another nineteen thirteen without my knowledge might furnish amount requested.'[1] The 'money withheld' referred to here was some £7,500, which Foran and John O'Neill, secretary of No. 1 branch, laid aside out of the lockout funds subscribed in 1913. They told Larkin at the time they had the money, but refused to tell him how much because they were afraid if he knew he would ill-advisedly expend it. Some £1,100 of the total £7,500 went in a strike pay bonus at Christmas, 1913. A further £600 went in legal fees, while £1,800 was spent to aid those victimized when the lockout was lost in early 1914. The remaining £3,500 went into the purchase of Liberty Hall in March, 1914. Since he did not know the total amount Larkin, unfortunately, assumed all the money had not been expended and called for the supposed balance to pay for the 'food ship' project.

Shortly after this exchange of cables, the Executive Committee called a special Delegate Conference to meet in Dublin on April 24 and 25, Foran and O'Brien in their capacities as General President and General Treasurer respectively, the other seven members of the Executive Committee and seventy-five delegates from the branches attended. The main purpose for calling the Conference was to amend the Rules of the Union in order to definite the relationship between the membership, the Delegate Conference, the Executive Committee, and the officials. In his opening remarks to the delegates Foran said, 'It was proposed to make the Conference an annual affair, and in the future it would be the Parliament of the Union.'[2] 'Power in the future,' he continued, 'would be in the hands of the Delegate Conference, and they could deal with any person or anything in the Union as they thought fit.' Referring to the exchange of cables between Larkin and himself, he said, they 'seemed to set up the position that one man could be a law to himself, and he hoped that that was a proposition that would never be accepted.'[3] Foran

---

[1] *Attempt to Smash, op. cit.*, p. 142, cable dated March 28, 1923.
[2] *Ibid.*, p. 143.　　　　　　　　　　　　　　[3] *Ibid.*, p. 144.

---

however, he told a delegate Conference of the Union. 'As to the criticism from the Communists and others, why take notice of these little wasps? . . . He knew about people using his name, but he would be the first to defend his friends who were working for the Union.' *Attempt to Smash, op. cit.*, p. 148.

then explained the reference by Larkin to the matter of the alleged money withheld. The delegates were asked to uphold the action of the Executive Committee in refusing to send the £5,000 for the 'food ship.' A motion to that effect was put and carried unanimously with the qualification—'that further consideration of the matter be deferred until Larkin's return.'[1]

The following day, April 25, was devoted entirely to the proposed changes in the Rules of the Union. O'Brien explained to the delegates that the Executive Committee 'was aware that the Delegates had not had sufficient time to study the draft new Rules in detail. It was not, therefore, proposed that every Rule should be gone through, but he had made up a list of those new Rules, which materially altered the old ones, or which brought in new matter, and he would suggest that these should be taken up and discussed.'[2] The effect of these new Rules would be to consolidate the power of the Executive Committee under a new title, the National Executive Council, which would be responsible to an annual Delegate Conference responsible in turn to the membership through the various branches. The real basis of power then lay with the new National Executive Council, and with the man or men that could command a majority of the Council. The new Rules were approved almost unanimously by the Conference. They were to be submitted to the branches, and if a majority of those who responded approved they would become official. The Conference then adjourned to await the pleasure of welcoming Larkin home.

Four days after his return, Larkin attended a meeting of the Executive Committee, and expressed his disappointment about them not sending him the £5,000, since he thought they 'should have known him sufficiently well to trust him.'[3] He said he was 'going to Russia immediately, where he had important work to do, and he would not allow the E.C. or any other body to prevent him doing the work he felt it his duty to do.' He then announced that he would resign as General Secretary the following day. After some discussion Foran and several others prevailed on Larkin to make a two-month tour of the Branches and not resign. At Larkin's request it was agreed there should be no public mention of his having any difference with the Executive Committee. The adjourned Delegate Conference, it was decided, should meet on Monday, May 14, 1923,

[1] *Attempt to Smash, op. cit.*, p. 144.
[2] *Ibid.*, p. 145.   [3] *Ibid.*, p. 143.

to allow the delegates to attend the meeting in commemoration of the execution of Connolly to be held on Sunday, May 13.

In greeting the Delegate Conference Larkin was more than reasonable, he was statesmanlike. With regard to the £5,000 he said, 'the E.C. had considered they had not sufficient particulars before them to warrant their sending the money, and he made no complaint on that score.'[1] As to the proposed Russian trip, he explained, he had 'arranged a monopoly of trade between Ireland and Russia,' and he was 'going to Russia shortly with the permission of the Union, but would not be very long away.'[2] One delegate was so impressed with Larkin's temperate tone that he said 'of all the meetings he had ever attended he had never been better pleased than here today. The people who had been prophesying about what Larkin would do on his return would evidently be disappointed. . . .'[3] Foran then explained the matter of the £7,500 and the purchase of Liberty Hall again, and Larkin appeared to accept the story at its face value. When the subject of the new Rules came up, Larkin objected only to 'the proposal to establish a Political Secretary, and if such a post was established he thought the official should be a subordinate official under the control of the E.C. He would ask the Branches to alter that rule.' O'Brien suggested that 'this proposal might be considered at a future Delegate Conference,' and Larkin agreed this 'might be done.'[4] In concluding Larkin advised them, 'Don't submit your minds to any one man. Think these problems out for yourselves. A leader who can lead you out of the wilderness can lead you back again. If there is a thinking, intelligent movement, no leader can mislead you.' He then gave his benediction by quoting St. Augustine—'In things essential, unity; in things doubtful, liberty; but in all things, charity.'[5]

All appeared to be well as Larkin began his tour of the Branches the following week. He was given excellent publicity by the *Voice of Labour*, which noted, 'Jim is coming as a tonic to many who were wearying in the march. . . . The One Big Union will make immense strides forward.'[6] Suddenly, at the end of May, in the second week of his tour he appeared back in Dublin without offering an explanation to anyone. That Sunday, June 3, 1923, in Dublin at the La Scala Theatre, he greeted Branch No. 1, which in Foran's words 'had been

---

[1] *Attempt to Smash, op. cit.*, p. 147.   [2] *Ibid.*
[3] *Ibid.*, p. 148.   [4] *Ibid.*   [5] *Ibid.*
[6] *Voice of Labour*, May 26, 1923.

the cradle of the Union,' and was now 'the heart of the Union.'[1] At this meeting Larkin unexpectedly declared open war on O'Brien and, presumably, all those who would take his part. He had told Foran 'he could no longer work with this man O'Brien.'[2] It was obvious from Larkin's long speech, which might be better described, perhaps, as a harangue, that he became aware of two things on his tour of the Branches. One being the very real power and influence of O'Brien in the Union and the other, the realization that the new Rules were designed less to secure the democratic representation of the members, and more to limit his own personal power.[3] The delegates he had met in Conference on May 14, 'should have been elected by the members of the Branches, but in Cork, Clonmel, Newbridge and other places,' Larkin claimed, he had 'been told the Delegates were not appointed by the members.'[4] Reading out the names of the No. 1 Branch delegates to the April and May Conferences, he asked if they had elected these delegates? Cries of 'No' greeted his question. He later asked a delegate, who represented Branch No. 1 at the Conference, who had appointed him? The delegate replied 'he was elected by No. 1 Branch Committee.' 'They packed that place,' said Larkin, referring to the Delegate Conference, 'for a certain purpose.' 'Tammany Hall,' he declared, 'never had a machine like this. All to down one man.' Foran did his best to stem the tide, but he was no match for Larkin. He did warn, however, that the 'General Secretary had struck a note here that might mean a rift in the Union.' 'If they were to come to a parting of the ways,' he asked, 'let them do it, but let the Union remain solid.'[5]

Within the week there was a civil war raging in the Irish Labour Movement. Two days after the La Scala meeting Larkin walked out of an Executive Committee meeting, summoned at his request, because they insisted on accepting as valid the new Rules of the Union.[6] Larkin claimed the new Rules were illegal, and should not have been registered, therefore, because they had not been revised by the method prescribed under the old Rules. The following Sunday,

---

[1] *Attempt to Smash, op. cit.*, p. 149.   [2] *Ibid.*, p. 153.

[3] 'Carney Memoir,' *op. cit.*, p. 10. 'Larkin then toured the country calling for peace. I went with him. He talked with the members of the Transport Union branches and discovered that the annual congress was being rigged against him. O'Brien had fixed the Delegates. Some of those friendly to him had been appointed, *not* elected, as Delegates. Any appeal that Jim might make to the Conference would be futile.'

[4] *Attempt to Smash, op. cit.*, p. 151.   [5] *Ibid.*, pp. 153–56.   [6] *Ibid.*, p. 158.

June 10, 1923, he appealed to the rank and file over the heads of the Executive Committee at meetings of the strategic and numerically powerful Dublin No. 1 and No. 3 Branches. At these meetings he secured the suspension of Foran and O'Brien, Thomas Kennedy and Michael MacCarthy, members of the Executive Committee, and John O'Neill, Secretary of No. 1 Branch.[1] The next morning Larkin and a number of his friends seized control of the Union's offices at Parnell Square and Liberty Hall, and refused to allow the suspended officers to enter the premises.[2]

The Executive Committee countered by suspending Larkin as General Secretary, and applied for an injunction to prevent him or his agents from interfering with their efforts to carry on their duties as officers of the Union.[3] The court complied and matters were legally restored to what they had been before the dispute broke out. Efforts were made meanwhile to patch things up inside the Union, but they came to nothing. The split was widened and deepened by the bitterest of personal recriminations on both sides. The newly launched Larkinite *Irish Worker* extended the split to the Irish Labour Party. 'We had the honour,' wrote Larkin, 'of initiating the Irish labour movement. We return to find a Labour Party lost to all sense of dignity, manipulated by ambitious self-seekers, a feeble imitation of the English Labour Party, and which, parrot-like, repeats the phrases of its prototype, but in a less vigorous manner.'[4] The split was now complete on both the trade union and political sides of the Irish Labour Movement. Larkin, however, was in serious difficulties because his influence was limited to Dublin and the Irish Labour Movement was no longer confined only to Dublin. Of the Transport Union's 100,000 members, over two-thirds were found outside Dublin, and they had been organized without Larkin's help. Further, of the eighteen members of the Irish Labour Party sitting in the Dail, only one, William O'Brien, sat for Dublin City. True, the hard core of the Union was found in Dublin, and Larkin was in a strategic position, but the machinery of the Union and the Party, on the other hand, was firmly controlled by his enemies, and there was little likelihood they could be upset unless the courts upheld Larkin in his view that the new Rules were illegal.

That the Irish Labour Movement should split at all was most unfortunate, but that the split should have come when it did was

[1] *Freeman's Journal*, June 12, 1923. [2] *Ibid.*
[3] *Ibid.*, June 19, 1923. [4] *Irish Worker*, June 15, 1923.

nothing less than catastrophic. Not only was the Irish Labour Party faced with a general election at the end of August, but the entire trade union movement was grimly awaiting the concerted onslaught of the Irish employers and their policy of wage cuts. The British employers, after calling the bluff of the Triple Alliance, and breaking the Miners' resistance in June, 1922, forced their workers to accept wage cuts amounting to £10 million a week.[1] The movement to reduce wages was long overdue in Ireland, and the prospects for the Irish workers were not pleasing. In fact the wage-cutting movement had begun in Ireland's basic industry, agriculture, shortly before Larkin's return. The farmers in the Waterford area attempted to force reductions among their agricultural labourers who had only recently been organized by the Transport Union.[2] After five months' firm resistance, the Executive of the Transport Union called the strike off in December, 1923. Needless to say Larkin was bitterly critical, and accused the Executive of 'selling the strike all along, and it was only a matter of time before they sold out completely.'[3] Actually, however, the Executive could not have done much more than it did. By December the harvest was long over and the agricultural labourers had no tactical advantage over their employers. In fact with the coming on of winter the advantage now lay entirely with the farmers. Once again, as in 1913, the task of organizing agricultural labour proved too much for the Transport Union.

Meanwhile the employers in the transport trade in Dublin launched their long expected offensive. They announced on Friday, July 13, 1923, that the dockers would have to accept a reduction of 2s. a day.[4] The average wage hovered about the 'dockers' minimum' of 16s. a day secured in early 1920 by Ernest Bevin. The dockers refused to take the cut, and on Monday, July 16, some 1,500 men with Larkin in command were out on strike.[5] All the men in the transport trade realized that if the dockers, who were in the best position to resist, were forced to take the reduction it would only be a matter of time before they would be obliged to submit as well. The Transport Union Executive was in an extremely awkward position. They could neither refuse strike pay, nor could they prevent Larkin from taking charge of the strike and increasing, thereby, his

[1] Keith Hutchison, *Decline and Fall of British Capitalism* (1951), p. 214.
[2] *Voice of Labour*, November 19, 1922. See Archie Heron, 'The Need for a Land Policy.'   [3] *Irish Worker*, December 8, 1923, 'Another Betrayal.'
[4] *Freeman's Journal*, July 14, 1923.   [5] *Ibid.*, July 17, 1923.

power and influence among the members. Whatever went wrong the Executive were sure to be blamed for it, and whatever went right Larkin would undoubtedly accept the credit for it. The strike dragged on well into October, with the dockers resisting every attempt to impose any cut at all.

Finally the Transport Union Executive took the bull by the horns on October 26, 1923, and declared the strike over.[1] They accepted as a basis for settlement President Cosgrave's mediation offer of a reduction of 1s. a day and no victimization. The Executive refused to recognize a ballot vote of the dockers which showed 443 for the Government proposal and 687 against. Larkin was furious and declared that that settlement had been offered to him eleven weeks ago, 'but he would not soil his soul, and let down those of his class.'[2] Despite Larkin's protests a large number of dockers returned to work rather than face the prospect of remaining out without strike pay. A few days later the coal merchants attempted to force the reduction of 1s. a day in the coal trade.[3] Five hundred coal men then struck work and refused to accept the cut claiming they did not come under agreement covering the dockers. The grain men were next, and Larkin advised both the coal and grain men to accept no reduction.[4] The next day resistance on the part of the men collapsed completely as the entire port—dockers, carters, coalheavers, grain men, seamen, and firemen—submitted to the 1s. a day reduction. Though very unhappy, Larkin advised the men to accept. 'The employers thought they had obtained a victory,' Larkin declared defiantly, 'but it would prove a Pyrrhic victory.' 'Defeat would have been inevitable,' he continued, 'if they had decided to remain out without strike pay. No doubt the Executive thought that was what he would advise.' 'Instead, however,' he concluded, 'they would go back like an army at a cut of 1s., but the day could come when they would demand that 1s. back from the employers.'[5] The game was lost, however, for the Irish employers had broken the core of resistance, and wage cuts were enforced in almost all areas of employment.

While the industrial arm of the Irish Labour Movement was thus

---

[1] *Freeman's Journal*, October 27, 1923.

[2] *Ibid.*, October 29, 1923. See also *Irish Worker*, July 28, 1923. 'Employers' Conspiracy Unmasked.'

[3] *Ibid.*, October 31, 1923.

[4] *Ibid.*, November 2, 1923.   [5] *Ibid.*, November 5, 1923.

IRELAND'S EYE

2d

Vol. 1. No. 11.   JANUARY 27, 1923.

From 'Ireland's Eye', 27th January, 1923.

A world-famous photograph of Big Jim Larkin in characteristic attitude, addressing a huge Labour meeting in Upper O'Connell Street, Dublin, after his return from America in 1923.

being severely mauled by the employing classes, the political arm was being studiously ignored by the Irish voter under a complicated system of proportional representation. In the general election of late August, 1923, the Irish Labour Party offered forty-three candidates for the 150 seats in the Dail. When the dust settled, instead of increasing their numbers, the Labour Party was reduced from seventeen to fourteen members. 'The results of the elections,' wrote Larkin, 'proves the hypocrisy of political parties, stupidity of electors, and the fallacy of geographical representation.'[1] Still, there is more to be accounted for in Irish Labour's political eclipse, especially when its future seemed most assured, than will be explained by either the traditional faults of political parties and electors, or proportional representation. The unhealthy political atmosphere created by civil war, the steadily worsening economic situation, and Labour's rising star in Britain all pointed to a Labour triumph in Ireland. Why did Irish Labour fail so miserably in this the most crucial of general elections?[2]

The lack of organization, funds, candidates, political consciousness on the part of the worker, and the continued ascendency of Nationalism over all other ideas go far in accounting for Irish Labour's political eclipse in August, 1923. None, however, go further in explaining that debacle than the civil war that was then raging in the Irish Labour Movement. Whether the Irish Labour Party could have ever become a national Party is a moot point, but there is little doubt that whatever its chances might have been they were ruined by the split that developed on Larkin's return. The Irish voter simply could not have been expected to place his confidence in a Party that was unable to manage its own house while promising to solve the complicated problems that faced the nation. There is little doubt that the responsibility for forcing a split in the Irish Labour Movement was Larkin's, but whether the split was justified is a more difficult question.

First of all Larkin grossly overestimated O'Brien's influence and power in the Transport Union. Actually, at this stage, O'Brien's future in the Union depended entirely on his retaining the support of Foran, who was torn in his loyalty to Larkin as his friend and

---

[1] *Irish Worker*, September 8, 1923. 'The Dail Elections.'

[2] *Ibid.*, November 17, 1923. See Henry W. Nevinson, 'Why Irish Labour failed'. Reprinted from *The Nation* (New York), and dated September 17, 1923. 'The Labour Leaders expected 27 or 30 seats in the New Dail.'

mentor and his obligations to O'Brien as a colleague.[1] The attempt by Larkin to purge Foran as well as O'Brien by an arbitrary appeal to the rank and file left Foran no choice but to defend himself in alliance with O'Brien. Further, Larkin overestimated his own influence in the Union. Though the bulk of the rank and file in Dublin would support him, his influence in the country was slight. Then, too, the leadership in the Transport Union all supported the Executive against Larkin, and not because they were simply the 'tools' of Foran and O'Brien.[2] Since they were in their own right men of some experience and local prominence, they were not willing to accept as infallible the judgment of a man who had been away for nearly ten years, while they had been through a world, an Anglo-Irish, and a civil war. To make matters even worse, Larkin took little notice of the general feeling in the Irish Labour Movement. As a result, two of the most prominent and influential men in the Movement, Thomas McPartlin and Thomas Johnson, sided with Foran and O'Brien, as did, indeed, nearly every Labour man of any consequence in Ireland.[3] It is all too obvious that Larkin's analysis of the situation both in the Transport Union and the Labour Movement was defective in the spring of 1923.

The question, however, goes deeper than a want of judgment with regard to tactics, for there were larger questions reflected in this struggle for power between Larkin and O'Brien in the Transport Union. These two men, the one radical by temperament and the other conservative, mirror in their personalities not only two conceptions of what a trade union should be—a revolutionary or a reformist instrument for change—but two examples of what a trade union needs in leadership in its several stages of development. When a union is in its infancy, and every day is a struggle for survival, the perpetual state of crisis demands and produces the leader who is a hero and a martyr. Because he had made great personal

---

[1] *Attempt to Smash, op. cit.,* p. 158. See Foran's attempt to mediate between Larkin and O'Brien.

[2] *Freeman's Journal,* June 26, 1923. See, for example, John Butler's remarks in Dungarvan with Foran present. Some of the most prominent officials in the Union who opposed Larkin were Richard Corish, Wexford, James Everett, Wicklow, and James Hickey, Cork.

[3] MSS., Thomas McPartlin to William O'Brien, no date, about May, 1923. McPartlin was anxious to avoid trouble and predicted that if it came, Larkin might have to be driven out of the Labour Movement to save it. Courtesy of William O'Brien.

sacrifices he can command them of his followers, and personal loyalty becomes the cement out of which their structure is made. When, however, the union has won recognition, and numbers its members and its funds not in the thousands but the hundreds of thousands, and has in fact, reached the level of an institution in society, its needs, especially with regard to leadership, are different. At this stage there is not only a breakdown in communications between the leadership and the rank and file, but, with the passing parade, the old bonds of personal loyalty become more and more an institutional loyalty. With these developments there is an increasing need for the men of organizational and administrative talents rather than men of heroic proportions. Happy, indeed, is the union, institution, or State, that finds combined in a single personality all the elements that go into not only the making of the revolution but the consolidating of it. There is little doubt that with reference to the leadership needs of the Transport Union, time and circumstances were on O'Brien's side and against Larkin.

The differences between the two men, however, went deeper than the long-term needs of the union, deeper even than their personalities, they went to rock bottom—principle. Larkin was convinced that trade unions were revolutionary instruments to be used on every occasion to hasten the Social Revolution. O'Brien, on the other hand, took the more traditional view that trade unions were effective instruments of social change within the existing fabric of society. Each man then represented a view that had long plagued the Socialist Movement—revolutionary or revisionist. But what of Ireland? Was it a time for attack or retrenchment? Could even a Larkin with a united Labour Movement solidly behind him have effected a revolution? Hardly! The party of the revolution under de Valera, which had a wider and deeper support under the aegis of Nationalism among the Irish people, had just suffered a resounding defeat. The crest of the revolutionary wave had passed in Ireland, and none recognized this more than Larkin when he called on the Republicans to lay down their arms and come into the nation. Yet his own justification for splitting the Irish Labour Movement was that it was not a genuine revolutionary movement, and to make it such he would have had himself to go out of the nation in order to achieve the Social Revolution. In short Larkin's position in 1923, whether considered from a tactical, practical, or ideological point of view, was untenable.

Still, a word must be said for his sublime self-confidence, his doggedness, his moral courage in the face of all adversity. In summing up at the end of 1923, he admitted that his work did not satisfy for that year.

We arrived in Westland Row, Dublin, on April 30th [he wrote sarcastically], and since then life has been one long sweet song. We found the country torn with fratricidal strife. . . . To differ with or dissent against any Doctrine promulgated by the Tin Gods of any faction meant denunciation at least. A dozen would-be Mussolinis stood on the high places and issued their edicts. Lay theologians were as plentiful as mushrooms and just as dependable. The press of the country was the hired prostitute, as always, of the finance-capitalists. . . . Men who, in other days, had held the Flame of Liberty alight had become hucksters in the market place selling their soul, their power of expression and poetry of phrase. . . . The class in Ireland who had in all ages, under all forms of native and foreign oppression kept the torch of liberty alight, faint maybe at times, yet still alight, the Irish Working Class, they too, misled by a compromising, selfish, self-seeking group of place and fortune hunters masquerading as Labour Leaders had slunk into a slough of despond. . . .

Our Resolution, 1924 [concluded Larkin], 'No Compromise'—Truth, Moral Honesty, Class Solidarity will win and the Irish Working Class, often misled and betrayed, will again realise their responsibility and close their ranks and march breast forward, an Intelligent, Disciplined Army of Workers.[1]

[1] *Irish Worker*, January 5, 1924.

XII

COMMUNIST

THE serious nature of the successive problems encountered by Larkin on his return to Ireland caused him to continually postpone his long-projected trip to Russia. When he received an invitation from the Third or Communist International to represent Ireland at the Fifth Congress opening in Moscow on June 17, 1924, he applied to the Free State Government for passports for himself and his son to travel via Germany.[1] He was refused a passport, but undaunted he left Ireland at the end of May, a change of collars and a few books as baggage, and arrived in Leningrad by boat in early June.[2] In Moscow he was already well known by reputation. Two years previously, while still in Sing Sing, he had been elected to the Moscow Soviet by a group of tailors, most of whom had only recently returned to Russia from the United States.[3] Further, when he had been temporarily released in the spring of 1922, Zinoviev, second only to Lenin at the time in the Bolshevik inner circle, and President of the Comintern, had cabled his congratulations.[4] Since Lenin's death in January, 1924, Zinoviev was senior partner in the Triumvirate governing the Soviet Union. Finally, Larkin had caught Lenin's eye as long ago as 1913 during the Dublin lockout, and had earned his praise.

The Irish proletariat that is awakening to class consciousness [Lenin had written], has found a talented leader in the person of Comrade

[1] London *Times*, January 23, 1924.

[2] *Irish Worker*, September 27, 1924, 'From Dublin to Leningrad,' See *ibid.*, September 20, 1924, 'On May 27 there was opened a regular freight passenger line from Leningrad to London. The steamer *Roshal* made the first trip flying the Red Flag.'   [3] *New York Times*, February 1, 1922.

[4] *Workers' Republic*, June 3, 1922.

275

Larkin, the Secretary of the Irish Transport Worker's Union. Possessing remarkable oratorical talent, a man of seething Irish energy, Larkin has performed miracles among the unskilled workers—that mass of the British proletariat which in England is so often cut off from the advanced workers by that cursed petty bourgeois, liberal, aristocratic spirit of the British skilled worker.[1]

Though Lenin had been dead five months when Larkin arrived in Moscow, his words had already begun to take on the authority of scripture.

Larkin spoke only twice during the thirty-odd Comintern sessions in St. Andrew's Hall in the Kremlin. He intervened at the tenth session to uphold the British delegation's contention that the British Communist Party should attempt to form a 'united front' with the British Labour Party.[2] 'If we opposed any Labour Party candidate,' Larkin explained, 'the door would be shut upon us, and every Communist member excluded from the Labour Party. We should become sectarian and that was opposed to the whole spirit of Leninism.'[3] He also claimed to be expressing the unanimous view of the British Delegation when he said, 'although the Russian Party had lost its great leader, it was still from its experience and history fitted, beyond the possibility of challenge to provide the leadership of the Comintern.' A week later at the twenty-second session, he was invited by Zinoviev to address the delegates with reference to Ireland as part of a general discussion on National and Colonial questions. 'I mount this tribune with some deference,' Larkin began, 'and only at the request of Comrade Zinoviev who said that the Congress was interested in Ireland.'[4] 'I have failed to notice it,' he continued. 'The Congress seems interested only with those parties which have the largest membership.' 'The Irish proletariat, however,' noted Larkin pointedly, 'rose in 1916, not 1917. They went out as conscious revolutionaries because they had educated themselves for many years as revolutionaries.' 'I appeal to you, comrades,' he concluded, 'to turn your eyes to the Irish proletariat. We are not confined to

[1] V. I. Lenin, *Lenin on Britain* (London, 1934), p. 128.

[2] *Fifth Congress of the Communist International Abridged Report of Meetings held at Moscow, June 17th to July 8th, 1924*. Tenth Session, June 24, pp. 74–75. Larkin is listed as 'Brown' in the debates in the English Abridgement, but is corrected in the complete French and Russian versions. For British Delegations' point of view see Fifth Session, June 20, pp. 48–49, especially J. T. Murphy.

[3] *Ibid.*, Tenth Session, June 24, p. 74.

[4] *Ibid.*, Twenty-second Session, July 1, p. 204.

Ireland. We have millions in England, Scotland, the United States, Australia and South Africa. It is the duty of the Communist International to get this great mass, mostly proletarians, interested in the great Communist movement.'[1] At the closing session of the Comintern on July 8, 1924, Larkin was elected to the Executive Committee of the Communist International. This Committee was responsible for Comintern affairs between the Congresses.[2]

That same day the Third Congress of the Red International of Labour Unions, or Profintern, began its deliberations.[3] At the fourth session, on July 11, 1924, Larkin stressed the importance of the Co-operative Movement to the trade unions in their revolutionary struggle, for 'the mistake of the trade unions was to throw the masses into the fight without giving a thought to their stomachs.'[4] At the same session he also maintained that the 'Transport Workers represented a truly international force.' 'The merchant marine, well organized,' continued Larkin, 'represents an excellent way to tie the revolutionary elements of all countries together.' 'When the decisive hour shall sound,' he concluded, 'they must be prepared to answer the revolutionary call.'[5] Several days later, Tom Mann, the British Syndicalist, presented a report on 'The Position in England and Our Immediate Tasks.'[6] At the same session Kalinin, a top Bolshevik, presented a report 'On the Trade Union Movement in Great Britain.' In the debates which followed the reports, Arthur MacManus, Chairman of the British Communist Party, criticized both Mann and Kalinin for their analysis of tendencies in the British trade union movement.[7] He argued that the so-called 'left-wing,' composed of men such as Robert Williams and Purcell, was not left at all, but had been forced into that position temporarily by the pressure of the rank and file. Larkin rose to acknowledge MacManus's efforts to bring the debate within the realm of 'British actuality.'[8] 'It is amazing,' said Larkin, referring to the Socialist as opposed to the Communist International, 'that we should accuse the Amsterdam people of unreality while we ourselves have been nursing all the illusions that have been spread in the course of this single session.' 'For example,'

[1] *Fifth Congress of the Communist International Abridged Report of Meetings held at Moscow, June 17th to July 8th, 1935.* Twenty-second Session, July 1, p. 204.
[2] *Ibid.*, Thirty-first Session, July 8, p. 277.
[3] *La Vie Ouvrière* (Paris), July 25, 1924. For a full report see *ibid.*, 'Compte Rendu Analytique du IIIe Congrès de L'I.S.R.,' August 1 and September 26.
[4] *Ibid.*, August 8, 1924. Fourth Session, July 11, 1924.   [5] *Ibid.*
[6] *Ibid.*, September 5, 1924. Tenth Session, July 15, 1924.   [7] *Ibid.*   [8] *Ibid.*

he pointed out, 'some comrades have said that England was on the verge of revolution, that the revolution was already knocking at the door. But has anyone understood the true situation in Great Britain?' 'No!' Larkin maintained, for the English worker, 'the Empire goes before everything. Such is the way of thinking that is particular, not only to the leaders, but to the masses.' 'And what did Ben Tillett say lately?' Larkin asked. 'He said,' answered Larkin, ' "Although I am old, if the King calls for me, I shall answer his call." ' 'There are, however,' concluded Larkin, 'some people in Great Britain that are ready to struggle for revolutionary goals; they are convinced that the Empire must be destroyed, for otherwise, working-class humanity will have no hope of emancipation.'

The final contribution by Larkin to the Third Congress of the Profintern was in the debate that centred on the report by Losovsky, another top Bolshevik, on 'The Strategy of Strikes.'[1] Larkin objected strongly to any firm analogy being drawn between military strategy and the strategy of strikes. 'Is this a new application of Leninism?' he asked.[2] 'Does one have to study Klausewitz in order to galvanize the working classes into action?' he asked again. 'If so, why not follow the Hindenburg school?' 'I have taken part in a great many strikes,' he continued, 'and I dare assert that I know their mechanics. I have led campaigns among the most heterogeneous elements in Latin America and in the United States, where one finds subjects particularly impervious to propaganda.' 'Why, I declare,' he continued, 'that when someone tells me that a strike is a movement that can be run on paper, or directed from an information bureau, I assert that those who say that don't know what they are talking about.' 'One must see men as they are,' said Larkin, 'one must understand human emotions, the psychology of the workers. A motive that will find an echo among Russian workers will encounter indifference among British workers. That is why one must approach them differently. The ends may be the same, but the tactics must be different.'[3] The pragmatic roots ran deep in Larkin, and doctrinaire approaches to ways and means, when they were not his own, did not impress him much.

After an absence of nearly three months Larkin returned to Dublin on August 25, 1924.[4] The same evening a gigantic welcoming-

---

[1] *La Vie Ouvrière* (Paris) September 12, 1924. Twelfth Session, July 17, 1924.   [2] *Ibid.*   [3] *Ibid.*
[4] *Freeman's Journal.* August 26, 1924.

home procession, which featured a scarlet banner presented to Larkin in Moscow, paraded the principal streets of Dublin. On one side of the banner, inscribed in Russian, was, 'To the Revolutionary Transport Workers of Dublin, Greetings—From the Moscow Transport Workers,' while on the other, 'Proletariats, Unite in the Soviet Federated Republics.'[1] After the procession Larkin addressed his enthusiastic followers at a meeting in the Mansion House. He began by remarking that he left Ireland without the permission of the Government, and 'he would do so again and return to it when he thought fit, without asking their leave.'[2] 'He brought back a message of hope,' he claimed, 'for he had . . . an agreement and pledges for the establishment of direct commercial relations with Russia, which was the wealthiest country in the world.' 'He had,' he continued, 'been elected by the working classes of 32 countries of the world, as one of the 25 Commissioners [*sic.*, Commissars] to rule and govern the earth.' He had travelled 11,000 miles of Russia, mixed freely with all classes of the population, including the Red Army, and he declared 'that the greatest civil and religious freedom was enjoyed by every section of the community.'[3] 'In the course of his travels,' he claimed, 'he had sat on the throne formerly occupied by the Czar Nicholas, whose body was now lying in a well, and his power and position transferred to the workers and the people.' 'The Third Internationale,' he proceeded, 'was prepared to respond to the appeal of the Irish workers, and two and a half millions of the men of the Red Army, of which he was made a chief of Battalion, had pledged themselves to move their assistance to Ireland when called upon.' 'Perhaps the Red machines,' he romanticized, 'would fly soon in Northern skies, and then they would order England in decided tones to clear out of Ireland.'[4]

This eyewash, however, would not serve to solve the immediate and pressing problems faced by Larkin on his return. Before he had left for Russia, the several law suits which had been dragging on for over seven months between him and the Executive of the Transport Union came to trial in a consolidated action on February 12, 1924. The burden of Larkin's case had turned on the crucial question of whether the Rules of the Transport Union, as amended and registered on December 20, 1918, were legal. If these Rules were invalid,

---

[1] *Freeman's Journal*, August 26, 1924.　　　　　[2] *Ibid.*

[3] *Ibid.* See also *Irish Worker*, September 20, 1924. Larkin claimed to have visited 'Novogorod, The Caucasus, and Trans Georgia.'　　　[4] *Ibid.*

then the Executive Committee as it was constituted, and all their sub-sequent actions, including the Rules amended and registered on June 2, 1923, had no legal substance. After eight days of extensive hearing, with Larkin acting as his own counsel as usual, the Master of the Rolls found against Larkin and for the Executive.[1] On March 3, 1924, William O'Brien, in the name of the Executive Committee, informed Larkin by letter that he would be given the opportunity at their next meeting to explain why he 'should not be suspended or expelled from the membership of the Union.'[2] Larkin replied, in effect, that the Executive as constituted was illegal, and since the Order of the Master of the Rolls would be appealed when it was issued, no action could or should be taken.[3] The Executive Com-mittee, however, voted unanimously to expel Larkin from member-ship in the Union on March 14, 1924.[4]

Both sides settled down to wait each other out, but the dispute that broke out in the Dublin Alliance and Gas Consumers' Com-pany in the middle of May, 1924, soon brought matters to a head. The trouble began over the refusal of a clerk who was promoted to a collector of accounts to give up his membership in the Transport Union.[5] The Company insisted, and the Secretary of No. 1 Branch, John O'Neill, a supporter of the Executive against Larkin, sanctioned the strike, and applied to the Executive for strike pay for the Gas Workers' Section. O'Brien wrote in reply 'that in view of the action of this section in rejecting the advice of the Union and placing the control of the dispute in the hands of a non-member of this Union, no dispute benefit can be sanctioned.'[6] The Gas Workers by a ballot vote of 407 to 44, on May 20, 1924, at Liberty Hall, invited Larkin to attend their meeting at the Mansion House.[7] In a general appeal to all the members of the Transport Union to support the Gas Workers, Larkin advised them—'Pay your contributions this week, and as much more as you can afford into the Dispute Committee of the Gas Workers at Liberty Hall. Pay no shop steward this week . . . keep your cards just within the eight week limit—let not your

[1] *Attempt to Smash, op. cit.,* pp. 1–125. Judgment was delivered February 20, 1924.

[2] *Irish Worker,* March 22, 1924. See for full correspondence.

[3] *Ibid.* Larkin to O'Brien, March 13, 1924.

[4] *Ibid.* O'Brien to Larkin, March 18, 1924.

[5] *Freeman's Journal,* May 29, 1924.

[6] *Irish Worker,* May 24, 1924. O'Brien to John O'Neil, May 17, 1924.

[7] *Ibid.* B. Finnigan to Larkin, May 20, 1924.

arrears exceed seven weeks.'[1] In this way Larkin was able to impose the threat of holding the dispute together for at least seven weeks, and still have his supporters retain their membership in the Transport Union.[2]

A week later the Gas Company gave way to the men, and in the agreement signed between them, the Transport Union was not a party.[3] A few days prior to the settlement, Liberty Hall was surrounded by government troops 'accompanied by an armoured car and a machine gun mounted on a lorry,' and forty-five of Larkin's supporters, who had occupied the premises the previous evening, were arrested.[4] The same afternoon, a Sunday, Larkin defiantly spoke from the window of Liberty Hall, and the next morning he paralysed the port of Dublin with a lightning strike.[5] He called it off only when the forty-five men were released on bail that afternoon. The Transport Union repudiated the strike, but the stoppage was effective. Rumours began to fly of a 'New Larkin Union?' especially since the 'attempt to induce a section of the men to withhold their membership contributions to the organization under the executive.'[6] O'Brien denied that there was any truth whatever in the current rumour 'that 18,000 members of the I.T.G.W.U. have declared themselves in favour of Mr. Larkin. . . .'[7] A week later, the charges of unlawful occupation and conspiracy to take forcible possession of Liberty Hall against the forty-five men were unsustained, but upon their refusal to undertake to post £5 each for their good behaviour, they all received a month in jail.[8]

When Larkin departed for Moscow on May 27, 1924, he left his brother Peter in charge until he should return. On May 30, 1924, a 'Notice' was issued by the Port, Gas and General Workers' Provisional Committee' to the members of the Transport Union.[9] 'The Committee representative of all Sections of Workers,' it was announced, 'will receive All Monies until further notice and will issue receipts for same.'[10] The reason given was that—

[1] *Irish Worker*, May 24, 1924. Finnigan to Larkin, May 20, 1924.

[2] *Ibid.*, June 7, 1924. Each man received £1 and each boy 10s. per week during the dispute.

[3] *Freeman's Journal*, May 29, 1924. See also *Irish Worker*, May 31, 1924, for text of Agreement.   [4] *Ibid.*, May 26, 1924.

[5] *Ibid.*, May 27, 1924.   [6] *Ibid.*, May 28, 1924.   [7] *Ibid.*

[8] *Irish Worker*, June 7, 1924. See this for full Report of Magistrate's Hearings. See *Ibid.*, July 5, 1924, for their release.

[9] *Ibid.*   [10] *Ibid.*

In view of the fact that all buildings which are the property of the Members of the I.T. & G.W. Union are now under *Armed Guard*, placed there by the *Junta* calling themselves the Executive Committee of the above Union, the Committee calls upon all Union men and women to disassociate themselves from any Act or Word of Recognition of the said E.C., the members of which have repeatedly proven themselves to be Tools of the Employers, and Agents of the Government.[1]

After this notice of excommunication, Peter Larkin, at a meeting of the Inchicore Branch of the Transport Union on June 8, explained 'why the rank and file decided to take things into their own hands, and as a result of which the Provisional Committee came into being.'[2] In putting 'the issue to them straight,' he asked, 'were they going to continue being robbed by the E.C., or were they going to take their stand with the Provisional Committee?' Needless to say, the entire Branch, except the officials, voted to support the Provisional Committee. This Committee took another big step towards setting up a separate Union in Dublin when they ordered a number of men in the British and Irish Steam Packet Company to appear before them to answer certain charges.[3] The men refused and protested that they did not recognize the Committee. The great majority of their workmates, however, refused to work with them until they submitted to the Committee. A deputation of the men on strike visited the owner of the Steam Packet Company and persuaded him not to hire any man who was not recognized by the Committee.[4] A few days later, the *Irish Worker* declared that holding a card in the Transport Union was tantamount to 'Scabbery.' 'Our advice,' read the editorial in part, 'to those who have no cards—or wrong cards—is: "Act quickly," and join with the right body of men, because if you don't join willingly, perhaps you may join unwillingly.'[5] The following evening, Sunday, June 15, 1924, at a meeting in Beresford Place, Peter Larkin formally launched the Workers' Union of Ireland.

Within the month, two-thirds of the Dublin membership, or 16,000 men, transferred to the new Union.[6] In the country, however, only twenty Branches out of some 300 came over,[7] while very few of

---

[1] *Irish Worker*, June 7, 1924.   [2] *Ibid.*, June 14, 1924.

[3] *Ibid.* See letter dated June 11, 1924, from the Committee explaining the situation.   [4] *Ibid.*   [5] *Ibid.*

[6] File 369 T, Registrar of Friendly Societies, Ireland. Workers' Union of Ireland. Also William O'Brien, personal interview.   [7] *Ibid.*

the Branch officials either in the country or Dublin imitated their members.[1] The Rules of the new Union were duly registered on July 14, 1924, but the Executive Committee was listed as 'Provisional' and the officers, the General President and General Secretary had not been, as yet, elected.[2] The question now was—what would Larkin do when he returned? Larkin 'before he left told his brother Peter under no circumstances to allow the members of the Union to break away from the I.T.G.W.U.'[3] But as Jack Carney has pointed out it was not perhaps a question of what Larkin would do when he returned, but rather what could he do. 'When Jim returned from Russia,' Carney wrote, 'he was faced with a *fait accompli*. He could do no other but accept it.'[4]

Now there began a whole series of disputes that had nothing to do with either wages or hours, but rather with which union was to have control over a particular job. Typical of these jurisdictional disputes was the one that broke out in the Marine Housing project.[5] The 300 builders' labourers employed on the job, with the exception of five men, decided to go over to the Workers' Union. The contractor refused to dismiss the five men who decided to remain in the Transport Union, and when the Workers' Union men struck work, he called on the Dublin Employers' Federation for assistance. The skilled men, mostly carpenters and bricklayers, then refused to cross the picket line, and the strike dragged on for months. Similar jurisdictional disputes broke out in the Dublin Fish Market and in the Cinemas and Theatres as the workers split between the Transport and Workers' Union.[6] The Transport Union was explicit in a long manifesto addressed, 'To the Workers of Dublin.'

> In future, both on the docks and in the city, members of the I.T. and G.W.U. will remain at work unless involved in a genuine trade dispute, and they will fill the places of Larkinite workers who are foolish enough to quit their employment at the behest of any of Larkin's agents. In this decision the Dublin workers have the full support of the Union and the Union is determined that in each case that arises the

[1] *Irish Worker*, June 21, 1924. 'The New Movement.'
[2] Registrar of Friendly Societies, Ireland, *loc. cit.*
[3] 'Carney Memoir,' p. 3. James Larkin, Jr., concurred in this, personal interview.
[4] *Ibid.* See *Irish Worker*, September 13, 1924, for Larkin's endorsement of Workers' Union.
[5] *Irish Worker*, June 21, 1924.
[6] *Ibid.*, September 20, 1924. 'A Fishy Story.' See *ibid.*, December 6, 1924, for Cinema Strike.

workers will have an opportunity of choosing between their jobs and Larkin's interest.[1]

The Workers' Union also outlined its position, tempering it only by sarcastically remarking that they had 'no enmity against the rank and file, however small,' of the Transport Union.[2]

> The principle is plain and definite. In jobs where there is a division, then the Transport cards are recognized; in jobs where only W.U.I. men are, then only W.U.I. cards, and no others, will be recognized. That is our position. It is neither overbearing or provocative. It need cause no divisions or turmoil, and if employers will recognize and abide by it, no dispute will arise.[3]

This was a long step back from the position taken in the previous August, when the *Irish Worker* had announced—'The Transport Union has ceased to exist—except as a scab herding organization. The Transport Union card is nothing but a pass to a scab. There is only going to be one labourers union in Ireland and that will be the Workers' Union, which has earned its place by right of conquest.'[4]

The two rival unions continued to engage in a kind of guerrilla warfare with jurisdictional sniping and resulting work stoppages the order of the day. The climax finally came in the middle of July, 1925, when the Coal Merchants' Association decided that they had had enough and closed down their yards. The lockout would continue they maintained 'until a satisfactory guarantee is obtained that the men employed there will work amicably together.'[5] Within a week the Transport Union disclaimed 'all responsibility for the situation that had arisen in the coal yards,' and maintained that it had 'no difference with the merchants.'[6] Meanwhile Larkin claimed that he was negotiating with Amsterdam for a shipment of German coal but that, in any case, English coal was on its way and would be distributed by the Workers' Union.[7] By July 29 the first of the coal was being sold at cost to the poor and needy of Dublin.[8] The lockout continued into August when the Dublin Employers' Federation Ltd. intervened on behalf of the Coal Merchants and promised them financial as well as moral aid.[9] The Dublin employers resolved, 'to give organized support to employers and constitutional labour, so

---

[1] *Voice of Labour* (Dublin), November 29, 1924.
[2] *Irish Worker*, March 21, 1925.   [3] *Ibid.*   [4] *Ibid.*, August 9, 1924.
[5] *Irish Times* (Dublin), July 17, 1925.   [6] *Ibid.*, July 22, 1925.
[7] *Ibid.*, July 21, 1925.   [8] *Ibid.*, July 30, 1925.   [9] *Ibid.*, August 14, 1925.

that liberty of action should be secured for employers and labour, irrespective of the union to which any worker may belong.'[1] The proposer of the resolution, David Barry, managing director of the British and Irish Steam Packet Company, went on to explain what he meant—'the employers claimed the same liberty and the same right to organize themselves for . . . protection against tyranny and Bolshevism.' He went on to explain that 'Mr. Larkin demands the right to become the sole dictator of the wage-earners of Dublin.' 'Such a claim we will not admit, whoever the individual may be,' said Mr. Barry. 'It is our intention to resist it at any cost.' The *Irish Times* put the case even more plainly:

> Mr. Larkin, who does not conceal his association with a malignant and alien power, has chosen his time cunningly. He has precipitated this crisis at a moment when the national mind is beginning to recover from the confusions of the last few years, when new works of construction are being taken in hand, and vital matters of economic development are in the balance. His triumph would be the triumph of anarchy in the Free State.[2]

Meanwhile the Coal Merchants made arrangements to unload their coal, but at the last minute 'the men who were willing to work were afraid to start on account of the intimidatory tactics of the Workers' Union. . . .'[3] Finally, on August 12, the Coal Merchants were able to begin unloading their ships under police protection, and using men holding Transport Union cards.[4] Several days later violence broke out on the quays as Workers' Union men attacked the Transport men unloading coal.[5] Larkin managed to hold up deliveries, however, because most of the truck drivers were loyal to the Workers' Union, but the Transport Union countered by offering to provide the necessary drivers as well.[6] By August 24 the Coal Merchants announced that they were ready to make deliveries, but Larkin threatened that trade unionists would walk out of any firm that accepted a delivery.[7] The Gas Workers, who were militantly pro-Larkin, however, were the only group who struck in sympathy, but they bowed the next day when they went back to work agreeing to 'obey orders.'[8] Early in September, the Workers' Union men shot

[1] *Irish Times* August 14, 1925,
[2] *Ibid.* See Editorial, 'Danger and Opportunity.' [3] *Ibid.*
[4] *Ibid.*, August 13 and 15, 1925. [5] *Ibid.*, August 18, 1925.
[6] *Ibid.*, August 22, 1925. [7] *Ibid.*, August 24, 1925.
[8] *Ibid.*, August 28, 1925.

their final bolt in a mass attack on Transport Union men unloading coal in the Alexandra Basin.[1] Stones, lumps of coal, and anything they could get their hands on proved to be of no avail, for by the end of the first week in September, the Coal Merchants with the help of the Transport Union had consolidated their position.[2]

By 1926 it was obvious that the Irish trade union movement was in a serious decline. Though this decline was due perhaps more to the generally deteriorating economic situation in the British Isles, than to the civil war raging in the Irish Labour Movement, the fratricidal struggle made a bad situation worse. In 1923, when Larkin returned to Ireland, there were some 130,000 trade union members in Ireland, with the Transport and Distributing trades accounting for about 100,000 of them.[3] By 1926 the total had shrunk to some 95,000, with the Transport and Distributing trades absorbing almost the whole of the loss in listing about 67,000 members. In 1926, then, the Irish trade union movement was numerically back where it had been before the First World War, and in actual ability to resist the employing classes it was weaker because disunited. A sad commentary indeed on a Movement that had showed so much promise and hope.

With the trade union movement in shambles and economic action, therefore, out of the question, the pendulum began to swing to the great alternative—political action. Occasion, however, did not present itself, until the summer of 1927, when the Minister for Justice, Kevin O'Higgins, sometimes erroneously described as Ireland's Mussolini, was assassinated on a Sunday morning while on his way to Mass. In a panic the Government passed a stringent Public Safety Act that all but suspended civil liberties. Larkin called a public meeting in College Green to protest against the 'Czarist Methods' of the Government, but the meeting was prohibited and the police refused to allow him to speak when he appeared.[4] Instead, Larkin addressed his meeting from a window in Unity Hall, the headquarters of the Workers' Union in Marlborough Street, and proposed the following resolution:

---

[1] *Irish Times* September 4, 1925. [2] *Ibid.*, September 8, 1925.

[3] *Irish Worker*, December 19, 1931. See for Figures. Further, the figures for 1929 resulted in the total shrinking to 85,000, with the transport and distributing trades declining even more markedly to about 56,000 members. In 1923 Irish Trade Unionists contributed £183,617 to their Unions; in 1926, £98,461; and in 1929, £78,052. [4] *Irish Times*, August 4, 1927.

Head of Larkin by Mina Carney, wife of Jack Carney,
one of Larkin's closest friends in America and later in
Dublin.

Yours Fra.
Jim Larkin
Jan. 1ˢᵗ 1944,

From a drawing by Sean O'Sullivan, R.H.A., done in 1942.

That this mass meeting of citizens, union officials and union men and women, holding diverse political views, submit that in this crisis the leader of the second largest party elected to the Dail should summon immediately by advertisement a meeting of representative men and women of all parties and groups opposed to the Government and the elected representatives who have not taken their seats, with a view to organizing a conference, and that such conference shall draft a line of policy and draw up a programme with a view to meeting the tyrannical measures of the Government, and to find a common denominator in defence of the lives, liberties and rights of the common people.[1]

A deputation was sent to Eamon de Valera, who promised to put the resolution before a meeting of the leaders of his newly formed party, Fianna Fail (Soldiers of Destiny), the next day. After the meeting the following communication was issued to the Press by de Valera:

A CHARA,—Following on a request sent me from a mass meeting of workers held in the city last night, I hereby invite two members of the Labour Party, two members of the Farmers' Union, two members of the National League, two members of Sinn Fein, two representatives of the Transport Workers' Union, two representatives of the Irish Workers' Union and two members of Fianna Fail to meet to consider the present position with a view to deciding upon such lines of joint national action as will save the country from the consequences of the legislation now being passed through the Free State Assembly. The meeting will be held tomorrow morning at 10 a.m. at Wynn's Hotel, Lower Abbey Street.[2]

Only Larkin and de Valera attended, however, and after a short conference of less than ten minutes they broke up. Both the Farmers' Union and the National League, which generally supported the Government in the Dail, had written they would not attend. On behalf of the Labour Party Thomas Johnson, its leader, had written that the best way for Fianna Fail to check the Government would be for its members to take their seats in the Dail. Sinn Fein, from which de Valera had recently seceded with a majority to form Fianna Fail, refused to compromise with constitutionalism and did not even deign to reply. That same evening at Unity Hall, Larkin asked his followers, 'What about Sinn Fein now?'[3] 'Under the Electoral

[1] *Irish Times*, August 4, 1927.
[2] *Ibid.*, August 5, 1927.
[3] *Ibid.*, August 6, 1927.

Act,' he explained, 'they were denied the opportunity of presenting themselves for election without taking the oath, so that they would automatically be dissociated from every reform of representative Government.' 'There were only two other ways,' he maintained. 'One was by passive resistance; the other way was by revolution.' 'And where was the person,' he asked, 'who could tell him that this country was ready for revolution at present, either mentally or physically, for God knows they had more reason for a revolution than any country in the world?' 'There were therefore,' he concluded, 'two lines upon which they could go—inside the Dail or by passive resistance.'[1]

The upshot of all this was that Fianna Fail, led by de Valera, decided to take their seats in the Dail if elected in the general elections called by the Government for the middle of September. Larkin decided to contest North Dublin.[2] His newly created political organization, the Irish Workers' League, which also nominated his son James for County Dublin, and John Lawlor, General President of the Workers' Union, for South Dublin, had actually been in existence since early September of 1923. The League had been formed by Larkin on his return from America as a sort of Clarion Fellowship, and he was very careful in the beginning to point out it was a social and not a political or economic organization.[3] Later on, when the split in the Labour Movement became irreparable, the organization was given a Constitution, which had the effect of modifying its purely social character.[4] By the end of August, 1927, the League was a full-fledged political organization.[5] Larkin explained to a meeting of Irish Workers' League delegates that 'they had not intended to enter on active political work until the next general election, but circumstances had arisen during the past few weeks which called for immediate action.'[6] He then entered into a description of the distressing economic state of the country.

The position of the workers was growing worse hourly; unemployment was becoming more acute; wages and conditions were being attacked by every section of the employing class. The Government

[1] *Irish Times*, August 6, 1927. [2] *Ibid.*, August 31, 1927.
[3] *Irish Worker*, September 8, 1923.
[4] *Ibid.*, May 3, 1924. See Mansion House Meeting, April 27, 1924.
[5] *The Communist International between the Fifth and the Sixth World Congresses —1924–1928* (London, 1928), p. 135. See Report on Ireland, pp. 133–37.
[6] *Irish Times*, September 1, 1927.

claimed that it was interested in the development of trade and industry, but some mills were in a parlous condition, while others had closed. . . . Two-thirds of the unemployed were not receiving unemployment benefit.[1]

'The Free State Government was not alone to blame,' Larkin claimed, 'the alleged official Labour Party and many of the trade union leaders who represented British Unions in Ireland were directly responsible for that condition of things.' 'It was high time,' he concluded, 'they appealed over the heads of those so-called leaders of the workers to the rank and file of the Labour movement.'[2]

Larkin campaigned vigorously, and despite the fact that both he and Lawlor were designated as 'Communists' in the Press, he was elected in North Dublin on the first count under a complicated system of proportional representation.[3] His son James cost the very able leader of the Labour Party, Thomas Johnson, his seat in County Dublin by splitting the Labour vote. Though Lawlor lost in South Dublin, he destroyed any chance of the Labour Party capturing a seat there. Larkin, however, could not claim his seat in the Dail because he was an undischarged bankrupt, since he had refused, on principle, to pay the costs in the action he had lost to the Transport Union Executive.[4] His seat was declared vacant and a new election was called for early in April 1928. In the three-cornered fight between the Government, Fianna Fail, and himself, Larkin was extremely bitter about the Fianna entering a candidate. 'He had thought,' he said, 'that Fianna Fail, knowing his position—and they had been good enough to tell him personally that, thanks to his whirlwind campaign in the last election, he got them two or three seats they did not expect—would have left the fight open between himself and the Government.'[5] 'He was glad that Fianna Fail had done what they had done,' he continued, 'because it showed that the workers had to have their own party and their own movement.' In this contest Larkin was again referred to as 'the Communist candidate,' and his retort was that the electors 'were now being fooled by people who told them lies about what was happening in Mexico and Russia, while their own wages were being reduced and their hours lengthened.'[6] When the votes were counted, however, Larkin

[1] *Irish Times*, September 1, 1927.　[2] *Ibid.*　[3] *Ibid.*, September 19, 1927.
[4] *Voice of Labour*, January 24, 1925. See for Bankruptcy Hearing.
[5] *Irish Times*, March 26, 1928.　[6] *Ibid.*, March 28, 1928.

came in a poor third with 8,232 votes. The Government took the seat with a poll of 21,731, while the Fianna Fail candidate mustered 13,322 votes.[1] With 7,000 electors not voting, the Government probably would have lost the seat if Larkin had stepped down.

Between the election campaigns Larkin made his second and last visit to the Soviet Union. In February, 1928, he attended the sixth and final Executive Committee meeting of the Comintern between the Fifth (1924) and the Sixth (1928) World Congresses. Great changes had taken place in the Bolshevik hierarchy since his last visit in the summer of 1924. The Revolution, like the old sow, had begun to devour her young. Trotsky, discredited but unrepentant, was soon to go into exile. Zinoviev and Kamenev had been reduced to the state where they were reapplying for ordinary membership in the Party. Many had learned, and more were soon to learn, under the tutelage of Stalin, that the problem in revolutions is not so much in making them but in consolidating them. Oblivious of the vast implications, Larkin viewed the Trotsky–Stalin debate as simply a struggle for power in the Party. During a full-dress Comintern debate, at which both Stalin and Trotsky spoke, Bukharin, who had replaced Zinoviev as President of the Comintern, asked Larkin if he would like to speak. In refusing Larkin explained that 'the issue was one between the men and women of Russia,' and 'that it would be an impertinence on his part to take sides.'[2]

He did, however, speak at a meeting of the Moscow Soviet of which he was a member. For over an hour he spoke to an audience of 2,000 people, of whom perhaps not a hundred understood English, yet 'he held the meeting in the hollow of his hand.'[3] His theme was Ireland, and of the necessity for the trade union movement to understand the peasantry. The picture he drew, wrote Jack Carney, who was there, of an 'Irish peasant struggling with the soil "in the agony of bloody sweat" was the moving part of his speech.'[4] 'During his speech,' wrote Carney, 'he must have been thinking of the proceedings of the Communist International for he wound up by asking the audience to hold up the hands of Stalin, a Biblical reference to Joshua. When the interpreter came to this part of his speech the audience rose and cheered for several minutes.'[5] During this visit to Moscow, the question of Larkin's professed Catholicism came up.

[1] *Irish Times*, April 5, 1928. [2] 'Carney Memoir,' *op. cit.*, p. 1.
[3] *Ibid.*, p. 2. [4] *Ibid.* [5] *Ibid.*

The Russians looked upon Jim as some kind of enigma. Bukharin had asked him about his Faith, being under the impression that Jim avowed himself a Catholic for opportunistic reasons. To the surprise of Bukharin, Jim said he had faith there was a God. Bukharin had asked him if he *believed* there was a God. Jim insisted that he had Faith there was a God and he would hold to such a Faith until he had been proved to be wrong. There was no shaking him. Although he had the opportunity of going to Mass in Moscow he did not go, which added to the mystery.[1]

The order of business that most concerned Larkin at the meetings of the Comintern Executive Committee, however, was future Communist Party policy in Great Britain. A majority of the British Party argued that a change in policy was necessary, and submitted their views in 'The Report of the British Commission.' At the Fifth Congress (1924), the British delegation, with Larkin in the forefront, had urged a policy of 'united front' with the Labour Party. Now, it was generally argued, the Labour Party 'leadership as a whole had swung still more to the Right than it was at the time of the Fifth Congress, the pseudo-Left wing led by Lansbury, Purcell and the rest, that emerged prior to the big strike movements, had sunk back into the fold of the Right wing, and has completely merged itself with it.'[2] In the light of this state of affairs, the British Commission recommended, 'that the Party should aim, and do its utmost, to put forward as many candidates as possible of its own in all constituencies in order to make clear the policy of the Communist Party.'[3]

With his own recent victory against an official Labour Party undoubtedly in mind, Larkin fully supported a change in the policy he had helped formulate. 'I hold the line advanced by the Commission is correct,' he argued, 'the new tactics will lead to the consolidation of the bureaucrats both in the Labour Party and in the trade unions. But it is from the reformist party to a real fighting party.'[4]

---

[1] 'Carney Memoir,' *op. cit.*, p. 2.

[2] 'The Communist International,' *op. cit.*, p. 117. See for full Report on Great Britain, pp. 111–32.

[3] *Communist Policy in Great Britain. The Report of the British Commission of the Ninth Plenum of the Comintern* (London, 1928). See for Resolutions, pp. 191 ff.

[4] *Ibid.*, p. 129. See also pp. 69–71 for Larkin's remarks on Labour Party. See especially p. 69, where he comments on the 'Rationalisation' of Industry in Great Britain.

In answer to the scriptural argument that Lenin had advocated in 1920 a pushing to power of the Labour Party, Larkin maintained— 'We do not diverge from the Leninist line—it is true Leninism to change your tactics according to the difficulties, the obstacles and the changed conditions that confront you.' 'On the question of the immediate task, I hold,' said Larkin, 'that a daily newspaper is of the utmost importance.' 'There is hardly one out of ten workers,' he pointed out, 'who would read the "Daily Herald" if they could get a daily Communist paper.' 'Our Comrades of Great Britain with the help of the Comintern,' concluded Larkin, '. . . are going to carry their Party and the British working class to a social revolution. (Applause.)'[1] Since he had to return to fight the by-election in North Dublin in early April, 1928, Larkin could not wait for the Sixth Congress held in July and August. He did leave Carney behind, however, to represent Ireland at the Sixth Congress and to write an interim report on Ireland for the Comintern between the Fifth and Sixth Congresses.[2]

On his return from the Soviet Union, and after his election defeat, Larkin was presented with several proposals to bring the civil war in the Irish Labour Movement to an end. 'We have been importuned,' he wrote, 'by letter, by circular, by newspaper advertisement and by personal solicitation to come to two different conferences for the purpose of discussing this question.'[3] 'It was not a question,' he wrote, 'as set out in one of these reports and submitted to us and numbered in the order of their importance: 1—Representation; 2—Affiliation Fees; 3—National Political Factors.' 'No, Comrades, unity cannot be brought about on the lines that you suggest,' he continued, for '. . . political power can only arise out of and express itself in a class sense and with full effect and purpose, if it is based on industrial solidarity. . . .' To Larkin, then, political unity was impossible without some agreement between the Transport and Workers' Unions, which, as far as both he and O'Brien were concerned, was out of the question.

---

[1] *Communist Policy in Great Britain. The Report of the British Commission of the Ninth Plenum of the Comintern* (London, 1928), p. 130.

[2] *Protokoll—Sechster Welt Kongress de Kommunistischen Internationale, Moskau, 17 Juli–1 September 1928* (Hamburg–Berlin, 1928), III, 122–23. See this for full report of Carney's remarks on Ireland. For Carney's written report on Ireland see 'The Communist International,' *op. cit.*, pp. 133–37.

[3] *Irish Worker*, May 12, 1938. 'Labour Unity.'

Could the position of the Irish Labour Movement have been much more difficult on the eve of the worst of all the economic convulsions that have shaken modern Capitalism? Dispirited and disunited, the Movement was a far cry from the hopes expressed for it five years before by Larkin on his return from America as the force that would resurrect the Irish nation. But worse was to follow with the advent of the Great Depression. Divided, shrunken in members, without appreciable funds, the trade union movement was unable to resist the further wage reductions imposed by the Irish employers. The Irish Labour Party, reduced in numbers, leaderless and impotent, marked time in a Dail that made a mockery of minority rights with its coercive legislation in the form of Public Safety Acts. Emigration was no longer a palliative for unemployment, for America and Britain were themselves in the throes of the Great Depression. Much, indeed, has been said about the effect of the Depression on Capitalism, but much more could be said about its effect on Labour. After 1928 Larkin's popular fortunes went into a decline from which they never really recovered, and he soon ceased to be a figure of international importance.

XIII

DECLINE

TO chronicle nearly twenty years of decline is depressing. That so rich, so active, and so fruitful a life should come to such an end is nothing less than anti-climactic. In 1928, however, at the age of fifty-two, Larkin had no idea that he was at the beginning of his end. Sustained by his sublime faith in the working class, he was still confident that he would lead them out of their land of bondage. He struggled in his declining years to keep the flickering hope alive that the working classes, if they had only the courage to will it, would come finally into their own. As the Depression deepened in late 1930 he had not yet lost heart.

> For I dipt into the Future,
>   as far as human eye could see
> Saw the Vision of the World,
>   and all the wonder that would be . . .
> Till the war-drum throbbed no longer,
>   and the battle-flags were furled
> In the Parliament of Man,
>   the Federation of the World.[1]

'What a beautiful dream!' he wrote, 'but to realize this glorious dream requires an acceptance of the dream and determination to realize it.'[2] 'Comrades,' he implored a few weeks later, 'I am giving everything human nature will permit. I could do more if you would give me of your strength.'[3]

[1] *Irish Worker*, October 11, 1930. Quoted from Tennyson's *Locksley Hall*.
[2] *Ibid.*
[3] *Ibid.*, October 25, 1930.

294

> Come then! For what are you waiting?
> The day and the dawn is coming
> And forth the banners go![1]

The Irish workers, however, were no longer inspired by their Prophet.

Oblivious of the lack of faith Larkin continued to fight in the only way he knew. Appointing himself keeper of the public conscience, he denounced all and sundry who, in his opinion, stood between the workers and their promised land. When, for example, Sean Lemass, one of de Valera's chief lieutenants, predicted in October, 1930, the eclipse of the Irish Labour Party, without even saying 'a prayer for the departed,' Larkin, though a sworn enemy of the Party, was indignant. 'It is not,' he wrote, 'that they hate this heterogeneous grouping which calls itself "the Irish Labour Party," it is because today as in the past, they hate the very idea of a conscious, organized disciplined Irish Labour movement.'[2] As if to prove his impartiality a few weeks later in referring to the failure of the Labour Party to advise the workers on how to vote in a by-election, he thundered— 'In this land of nepotism, hypocrisy, and moral cowardice, at least a thing of wood with a brass belly might dare emit a sound.'[3] This was milk and toast, however, when compared to his denunciations of the Free State Government. 'The Government,' he declared, 'have betrayed the nation, dishonoured the dead, derided the poor and needy and have demonstrated their hatred of the working class.'

> They are unnational!
> They are unmoral!
> They are unpractical!
> They are unhung!
> The pity of it!!![4]

The public, however, paid no attention to his moral instruction, and ignored his moral indignation.

Though his difficulties increased in the early years of the Great Depression, Larkin did not grow more cautious. With the approach of the general election in early 1932, the Government, uneasy over the prospects for a peaceful transition within the democratic process, passed a Public Safety Act in October, 1931, that virtually suspended 'due process of law.' 'We learn,' Larkin commented caustically, 'the

---

[1] *Irish Worker*, October 25, 1930. [2] *Ibid.*, November 1, 1930.
[3] *Ibid.*, December 6, 1930. [4] *Ibid.*

Constitution is to be wrapped up in cotton-wool and placed in a glass case in Trinity College so that in the years to come the people will see what the people fought for.'[1] Several weeks later the Minister for Justice prohibited for Saturday, November 7, 1931, 'the public meeting proposed to be held to celebrate the 14th anniversary of the Russian Revolution.'[2] Larking issued a 'Stop Press,' which advised— 'IMPEACH THE MINISTER FOR JUSTICE,' but the meeting was not held. Though the trumpet still gave no uncertain sound, there were none to do battle.

In this atmosphere the country prepared to go to the polls in February, 1932. Larkin decided to contest North Dublin where he had polled over 8,000 first preference votes in 1928. The Dublin Press virtually ignored Larkin's campaign, and the voters very nearly did the same. In losing, Larkin polled less than 4,000 first preference votes.[3] Fianna Fail led by de Valera with the support of the Labour Party's seven seats, put the Government out, but uneasy over his dependence on Labour de Valera called for new elections within a year. Once again, in January, 1933, Larkin was campaigning in North Dublin. This time, he suffered a most humiliating defeat, polling less than 2,800 votes, and actually receiving some 1,200 votes less than the official Labour Party candidate in what was once considered his personal stronghold.[4] De Valera and Fianna Fail were returned with a majority that guaranteed them a full five-year term in office.

By 1933 the situation was desperate for both Larkin and the Irish Labour Movement. The *Irish Worker* had collapsed the previous year from want of funds, and the membership of the Workers' Union was shrinking.[5] The Depression had made a shambles of the entire Irish trade union movement and destroyed any hope of economic action on the part of the workers. Now the victory of Fianna Fail at the polls effectively limited the political alternative for at least five years, since the Labour Party had only eight seats in the Dail. Larkin was himself further humiliated some months later in the local elections when he lost his seat on the Dublin Municipal Council.[6]

The most important single factor in accounting for Larkin's

---

[1] *Irish Worker*, October 24, 1931. See for text of new judicial procedures by military tribunals in civil cases.　　　　　　[2] *Ibid.*, November 14, 1931.
[3] *Irish Times*, February 18, 1932.　　　　　[4] *Ibid.*, January 27, 1933.
[5] *Irish Worker*, March 19, 1932. This was the final issue.
[6] *Minutes*, Dublin Municipal Council, 1933.

popular decline in the early thirties was, undoubtedly, his 'Communist' affiliations. At the general election in 1932 he was listed as a 'Communist' candidate in the Press.[1] Though he did not protest the label, it was, in 1932, a good deal less than the truth. Actually, after his last trip to Moscow in the winter of 1928, he had drifted out of the Communist current. Until 1928 he had made no secret of his membership in the Comintern and Profintern. He had in fact received financial aid, though modest indeed, from the Comintern.[2] The breach had been opened in 1928 in Moscow, when Larkin quarrelled so violently with Losovsky, Chairman of the Profintern, that the two men very nearly came to blows.[3] He had already crossed swords with Losovsky in Moscow in 1924, it will be remembered, when the Russian maintained there was a parallel between military strategy and strategy in strikes.

More significant, however, was the fact that he had nothing to do with the production of the *Workers' Voice*, which appeared in April, 1932, replete with hammer, sickle, and Soviet star, only a month after the collapse of his *Irish Worker*.[4] The title of the new paper was changed to the *Irish Workers' Voice* early in 1933, and when the Communist Party of Ireland was relaunched in June, it became the official organ of the Party.[5] Larkin studiously ignored the Party and its paper, though it gave him the 'elder statesman' treatment. It became obvious to all who cared to notice, that by 1934, though he never made a public recantation, he had quietly disassociated himself from the international Communist Movement.

The years between 1928 and 1935 were a sad testimonial to a man who lived to serve; but they are not tragic years, for, in the deepest sense Larkin had not been defeated. He had refused to compromise even in the interests of those who gave meaning to his work, and he never became less, therefore, than what he conceived himself to be. After 1935, imperceptibly, the tragic personal decline begins, for the man who for thirty years had believed himself to be the Irish Labour Movement incarnate began to realize he was only a part of it. This

[1] *Irish Times*, February 18, 1932.

[2] Ernest Blythe, personal interview. Mr. Blythe was a former Minister in the Free State Government up until 1932. Also Jack Carney, personal interview. Mr. Carney confirmed the fact that Larkin received the funds which arrived by courier.

[3] James Larkin, Jr., personal interview. Mr. Larkin was in Moscow attending Lenin College at the time.

[4] *Workers' Voice* (Dublin), April 9, 1932.

[5] *Irish Workers' Voice* (Dublin), June 11, 1933.

decline was paralleled by the growing right-wing reaction in Ireland. The rise of General O'Duffy and his Blueshirts in 1934 was the Irish reflection of a worldwide Fascist phenomenon. When the Spanish Civil War broke out in 1936, the Republican and Socialist left in Ireland were more hard-pressed than ever. The pro-Franco pressure became so great that the Executive Committee of the Workers' Union, with Larkin's tacit approval, passed a resolution forbidding any official of the Union from appearing on any but a trade union platform. This was directed against those officials, and Jack Carney in particular, who spoke from Irish Republican platforms in support of the Republican Government in Spain. Carney immediately protested the resolution as an insupportable infringement on his personal liberty, and receiving no satisfaction from Larkin resigned his position in the Union and left for England.[1] Larkin had achieved greatness because he never counted cost, either to himself or his followers, when he deemed a question of principle to be at stake. That he failed to distinguish principle in this case can hardly be mitigated by the fact that circumstances made such distinctions more difficult.

Meanwhile, when it seemed that there was nothing left to Larkin except hope, his popular fortunes began to revive a little. In the summer of 1936 he regained his seat in the Dublin Municipal Council,[2] and in the general election the following year he won a surprising upset victory in North-East Dublin.[3] The continuing Depression, deepened in Ireland by de Valera's disastrous economic war with Britain, had resulted in much dissatisfaction. De Valera lost his majority in the Dail and was only able to form a minority Government with the support of Labour's thirteen seats. Though he had run as an independent Labour candidate, Larkin generally supported de Valera and his policies. In the Dail, he had surprisingly little to say, though there were occasional flashes of the old Larkin. In the course of one debate he remarked to a member of the Fine Gael, or Conservative Party—'You have neither policy nor morals. Your religion is to get all you can for yourselves.' He was heckled in turn by another Conservative member who added—'And to get you out of the country.' Furious, Larkin turned on the heckler and exploded—'No Blueshirt bastard like you will put me out.'[4] The explosions.

---

[1] Jack Carney, personal interview.

[2] *Minutes*, Dublin Municipal Council, 1936.

[3] *Irish Times*, July 5, 1937.   [4] *Dail Debates*, 1937, vol. 69, cols. 743–44.

however, were becoming fewer and further between. Meanwhile, de Valera, uneasy over his dependence on Labour, dissolved the Dail, and Larkin for the second time in a year was campaigning in North-East Dublin. In the interim de Valera had negotiated in early 1938 an agreement with the British Government which returned to Ireland those naval bases Britain had retained under the terms of the 'Treaty' signed in 1921. The Irish were overjoyed with de Valera's diplomatic stroke, since a European war appeared to be inevitable, and Ireland was determined to remain neutral. De Valera, therefore, was returned with a comfortable majority that ensured him a full five-year term in office. Larkin lost his seat in a hard-fought contest but demonstrated that there was still enough magic in the name of Larkin to muster a hard core of 5,000 supporters.[1]

The last of the great turning points in Larkin's life came in early 1941 when the Government passed the Trade Union Act. With most Irish trade unionists Larkin viewed the Act as a serious threat to the Constitutional right of freedom of association.[2] Soon after the Act was passed, Larkin and his son James among thousands of others, applied for membership in the Irish Labour Party.[3] Both were admitted in December, 1941, and in the local elections the following summer, with Larkin as an official Labour candidate, the Party gained its first significant municipal victory, becoming the largest single Party in the Council. The Party was now confident that real gains could be made at the general election scheduled for the spring of 1943. William O'Brien, however, supported by his colleagues in the Transport Union, was not a man to either forgive or forget.

Anxious to avoid any rupture with the officers of the Transport Union over Larkin's proposed candidature for North-East Dublin, the Administrative Council of the Labour Party appointed a delegation to approach both sides in an attempt to arrive at a satisfactory arrangement. The officers of the Transport Union were adamant, pointing out that Larkin had tried to disrupt their Union, and failing

---

[1] *Irish Times*, June 22, 1938.

[2] Irish Trades Union Congress, *Forty-Seventh Annual Report*, 1941, pp. 29–31. See also *Forty-Eighth Annual Report*, 1942, pp. 25–28.

[3] The Labour Party. *Official Statement relating to the disaffiliation from the Labour Party of the Irish Transport and General Workers' Union*, prepared by the Administrative Council for the information of Party Branches, Divisional and Constituency Councils and the affiliated Corporate bodies, p. 2.

in this promoted a rival union, and added that there was no guarantee he would abide by his professed undertakings. The delegation, headed by William Norton, leader of the Labour Party, prevailed upon Larkin to put his submission in writing. He wrote Norton, in part, on May 14, 1943:

> For myself, I assure you most sincerely that I am willing to work loyally with any member of the Party regardless of previous personal differences and antagonisms and to put aside all divisions and conflicts. . . . You may be assured that this declaration will be scrupulously observed by me and I shall at all times accept the judgment of the Administrative Council as to whether or not I have been faithful to that declaration.[1]

Armed with Larkin's submission, the delegation again approached the officers of the Transport Union, who now pointed out that, despite Larkin's assurances, he 'had not anywhere in his letter expressed regret for his part in the earlier conflict with the Union.'[2] The delegation then informed Larkin of the seemingly final obstacle in the way of putting an end to the twenty-year feud. In what must have been an herculean effort for an enormously proud man, Larkin delivered up the required 'pound of flesh.' He wrote Norton on May 22, 1943:

> I am deeply sensible of the efforts which you, personally, and the other leaders of the Party are making to resolve the present difficulties and I, on my part, am willing to do all possible to assist you short of coming in conflict with my own self-respect and principles. . . .
> I have fully considered the points you put to me in our last conversation and I will respond to your viewpoint by stating that if in the heat of past conflicts statements were made by me, I regret having made such statements if those statements today appear as obstacles in the way of a united effort by all members of the Party at the present moment.[3]

When the officers of the Transport Union refused to accept this apology, the Administrative Council of the Labour Party, eight of whose seventeen members were Transport Union representatives, pressed for a vote on Larkin's nomination. The eight Transport Union representatives voted solidly against Larkin, and since two of the other nine members were absent though they would have voted

---

[1] *Ibid.*, p. 4. The whole of the letter is quoted on pp. 4–5.
[2] *Ibid.*, p. 5.   [3] *Ibid.*

for Larkin if present, the endorsement was lost, 8 votes to 7. The Dublin Executive of the Labour Party then took matters into its own hands by endorsing Larkin's nomination as an official Labour candidate shortly before the election, and presented the Administrative Council with a *fait accompli*.[1] Larkin fought a whirlwind campaign in Dublin, and while admitting that—'It was true that there were men in the Labour Party who held diverse views about the strategy of the Labour movement . . . Labour's supporters would go to the polls not to vote for personalities, but for the Labour movement—the only movement that would solve the problem of poverty —poverty of the body and poverty of the soul.'[2] There were moments in the campaign when he looked and sounded like the Ishmael who had come to Dublin thirty-five years before.

> They were living in a city where the doctors spent half their time dealing with diseases that were due to malnutrition—a country from which 150,000 men had been driven to join the British Army and another 150,000 to make munitions. The reason these people had been allowed to go was that the Government realized that, but for the remittances sent home by these men—in money orders six millions a year—there would have been a revolution in the city of Dublin.[3]

When the returns were in, Labour had gained eight of the ten seats de Valera's Fianna Fail had lost. Larkin won in North-East Dublin with nearly 6,000 first preference votes, while his son captured his first seat in South Dublin.[4] Labour now mustered its greatest strength since the early twenties, holding some seventeen seats. The fruits of victory, however, were not to be long enjoyed. The Executive of the Transport Union decided to disaffiliate from the Labour Party because the Administrative Council of the Party refused by a vote of 9 to 8 to expel those officers of the Dublin Executive who had been responsible for endorsing Larkin as an official candidate. Of the seventeen members of the Labour Party in the Dail, eight were Transport Union officials, and five of them left the Party at the bidding of their Executive. In a joint statement, dated January 26, 1944, the five seceding Deputies introduced a new issue. They asked what action 'has been taken to remove the Communists and Communist influence from the Party?'[5] Further, in a long pamphlet

[1] *Ibid.*, p. 3.   [2] *Irish Times*, June 22, 1943.   [3] *Ibid.*
[4] *Ibid.*, June 25, 1943.
[5] 'The Labour Party,' *op. cit.*, p. 7. Quoted in this pamphlet.

rebutting the Labour Party's defence of its position, and issued over the name of William O'Brien for the Transport Union, Larkin's earlier differences with the Union were presented in a new light and some unique conclusions were drawn from them.

> The really significant aspect of that campaign of disruption *was that Larkin was not alone in it.* He had then as he has now the active and sinister backing of the Communist Party. Then, and all through the conflict, those apostles of chaos assailed the Union and the Labour Party by almost every method of gangsterdom, *and in the height of the campaign Mr. Larkin was lionised in Moscow, where the Third International invested him with a twenty-fifth share in the rulership of the earth.* The Communist hatred of the I.T. & G.W.U. has never abated; while on the other hand their alignment with Larkin is as close today as it was then.[1]

The upshot of the split in the Labour Party was that de Valera called for new elections in the spring of 1944 and recaptured nine of the ten seats he had lost the previous year. The five Deputies who left the Party put themselves forward as 'National Labour' candidates and were reduced to four.[2] The remaining twelve members of the Party were reduced to eight, as Larkin lost his seat, though his son retained his in South Dublin with an increased vote.[3]

To make matters even worse, trouble was also brewing on the trade union side of the Irish Labour Movement. The storm finally broke early in 1945, when a number of Irish unions, led by the Transport Union, seceded from the Irish Trades Union Congress and set up a rival organization, the Congress of Irish Unions.[4] The justification offered by the seceders for the split was that the growing influence of the British Amalgamateds (British based unions with branches in Ireland) was undermining the independence of the Irish Labour Movement.[5] The claim was made that the Amalgamateds dominated the National Executive of the Irish Trades Union Congress. The only way to meet this threat, the seceders maintained, was to reorganize the Irish trade union movement on purely national lines, with only those unions having their headquarters in Ireland being eligible for membership. The Irish Trade Union Congress lost

---

[1] *Irish Transport and General Workers' Union and the Labour Party. The Union's Reply to the Labour Party's Statement*, p. 4.

[2] *Irish Times*, June 2, 1944. [3] *Ibid.* [4] I.T.U.C., *Report*, 1945, pp. 29-37.

[5] *Council of Irish Trade Unions. Report of the Special Delegate Conference*, March 21, 1945.

some 60,000 members, or approximately one-third of its membership, to the Congress of Irish Unions.[1]

Meanwhile, as a delegate from the Dublin Trades Council to the I.T.U.C., Larkin had been trying for years to secure recognition for his Workers' Union.[2] His efforts year after year were successfully blocked by O'Brien, who dominated the National Executive of the Congress. In his effort to keep Larkin out O'Brien's iron discipline aroused a great deal of resentment, and Larkin began to find a more sympathetic hearing at each succeeding Congress.[3] Finally, after some ten years of applications, the National Executive approved the affiliation of the Workers' Union to the Congress in 1945.[4] But now that Larkin and his 8,000 members were officially part of the Labour Movement, O'Brien and some 60,000 others were out of it, and after twenty years of civil war the Movement was more seriously split than ever.

Approaching seventy in 1945 Larkin had begun of late years to rely more on his very able son James. An intellectually convinced Socialist, an astute politician, and an able administrator, 'young' Larkin, though very much like his father physically, was quite unlike him in temperament. Thoughtful and taciturn by nature, he lacked his father's flamboyance, rhetoric, and colour, and above all, his personal magnetism. If Larkin had been designed to make a revolution his son, undoubtedly, had been designed to consolidate it. The difficulty was that there was not much left to consolidate in the Irish Labour Movement.

In taking the pace somewhat more slowly Larkin visited his old friend Sean O'Casey in lovely Totnes in Devon in the last summer of his life. 'Jim,' commented O'Casey, 'was a man interested in everything that embraced the full life of man.'[5] He talked about politics, past and present, his union, the theatre, the vagaries of an apple tree, 'and how fine a broad spray of snowy hawthorne looked draping itself over the wall of the back garden.' When he returned to Ireland O'Casey wrote and asked him to begin his memoirs. 'Maybe I will turn my mind in that direction,' he wrote Jack Carney in

---

[1] I.T.U.C., *Report*, 1945, *op. cit.*, p. 31.   [2] *Ibid.*, *Reports*, 1937–45.

[3] *Ibid.*, *Report*, 1941. See especially for William O'Brien's heavy-handed treatment of the delegates as Chairman of the Congress.

[4] *Ibid.*, *Report*, 1945, p. 19.

[5] Sean O'Casey, 'James Larkin, Lion of Irish Labour,' *The Irish Democrat*, March, 1947, 'Larkin Memorial Number,' p. 5.

London, and then commented in characteristic fashion—'Of course I would not have any interference—it would have to run as written.'[1]

He did not, however, turn his mind to his memoirs, and shortly before Christmas of 1946, while he was inspecting some repairs being made in the Union hall, he slipped, fell, and injured himself internally. As was usual with him, he ignored all advice, but early in January he had to be admitted to the Meath hospital. His condition did not improve, and towards the end of January, 1947, it was apparent that he would not recover. He died in his sleep in the early morning of January 30, 1947. 'In a hush, broken only by the strains of the "Dead March" in "Saul," and the thud of hundreds of shoes on snow and slush,' his body was taken the following evening to the Union hall in College Street where he lay in state.[2] For two days his friends and followers came to take their last leave of him. On Monday, February 2, 1947, a bitter winter day, he was buried by those he loved among his peers in Glasnevin.

[1] MS., James Larkin to Jack Carney, September 6, 1946. Courtesy of Mina Carney.

[2] *Irish Times*, February 1, 1947.

APPENDIX A

THE BACKGROUND AND EARLY LIFE OF JAMES LARKIN

THE background and early life of James Larkin as presented in this chapter is a composite picture drawn from various sources. The first and most important source, both materially and chronologically, is a biographical sketch of Larkin presented by his friend George Dallas, then Secretary of the Scottish Independent Labour Party Federation, in the Glasgow *Forward* from October 9 to October 30, 1909. At the time Larkin was on trial for an alleged fraud, and the sketch was published with the view of raising funds for his defence. Though the series is a gaudy and idealized account, with much direct quoting by Larkin included in it, aside from the obvious adornment, it is possible to follow the main turning points in his early career.

The second main source is the thousand-odd-page typewritten manuscript of a court stenographer's transcript of the Minutes of Larkin's trial for criminal anarchy in New York City in April, 1920. Larkin acted as his own counsel, and when he examined himself as the chief witness in his own defence, he was able to give more than the usual short pertinent biographical sketch demanded on such occasions. In his summation to the jury Larkin pointed out that his position could hardly be understood unless his background was given ample consideration, and once again he unrolled the vast panorama of his past. Aside from a few flamboyant statements this transcript corroborates and supplements the account in the *Forward*.

The third important source is the account of Larkin's life by J. D. O'Reilly in the Dublin *Sunday Chronicle*, beginning November 23, 1947, some ten months after James Larkin's death. This account is valuable in that it embodies the recollections of Larkin's early career

305

by his sister Delia, Mrs. P. Colgan. This account is further supplemented by J. D. Clarkson's essay, 'Big Jim Larkin: Footnote to Nationalism,' in *Nationalism and Internationalism* (1950), edited by Edward Mead Earle. Professor Clarkson's account of Larkin's early career rests mainly on information supplied by the now deceased Mrs. Colgan.

All these accounts have been in turn supplemented by personal interviews with all who could supply pertinent information. In particular, James Larkin, Jr., Thomas Johnson, who first met Larkin in Liverpool about 1895, and Jack Carney, who met Larkin in 1905 and was later his close friend and associate for many years, were most helpful in filling in the many gaps. There are also the countless number of passing remarks made by Larkin in the course of his long career as an agitator that take on an added meaning when placed in their proper perspective.

Pages 1–6 depend mainly on the three main sources mentioned above. With Larkin's return to Liverpool in the latter half of 1894, it becomes possible to cross-check some of his statements. The notes in the *Clarion* from Liverpool, in particular, in the years following 1894, have substantiated in the main Larkin's own accounts, though his name is not specifically mentioned. The *Liverpool Labour Chronicle* also substantiates Larkin's accounts of the times, but like the *Clarion* 'Notes,' there is no specific mention of him. Where cross-checking was possible after 1894, the reference will be found in the footnote.

APPENDIX B

LIVERPOOL IN THE 1870s

The condition of Liverpool, whether from a sanitary or a moral point of view, is as far as possible from satisfactory. The death-rate of the town has for many years past far exceeded the average of English mortality, and by the last returns of the Registrar-General it is absolutely the highest of any of the eighteen large English towns of which particulars are supplied. We are informed further that Liver-

pool is one of the places in which 'scarlet fever continues fatally prevalent,' and every doctor will know how such a statement is to be interpreted. The police statistics . . . will scarcely be thought more encouraging. It appears, indeed, from them that theft in Liverpool has
declined during the present year, but at the same time they admit
and even prove that brutality has become much more rampant. . . .
It would seem, upon a review of the whole evidence, that the criminal
statistics and the health statistics of Liverpool point to the same conclusion. Liverpool is a town whose leading inhabitants are negligent
of their duties as citizens. It must be by their fault that the sanitary
condition of Liverpool has so long remained very far from satisfactory.
Nor can we acquit them of blame for the facts which we quoted yesterday from our Liverpool contemporary. The case of Liverpool, it should
be borne in mind, is in one sense peculiar. Crimes of violence are, indeed, committed almost as frequently in other places; but in no other
town do they occur under the same circumstances. In Manchester, in
Salford, in Oldham, and in the other manufacturing towns of Lancashire they are at least comparatively unknown. With the single
exception of Liverpool, they are aliens and exotics elsewhere than in
the colliery districts, which are their natural home. It is not, of course,
within the power of the great merchants and of the other leading men
of Liverpool absolutely to prevent the recurrence of the savage scenes
for which their town is now beginning to be notorious, but we might,
at least, expect them to do all they could towards the formation of a
sounder public opinion than that which at present prevails in it. The
control of this is, to a great extent, placed naturally in their hands,
and, if they decline the duty thus laid upon them, we shall in vain
expect that those below them in station will have either the wish or
the power to make up for their shortcomings. . . .

London *Times*, December 26, 1874.

This is partially quoted and mitigated to some extent by Ramsay
Muir in his *History of Liverpool* (1907). It is also quoted in Anne
Holt's *A Ministry to the Poor* (1936). Chapters VII–IX of Margaret B.
Simey's *Charitable Effort in Liverpool in the Nineteenth Century*
(1951) include a good description of prevailing social conditions
from 1875 to 1900.

Gerard Manley Hopkins, the Jesuit poet, laboured among the
immigrant Irish of Liverpool and, as his biographer, Eleanor Ruggles,
relates in *G. M. Hopkins, A Life* (1944), 'His commitments lay
throughout that section of the city, crowded with immigrants,
where in 1879 a vicious poverty reigned. Drunken laborers sat weep-
ing in the gutters, prostitutes ranged the thoroughfares, while at

every street corner children between three and four years old stand silently extending toward the passers-by a bunch of lucifer matches. Work and food were scarce; the death rate was terrifying . . .' (p. 185). Bryan D. White's *A History of the Corporation of Liverpool, 1835–1914* (1951), is excellent on health and housing after 1870, in Chapters X and XI. See also, for housing conditions in Liverpool, H. Taine, *Notes on England* (1872).

APPENDIX C

THE SHIPPING FEDERATION

THE Shipping Federation was an anathema to trade unionists the world over between 1890 and 1914. The Federation was the most formidable employer association that existed during this period. It had been founded in 1890 to meet the challenge offered to the shipping industry by the National Sailors' and Firemen's Union, which had been founded in 1887 by J. Havelock Wilson. By 1913 the Federation included 1,000 of the 1,050 owners of vessels of over 300 tons gross register. The fifty-odd shipowners outside the Federation, however, were not as insignificant as their numbers might indicate. Their gross tonnage came to something about $3\frac{1}{2}$ million tons, while the tonnage of those owners who were members of the Federation approximated some $13\frac{1}{2}$ million. The unorganized owners were situated chiefly in Liverpool and were, like the Cunard and White Star lines, mainly engaged in the Atlantic passenger service. The main purpose of the Shipping Federation was to handle the general labour problems encountered by its members. The provincial branches of the Federation set the local rates of wages, hours, and conditions, subject to the general policy established by the central office in London.

While the Federation claimed it was not against trade unions *per se*, and did not object to any man belonging to a trade union, it was determined to prevent any attempt to establish a 'closed shop' in the shipping industry. In its effort to uphold the so-called 'freedom of contracts,' the Federation introduced the Shipping Federation 'ticket.' The principal rule on the 'ticket' read: 'Every seaman, by registering pledges himself to carry out the agreement in accordance with the Merchant Shipping Act, and to proceed to sea in any vessel in which he signs articles, notwithstanding that other members of the crew may or may not be members of any seamen's union.' In other words, a seaman registered for his 'ticket' at the Shipping Federation offices and presented it to the master of the ship he proposed to sail, so that the master might know he was not a man 'who would strike after signing contracts because, perhaps, there was one non-union man on board.'

Trade unionists were violent in their objections to the Shipping Federation, and especially the 'ticket.' They complained the 'ticket' was discriminatory, since men who showed their 'ticket' were taken on first. For all practical purposes, therefore, registering for a 'ticket' meant joining a 'company union,' and no trade unionist would accept that. Further, sailors and firemen were in the unfortunate position, owing to the nature of their work, of having no permanent stake in their jobs. They signed on for a voyage and when it was over they were through. They were, therefore, like all itinerants and casuals, very difficult to organize and keep organized. Without a 'closed shop' it would be practically impossible to maintain a trade union in the shipping industry. Then, too, since a man could not strike before he had a job, and if he were forced to promise not to strike to get a job, what chance did he have of ever improving his working conditions? In addition to which, the men who remained outside the union benefited to the same extent as those who had taken all the risks and endured all the hardships in agitating for improvement.

Not only did the sailors and firemen view the Shipping Federation as the employers' instrument to keep them weak and divided, but the other waterside trades, particularly the dockers, were also vehement in their denunciation of the Federation. Whenever a dispute broke out in any port, the Federation was always prepared to furnish its members with a ready supply of 'free labour' to break the strike. The Federation recruited these professional strike-breakers, and the individual shipowner paid their wages and maintenance. These 'blacklegs' were generally housed aboard the vessel involved in the dispute or in the sheds on the dock estate, usually well outside the reach of the strikers' pickets. Throughout the shipping world, and in the waterside trades especially, trade unionists could not find words low enough to express the contempt and hatred they felt for the Shipping Federation.

The factual basis for this appendix may be found in the evidence of Cuthbert Low, General Manager of the Shipping Federation, in the Report of the Industrial Council on Inquiry into Industrial Agreements. Minutes of Evidence, *Parliamentary Papers*, 1913, XXVIII (Cd. 6953), pp. 567 ff.

APPENDIX D

THE RISE OF THE INDEPENDENT ORANGE ORDER, THE ANCIENT ORDER OF HIBERNIANS, AND THE BELFAST LABOUR PARTY

THERE is a general impression abroad that:

> By 1906 it was clear that Orangeism was a marvellous combination of the ruling class in Ulster, of the working classes in Belfast, and the majority of the Protestant farmers of the North. Belfast was its stronghold, its disciplined strength was impressive. . . .[1]

This is simply not so, for the Orange Order was hard pressed in 1906 to retain its control of Belfast and the surrounding countryside. The conditions described above were not to be such until 1910, when Home Rule became a menacing reality for Orangemen and Sir Edward Carson assumed the leadership of the near moribund Unionist cause in Ireland from the temporizing Walter Long. Up to that time the situation was in a state of flux, and before 1910 things had been going hard against the 'good old cause' in general, and Orangism in Belfast in particular. This was true for three important reasons—the rise of the Independent Orange Order, which challenged Orthodoxy in the name of humanity; the growth of a strong

[1] Edmund Curtis, *A History of Ireland* (1952), p. 396.

and popular Labour Movement in Belfast; and the development of an effective Catholic-Nationalist political machine in the guise of the Ancient Order of Hibernians, the Catholic counterpart of the Protestant Orange Order.

The rise of the Independent Orange Order is one of those curious paradoxes so often encountered in Irish history. For, out of the bigoted and ultra-militant Belfast Protestant Association came this most humane and truly patriotic of organizations. Just before the turn of the present century, when the Home Rule bills of '86 and '93 were becoming dim figures in a rapidly receding past, and the very real Tory ascendancy at Westminster afforded assurance that it would be some time before such a solution would be tried again, the Orange Order began to relax and did not beat the Protestant drum with as much vigour and enthusiasm as in former days. As a consequence, within the Orange lodges in Belfast there was a considerable amount of dissatisfaction with the attitude of the Grand Master, Col. E. J. Saunderson, and his hierarchy of lodge officials.[1] The result of this discontent was the formulation of the ultra-militant Belfast Protestant Association by Arthur Trew and T. H. Sloan. The Grand Orange Lodge watched the B.P.A. with the suspicious and waiting eye that all orthodoxy fixes on its rigorists, but it had to tread carefully because the rank and file of the Order vigorously backed Trew and his Association. There was also an indication of a split along class lines, as 'the majority of the Grand Lodge were well-to-do merchants, Justices of the Peace, and clergymen having little in common with Trew and his supporters,' who were chiefly working-men.[2]

Every Sunday afternoon, at the Custom House steps, Trew treated his largely attended B.P.A. meetings to an anti-Catholic diatribe, and in time he produced the violence he so pugnaciously preached. For inciting his fellow Protestants to riot against a Catholic *Corpus Christi* procession in 1901, Trew received twelve months at hard labour.[3] The B.P.A. greatly increased its membership after Trew's 'martyrdom,' and his place at the Sunday meetings was ably filled

---

[1] Statements by Thomas Johnson and Ernest Blythe, personal interviews.

[2] MSS., Thomas Carnduff, *North of the Eire Border*, p. 42. These are Mr. Carnduff's unpublished memoirs, which he was kind enough to let me use. They are extremely valuable in that they throw much light on the inner working of the Independent Orange Order, of which he was a member.

[3] *Ibid.*, p. 43.

311

by T. H. Sloan, a shipyard cement worker. Sloan was somewhat less of an agitator than Trew, but infinitely his superior in recognizing an opportunity. When William Johnston, Conservative member for South Belfast, died in the summer of 1902, Sloan decided he heard the knock and contested the seat. He declared himself the 'Democratic Candidate,' and beat the Tory offering, a County Down landowner, by some 800 votes in a poll of nearly 6,000.[1]

When Sloan was returned for South Belfast, the County Grand Lodge of Belfast suspended him for two years for some remarks made about Col. Saunderson, the Grand Master. His 'sentence' was reviewed at the Grand Lodge of Ireland, at Armagh. After the review, Sloan explained to a large group of his followers in Belfast that his suspension would be lifted if he apologized in writing to Col. Saunderson. He declined to apologize because he could not allow his dignity as a public man, since he was now a Member of Parliament, to be insulted. Sloan also declared that within the Grand Lodge of Ireland he had support, for many members were indignant at the way the Belfast Lodge 'had attempted to place the iron heel on the face of the democracy of Belfast.'[2] Several lodges in South Belfast protested Sloan's suspension, and were in turn suspended. In a defiant and fighting mood they formed the Independent Order of Orangemen, and were joined by many lodges in North Antrim and West Down, which indicated more than a nominal dissatisfaction in the countryside as well.[3] A few more lodges were added from Dublin by R. Lindsay Crawford, a Dublin Orangeman, and editor of the *Irish Protestant*.[4] Crawford, who was a gifted speaker, as well as a talented journalist, was elected Imperial Grand Master of the new order. Under the guidance of Crawford, the new Order began to turn from the militant bigotry of the Trew-dominated B.P.A. and adopt a more tolerant tone with regard to religion. Even more surprisingly, the new Order tried to strike roots in a humane and rational patriotism. On July 12, 1905, significantly enough, the new Order issued a manifesto 'To All Irishmen Whose Country Stands

[1] *The Constitutional Yearbook*, 1911, p. 213. T. H. Sloan (I.C.), 3,795; C. W. Dunbar-Buller (C.), 2,969.

[2] *Belfast Newsletter*, June 4, 1903. I am deeply indebted to Dr. John W. Boyle, who called my attention to this quote on reading this appendix.

[3] R. M. Sibbett, *Orangism in Ireland and Throughout the Empire* (1914), II, 606–7.

[4] Carnduff, *loc. cit.* For tone of paper see Sean O'Casey, *Drums under the Window* (1947), p. 348.

First in Their Affections,' which indicated the triumph of the new spirit. The manifesto said in part:

The victory of our forefathers at the Boyne was not a victory over creed or over race, but a victory for human liberty, the fruits of which our Roman Catholic countrymen share no less than ourselves. . . . As Irishmen we do not seek to asperse the memory of the hallowed dead whose fortunes were linked with those of the ill-starred house of Stuart, and whose courage and daring were proved on many a hard-fought field. We stand once more on the banks of the Boyne, and not as victors in the fight, not to applaud the noble deeds of our ancestors, but to bridge the gulf that has so long divided Ireland into hostile camps, and to hold out the right hand of fellowship to those who, while worshipping at other shrines, are yet our fellow countrymen— bone of our bone and flesh of our flesh. We come to help in the Christian task of binding up the bleeding wounds of our country, and to cooperate with all who place Ireland first in their affections. . . .

In an Ireland in which Protestant and Roman Catholic stand sullen and discontented, it is not too much to hope that both will reconsider their positions, and, in their common trials, unite on a true basis of nationality. The higher claims of our distracted country have been too long neglected in the strife of party and of creed. The man who cannot rise above the trammels of party and of sect on a national issue is a foe to nationality and to human freedom.[1]

Both Sloan and Crawford were among those who signed the manifesto, but it was soon evident that the spirit was in the voice of Crawford, while the signature was but the hand of Sloan. For Sloan seasonably repudiated a good deal of the manifesto in his successful effort to retain his seat for South Belfast in the general election some six months later.[2]

The Ancient Order of Hibernians, like the Independent Orange Order, did not become a power in Belfast politics until after the turn of the century, though it had pretensions to a rather tenuous tradition of some two hundred and fifty years. Tracing its origins to the Irish Rebellion of 1641, the A.O.H. claimed lineal descent through the agrarian secret societies that plagued Ireland in the eighteenth and early nineteenth centuries. The Defenders, the Whiteboys, and the Ribbon Societies with their colourful names—Caravats, Shana-

[1] *Magher Amorne Manifesto*. Reprinted from the *Irish Protestant* of July 22, 1905. Courtesy of Thomas Johnson.

[2] *Belfast Newsletter*, January 1, 1906. See Sloan's letter, also quoted in F. S. L. Lyons, *The Irish Parliamentary Party, 1890–1910* (1950), p. 136 n.

vests, and Molly Maguires—were the nominal forerunners of the A.O.H. The latter title was officially adopted in the United States in 1838, but it only gradually found favour with the divisions or lodges in Ireland. The A.O.H., if indeed it was ever an effective force in Ireland in the nineteenth century, was further handicapped by a serious split in 1884 in both the American and Irish branches over the question of admitting members of Catholic-Irish descent instead of by birth alone. The breach was finally bridged in Ireland in 1902, when both groups agreed to a probationary joint executive, called the Board of Erin, for a period of two years. At a national convention summoned in Belfast in 1904, Joseph Devlin was elected first National President of the united organizations. 'Wee Joe' Devlin, a Belfastman, Member of Parliament for North Kilkenny, and a rising luminary in the recently reunited Irish Parliamentary Party under John Redmond, was able to build in Belfast, in a very short time, a powerful personal political machine of the Catholic raw material mobilized in the A.O.H. divisions.[1]

By 1906 Devlin was ready to test his new machine in West Belfast, in the general election. Though West Belfast contained a large Catholic-Nationalist electorate, it had not been contested since a Nationalist lost the seat by some 800 votes in 1892. Devlin not only had the support of his pet political machine behind him, but received considerable support from quasi-Liberal sources. William J. Pirrie, shipbuilding magnate and chairman of the Belfast firm of Harland and Wolff, was unhappily disappointed when in 1902, on the death of William Johnston, he did not receive the Unionist nomination for South Belfast. The nomination went instead to a County Down landowner. Bitter and in a revengeful mood, Pirrie backed T. H. Sloan, the independent candidate, and by helping elect a working-man to Parliament proved in his own way to his former Tory friends that an industrialist was as good as a landlord any day.[2]

In 1905 Pirrie was prepared to forgive and forget and once again offer himself as the Unionist candidate for West Belfast in the coming general election.[3] But the Conservative caucus would have none of him and nominated instead Capt. J. R. Smiley to oppose Joseph Devlin, the Nationalist candidate. For a second time Pirrie

---

[1] J. J. Bergin, *History of the Ancient Order of Hibernians* (1911). This is an 'official history,' but it is very sketchy.

[2] Herbert Jefferson, *Viscount Pirrie of Belfast* (1947), p. 135.

[3] *Ibid.*, p. 100.

proved to his Tory friends he was a dangerous man to cross, as he not only declared himself a Liberal, but 'subscribed generously' to the Liberal war chest in both London and Belfast.[1] Some ten Independents and Liberals were enabled by the now financially solvent Liberal Association in Ulster to contest seats seldom bothered by a hard-fought election. In West Belfast itself, Pirrie once again had his revenge through an extremely slick political manoeuvre. To upset Unionist chances in what everyone viewed a very close contest, Pirrie's brother-in-law, A. M. Carlisle, declared himself an independent candidate for the West Belfast seat, and thereby ensured a split in the Unionist vote. Though Carlisle received only 153 votes in a poll of over 8,400, a striking tribute to the effectiveness of the Orange-Unionist political machine, the manoeuvre worked, for the Nationalist candidate, Joseph Devlin, squeezed through with a plurality of only 16 votes to win the seat.[2] Pirrie, for his strenuous and effective efforts on behalf of the Liberal cause in this general election, was elevated to the peerage as Baron Pirrie of Belfast in June, 1906. The new Lord Pirrie did not flag in his new-found faith once he achieved his reward, however, since he further attempted to enlarge Liberal horizons in Ulster by an open alliance with the growing Independent Orange Order. In January, 1907, R. Lindsay Crawford, President of the Independent Orange Order, was appointed editor of the chief Liberal organ in northern Ireland, the *Ulster Guardian*.[3] Crawford immediately instituted a feature column headed 'Independent Orange Notes,' and perhaps even more significantly, from one point of view, began to sound working-class interest by sympathetic news reporting and a column covering 'The Labour World.'

By 1906 Labour was also a political power in Belfast, but like their British brethren, the Belfast Socialists spent long years in the wilderness, seeming always to reap less than they sowed. As early as 1885 the trade unionists of Belfast made an assault on the Parliamentary constituency of North Belfast in a 'Lib–Lab' alliance. Their champion, Alexander Bowman, a flax dresser and trade union official, was decisively defeated. Little was heard about Labour or Socialism

[1] Herbert Jefferson, *Viscount Pirrie of Belfast* (1947), p. 136.
[2] Yearbook, 1911, *op. cit.*, p. 213. West Belfast: J. Devlin (N.), 4,138; Capt. J. R. Smiley (I.U.), 4,122; (Rt. Hon.) J. A. M. Carlisle (L.U.), 153.
[3] *Ulster Guardian*, December 28, 1907. See libel action by William Moore taken against the *Guardian*. Crawford insisted he be made editor, January 12, 1907.

until the founding of the Belfast Labour Party in September 1892.[1] The 'Party' soon became a branch of the Independent Labour Party, which held its first conference in Bradford in January, 1893. The branch struggled manfully in the sea of 'bigotry and brutality' that was Belfast, sustaining itself on a rugged and earnest, yet good-humoured, optimism. On June 1, 1895, the branch reported from Belfast:

> We think it advisable to discontinue the Custom House meetings until the spirit of the pious and immortal William cools down a bit. On Saturday evening, however, we went to the Queen's Bridge. As usual bigotry and brutality were well represented in the audience; but amidst cries of 'Throw him in the dock!' 'You're a Home Ruler!' 'Drown him!' Walker held his ground, and said all that he went there to say. A large crowd followed us through the streets, but we divided. Walker jumping on a tram car, and they dispersed. We sold fifty 'Merrie Englands' at the meeting. We advertised it as an exposure of Socialism; that sells it and minimises the risk of getting hit with something.[2]

In January, 1896, the local branch, drawing strength from a serious shipbuilding strike on the Clyde and the Lagan, proposed to run the well-known Socialist, Pete Curran, as the I.L.P. candidate for North Belfast.[3] The contest vaporized with the end of the strike and by early 1897 the Belfast branch faded completely, leaving only a handful of propagandists under the leadership of William Walker to carry on as the Belfast Socialist Party. When the Belfast Corporation was effectively thrown open to the working-class vote by an extension of the city boundary in 1896 and the division of the city into fifteen instead of five wards in 1897, Walker and six other trade unionists were elected as Councillors. During these early years of the present century Walker and his fellow Socialists dominated the Belfast Trades Council and made Belfast the Socialist stronghold in Ireland. In 1903 the Belfast Labour Party was founded, and in October, 1904, the *Belfast Labour Chronicle* was launched. The Party in early 1905 nominated Walker to contest a by-election in North Belfast which had not been seriously contested since Bowman

---

[1] *Belfast Newsletter*, September 4, 1893. Alexander Stewart, Chairman of I.L.P. meeting refers to the 'Belfast Labour Party' as a young organization founded September 29, 1892. I am again indebted to Dr. Boyle for this source.

[2] Millar, Jr., 'Notes From the Front,' 'Belfast,' *Clarion*, June 1, 1895.

[3] *Clarion*, January 18, 1896.

made the attempt twenty years before.[1] Walker did reasonably well in his first contest, and a by-election to boot, when he lost by less than 500 votes in a poll of over 8,400.[2] His opponent was hardly elected when Parliament was dissolved and a general election called. In his second attempt Walker lost by less than 300 votes in a poll of over 9,500.[3] With Labour victories everywhere, it seemed to the Socialists of Belfast that it was only a matter of time before the Orange stronghold of North Belfast would be theirs.

In 1906 Orange domination in Belfast was broken. Sloan held South Belfast, Devlin was the victor in West Belfast, and Walker rocked the Orange-Unionist machine in North Belfast in two elections running. Only East Belfast could now be counted as a safe Unionist seat. More than that, it seemed, in 1906, as if Orange-Unionist control of the whole north-east was in jeopardy. For, on the tide of the tremendous Liberal victory that swept Great Britain, some nine candidates outside Belfast contested seats seldom bothered by a hard-fought election. Of the nine, six were Independents, two Liberals, and one Independent Orangeman. The Independent Orangeman, R. G. Glendenning, won in North Antrim by a comfortable margin,[4] as one of the two Liberals squeezed home in North Tyrone by nine votes,[5] and one Independent captured South Tyrone.[6] In this general resurgence against orthodox unionism in Ulster the opposition won five of the twelve seats contested, and, indeed, it is not too much to say that a new era appeared to be in the offing for northern Ireland.

[1] Clarkson, *op. cit.*, p. 351. See also W. P. Ryan, *The Irish Labour Movement* (1919), p. 183.

[2] Yearbook, *op. cit.*, p. 213. (Rt. Hon.) Sir Daniel Dixon, Bt. (C.), 4,440; William Walker (Lab.). 3,966.

[3] *Ibid.*, p. 213, Rt. Hon. Sir Daniel Dixon, Bt. (C.), 4,907; William Walker (Lab.), 4,616.

[4] *Ibid.*, p. 204. R. G. Glendenning (L.), 3,757; W. Moore, K.C. (C.), 2,969.

[5] *Ibid.*, p. 211. W. H. Dodd, K.C. (L.), 2,966; D. S. Henry, K.C. (L.U.), 2,957.

[6] *Ibid.*, p. 212. T. W. Russell (L.), 2,954; A. L. Horner, K.C. (C.), 2,271.

APPENDIX E

THE BELFAST STRIKE, 1907

THERE are accounts of the Belfast strike from nearly every point of view. The employers' point of view was presented before a Royal Commission in 1912 by Alexander McDowell, and is found in the Report of the Industrial Council on Inquiry into Industries Agreements. Minutes of Evidence, *Parliamentary Papers*, 1913, XXVIII (Cd. 8953), pp. 405–15. McDowell, a solicitor who represented the Belfast employers in their labour disputes, ably sketched, from this point of view, employer–employee relationships from the spring of 1907 to 1912. The strikers' point of view was presented by Richard Elliot, a member of the Belfast Strike Committee's delegation to Glasgow, in the *Forward*, August 17, 1907, under the title of 'The History of the Belfast Strike.' From the arbiters' point of view, Lord Askwith is very effective in his handling of the facts in his memoirs, *Industrial Problems and Disputes* (1920), pp. 109–14. Thomas Carnduff, in his unpublished autobiography, *North of the Eire Border*, also gives an excellent account of the strike from the workers' point of view, in Chapter IV, entitled 'Industry.' J. D. Clarkson, in his *Labour and Nationalism in Ireland* (1925), pp. 215–20, is partial to the Labour point of view, but takes his account of the facts from one of the chief Orange newspapers in Belfast, the *Northern Whig*. The account presented here is taken mainly from two daily Belfast newspapers, each of which took a decided stand on the issue of the strike. The *Irish News*, the Catholic-Nationalist organ of the Irish Party and the Ancient Order of Hibernians, was very partial to the strike and the strikers in its columns, while the *Northern Whig* came down heavily on the side of the employers in the struggle. R. Lindsay Crawford, in the *Ulster Guardian*, was very partial to the strikers, as was, of course, the Belfast correspondent in the Glasgow *Forward*. Both weeklies provided much excellent material on the strike. The *Minutes* of the Belfast Trades Council, however, were surprisingly meagre in the period covered by the strike. In the plays of St. John Ervine the troubled spirit of the times in Belfast is admirably presented.

Especial mention must be made of his play, *Mixed Marriage*, which gives an excellent picture of the labour conflict in Belfast in 1907 and its effect on religious problems in that city. The account presented here is an amalgamation of the various sources mentioned above.

APPENDIX F

WHY JAMES LARKIN LEFT IRELAND IN 1914

LONG before the war began Larkin had been thinking about touring America to raise funds for the Transport Union.[1] He continued to postpone the trip because of the chaotic situation that existed in Dublin after the lockout.[2] When the resignation crisis was settled, in June, 1914, and the situation in Dublin somewhat more composed, Larkin began to make preparations for a lecture tour in the United States.[3] The outbreak of the war delayed his departure again, but by October, 1914, he was ready to sail. Now the problem to be faced was who was going to take over the Union in Larkin's absence. The leadership could only devolve on one of two men, P. T. Daly or James Connolly. Each had developed a strong claim to succeed Larkin. Daly had been an unswerving and loyal supporter through the Union's most difficult days. He had played a most prominent part in the Union when Larkin was in jail in 1910, and had increased the membership and added to the depleted treasury. He was most responsible for the Wexford strike being carried to a successful conclusion, though arrested and jailed. In the Sligo troubles, in

[1] *Freeman's Journal*, December 15, 1913. Larkin probably got the idea of touring America from 'Big Bill' Haywood. See Haywood's account of his trip to Ireland and, with Larkin, through England in *Bill Haywood's Book* (1929), pp. 272–74.

[2] *Forward*, June 14, 1914. See Michael M'Keown's letter dated February 12, 1914.

[3] *The Attempt to Smash the Irish Transport and General Workers' Union* (1924), pp. 165–66.

1913, Daly was also in the thick of the fight. Throughout this whole period Daly was naturally viewed as Larkin's chief lieutenant.

Connolly, on the other hand, only became an official of the Union in June, 1911, and spent most of his time in Belfast as branch secretary of the Union. He was out of touch with Dublin and was, by his own accounts, not in Larkin's good graces.[1] As for ability and intelligence, there was no question but that Connolly was markedly superior to Daly. Connolly's position in Belfast had been an extremely difficult one. Larkin's harangues and rebukes to Connolly over the poor returns and membership were often not deserved. Belfast of 1912 was not the Belfast of 1907, for the Orange core had hardened in the fanatical opposition to Home Rule. In Sir Edward Carson the Orange-Unionist machine had at last found a man of real ability and dogged determination. The leader of a 'Papist' trade union, even if he were a Larkin, could not be expected to get much done in these years in Belfast. In late August, 1913, when Larkin was first arrested, O'Brien hurriedly sent Connolly a telegram telling him to come to Dublin. When Larkin was avoiding arrest the Saturday before 'Bloody Sunday' in O'Connell Street, O'Brien posed the question of leadership in the event he should be arrested.[2] Larkin told O'Brien that Connolly was to take over the Union. O'Brien asked Larkin to put it in writing, and Larkin did so in a short memorandum in red ink.[3] When Larkin was later jailed in November, he appointed Connolly his successor. After release, and while he was away on his 'fiery cross' campaign, Connolly was in charge in Dublin and edited the *Irish Worker*. By the end of 1913, through sheer ability Connolly had become Larkin's second-in-command.

When in the first week of October, 1914, Larkin told Connolly that he was leaving for America and that he wanted him to take over the *Irish Worker* and the Insurance section, while Daly took over the Union, it was small wonder Connolly wrote O'Brien:

> I said that I hated the Insurance end of the work, but expressed no opinion about Daly. But you know as well as I do that such an arrangement would be unbearable and unworkable. For one thing, we could never hope to maintain an understanding with the Nationalists

[1] *Ibid.*, pp. 162–64.
[2] William O'Brien, personal interview.
[3] *Ibid.* Mr. O'Brien retains the memorandum.

if Daly was in command of the Transport Union. They would not trust him, or co-operate with him, and the Transport Union would become a mere dues-collecting Union if a man with the character of Daly for evading difficulties was in charge. Other reasons you will readily see. I think you should at once get hold of Foran and tell him Jim's proposition, and get him to see that the Committee makes it clear that they will not agree to any such proposal. The danger is that Larkin will publicly announce it first, and that would make it as difficult to be altered as it would be to carry out. The Committee could avoid this by meeting immediately and raise this among other questions before any public announcement is made.

Yours in haste,
JAMES CONNOLLY[1]

O'Brien immediately wrote Connolly not to accept any post subordinate to Daly, and suggested the lines on which he should write to Larkin about it. Connolly promptly replied, and enclosed a copy of the letter he was sending to Larkin. Connolly wrote O'Brien, 'At present I feel like declining the "honour" of serving under Daly, even if it meant losing my position in the Union.'[2] That Connolly, incidentally, like Larkin, had been swallowed by the National Being was evident from the rest of his letter:

> As I see things now, there is a magnificent chance for the Transport Union all over Ireland as the one Labour organisation aggressively active on the true Nationalist side. It has an opportunity of taking and keeping the lead. But if a man who is distrusted by both Nationalists and Labour men is in charge of that Union, I see nothing before it but decay and disorganisation, and the absolute loss of Labour support to the Nationalist cause as of Nationalist support to the Labour cause.[3]

In his letter to Larkin, however, Connolly clearly made the point that it was a choice between Daly or himself.[4] O'Brien showed the copy of Connolly's letter to Larkin to Thomas Foran, General President of the Transport Union. Since there was to be a meeting of the Executive Committee that same day, Foran spoke to several members

---

[1] *The Attempt to Smash, op. cit.,* p. 164. See letter from James Connolly to William O'Brien, undated, received October 6, 1914.

[2] *Ibid.,* p. 165. Letter, Connolly to O'Brien, October 7, 1914.

[3] *Ibid.*

[4] MSS., Letter, Connolly to Larkin, October 7, 1914. Connolly refuses in this letter, which is in the possession of William O'Brien, to accept a subordinate position to Daly.

and persuaded them to support Connolly. When Larkin proposed that Daly should take over the Union in his absence, it was suggested to him that Connolly would be the better choice, and after much discussion Larkin finally said, 'Have it your own way.'[1]

In his lengthy farewell message in the *Irish Worker*, Larkin explained that he found it necessary to go to America for the benefit of the Union. Much has been said, and more left unsaid, about Larkin's motives for leaving Ireland at this particular time. His detractors have intimated that he cleared out because he knew that an insurrection had been planned by the Irish Republican Brotherhood. It was not likely that Larkin knew about the proposed insurrection, for no concrete plans had been laid, or any date set at the August meeting of the Supreme Council of the Brotherhood.[2] It was only decided that an attempt would be made before the end of the European war. There was some reason to believe that Connolly knew of the decision of the Supreme Council to stage an insurrection and that he hinted as much to Larkin.[3] Still, Tom Clarke, the man most responsible for the insurrection in Dublin in 1916, gave Larkin an introductory note to John Devoy, the chief contact of the Brotherhood in the United States.[4] Clarke would hardly have helped Larkin contact Devoy if he felt Larkin was leaving Ireland to avoid an insurrection.

All available evidence indicates that Larkin needed and wanted a change of scenery. Connolly himself had suggested, at the resignation crisis in June, 1914, that 'the price Jim had paid was that he had broken down physically, run down mentally, and almost worn out.

[1] William O'Brien in a letter to the author dated October 17, 1957.

[2] P. S. O'Hegarty, *A History of Ireland under the Union, 1801–1922* (1952), p. 697. Mr. O'Hegarty was a member of the Supreme Council at the time.

[3] *The Attempt to Smash, op. cit.*, p. 164. Letter, James Connolly to William O'Brien, September 5, 1914.

[4] MSS., National Library of Ireland, 2112. Letter, John Devoy to Frank Robbins, September 21, 1923. Courtesy of William O'Brien. Patrick Pearse, who commanded the Irish forces in the Easter Rebellion in 1916, wrote, in October, 1913, in *Irish Freedom*, 'I do not know whether the methods of Mr. James Larkin are wise methods or unwise methods (unwise, I think, in some respects), but this I know, that there is a most hideous wrong to be righted, and that the man who attempts honestly to right it is a good man and a brave man.' Pearse, who founded St. Enda's School, accepted Larkin's two oldest boys as pupils. Pearse would hardly have done this if he suspected Larkin of want of honesty. In short Larkin had won the respect of the extreme nationalists, if he had not won their confidence.

Hence he did not realise himself that what he needed was a rest. . . .
If he were to go to America and raise funds for the new Irish Labour
Party it would recuperate him, and he would be back in seven days
if needed.'[1] Even after the reassuring vote of confidence in June, he
wrote to an American friend in August, 'I have not had a holiday for
years, and I am not in love at present with the work here, and maybe
the change would do good all round.'[2] Like most people who are
upset and disappointed as well as exhausted, Larkin welcomed a
change and a chance to freshen his perspective. He sailed in the last
week of October, 1914 from Liverpool for New York, little realizing
he would not set foot in Ireland again for nearly nine years.

[1] *Forward*, June 27, 1914.
[2] *The Attempt to Smash*, *op. cit.*, p. 166. Letter, James Larkin to Patrick L.
Quinlan, August 18, 1914.

INDEX